The Emerging Child

PATRICIA KIMBERLEY WEBB
SOUTHERN METHODIST UNIVERSITY

The Emerging Child
Development through Age Twelve

MACMILLAN PUBLISHING COMPANY
NEW YORK
Collier Macmillan Publishers
LONDON

Copyright © 1989 by Macmillan Publishing Company,
a division of Macmillan, Inc.

PRINTED IN THE UNITED STATES OF AMERICA

All rights reserved. No part of this book may be reproduced or transmitted in any form or by any means, electronic or mechanical, including photocopying, recording, or any information storage and retrieval system, without permission in writing from the Publisher.

Macmillan Publishing Company
866 Third Avenue, New York, New York 10022

Collier Macmillan Canada, Inc.

LIBRARY OF CONGRESS CATALOGING-IN-PUBLICATION DATA

Webb, Patricia Kimberley.
    The emerging child / Patricia Kimberley Webb.
      p.   cm.
    Bibliography: p.
    Includes indexes.
    ISBN 0-02-424920-3
    1. Child development.   I. Title.
HQ767.9.W43 1989   88-11090
305.2′3—dc19   CIP

Printing: 1 2 3 4 5 6 7   Year: 9 0 1 2 3 4 5

*To my daughter
Joy Kimberley,
and to her many friends who provided
a living laboratory for my observations
of child growth and development*

Preface

In the fable of the blind men and the elephant, a heated debate broke out when one man described the elephant as "like a fan" because he felt its ear, another insisted that the animal must be "like a wall" when he fell against its side, and the third declared that even a simple person must agree that the beast was "very like a tree" as he wrapped his arms around one leg. Each was offering a bit of truth, but none was describing the elephant completely. In like manner, the child may be described in many ways and considered from many points of view.

This book is designed as a comprehensive introduction to child development. I hope it will prove interesting and useful to undergraduate students, to child-care personnel, and to parents. In writing this book, I have used an eclectic approach; I have included explanations from many different theorists in order to give as complete a description of the child as possible. I have tried also to provide a balance among description (what children are like), theory (why they are that way), and application (how this relates to the everyday process of working with them). Finally, I have arranged for active involvement of the reader through the use of Involvers, activities designed to expand the reader's understanding of the chapter topic through actual interaction with a child.

The topical approach is used in this text, since this structure allows the reader to see the progression and continuity of each aspect of development. It also allows for individual differences, since any particular child may be above age level in some areas of development and below age level in others. The chronological data indicating the ages at which certain characteristics are likely to appear are fitted into each chapter. I feel that this combination of topical and chronological approaches will give a clear and meaningful picture of development during these early years.

There is current concern with the use of sexist references in textbooks. In deference to the American Psychological Association guidelines and for the sake of clear sentence structure, I have avoided (s)he, he/she, and excessive use of plurals by using the generic "he" in odd-numbered chapters and the female referent "she" in even-numbered ones.

Organization

Part I, "Becoming Child Watchers," is designed to help the reader become active in child development research. Chapter 1 presents a brief overview of several theories that can be used to explain behavior. Each of these is included in later chapters as it relates to specific areas of development. Chapter 2 provides the reader with basic skills for becoming a more adept observer of children.

Part II, "In the Beginning: The Prenatal Period," stresses the importance of the first nine months prior to birth. Chapter 3 includes new research findings related to the influence of heredity, prenatal environment, and the birth process on the future well-being of the child.

Part III, "Early Child Development," describes the physical, cognitive, emotional, and social development of the child in contemporary society. Chapter 4 outlines the emergence of physical, motor, and perceptual skills. Proper nutrition and the consequences of an inadequate diet are the major concerns in Chapter 5. Chapter 6 analyzes the development of cognition, and Chapter 7 focuses on language acquisition. The emergence of "self" and its impact on emotional development is detailed in Chapter 8, and Chapter 9 describes the child's interactions with such socializing agents as parents, siblings, peers, and caregivers. Chapter 10 considers the effects of modeling, conditioning, and cognitive strategies on the development of moral behavior. The importance of play in the child's development is emphasized in Chapter 11. Chapter 12 explores the relationship of social and ethnic affiliation on development, with emphasis on similarities and unique needs rather than on between-group comparisons.

Part IV, "The Special Child," is included to familiarize caregivers with the needs of children who, in some way, differ significantly from the norm. Chapter 13 describes the cognitively and physically different, including children who are gifted, retarded, and learning disabled and those who have visual, auditory, speech, neurological, or orthopedic handicaps. Chapter 14 deals with relational dysfunctions: hyperactivity, lack of relatedness (autism), hesitant relatedness (phobias, depression, withdrawal, extreme shyness), and hostile relatedness (aggressive disorders).

PREFACE

Special Features

Organization and format are designed for readability.

- The outline at the beginning of the chapter provides an overview.
- Color is used throughout the chapter to highlight the major sections.
- Key words are emphasized by italic type and are immediately defined in the text.
- Chapter summaries help the student review the main ideas presented.
- The chapter is written in clear, lively prose and contains many everyday examples to which the reader can relate.
- The chapters are concise. Careful selection of topics and direct wording help make this a brief but comprehensive text.

Research is current, balanced, and well documented.

- Because of the many changes occurring in contemporary society, studies conducted during the past five years are emphasized (except for classic works).
- A partial list of current topics discussed includes day care, television, behavior management, sex role changes, fathering, one-parent families, child abuse, nutrition, creativity, developmental play, and handicapping conditions (mental, physical, emotional).
- Ideas drawn from major theorists are interwoven throughout the book to provide a balanced, eclectic explanation of child development.
- Statements are well documented, showing sources and dates.
- Selected Readings at the end of each chapter give the reader the opportunity to explore the chapter topic in greater detail.

Boxes, visually highlighted by colored background or rules, are used to present special interest data.

- Charts summarize key points in the topic under discussion.
- In each chapter, a Case Study is presented to illustrate a major issue.
- The Involver in each chapter is designed to expand the reader's understanding of the topic through first-hand experience with a child.

A variety of illustrations is used.

- In a single line, cartoons can present the essence of an idea in a humorous way that will long be remembered.

- Pictures capture both activities and feelings. They make the children being discussed "come alive."
- Drawings accurately depict many concepts that cannot be photographed.

Text supplements are available for both student and teacher.
- The Student Study Guide contains chapter summaries, study questions, sample quizzes, and suggestions for additional projects with children.
- The Instructor's Manual contains chapter outlines, suggested topics for discussions and individual research, ideas for additional Involvers, a catalogue of related audiovisuals, and a test item file including true-false, multiple-choice, and essay questions.

Acknowledgments

This book has been developed through the efforts of many people. It would not be possible to list all who have helped me in some way during the time this work has been in preparation, but to each I am grateful. I should like first to thank my family and friends for their continued encouragement and interest. Particularly, I should like to express appreciation to my mother, Letha Conner Kimberley, for her unflagging support of the project from its inception to its completion.

Professional colleagues have also given invaluable assistance through their careful reading and critiquing of the manuscript. For the knowledge they shared and the suggestions they made, I should like to thank the following reviewers: David L. Brown, East Texas State University; Anne G. Dorsey, University of Cincinnati; Marjorie Fields, University of Alaska; Megan P. Goodwin, Central Michigan University; Shirley Hill (retired), California State University/Fullerton; Ruth A. Hough, Georgia State University; Marjorie W. Lee, Howard University; Lynn J. Lessie, Atlantic Community College (NJ); Mary Ann McLaughlin, Clarion University of Pennsylvania; Sherry Shugarman, University of Dayton; and Judy Spitler McKee, Eastern Michigan University.

I should also like to acknowledge that my seminal work in affective development appeared in a chapter entitled "Becoming: Affective Development in Early Childhood," which I wrote for *Guiding Young Children's Learning*, a McGraw-Hill publication by S. W. Lundsteen and N. B. Tarrow. Selected topics and references that were included in this earlier work appear in this volume with permission of McGraw-Hill Book Company.

Many of the pictures used throughout the book were taken at local childcare facilities and schools. I should like to thank the following persons for their cooperation and assistance: Dr. Sue Francis, Hamilton Park

Elementary School; Glenda Sellers, Creative School; Jan Songstad, The Academy, and Connie Stanhouse, Highland Park Methodist Child Development Program.

I am particularly indebted to those who assisted in the production of this book: to editor Lynn Greenberg, who worked with me during the early stages of manuscript preparation; to editor Robert Miller and assistant editor Sharon Balbos, whose kindness and patience during the completion of the work will always be remembered; and to Barbara Chernow and her staff, whose efforts were invaluable.

Finally, I should like to express thanks to all the children with whom I have worked over the years. From them I learned so much and through them I experienced repeatedly the wonder of childhood.

P. K. W.

Contents

PART I
Becoming Child Watchers — 1

CHAPTER 1
Theories of Development — 3

Psychoanalytic Theory: Freud, Erikson   4
Behaviorist Theory: Skinner, Dollard, and Miller   13
Maturational Theory: Gesell   17
Developmental Tasks: Havighurst   18
Cognitive Theory: Piaget   21
Self Theory: Rogers   24
Summary   27
Selected Readings   28

CHAPTER 2
Child Study through Research, Observation, and Interaction — 29

Types of Research   31
Personal Involvement in Child Study   40
Ethical Child Watching   50

Summary 51
Selected Readings 52

PART II
In the Beginning: The Prenatal Period   55

CHAPTER 3
The Prenatal Endowment Fund: Influences on Development   57

Conception 59
Heredity 60
Periods of Prenatal Development 70
The Prenatal Environment 74
Birth 79
Nature and Nurture: Forces Interacting to Shape Development 85
Summary 88
Selected Readings 89

PART III
Early Child Development   91

CHAPTER 4
Physical Development   93

Principles Governing Growth and Development 95
Physical Characteristics and Needs 95
Motor Development 107
Perceptual Development 116
Coordination of Physical, Motor, and Sensory Development 124
Summary 125
Selected Readings 127

CONTENTS   *xv*

CHAPTER 5
Nutrition and Development   *128*

Nutritional Status of Children   129
Analysis of Needed Nutrients   131
Problems of the Malnourished   145
Programs for Fostering Better Nutrition   150
Summary   154
Selected Readings   156

CHAPTER 6
Cognitive Development and Learning   *157*

Mental Development: Intelligence and Cognition   159
Construction of Knowledge   160
A Sequence of Cognitive Development   162
Cognition as an Information Processing System   173
Cognitive Learning Styles   180
Evaluation of Cognitive Development   183
Summary   188
Selected Readings   190

CHAPTER 7
Language Development   *192*

Components and Functions of Language   194
Theories of Language Development   197
Sequence of Language Development   206
Relationship of Language Development to Other Factors   218
Summary   224
Selected Readings   226

CHAPTER 8
Personality Development   *227*

What Is Personality?   229
The Mosaic of Self: Self-Personality Development
    from Basic Elements   229

The Process of Becoming 237
Negative Roadblocks 245
Facilitating Personality Growth 251
Summary 253
Selected Readings 255

CHAPTER 9
Social Development — 257

From "I" to "We": Foundations of Socialization 258
Agents of Socialization 264
Social Pluses and Minuses 278
Summary 285
Selected Readings 287

CHAPTER 10
Moral Development and Behavior Management — 289

Moral Behavior: Major Components 291
Factors That Affect Moral Behavior 291
How Moral Behavior Develops 294
Strategies for Developing Moral Behavior 305
Summary 318
Selected Readings 319

CHAPTER 11
Integration of Development through Play — 321

What Is Play? 323
Developmental Sequence of Play Behavior 325
Functions of Play 331
Facilitating Children's Play 340
Summary 343
Selected Readings 345

CHAPTER 12
The Child and the Socioculture: Contributions of Society to Development — 346

Sociocultural Shaping   348
   Group Traditions   348
   Family Structure   351
   Socioeconomic Status   355
   Communication Patterns   359
   Educational Opportunities   361
Current Concerns for Which Society Needs Support Systems   364
   Child-Care Facilities   365
   Divorce   369
   Child Abuse   373
Summary   376
Selected Readings   378

PART IV
The Special Child — 381

CHAPTER 13
Cognitive and Physical Differences — 383

Cognitive Variations   385
   Giftedness   385
   Retardation   390
   Learning Disabilities   393
Physical Variations   397
   Visual Handicaps   397
   Hearing Impairments   400
   Speech and Language Disabilities   403
   Neurological Impairments   405
   Orthopedic Handicaps   407
Summary   410
Selected Readings   411

CHAPTER 14
Relational Dysfunctions — 412

Excessive Reaction: Attention Deficit Disorder (Hyperactivity) 414
Lack of Relatedness: Autism 418
Hesitant Relatedness 421
  Phobias 421
  Depression 423
  Withdrawal 426
  Extreme Shyness 427
Hostile Relatedness: Aggressive Disorders 431
Summary 435
Selected Readings 436

BIBLIOGRAPHY 439

SUBJECT INDEX 467

NAME INDEX 480

PART I

Becoming Child Watchers

CHAPTER 1

Theories of Development

CHAPTER OUTLINE

    Psychoanalytic Theory: Freud, Erikson
        Psychoanalytical Development: Freud
        Psychosocial Theory: Erikson
    Behaviorist Theory: Skinner, Dollard, and Miller
        Operant Conditioning: Skinner
        Social Learning Theory: Dollard and Miller
    Maturational Theory: Gesell
    Developmental Tasks: Havighurst
    Cognitive Theory: Piaget
    Self Theory: Rogers
    Summary
    Selected Readings

While Marcy carefully waters some plants, Joy stares intently at the fish in the tank. Greg asks the tenth question in five minutes, and Sandi struggles with Carolyn over possession of a favorite doll. Jan clobbers Nancy with the receiver of the toy phone, and Dennis sits in the corner of the room oblivious to it all. What accounts for the differences in children's behavior? Theorists have offered a variety of explanations.

Psychoanalytic Theory: Freud, Erikson

The psychoanalytic theorists concentrate on a careful examination of the individual's mind. They consider how the personality is formed as a result of experiences at crucial points in life. Freud believes that the personality structure is formed during the first five years and that later behavior is based on this foundation. Erikson, a later follower of the psychoanalytic tradition, feels that society plays a greater role in personality, and he has identified key developmental conflicts that need to be resolved throughout the life cycle.

Psychoanalytical Development: Freud

Sigmund Freud studied human behavior by analyzing the structure of the mind (psychoanalysis). He believed this personality structure was made up of three parts which he named the id, the ego, and the superego. The development of these parts—their interactions with each other and with the environment—determines how people will behave (S. Freud, 1970).

THEORIES OF DEVELOPMENT

Sigmund Freud (*Source: Archiv/Photo Researchers, Inc.*)

PARTS OF THE PERSONALITY.   Freud described the id as everything that is inherited, that is present at birth, and that is fixed in the constitution of the individual. The purpose of the id is to insist on satisfaction of innate needs such as hunger, physical comfort, and emotional desires. The infant's id says, "I'm wet; I'll scream!" The young child's id says, "I'm lonely and bored; I'll suck my thumb till I feel better."

As the child develops, the second part of his personality structure, the ego, emerges from the id. This change takes place as the child interacts with people in his lifespace and discovers that he cannot always have his way. The purpose of the ego is to help the individual relate to the outside world. The ego controls the instincts of the id by deciding which demands will be met and by determining the appropriate time and circumstance for such action. The child's ego says, "Yes, you may have that toy, but you must wait your turn." The ego also learns to deal with the environment. It makes the individual aware of elements in the environment (for learning) but avoids overstimulation. (Experiences that are too hard or too painful may result in running away from the conflict or refusing to think about the situation.) The ego stores perceptions and memory traces to be used in future decision making. Based on this information, the ego considers options and selects what it perceives to be advantageous solutions.

The third part of the personality structure, the superego, is the internalization of what others have taught the person is right and wrong. Since the content of the superego is based on personal experience, individuals may vary greatly in their concepts of what should be forbidden (conscience) and what should be desired (ego-ideal). Freud states that an individual's basic task in life is to coordinate the demands of the id, ego, and superego so the needs of all three parts are met simultaneously.

ANXIETY.   When the self perceives that it is in danger, anxiety results. This fear reaction may relate to some real threat (reality anxiety), to an intense feeling of powerlessness (neurotic anxiety), or to a feeling of guilt (moral anxiety). If anxiety is not constructively relieved, the individual may become immobile (S. Freud, 1936).

ADJUSTMENTS TO ANXIETY.   One positive method for overcoming feelings of helplessness is through identification with a person who possesses desired power and/or accomplishments. Through this close association and modeling, the individual hopes to increase his own status and desirability. The mature personality will comprise many such identifications. The success of identification in relieving anxiety depends partly on the actual competence gained from the modeling and partly from the perceived increase in capability.

When anxieties and fears are so great that the individual cannot face

---

BOX 1.1
Defense Mechanisms: Characteristics and Examples

Defense Mechanism	Description	Example
Repression	Unconsciously refusing to remember objectionable experiences, impulses, or ideas	"I have never acted like that." (Everyone sees it but me.)
Regression	Going back to behavior of a previous stage	"Since the new baby came, Susie has started soiling again." (Susie won't let that baby have all Mother's attention.)
Rationalization	• Making up excuses rather than facing mistakes • Refusing to recognize and/or admit unfulfilled desires	• "The test was too hard." (That's why I cheated.) • "I didn't want to go." (I wasn't invited.)
Undoing	Believing one can nullify past guilt-evoking actions	"I give that child my undivided attention." (I do penance for previous neglect.)
Projection	Accusing others of a weakness one possesses	"Everyone here is so fussy." (I have a rotten temper.)
Reaction-formation	Doing the opposite of what one feels to avoid guilt feelings	"I'm always very courteous to Mary." (I can't stand her.)

SOURCE: A Freud, 1967; Wolman, 1968.

them, they are pushed to the unconscious level, and reality is distorted. Some of these distorted reactions are called defense mechanisms. Box 1.1 contains descriptions and examples of six major defense mechanisms.

IMPLICATIONS FOR WORKING WITH CHILDREN. After intensive study and research in psychoanalytic theory, Anna Freud (1973) offered the following suggestions to parents and teachers:

1. Evaluate behavior in terms of the age at which it occurs. Selfishness and physical aggression such as biting, hitting, and kicking are normal in preschool children, because they still think only in terms of themselves and have not learned to consider the feelings of others. The same behavior from an upper elementary grade student could indicate social maladjustment.

2. Understand that the child's reactions are based on which part of the personality is predominating at a given time. The young child's personality comprises the id or instinctual life (original childish behavior), the ego (the emerging responsible self), and the superego (derived from relationships with parents/caregivers). In a given situation, will the disciplining force of the superego (what he's "supposed" to do) be strong enough to counteract his basic instinctual desires (his childish, self-centered tendencies)? "I know I shouldn't snatch toys from other children but I want that truck!" "I know Mother won't allow me to scream back at her, but I'm so angry!" This behavior is best managed by recognizing the struggle within the child and encouraging him to develop self-control. When the responsible self prevails, the child desires praise. When he exhibits immature behavior, patient but firm redirection of behavior is often more profitable than anger and aggression on the part of the adult. Many suggestions for working with children in the development of self-management can be found in Chapter 10.

3. Help the child to understand "why" rather than merely to memorize rules of conduct. The internalization of the mandates from parents, teachers, or other significant persons without understanding can be a dangerous step, since these prohibitions and demands tend to become fixed in the mind. An individual may attempt to continue to follow the dictates of these persons years later under totally different circumstances. If these significant others were present at that future time, they would have the opportunity to consider new developments and make appropriate revisions in thinking. The "authority figure in the mind," by contrast, can only parrot what was said years before in a different context without adjusting to the current situation. Another problem arising from not understanding "whys" is that the child often

Adult talking with child   (*Source: MacDonald/Envision*)

fails to apply rules correctly. Many a caregiver has been exasperated when the child did something inappropriate and defended his action with "but you said." See Chapter 9 for further discussion of the impact of various agents of socialization.

How do you help the child understand "whys?" Both parents and teachers might consider the following strategies:

- Talk with the child about his feelings and those of others.
- Explain to him that what we do must be fair to both ourselves and other people.
- In many instances, let the child verbalize what needs to be done in given problem situations to be fair to all concerned. (If this behavior

becomes a habit for the child, it can be applied to many situations, and there will not be a need for so many rules.)

Since people do not realize that they are using defense mechanisms, it is often difficult to get them to change these behaviors. They assume that their reactions are caused by some other person or circumstance and are appropriate responses. Often much counseling is necessary before these defensive individuals can more realistically appraise their problems and make rational decisions.

STAGES OF DEVELOPMENT. Freud believed the child's experiences during the first five years of life were crucial to later adjustment. He divided this period into three stages, named for the child's primary sources of pleasure/stimulation during this time: oral, anal, and phallic.

The oral stage occurs during the first year. The child's major avenue for pleasure at this time is his mouth. Through feeding and sucking, major needs are met, and a feeling of warmth and trust toward the environment is established.

The anal stage runs through the second and third years. The child experiences great satisfaction from learning to control elimination. Part of this pleasure comes from the encouragement and praise he receives from his caregivers. Part also comes from the actual physical sensations associated with these body processes.

The phallic stage transpires during the fourth and fifth years. At this time, pleasure centers on the genitals. Exploration and/or masturbation are not unusual as the child seeks to understand and establish sexual identity. At first, both boys and girls relate very closely with the mother, since she has been a major source of nurturance during infancy. At about age five, most boys will shift identification to the father, who, from that time on, will be the role model.

If the child receives adequate and appropriate satisfaction during each of these stages, his emotional development is likely to be healthy. If, however, he is overindulged or if he is neglected during one of these periods, certain lifelong problems may occur. Freud believed that problems during the oral stage could result in behavior such as alcoholism, overeating, or nailbiting. Maladjustments during the anal stage could lead to stinginess and overconcern for order (holding in) or messiness and compulsive excessives (expelling). Phallic difficulties could be manifested as extreme selfishness, bragging, and pompousness. Many research studies have failed to support these observations. These three stages are followed by a latency period which begins at about age six and extends until adolescence. During this period there is a lull in sexual development. Freud believed that during this time many of the psychological conflicts of the oral, anal, and phallic stages are suppressed from conscious memory although they still affect behavior. In therapy, this "forgotten" material must be remembered in order to deal with problems that result from these early impressions.

Breger (1981) describes Freud's psychoanalytic theory as an "unfinished journey" since much more research is needed to make necessary modifications in his theory. He pointed out that since a large number of Freud's research subjects were upper-middle-class European women of the nineteenth century, Freud's ideas were both time- and culture-bound. Although Freud's contributions were unquestioningly significant, current cross-cultural research is needed to test and revise his theories about the causes of behavior. Personality problems are very complex and may result from a combination of many factors that occur throughout life.

Psychosocial Theory: Erikson

Erikson was trained as a psychoanalyst in the tenets of Freud. He later expanded on Freud's theories in order to stress the effects of society on our psychological and social development. In his classic book *Childhood and Society*, Erikson identified eight stages of development through which he believes all people must pass. "There is in every child at every stage a new miracle of vigorous unfolding, which constitutes a new hope and a new responsibility for all" (Erikson, 1963, p. 255). We shall examine the first four of these stages, since they relate to young and elementary age children.

Erik Erikson

THEORIES OF DEVELOPMENT

BASIC TRUST VERSUS BASIC MISTRUST: HOPE. The child begins to develop trust or mistrust as he notices whether or not his basic needs for food, cleanliness, and human contact are being met. Erikson believes it is the quality or feeling that a conscientious caregiver transmits that helps the child develop an inner certainty that his world is a good and nurturant place. The warm smile the infant sees on the approaching caregiver's face and the rocking and crooning the young child enjoys when discomforts make him fretful are but two examples of caregiver responses that engender trust. By contrast, an unstable or unresponsive environment at this time can lead to a lifelong tendency toward "a depressive state involving excessive caution and withdrawal in relations with the world—an inability to trust others or oneself" (Stevens, 1983, p. 44).

AUTONOMY VERSUS SHAME AND DOUBT: WILL. At about the age of two, the child's motor maturation enables him to move independently, and his emerging language skills enable him to express himself. "No" seems to be a favorite expression at this age. In essence the child is saying, "No, I am not a part of someone else, I am a separate person." The development of this separateness is of far-reaching importance. It serves as the foundation for assuming personal responsibility. (This little individual who can say "No" can also learn to be responsible for doing things that need to be done and for monitoring his own behavior.) What the child does with this new freedom, however, may give rise to the phrase "terrible twos."

There are many activities that help the child to develop a "can do" attitude. The child can learn to dress himself, to eat independently, to clean up when he litters, and to express simple courtesies such as "please" and "thank you." In all of these, adults play a crucial role. They should encourage and praise the child for pursuing constructive goals while protecting him from asserting himself simply for the pleasure of having his own way. Being successful at doing for themselves at this stage helps children develop a sense of autonomy and self-assurance. Excessive shaming during this period may cause children to doubt their personal worth and their ability to act independently.

INITIATIVE VERSUS GUILT: PURPOSE. The child between the ages of three and five has boundless energy and delights in starting things (not necessarily in finishing them). Great wisdom is needed on the part of the caregiver to be able to guide the child into projects in which he has a good chance for success without squelching his desire to tackle virtually anything. (I started a tunnel under our back fence at age four. I can still remember how puzzled I was when it kept caving in!)

Children at this stage may also feel the sting of jealousy when they compare their efforts with the accomplishments of older, more competent children. Siblings should be encouraged to be supportive and not tease younger children in the family about their first initiatives. Children may also experience jealousy with reference to the attention their parents give to each other. Since attachment to parents at this age is very strong and often possessive, a child may make many frustrated attempts to compete with one parent for the love and attention of the other. In such cases, both parents need to find opportunities to help the jealous child feel loved, accepted, and needed. As they get older, children include heroes of screen, sports, and neighborhood as models whose accomplishments may be imitated.

If the child can do many of the things he tries, and if his efforts are respected, he is likely to continue to initiate. If not, he is likely to feel guilty about his lack of ability and is apt to try constantly to get others to do for him.

INDUSTRY VERSUS INFERIORITY: COMPETENCE. The child of elementary school age learns to derive satisfaction and approval through producing things. He becomes adept in the use of the tools and skills of his society. By contrast to the younger child, who is content merely to start projects, the child from six to twelve gradually develops a sense of pleasure in working industriously and in completing projects. If the child's efforts are not successful, he is apt to internalize feelings of inferiority. The child who comes to school ill-prepared for academic tasks or the one who feels unworthy because of his ethnic group or social status is likely to accept defeat at this early age and achieve far below his actual potential. An overstress on success as the measure of worthiness may also produce an individual who is either a slavish nonconformist with a fear of creativity or an antisocial person who feels that anything is "fair game" if it works to his advantage.

All children experience some feelings of mistrust, doubt, guilt, and inferiority. The ages mentioned in the preceding paragraphs merely reflect the time at which the characteristic first appears in most people. According to Erikson, it is the ratio or number of positive versus negative experiences internalized by the child that determines his psychological health. Think of the labels of each of these stages as points on a continuum rather than as all-or-nothing attributes.

If the child develops a strong sense of autonomy, for example, he may move on to the next stage with ease and confidence. If he has only moderate success at autonomy, however, he may have difficulty having enough faith in his own ability to initiate many things in the initiative versus guilt stage. But what happens to the child who has very little opportunity to develop the characteristics of a given stage? Erikson says that he fixates,

THEORIES OF DEVELOPMENT

or gets stuck and remains in this stage. Such a child will not be able to function at the next stage and may meet with great discrimination and pressure from both peers and caregivers. Children who develop trust, autonomy, initiative, and industry more than mistrust, shame, guilt, and inferiority are likely to be happy with themselves and successful in their relations with others. Erikson stressed the constant interactions among the capacities of the individual, the expectations of society, and the many situations that occur. A person is capable of behaving in many ways and becoming many things. Different subcultures within a society stress different values and skills. Many situations related to such factors as opportunity, health, and fortune occur—some by accident and some as a result of individual effort. Each factor interacts with other elements to affect what the person will do and become. For more information relating to Erikson's theory, see Chapter 9.

Behaviorist Theory: Skinner, Dollard, and Miller

The noted psychologist J. B. Watson coined the term *behaviorism* in the early 1900s. He was concerned about the speculation by Freud and others concerning internal thought processes. Watson felt that more accurate work could be done if psychologists concentrated on the behaviors that could actually be seen and measured. Because of this emphasis on observable behaviors, the followers of this trend became known as the behaviorists.

Operant Conditioning: Skinner

Whereas Freud believed it is necessary to know the cause of behavior in order to change it, Skinner believes the response a person receives following his behavior determines whether or not he is likely to repeat the act (Holland and Skinner, 1961; Skinner, 1974).

WHAT IS OPERANT CONDITIONING?   With every response we make, we operate on the environment by changing it in some way. When Seth responds to an argument by biting his playmate, he has operated on his friend. When Denise scatters toys, she has operated on the play area. The response made by the playmate or teacher to these actions affects the probability of their recurrence. Although much behavior in very small children is impulsive and without premeditation, the child soon learns to consider the consequences that followed previous similar behavior in determining how he wants to act in a given situation. The child operates on the environment and is conditioned by the results (operant conditioning).

B. F. Skinner   (*Source: Courtesy, B. F. Skinner, Harvard University. Photo by Christopher S. Johnson*)

REINFORCEMENT.   A reinforcement is anything that happens following a behavior that increases the chances the person will act that way again. If behavior is not reinforced, it will occur less frequently. Eventually behavior that is not reinforced in some way will be given up entirely (extinguished). There are two kinds of reinforcement—positive and negative.

Positive reinforcement involves responding to behavior with something the individual likes. Reinforcements frequently valued by children include attention, approval, affection, food, stars/checks, tokens, favorite activities, and free time. To be effective, the caregiver must learn which child likes which response. To one child, a smile or a pat may be very rewarding; to another, such teacher attention may threaten peer status and be very unwelcomed. Caregivers must also be careful not to positively reinforce undesired behavior. The teacher who puts the child in the hall as punishment may actually be rewarding him. That youngster may find more interesting things to do in the hall than in the classroom.

THEORIES OF DEVELOPMENT *15*

Negative reinforcement involves the ending of an unpleasant experience. If the child has been required to sit on the sideline during a game because of misbehavior, the teacher applies negative reinforcement when she lets him rejoin the group. The good feeling that a child has when he is able to end an undesired condition encourages him not to repeat the act that caused the restriction or punishment. He realizes he can continue in this pleasant state if he does not repeat the offending behavior. Both positive reinforcement (giving the child something he likes) and negative reinforcement (removal of an unpleasant situation) will tend to increase the frequency of the behavior they follow.

PUNISHMENT. Punishment is not the same as negative reinforcement. Punishment occurs when behavior is followed by (1) the removal of something the individual likes (e.g., taking away privileges) or (2) the administering of something the person doesn't like (e.g., scolding). The effectiveness of punishment is questionable, since research indicates that it is impossible to predict in advance whether or not the child, when punished, will change his behavior and if so, in what direction.

TWO NECESSARY CONDITIONS. Two conditions are necessary if operant conditioning is to be successful: (1) the reward for the desired behavior must be administered immediately, and (2) the reward must be something the individual values and wants. Further details on shaping behavior and scheduling rewards are included in Chapter 10.

Social Learning Theory: Dollard and Miller

Social learning theory stresses the role of social and cultural factors in determining what a person is likely to do and the conditions under which he is apt to express or inhibit certain actions. In their classic work, Miller and Dollard (1941) stated that learning involved drive, cue, response, and reward. These occur in sequence to produce behavior. The following ideas are based on their work.

A drive is a desire that is strong enough to impel action. Some of these drives, such as pain and hunger, are innate. Other drives are acquired as they are learned from one's society. Approval is an example of a drive acquired as the individual learns that many of his needs and wants can be satisfied by others if their approval is won. Powerful motivation to do or to have something often results from a combination of drives.

Cues are objects or occurrences in the environment that determine when and where an individual will respond to a drive and which response he will make. For example, the child who buys cookies in the grocery store may be faced with competing cues. The sight of the cookie bag cues him to open it immediately in the store. The appearance of a watchful mother who shakes her head "no" cues him to wait until he gets home. Anything that can be perceived by the senses can serve as a cue. These can be either internal (body sensations) or external (persons, places, things, events).

A single cue may elicit different responses according to its distinctive features. A strong noise may be frightening and cue flight, whereas a soft one may be relaxing and induce sleep. Many jokes have been made about the child who never follows directions until the parent says the words in a certain tone of voice.

Response is the action a person may make to a cue. Some responses are almost automatic (removing the hand after touching something hot). Other responses are learned as a result of reward systems. The individual tends to repeat acts he finds rewarding and refrain from those that are not. (These basic ideas were presented in the section concerning operant conditioning.)

A reward is something an individual desires. It may be material (possessions), social (friends, group membership), or psychological (feeling of success or accomplishment). Rewards have different value intensities. There are some things for which we will work very hard; other things we will do only if they come easily. Influencing the behavior of another person, whether in an academic or a social setting, depends on an understanding of how much that individual wants a particular thing.

MATCHED-DEPENDENT AND COPYING BEHAVIORS. Two types of action demonstrate imitation. Each involves important concepts related to explaining behavior. The first is matched-dependent behavior, which involves a leader/follower relationship. The person who is the leader is often older or more experienced in the given setting. He notes the cues and behaves in a way he feels is most advantageous. The follower simply "goes along"—doing what he sees done in the immediate present. Many times a child's behavior is matched-dependent. When the adult asks why he did something, he will simply say, "Because John did it." Matched-dependent behavior is often done without independent thought on the part of the follower and may reflect only the values of the leader.

The second type of imitative behavior is copying. The copier observes someone who has possessions or skills he desires. He then consciously works to copy the behavior of the model. He believes that if he can become enough like the model he will come into possession of the things he desires. Further data on the effects of social learning and imitation on development are found in Chapter 9 (social) and Chapter 10 (moral).

Maturational Theory: Gesell

Arnold Gesell believed that development was based more on the maturation of an individual's body systems than on environmental factors. Therefore, he conducted surveys to document the small changes that occur in a child's development as a result of age and maturation (Gesell, 1945). Using samples of children at each age level (e.g., twos, threes, fours), Gesell and his research teams did detailed studies of children's behavior. Direct observation in the home, extensive photography, and psychological examination provided data which were compiled into developmental schedules.

Gesell felt this information would be of great value to parents, teachers, and clinicians in working with children. The first-time mother may be less discouraged by Jason's "No, no, no!" if she understands that assertiveness is typical of a "terrible two." The caregiver preparing to work with a given age level can gain "presight" by studying the physical, cognitive, social, and emotional characteristics of these youngsters. Clinicians can use the schedules as a basis for differentiating between typical and atypical behavior.

From his research, Gesell concluded that behavior develops in cycles.

> At some ages the child seems to be in good equilibrium; at others, in rather marked disequilibrium. There are ages when he is compliant and restrained; others when behavior is definitely out of bounds.
>
> All of this occurs in such a systematic way and so similarly from child to child that we have come to think of developing behavior as spiraling, moving upward and doubling back like a spiral set at an upward angle.
>
> This, of course, does not mean that all 2½-year-olds are difficult at all times or in all situations, or that all threes are continually calm and amenable. Behavior can vary from hour to hour as it does from child to child. But in general we have found these characterizations to be accurate and to help in our understanding of the inevitable behavior changes which will take place as any given child matures. (Ames et al., 1979, p. 18)

These data are reported in several age level books (Ilg and Ames, 1981; Gesell and Ilg, 1986). These volumes contain detailed information concerning behavior that is typical of the child at each age level. For the youngster under three, the descriptions are written at half-year intervals. Areas of

BOX 1.2
Sample "Age-Stage" Data: Gesell

Behavior profile: summary of about ten pages on how the child will likely act at a given age
Maturity of traits: specific information concerning a child's characteristics in such categories as:

- motor proficiency
- personal hygiene
- emotional expression
- fears and dreams
- self and sex
- relations with others
- school life
- play and past

---

development included are motor, adaptive (use of materials such as paper/pencil, cubes, and formboards), language, and personal-social. A sample of the information that can be found for each age level is presented in Box 1.2.

Gesell's research is now being carried on by the Gesell Institute. One interesting outlet for their research findings is a television talk show to which problems in child behavior are submitted by studio guests and by letters from the viewing audience.

One serious criticism of Gesell's work is that the research samples mainly comprised upper-middle-class Anglo children in Connecticut. To better understand ethnic differences among children and the effects of culture on development, the reader is encouraged to become familiar with such books as *Black Children: Their Roots, Culture, and Learning Styles* (Hale, 1982) and *Education: A Theoretical Analysis* (Weber, 1984). Findings from these authors will be reported in subsequent chapters.

Developmental Tasks: Havighurst

As the child matures physically he is able to walk; as he develops neurologically he can talk and reason. With these emerging abilities comes the expectation from society that the child will master a series of developmental tasks. Successful mastery of a given task leads to personal satisfaction and social approval; failure at mastery results in negative self-feelings, discrimination from others, and difficulty with future tasks (Havighurst,

THEORIES OF DEVELOPMENT   *19*

Robert J. Havighurst

1979). For instance, somewhere between two and four years of age, most children learn to control elimination. If the task is successfully mastered at this time, the child feels good about himself and moves on to other tasks. If he does not succeed at this time, others disapprove of his behavior, he feels bad about himself, and he may not be able to participate without embarrassment in many future activities.

INFANCY AND EARLY CHILDHOOD TASKS. Havighurst has divided life into time periods—infancy and early childhood, middle childhood, adolescence, early adulthood, middle age, and later maturity—and has identified the major developmental tasks for each of these periods. The major tasks for middle childhood are presented in Box 1.3.

REASONS FOR TASKS. From Box 1.3 one can see that some tasks result primarily from maturation (e.g., learning to walk, controlling elimination).

BOX 1.3
Havighurst's Developmental Tasks: Middle Childhood

- Learning physical skills necessary for ordinary games
- Building wholesome attitudes toward oneself as a growing organism
- Learning to get along with age-mates
- Learning an appropriate masculine or feminine social role
- Learning fundamental skills in reading, writing, and calculating
- Developing concepts necessary for everyday living
- Developing conscience, morality, and a scale of values
- Learning to personal independence
- Developing attitudes toward social groups and institutions

Other tasks are created from the pressures of society (e.g., getting ready to read, developing a sense of right and wrong). Finally, individual personal values that one forms may serve as a basis for later tasks. Throughout life most tasks will be based on an interaction of all three—maturation, societal pressures, and personal values.

TASK ANALYSIS. Havighurst used the following format in analyzing each developmental task (Havighurst, 1979). First he gave a brief definition of the task. Then he discussed biological bases (e.g., maturation, physical differences) and cultural bases (e.g., variance from culture to culture). He concluded with educational implications—how caregivers can assist the individual in accomplishing the task.

The following example is drawn from Havighurst's analysis of getting ready to read (Havighurst, 1979). The nature of the task is defined as learning that signs represent words, being able to discriminate among several different symbols, and acquiring a large vocabulary. The biological basis involves both the brain and the eye. The brain must contain a large store of words and meanings, and the eye must be able to focus on small objects (letters or words), move slightly and refocus (following a line of words on the printed page), and function for a period of time without eyestrain. The cultural basis for reading is vested in the number of experiences the child has had that may give the written words meaning and the vocabulary to which the youngster has been exposed. The educational implications are that reading readiness may be fostered by providing the child with (1) a variety of experiences for concept development, (2) practice in form perception, and (3) development in oral language.

THE TEACHABLE MOMENT. Havighurst believes there are sensitive periods during which some skills are best learned. "When the body is ripe, and society requires, and the self is ready, the teachable moment has come" (Havighurst, 1979, p. 7). Attempting to teach a skill too early may result in frustration and failure; waiting too late may result in low self-concept and negative societal reactions. A study of child development can assist caregivers in determining these "teachable moments."

Cognitive Theory: Piaget

Are we born with intelligence, or do we develop it from interaction with the environment? What effect does cognitive development have on other aspects of our lives? These are the questions the Swiss psychologist Jean Piaget has tried to answer (Piaget, 1963; Piaget and Inhelder, 1969; Modgil et al., 1983).

ACQUIRING AND STORING INFORMATION. What happens to the information we take into our minds? Piaget believes we form mental patterns which he calls schemas. The child who coos and waves his arms at the sight of a familiar face or pops his thumb into his mouth when he is tired is showing that he has developed behavior patterns. When these patterns are regularly repeated, the child is said to have developed a schema for that activity. These schemas may be motor responses (the way a child throws a ball), or they may be verbalizations (the ability to form grammatically correct sentences).

How do we develop these schemas? Piaget believes we take in, revise, and store information in our minds through two reciprocal processes—assimilation and accommodation. These processes are constantly active and account for our growth in an understanding of our environment.

When an individual puts new information into his cognitive system—when he sees, hears, feels, smells, or tastes—Piaget says that assimilation has taken place. This input becomes a part of our mental structure just as the food we eat is assimilated and becomes a part of our physical being. Both children and adults spend much of their time assimilating cognitive input from the environment. Many times the information we try to assimilate does not fit existing structures. In such cases, we may do one of two things. First, we may take it in "as is" and get a distorted or incorrect view of something. (We may misidentify a sheep as a goat.) Second, we may change our cognitive structure to make use of the new data (called accommodation).

Very frequently the information we are assimilating contains some new data that we need to incorporate into an existing schema. Accommodation may occur (1) when an existing schema is changed to incorporate new information (horses may be black, white, big as a Clydesdale or small as a Shetland) or (2) when a new category is set up (the animal is a goat, not a sheep). In order to maximize cognitive functioning, the individual should maintain a balance, or equilibrium, between the amounts of assimilating and of accommodating that occur.

Of what value is this equilibrium between assimilation and accommodation? Assimilation provides a constant supply of new data from the environment. This new information can be used to expand and refine existing concepts through accommodation. If assimilation is limited, the new information needed for more clear or advanced thinking is missing. If accommodation does not constantly take place, assimilated data are not used to make the changes in existing schemas needed for increased comprehension. A lack of equilibrium between assimilation and accommodation, therefore, can result in thinking that is apt to be limited, out-of-date, or biased.

STAGES OF DEVELOPMENT. Piaget believes intelligence develops through a series of stages. These periods must occur in a particular order, since at each stage the individual becomes more effective in using input from the environment. Box 1.4 contains a summary of these periods.

When you examine Box 1.4, you can see how one stage builds on another. For instance, infants must have freedom to explore and see things before they can develop the perceptions they use during the preschool years. A wide variety of perceptual experiences must occur during the preschool period in order to develop the ability to analyze relationships and set up categories at the concrete level during the elementary school ages. Each level builds on the experiences that occur at the preceding level, and a limited learning environment during any period may significantly restrict cognitive development.

PROGRESSION THROUGH STAGES. What causes the individual to move from one stage to another? First, maturation furnishes the physical capabilities, both internal and external. The nerve endings become more refined so that impulses travel with greater speed and accuracy. The eyes, ears, and hands develop more mature functioning. Second, active experience enables the child both to discover the properties of objects and to understand the relationships necessary for organizing the environment. The child finds that objects can be hard or soft, round or square, solid or hollow, big or little. He learns that some things are part of a larger whole, that objects that are alike may go together in a set, that things of different

BOX 1.4

Piaget's Periods of Development

Periods	Approximate Age Range	Characteristics
Sensorimotor period	Birth–2 years	• Uses senses and motor abilities to investigate environment • Needs verbal and social interactions for language and personality foundations • Must have freedom to explore

Preoperational period	2–7 years	• Is developing representational thought:
		    Stores mental images of past experience
		    Can mentally "picture" future actions or wishes (e.g., a trip to the zoo, a visit from Santa)
		• Is rapidly increasing vocabulary and language facility
		• Is perceptually bound (can't distinguish likeness and differences unless visually apparent)
		• Thinking is affected by:
		    egocentrism—seeing things only from one's own point of view
		    centering—concentrating on only one attribute (e.g., size, color)
		    inability to follow transformations—cannot follow change and know things remain the same even if they look different (do number of objects change when row is shortened)
		    inability to form reversals—cannot see that original state or order can be restored by reversing an action

Concrete	7–11 years	• Uses more mature logic to analyze relationships and construct knowledge • Sets up meaningful categories • Understands conservation—if nothing has been added or taken away, it must be the same even if arrangement makes it look different
Formal	11+ years	• Can use abstract thought in analyzing concepts • Can think through propositions and hypotheses

sizes may be lined up in a series—small to large; first, second, third, and so on. Third, social interaction provides models for behavior and feedback concerning other points of view. Janice can't snatch toys away from other children because they will hit her. One of the ways Denise learns that ∴ is three, not four, is that another child corrects her. Finally, Piaget believes that within each individual is an inborn inclination to take in new experiences and incorporate these into meaningful thought patterns. Because we are human, we are impelled to try new things, evaluate the results, and use the knowledge we gain as the basis for additional action.

CONSTRUCTION OF KNOWLEDGE. The major emphasis of Piaget's work and the research related to it is the construction of knowledge. The child uses his physical capacities, environmental experiences, and internal responses to construct understandings of things in the world around him. As he explores, he may learn as much from his wrong ideas as from his right ones when he observes that some things don't work and determines why. This constant cycle of taking in information and revising present concepts helps the child build ever-more-precise schemas. Further discussion of Piaget's theory and its relation to cognitive development is found in Chapter 6.

Self Theory: Rogers

Carl Rogers believes that a well-adjusted, fully functioning individual is one who can recognize his feelings—his hopes, fears, values, and dislikes—and still feel that he is a person of worth (Rogers, 1951, 1961). According to Rogers, many mental health problems occur when an individual denies or distorts these true feelings because he deems such emotions shameful or unacceptable.

Rogers developed his theory over a period of years as he worked as a psychotherapist with both children and adults. His technique is called nondirective, client-centered therapy because Rogers does not tell the client what he should do or how he should feel; Rogers accepts the individual completely as that person is. Rogers has identified and described sixteen tenets related to self-development. The following is an annotated list containing seven of these ideas:

1. Everyone is the center of his constantly changing world. When the classroom is in an uproar, the teacher from her center may decry it as a "horrible day," whereas the students may view the time as delightful and exciting.
2. "Reality" for each individual is "how he sees it." Whether we feel a given situation is fearful, happy, successful, or unpleasant depends not only on what happens at that time but also on our past experience.
3. All people strive to develop and improve. People may appear to be unmotivated when they feel that they cannot succeed at a given task or when they do not see the activity as being related to their needs and goals.

Case Study 1

Feelings: True or False

Three-year-old Derek is greatly upset by the arrival of a little brother. Resenting the attention the baby is getting during a feeding time, Derek slugs the infant. Mother attempts to sound convincing as she says, "Why Derek, how naughty. You know you love little Timmy!" Derek scowls and darts away.

Derek doesn't love Timmy at this point in time, and denying or falsifying his true feelings won't change them. Mother could help Derek keep his true feelings intact by responding honestly, "I know you wish the baby didn't take so much of my time, but you and I are going to do something together after Timmy eats. And perhaps as Timmy gets a little older, you can enjoy doing things with him, too." (Even more effective would be to think of something the child would like to do with Timmy today.) In this way, Derek doesn't have to deny his present feelings in order to be a "good boy," and he can be encouraged by the thought that Timmy may be good for something someday.

---

4. The self structure is formed as a result of feedback from the environment, particularly from the evaluations of others. Much of what we believe about whether we are good or bad, attractive or ugly, clever or unsuccessful is based on the way others have reacted to us.
5. How a person behaves is greatly affected by what he thinks of himself. In many cases, a person will become whatever others think he is—whether good or bad!
6. When a person feels threatened, he becomes rigid. In the absence of threat, the individual may be willing to try some changes and new experiences.
7. When a person is able to understand and accept all of his own feelings and experiences, he will become more accepting and understanding of others.

During the course of therapy, Rogers encourages the client to discover his true feelings, accept himself as a good and capable person, and make his own decisions based on this self knowledge. As a result, it is hoped that the individual will become more accepting of self and others.

INVOLVER 1

Living the Theories

In this chapter, many explanations for behavior have been considered. The purpose of this involver is to relate these ideas to your daily life. Construct a chart as shown below. For the following three days, record experiences that relate to any of these theories (e.g., "My id prevailed over my ego, and I went shopping instead of studying" could be placed in the Psychoanalytic column).

THINKING IT OVER

What did you learn about yourself? Which theories did you understand better after having applied them? About which theories do you want to know more? Which theory do you feel best explains behavior, and why?

Psycho-analytic: Freud	Psycho-social: Erikson	Develop-mental Task: Havighurst	Cognitive: Piaget	Operant Conditioning: Skinner	Social Learning: Dollard and Miller	Self: Rogers

THEORIES OF DEVELOPMENT

Summary

- Freud described the personality as having three parts: the id (concerned with innate bodily needs), the ego (developed to analyze and deal with reality), and the superego (based on what the individual's society has said was right and wrong). He viewed anxiety as a fear reaction which may be alleviated through identification with a person of perceived strength and desirability or through the unconscious use of distorted responses called defense mechanisms (e.g., repression, undoing, projection).
- Four of the eight stages through which Erikson feels an individual passes occur during early childhood (trust versus mistrust, autonomy versus shame and doubt, initiative versus guilt, industry versus inferiority). If the child experiences more successes than failures at each of these stages, he is likely to be well-regarded by both self and others.
- Skinner believes that what happens to an individual immediately after an action determines whether he is likely to repeat that behavior. Operant conditioning involves (1) rewarding desirable behavior immediately and (2) finding and applying a reward that is valued by the subject. Reinforcement (reward) may be either positive (giving an individual something he likes) or negative (removing a condition he doesn't like). For behavior control, punishment is less effective than reward, since the child's response to punishment is less predictable.
- Dollard and Miller described the effects of drives, cues, responses, and rewards on behavior. They also explained how matched-dependent and copying behaviors are manifested in imitation.
- Gesell is best known for his "ages and stages" research. He and his associates have examined large groups of children at various age levels and have used these data to construct developmental scales based on the behavior of children at different ages. Several books describing these ages and stages have been published.
- Havighurst believes each individual must accomplish a series of "developmental tasks"—skills that, if mastered, will enable the individual to function successfully in his society and that, if not mastered, will result in personal frustration and rejection by society.
- According to Piaget, intelligence is developed as a person forms mental patterns (schemas) through the processes of assimilation (fitting new information into existing mental patterns) and accommodation (revising existing thinking to utilize new data). Because of maturation, experience, and environmental feedback, people pass through a series of stages.

At each of these, the individual becomes more competent in thinking ability.
- Rogers stresses the importance of recognizing and accepting our own feelings. If we feel sufficiently secure about our own worth, he believes we will be more accepting of others. We may also be able to make changes in ourselves without undue feelings of threat and fear.

Selected Readings

ERIKSON, E. H. *Childhood and Society* (2nd ed.). New York: Norton, 1963.
In addition to a comprehensive discussion of each of the eight stages of man, this book includes related case studies from other cultures.

FREUD, S. *An Outline of Psychoanalysis.* New York: Norton, 1970.
This work provides a brief but comprehensive summary of the basic tenets of Freud's theory.

GESELL, A., AND ILG, F. L. *The Child from Five to Ten.* New York: Harper and Row, 1986.
This work gives detailed information concerning emotional, social, physical, and cognitive development of the child on a year-by-year basis.

HAVIGHURST, R. J. *Developmental Tasks and Education* (3rd ed.). New York: Longman, 1979.
A separate chapter is devoted to an analysis of tasks related to each age level.

HOLLAND, J. G., AND SKINNER, B. F. *The Analysis of Behavior.* New York: McGraw-Hill, 1961.
This is a programmed text designed to teach the basic concepts of operant conditioning.

PIAGET, J., AND INHELDER, B. *The Psychology of the Child.* New York: Basic Books, 1969.
This is a good first book—simply written, yet including essential basic concepts.

ROGERS, C. R. *Client-Centered Therapy: Its Current Practice, Implications, and Theory.* Boston: Houghton-Mifflin, 1951.
This book includes both a description of client-centered therapy and a detailed discussion of each of Roger's sixteen tenets.

WADSWORTH, B. J. *Piaget's Theory of Cognitive and Affective Development* (3rd ed.). New York: Longman, 1984.
This is a concise summary written in lay terms—very readable.

CHAPTER 2

Child Study through Research, Observation, and Interaction

(*Source: Courtesy, National Science Teachers Association*)

CHAPTER OUTLINE

    Types of Research
        Historical Research
        Descriptive Research
        Experimental Research
    Personal Involvement in Child Study
        "Looking and Learning": Observation Techniques
        Interactions: Interviews, Assessment Instruments, and Creative Activities
    Ethical Child Watching
    Summary
    Selected Readings

The student teacher was asked to select one of the first-graders for a case study. When she chose a very quiet, self-contained little boy, the cooperating teacher cautioned that she might not get enough data because "that little boy never does anything." Curious, Kim decided to accept the challenge. After several observation attempts confirmed the classroom teacher's prediction, the student teacher decided to use time sampling and record exactly what this youngster was doing at thirty-second intervals. "Dan selected book . . . seated himself away from others . . . read attentively (fidgity child pulled up chair close by) . . . ignored child's attempts to talk to him . . . winced as child turned over chair and bumped against him . . . scowled as child lurched against him again . . . without looking up from book, quickly backhanded child knocking him sprawling onto the floor . . . continued to read attentively." The teacher, missing Dan's sleight of hand, saw the child on the floor, snatched him up, and said, "Why can't you find something to do quietly like Dan does?" The recently clobbered child looked bewildered at the teacher's lack of understanding, and Dan smiled shyly to himself as he continued to read attentively.

  Watching and interpreting the behavior of children is a fascinating activity. In this chapter, the reader first will be introduced to three basic types of research—historical, descriptive, and experimental. Then special emphasis will be given to techniques that can be used by the reader for gathering first-hand data through observation and interaction with children.

Types of Research

Research may be grouped into three basic categories—historical, descriptive, and experimental (Mook, 1982; Rosenthal and Rosnow, 1984). Each of these is used to explore different types of problems. The following survey should help to clarify the uses, possibilities, and problems associated with each.

Historical Research

WHAT IS HISTORICAL RESEARCH? Many times one wishes to investigate a current problem: What causes a child to be hyperactive? Do many children from one-parent families have cognitive and emotional difficulties? Information related to such problems can be garnered through historical research—the collection, synthesis, and interpretation of material that has already been recorded. Such data may include books, journal articles, diaries, letters, and artifacts. The quality of historical research depends on which facts are selected and how the material is organized and interpreted.

Primary source materials related to children include baby books and family scrapbooks. (*Source:* © 1988 Brent Jones)

USING PRIMARY AND SECONDARY SOURCES. Primary source materials are original documents and/or artifacts. Samples include legal papers (deeds, court records), personal notes (autobiographies, letters, diaries), and physical remains (clothing, pottery). Although the types of primary source materials are virtually limitless, many valuable specimens are lost because no one recognizes their historical potential. Family lore is often lost when an oldster dies unrecorded, houses no longer have attics for storing memorabilia, and the very explosion of paperwork in the twentieth century makes it difficult to determine what should be kept and what can safely be discarded.

Secondary source materials are reports that have been compiled after a study of the works of others. Research papers, textbooks, and encyclopedias are common forms of secondary research. When possible, both primary and secondary materials should be included in a research study, since each type has both advantages and disadvantages. Box 2.1 illustrates some possible strengths and weaknesses of primary and secondary materials.

BOX 2.1

Comparison of Primary and Secondary Sources

PRIMARY SOURCES

Pro	Con
• More detailed	• Limited to one person's view (may be biased)
• May contain interesting first-hand language	• Records only certain spots (fragmentary)
• Apt to convey feeling or emotional tone	• Accuracy hard to verify
	• Writer can evaluate only in terms of present (cannot perceive long-term effects)

SECONDARY SOURCES

Pro	Con
• Can present many points of view	• May cover too much material too fast (lacks depth needed for understanding)
• Can contain research relating to all aspects of problem	• May be dry and uninteresting
• Can infer accuracy from several concurring reports	• May present facts without conveying the "why"
• Can contain assessment of long-term effects	

PRODUCING QUALITY HISTORICAL RESEARCH. Attention to the following factors should improve the accuracy of historical research (Wiersma, 1985):

1. *Select the problem.* Interest in a particular area may come from such sources as personal experience, a study course, or related readings.
2. *Identify questions to be answered.* This helps to limit the topic. For instance, "prenatal development" is too broad and vague. "What are the effects of maternal nutrition on the unborn child?" narrows the problem. Questions also help in data gathering, since one knows specifically which information to collect.
3. *List possible sources for information.* Using a wide variety of quality sources generally improves the research. Check for validity, or trueness, of information by asking: "Is the author an authority in this subject area? Is there apparant bias? Was the conclusion backed by several reputable references?"
4. *Gather data.* Since you can't include everything without sounding like an almanac, you need to take notes selectively. Use the questions you developed in Step 2 to determine what to include and what to omit, choose references that are clear and concise, research widely, and report an unbiased sample of your findings (Mouly, 1982). Don't be like the student who said, "Help me find all the references that prove that Glaser's reality therapy is more effective than Freud's psychoanalysis."
5. *Sift and organize findings.* Organize the material so that it answers your questions. A summary of everything you have collected may be too detailed and/or meaningless. Omit the irrelevant and gather new data as needed.
6. *Interpret and draw conclusions.* "Facts have no meaning in and of themselves" (Mouly, 1982, p. 221). Accurately report what was found, try not to project personal biases in conclusions, and, if possible, offer several alternative explanations for your findings. It is also helpful to point out what was not found—what research still needs to be done in this area.

Descriptive Research

WHAT IS DESCRIPTIVE RESEARCH? Descriptive research is the systematic collection and interpretation of data that can be used to describe the current status of an individual or group or changes that take place over a period of time. *Cross-sectional research* refers to studies in which data are collected from a wide sample at one point in time. (A survey is conducted to identify the physical characteristics of four-year-olds; the socialization skills of a sample of fifth-graders living in a metropolitan area are compared with those of a corresponding sample from a rural setting.) By contrast, *longitudinal research* refers to studies in which an individual or group is followed for an extended period of time in order to note changes that may take place. (A group of children are observed from kindergarten through the sixth grade to determine what, if any, long-term effect attendance in a Head Start program has had on academic achievement.) Such data may be used in developing theories, inferring causes, planning treatments, and/or promoting understanding and empathy. There are many possible types of descriptive research. Each serves a particular function in describing or analyzing a given population. Examples used here to illustrate the strategies and possibilities of descriptive research are survey, case study, causal comparative study, content analysis, and follow-up study (Borg and Gall, 1983; Rosenthal and Rosnow, 1984; Best and Kahn, 1986).

THE SURVEY. The survey involves examining, questioning, or testing a large number of cases that belong to a particular group at a given time. Survey possibilities (Best and Kahn, 1986) include social issues (how many hours of television children watch), school problems (how many special education rooms are available), public opinion polls (who will win a seat on the school board), or market surveys (which toys are selling best). The instruments used in data collection may include questionnaires (administered by phone, mail, or personal interviews) or analyses of public records. In order to conduct an accurate survey, it is most important to "administer the same instrument in the same way to all subjects" (Borg and Gall, 1983, p. 188).

CASE STUDY. In contrast to the large number of cases examined in a survey, the case study involves the intensive and long-term examination of an individual or small sample in order to note changes and/or developments that take place during a specified period of time. A child's baby book or the records that a caregiver accumulates to document the social development of a given child are examples of case studies. Since the purpose of the case study is both to describe changes and to consider factors related to these modifications, many types of evidence should be collected and analyzed. Such data might include medical records, family surveys, direct observation, and conference reports from professionals.

CHILD STUDY THROUGH RESEARCH, OBSERVATION, AND INTERACTION

The case study of a child involves the long-term observation of that person. *(Source: © 1988 Jean Shapiro)*

Ethnographic research uses the case study method to record and analyze data concerning selected cultures or groups. These records comprise continuous logs of selected happenings. The researcher usually lives close to the target group and keeps carefully written records which may be supplemented by audio- and videotapes. This "live-in" experience is necessary in order to understand the value systems of the group being studied and to accurately interpret findings. Some of the advantages and disadvantages of ethnographic research are summarized below:

ADVANTAGES	DISADVANTAGES
• Based on long-term observations rather than on chance happenings	• Very expensive and time-consuming
• Recorded by observer who has had the opportunity to become familiar with group value systems	• May contain bias when observer is not a member of the target population
• Contains extensive detail	• May rapidly become dated if the group is in a state of change

CAUSAL COMPARATIVE STUDIES. Many times cause cannot be determined by experimentation for ethical reasons (e.g., child abuse cannot be administered to determine effects of such treatment on cognitive development). In such cases, causal comparative studies are often used. These studies are designed to discover possible causes for the presence of a particular characteristic in one group but not another. For instance, if a group of child abuse victims are found to have attention problems, they may be compared with a group of nonabused children by testing the attention spans of the children in both groups. If the average attention span for the abused group is found to be less than that of the nonabused group, the examiner may conclude that child abuse may affect attention span. Other factors that might explain the difference must be considered. Could age, sex, social class, nutrition, or motivation have caused the groups to differ? Although causal comparative studies can never prove that one condition caused another, possible cause and effect relationships can be explored in cases where direct experimentation cannot be used.

CONTENT ANALYSIS. Content analysis is widely used when careful examination of a document or process seems warranted. Books are checked for objectionable language and/or ideas, television programs are screened for violence, and company policies are reviewed for discrimination practices.

CHILD STUDY THROUGH RESEARCH, OBSERVATION, AND INTERACTION   37

FOLLOW-UP STUDIES. It is often necessary to measure and describe the lasting effects of a program or treatment. Follow-up studies are used for this purpose. Direct observation and testing instruments are employed to determine whether the individuals involved reaped any long-term benefits from the experiment. Care should be taken to evaluate in terms of the objectives of the program or treatment. For instance, if a Head Start program was designed to promote language development, then language skills, not social graces or creativity, should be measured to assess the success of the program.

Experimental Research

Experimental research is conducted to explore cause and effect relationships systematically. If two groups are initially alike and a special treatment is administered to one group but not to the other (e.g., language enrichment, perceptual training) or something is removed from one group but not from the other (e.g., negative comments on children's misbehavior, motor practice), differences then noted are believed to result from the thing that was added or taken away. The element that is put in or removed is called an *independent variable,* because the examiner can independently vary the condition of one group by adding this thing or taking it away. For instance, if one group of toddlers is given stair-climbing exercises and the other group is not, the training in climbing is the independent

---

BOX 2.2

Relationship between Independent and Dependent Variables

Independent Variable	*Dependent Variable*
• Physical fitness exercises	• Lung capacity
• Viewing violence on videotapes	• Number of aggressive acts committed
• Visual discrimination training	• Ability to see likenesses and differences

variable. The level of stair-climbing ability the children achieve is called the *dependent variable* since it is dependent on the training. Box 2.2 contains additional examples of independent and dependent variables and the relationship between them.

The group that is receiving this special treatment is called the *experimental group;* the one that receives no special instruction is called the *control group*. Control groups are very important, since they help the experimenter to determine what changes might take place automatically through maturation or as a result of circumstances other than the special treatment. In the stair-climbing incident, many children might have learned to climb without any special help as a result of maturation or other daily activities. Only if the climbing ability of the children in the training group significantly exceeds that of the control group might the treatment be considered a cause.

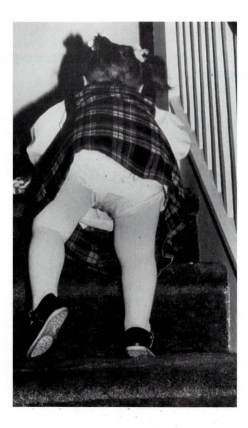

Does training change stair-climbing ability? (*Source: Grace Davies/Envision*)

CHILD STUDY THROUGH RESEARCH, OBSERVATION, AND INTERACTION   39

WHAT DETERMINES CAUSE?   Several factors must be considered in assigning cause. (1) Were both groups alike in the beginning? If not, differences noted might always have been there. (2) Did the assumed "cause" take place before the effect? Don't assume that because two conditions are present, one caused the other. The child from a one-parent family who is having temper tantrums may have been having these outbursts long before the divorce. (3) Are there other factors that might account for the effect? The autistic child may have cold parents, or he may have been born with impaired functioning.

RANDOMIZING OR MATCHING GROUPS.   How can the researcher determine if the two groups are basically alike before the experiment begins? One method is by randomizing. Randomization is used to ensure that no partiality was shown in the group assignments. To accomplish this goal, a table of random numbers (numbers in mixed order) is often used. Box 2.3 illustrates how a teacher assigned children to experimental and control groups using a table of random numbers.

Random assignment is based on the assumption that in this way the experimenter will have an approximately equal mixture of characteristics in each group. For some experiments, the researcher wants to be more exact. In this case, the subjects will be matched on any characteristics believed to be related to the treatment. For instance, if readiness scores,

---

BOX 2.3

Group Assignment by Table of Random Numbers

Random Numbers	Class Roll	Special Language Enrichment	No Special Language Enrichment
5	1. Jan	Kye	Maria
9	2. Tim	Josh	Jed
2	3. John	Tim	John
6	4. Graciela	Dennis	Carolyn
4	5. Kye	Graciela	Jan
1	6. Dennis		
8	7. Carolyn		
3	8. Jed		
7	9. Josh		
10	10. Maria		

intelligence quotients, and sex of the subject are believed to be related to success in beginning reading, the experimenter might compile a list of pairs of children who were matched on these characteristics. Then, from each pair, one child would be assigned to the experimental group and one to the control setting.

INSTRUMENTS: RELIABILITY AND VALIDITY.   If the research is to be accurate, the instruments (tests, measures, procedures) must be both reliable and valid. Instrument reliability means that the same score will always be awarded for a given response. For instance, a true-false test may be said to have high reliability, since everyone who selects the same response to a given question gets the same credit (or lack of it). By contrast, an essay test may have low reliability, because it may be difficult to determine whether John's response is equal to Michael's if what they wrote was quite different. Validity refers to whether the test measures what it is supposed to measure. A language-loaded mental abilities test would not be considered valid for a language-disabled child, since it would measure expressive skills as well as cognitive ability. A test that involved demonstrating or doing might have much higher validity in this case.

GENERALIZING.   After a research study has been conducted, the experimenter asks, "To what new situations can these conclusions be applied (or generalized)?" Care must be taken not to "overgeneralize" or apply conclusions incorrectly. If the experimenter found that black children in the inner city had limited vocabularies, she should not conclude that all black children are deficient in language skills. To correctly generalize a research finding to a new situation, one must consider not only how much alike the two circumstances are, but also what other factors could have accounted for the results that were noted.

Personal Involvement in Child Study

Observation and participation are two of the best ways to become personally involved in child study. First you will be introduced to some techniques that will help you to see more during the time you spend observing children. Next you will find a number of concrete suggestions for interactions that can be used with individual children or with small groups.

"Looking and Learning": Observation Techniques

Observations may be used for many purposes. They can help the observer investigate such factors as an individual's status, frequency of group participation, level of responsibility, attitudes, achievement and progress, and response to a variety of teaching techniques (Almy and Genishi, 1979). In planning observations, there are at least four possible aspects of the situation on which you can focus your attention—the individual child, the group, the caregiver, or the activity (Lindberg and Swedlow, 1980). Each of these will yield different types of information. A few possibilities are noted below:

Focus on individual child	• Learn more about that child
	• Investigate characteristics of a group (ethnic, sex, age level)
Focus on group	• Note interactions among children
	• See individual child's status in group
Focus on caregiver	• Notice arrangement of learning space
	• Observe facilitating or restricting behaviors
Focus on activity	• Determine how the activity relates to physical, cognitive, emotional, or social growth
	• Consider how motivation or interest is stimulated

To reap maximum benefit for the amount of time spent, you should identify in advance what your focus will be. You must also decide on a systematic method for recording your observations. Some frequently used notation systems include observation sheets, anecdotal records, event sampling and time studies (Walker, 1973; Cohen, 1976; Medinnus, 1976; Mook, 1982; Beatty, 1984).

OBSERVATION SHEETS. Some observation records are checklists used to collect specific information. These checklists may be in the form of questions the observer wishes to answer in order to better understand some facet of behavior. Checklists may also be used to indicate a child's level

BOX 2.4
Sample Observation Formats

FORMATS WITH QUESTIONS

- With whom does the child play? (Write out description—names of children, whether one only or group, sex of friends)
- What is the child's behavior in a group? (Circle all that apply.)

    a. quiet/noisy

    b. aggressive/passive

    c. hostile/friendly

    d. withdrawn/outgoing

FORMATS SHOWING DEGREE OF PROFICIENCY

- How is the child accepted by the group? (Circle number.)

    | 5 frequently chosen | 4 often chosen | 3 occasionally chosen |

    | 2 not noticed | 1 rejected |

- How often does the child assume responsibility? (Check one for each child.)

Name	Almost always	Frequently	Occasionally	Not yet
Mary				
Dennis				
John				

of achievement in a given area. Box 2.4 illustrates several observation formats.

Some observation sheets are much less structured and more open-ended (Lindberg and Swedlow, 1980). For instance, the observer might want to draw the floor plan of an early childhood room and determine how that particular arrangement of space and materials contributes to such factors as group interactions (spaces for children to work together), concentration (books away from blocks), and exploration (use of discovery materials). On another occasion, observation might involve examining and listing materials in each learning center in order to assess their value in physical, cognitive, language, and social development.

ANECDOTAL RECORDS. An observer often wishes to analyze individual or group behavior by writing descriptions of specific happenings. A collection of these observations is called an anecdotal record or a behavioral journal. Two crucial factors are knowing how to write objectively and deciding which episodes to record.

In order to report objectively, the writer should learn to note exactly what happened without interjecting personal feelings and evaluations. For example:

OBJECTIVE STATEMENT

- John kicked over Saul's block tower.
- Lori showed her picture to five children saying each time, "Isn't my house pretty?"

BIASED SOLUTION

- John had a tantrum.
- Lori feels insecure in the group.

In deciding which episodes to record, the following general recommendations may prove useful (Bonney, 1969):

- Observe the child in many settings to discover how she responds to different persons and situations.
- Record dates of episodes and names of all persons involved in the situation for clues as to when and with which persons the child is likely to act in a given manner.
- Try not to let the child know she is being watched lest she "act" for you.
- Don't limit study to problem children; at times concentrate on the "average" child to better understand normal behavior.

EVENT SAMPLING. If you want a better understanding of factors related to a given behavior, you may want to use event sampling—a detailed description of the situation in which a selected behavior occurs (Medinnus, 1976). Whereas an anecdotal record may include many different types of behavior, an event sampling focuses on one in particular (helping, quarreling, withdrawing). The observer must remember that conclusions cannot be drawn on the basis of a single observation. If, for instance, the withdrawal tendencies of a child are to be understood, a number of instances (events) of withdrawal must be recorded and compared. Event sampling may be unstructured (record as much detail about the incident as possible) or structured (use a checklist in order to compare episodes). Box 2.5 is a checklist designed to investigate withdrawal tendencies in a preschooler. By comparing the findings from several withdrawal episodes,

BOX 2.5
Event Sampling: Withdrawal

For each episode of withdrawal, record the following information:

- when or where withdrawal occurred
- how long episode lasted
- events immediately preceding withdrawal
- responses of others to withdrawal
- how long withdrawal lasted
- what was occurring when child became reinvolved with the group
- what child did immediately following reinvolvement

---

a caregiver might be able to identify the circumstances that cue withdrawal in this child.

TIME SAMPLING. When you are interested in the amount of time a child spends engaging in a particular behavior, time sampling is useful (Medinnus, 1976). Set up categories related to the behavior you want to analyze, and record what the child is doing at thirty-second or one-minute intervals. For instance, if you wanted to study a child's play patterns, you could place a checkmark in one of the following categories at timed intervals in order to compile a record of how she is spending her play time:

Solitary (alone)	I
Parallel (near but not with)	III
Cooperative (interacting with another child)	I

If you were trying to determine if a child's lack of progress was based on poor work habits, your categories might be "on task" and "not on task."

To be an effective observer, three cautions must be remembered (Almy and Genishi, 1979): (1) Avoid personal bias in recording. Your own past experience may cloud your objectivity. (2) Avoid "halos, horns, and averages." Unconsciously you may select what you expect to see—all the failures of the "bad" child and all the successes of the "good" child. The average child may be invisible. Many caregivers can describe their best and their most troublesome children but can't give much detail about many of those

CHILD STUDY THROUGH RESEARCH, OBSERVATION, AND INTERACTION 45

> ## INVOLVER 2
>
> ## *An Observation*
>
> Visit a preschool class and observe the children for a thirty-minute period. Then select one child who in some way is particularly interesting to you. Design an appropriate observation checklist based on one or more of the techniques discussed in the previous section. During two additional thirty-minute periods, use your checklist to record observations of the child you selected.
>
> **THINKING IT OVER**
>
> - What did you learn about the child you selected?
> - How does what you saw compare with what you have read or studied?
> - What kinds of activities would be appropriate for this child (for development, enrichment, and/or remediation)?
> - What questions did this observation raise that might serve as a basis for future observation or study?

in the middle. (3) Don't jump to conclusions. After a number of individual episodes are collected, the observer may note which actions have been repeated sufficiently to form a pattern of behavior and which may be mere chance happenings or reflect an "off day" for the child. Children are constantly changing. What you see is only a clue to the child's current state.

Interactions: Interviews, Assessment Instruments, and Creative Activities

Before you attempt to gain information about a child through interviewing, testing, or analyzing responses to planned activities, be sure the child has had ample time and opportunity to get acquainted with you. Fear and shyness must be overcome before the child is ready to share her ideas and feelings with others.

INTERVIEWS. An interesting way to gain insight into the child's thinking is by interviewing. Questions may be designed for either limited or open-ended responses. If you wish to compare children's answers by counting frequencies, use the limited response. Some examples of limited responses are yes-no answers; like me, not like me; very good-good, bad-very bad; or ☺ ☹ (have child mark happy or sad face on score sheet in response to questions).

If you want detailed information about a child's understanding of a subject, ask open-ended questions. These are questions that cannot be answered with a single word or short phrase. "How" and "tell me about" are good starters for questions that may get extended conversation from the child.

ASSESSMENT INSTRUMENTS.   Assessment instruments for young children may be classified into a number of categories including cognitive development, social/emotional functioning, and sensorimotor abilities (Walker, 1973; Goldman et al., 1983).

Cognitive development is estimated by noting the child's knowledge of her surroundings and her ability to do problem solving. Such development (Ames et al., 1979) may be demonstrated by:

· matching block play patterns such as building a tower or bridge
· copying forms

Adult interviewing child   (*Source: © Peter Anold, Inc.*)

CHILD STUDY THROUGH RESEARCH, OBSERVATION, AND INTERACTION 47

Case Study 2

Piaget's Interviews

Jean Piaget based his theory of cognitive development on insights gained through interviewing. He used a flexible system of open-ended questioning. After each response by the child, the interviewer designed her next question to further explore the child's ideas and understandings related to the topic being discussed. In this way, Piaget and his colleagues discovered the child's concepts in such areas as time, space, and causality. The following questions and responses are based on statements made during Piaget's investigation of the rules for playing marbles (Piaget, 1948):

Q. Where did the rules come from?
A. Oh, Noah's children played marbles this way when they came out of the ark.
Q. What would happen if someone cheated?
A. God would cause his marble to go wrong, and he would miss.

Try interviewing. It's refreshing and delightful to again see the world through the eyes of a child!

- drawing the missing parts on a "Draw-a-person" test
- writing own name, letters, numerals
- distinguishing colors
- counting
- naming objects or identifying pictures

Creative endeavors and problem-solving activities are also evidence of cognitive functioning.

From the preceding list, one can readily see that cognitive development is greatly influenced by experience. For this reason, estimates of cognitive ability made during early childhood may or may not accurately predict the level of cognitive functioning the child may possess at an older age.

A wide variety of social and emotional responses also may be checked. The following chart illustrates only a few of the many testing possibilities described by Walker in her book on socioemotional measures for young children (1973):

Characteristic	Test	Description
Attitudes	Family Relations Test (feelings about family)	Child selects family members from twenty cardboard figures; examiner reads forty statements depicting feelings; child attributes each to family member "it is most like."
Emotional adjustment	Human Figure Drawing Test (child's anxieties, concerns, and attitudes)	Child is asked to draw a "whole person"; thirteen special features such as size of parts and missing parts are assessed.
Interest	IT Scale for Children (sex-role preference)	Child selects toys she would like to play with from thirty-six pictures (stereotyped boy or girl toys shown).
Behavior traits	ETS Locus of Control Scale (whether child feels that happenings result from her behavior or from fate)	Child is shown twenty-two cartoon-type drawings and asked why the character succeeded or failed.

The child's large and fine motor development determine her ability to move through space and to use objects. Three important areas to check are fine motor, gross motor, and self-help skills (Ingram, 1980, p. 97). I have suggested some activities that can be used for assessing the child's proficiency in each area. Please note that these activities span a broad developmental range; the child should not be expected to become proficient in all these skills at the same age.

Motor Area	Skill	Testing Suggestions
Fine motor	Eye-hand coordination	• Cut with scissors • Remove dots with a hole punch • Pound nails
	Hand use	• Use lacing cards • Write words and numerals legibly
Gross motor	Walking Rolling Climbing Running Skipping	• Musical activities • Games • Use of playground equipment
Self-help	Eating	• Use of fork and spoon • Pouring without spilling
	Dressing	• Buttoning • Shoe tying

In addition to informal, self-made measures, there are a number of commercial tests, observation sheets, and rating scales available.

CREATIVE ACTIVITIES. Another fascinating way to learn more about children is through analysis of their activities and products. Youngsters exhibit many ideas, values, and feelings through both free play and planned activities. The following is intended to provide a few ideas to stimulate your thinking. The activity categories were taken from Almy and Genishi, 1979):

Activity	Motivation Suggestions	Possible Insights
Oral expression	• Let child finish story you started • Let child create story using pictures or puppets	• Language fluency • Sentence structure • Imagination • Cognitive level
Dramatic play	• Set up play house changing with such variations as school, doctor's office, grocery store	• Feelings, attitudes, and values • Knowledge of basic life • Home relations
Role playing	• Present a problem to the children through such means as discussion or story • Often select problem that group is actually having	• Ways a child usually responds to a given situation • Opportunity for child to "try out" new behaviors
Movement exploration	• Plan activities involving running, jumping, hopping, skipping • Use dance or rhythmics • Teach games	• Coordination • Balance • Ability to follow instructions
Art	• Use variety—crayons, clay, paint, scissors, wood • Make constructions	• Knowledge as evidenced through pictures and constructions • Eye-hand coordination feelings

Please use caution in interpreting creative expressions. Although the child may be demonstrating some great emotional need, she may merely be expressing an interest or exploring the use of materials. Her answer or product also may in no way be related to emotions. A kindergartner was sharing with me the picture she had drawn of her family. When I noticed that the baby was huge in comparison to the other family members, I immediately concluded that the child was troubled and felt displaced by her little brother. Wishing to confirm my guess, I said, "Tell me about your picture." "Well," the child replied, "that's me and Mommy and Daddy and Jason, and the reason Jason looks so big is that he's standing a lot

Dramatic play may give clues to the child's understandings and interests.

closer to you. Things look bigger the closer they get." I had completely misjudged the situation. Whereas I thought the child was feeling unloved, she actually was making a scientific observation.

Ethical Child Watching

Since a child who is too young to understand the nature and purpose of the research being conducted is often "volunteered" by the teacher and/or caregiver to participate, certain ethics must be maintained to protect her welfare (Lindberg and Swedlow, 1980; Hays, 1984).

RESPECT THE CHILD'S PRIVACY

- DO NOT identify the subjects of your studies. In written work refer to them under fictitious names or as Child A, B, Y, or Z.
- DO NOT discuss a child's problems in front of that child or the other children. Youngsters aren't deaf!
- DO NOT discuss findings outside the school setting. What you discovered about a given child is not the business of your friends or the child's neighbors.

PROTECT THE CHILD'S WELFARE

- DO NOT involve the child in any situation in which she will fail miserably. Stop testing when the child reaches the limit at which she can succeed (usually about three consecutive wrong answers).
- DO NOT involve the child in any interaction that will cause other children to ridicule or react negatively toward her.

The purpose of observation and interaction is to help the children involved. Thoughtless procedures can endanger both the child's self-esteem and her group status.

Summary

- Child study can be an exciting and informative pastime through the use of research, observation, and interaction with children.
- Three major types of research are historical, descriptive, and experimental.
- Historical research involves collecting, synthesizing, and interpreting available data related to a given topic. Primary source materials (original documents) add detail and human interest, and secondary source materials (the research findings of others) provide diverse points of view and assess the long-term effects. To produce quality research, one should define the problem; identify questions to be answered; list possible sources for information; gather data; sift, organize, and interpret findings; and draw conclusions.
- In descriptive research, the current status of an individual or group is examined. A survey involves questioning a large number of cases at a given point in time, whereas a case study is a long-term investigation of a single person or group. Causal comparative studies are conducted to explore the causes for differences between groups when, for ethical reasons, direct experimentation is not acceptable. Content analysis is used for the thorough examination of a document or process. Follow-

up studies are designed to determine the lasting effects of a treatment or program.
- Experimental research is used to explore cause and effect relationships. The independent variable is the element that is put in or taken out by the experimenter in an effort to produce the desired effect. The dependent variable is the activity or state that will be affected by the treatment. After the experiment, cause is inferred by measuring the difference between the experimental group who received special treatment and the control group who did not. Before assuming cause, one must determine whether the groups were initially alike, whether the "cause" preceded the "effect," and whether other factors might have accounted for the change. Instruments or procedures must be reliable (yielding consistent scores) and valid (measuring what they are purported to measure). Research findings should be generalized (applied) only to situations very similar to those in the study.
- Observation is vital in child study and may focus on the individual child, the group, the caregiver, or the activity. To record observations, a variety of checklists and other forms are helpful. A collection of written descriptions of a child's behavior is called an anecdotal record. If one particular type of behavior is selected for study, the procedure is called event sampling. When there is a need to determine how a child is spending her time, the activity in which she is engaged may be recorded at thirty-second to one-minute intervals (time sampling).
- Another important way to study children is through interaction, which may involve interviews, tests, or creative activities. Interview questions may be limited, requiring yes-no types of answers, or they may be open-ended, encouraging the child to extend her comments. A wide variety of teacher-made and commercial tests are available for use in assessing the child's cognitive development, social/emotional functioning, and sensorimotor abilities. Creative activities provide many additional opportunities to explore the child's development through her natural medium of play.
- Ethical considerations must always be included in child study. The researcher must always respect the child's privacy and protect the child's welfare throughout the course of the investigation. The major purpose of child study is to enhance the welfare of children.

Selected Readings

ALMY, M., AND GENISHI, C. *Ways of Studying Children: An Observational Manual for Early Childhood Teachers* (2nd ed.). New York: Teachers College Press, Columbia University, 1979.

This very readable book includes basic observation techniques, studying children in groups, questioning techniques, and analysis of creative expression.

BEATTY, J. J. *Observing Development of the Young Child.* Columbus, OH: Merrill, 1984.

This book includes summaries of research in various areas (e.g., emotional, social, cognitive, language development) and coordinated suggestions and checklists for observing this development.

BEST, J. W., AND KAHN, J. V. *Research in Education* (5th ed.). Englewood Cliffs, NJ: Prentice-Hall, 1986.

This is an excellent basic text describing historical, descriptive, and experimental research. It contains clearly written chapter summaries.

GOLDMAN, J.; STEIN, C. L.; AND GUERRY, S. *Psychological Methods of Child Assessment.* New York: Brunner/Mazel, 1983.

This reference is a must for selecting and evaluating assessment instruments to be used with children. Part I contains methodical and ethical considerations related to child study. Part II contains comprehensive information and evaluation of a very large number of instruments in the following categories: intelligence, achievement, development, projection, behavior, and neuropsychology.

MERCER, J. R. "What Is a Racially and Culturally Nondiscriminatory Test? A Sociological and Pluralistic Perspective." In Reynolds, C. R., and Brown, R. T. (eds.), *Perspectives on Bias in Mental Testing.* New York: Plenum Press, 1984.

In this article, the author reviews legislation related to nondiscrimination in psychological observation and outlines specific criteria to be used in analyzing instruments for racial or cultural bias.

TOULIATOS, J., AND COMPTON, N. H. *Approaches to Child Study.* Minneapolis: Burgess, 1983.

This book contains very specific instructions for using a wide variety of observational techniques, self-report methods, tests, scales, and projective techniques. The many samples and charts make this work especially clear and useful.

VASTA, R. *Strategies and Techniques in Child Study.* New York: Academic Press, 1982.

This book provides overviews of various developmental areas and makes specific suggestions for designing and interpreting original studies. Sample areas included are infancy, social skills, language, perception, cognition, prosocial behavior/self-control, and sex roles.

PART II

In the Beginning: The Prenatal Period

CHAPTER 3

The Prenatal Endowment Fund: Influences on Development

(Source: © 1988 Jean Shapiro)

CHAPTER OUTLINE

> Conception
> Heredity
>> Review of Genetic Process
>> Heritability
>
> Periods of Prenatal Development
>> Period of the Zygote (Conception to Two Weeks)
>> Period of the Embryo (Three to Eight Weeks)
>> Period of the Fetus (Eight Weeks to Birth)
>
> The Prenatal Environment
>> Time of Pregnancy
>> Nutrition
>> Maternal Diseases and Disorders
>> Harmful Substances
>> Radiation
>> Maternal Emotions
>
> Birth
>> Trends in Hospital Services
>> Variety of Delivery Settings
>> Evaluation of the Newborn
>
> Nature and Nurture: Forces Interacting to Shape Development
>> Individual Characteristics
>> Environmental Stimulation
>> Family and Peer Relations
>> Societal and Ethnic Affiliations
>
> Summary
> Selected Readings

Each day, as Joy entered the hospital to visit her grandfather, she hurried to the section where the new babies were kept. As she approached the viewing window, her face would shine with anticipation, then fall with disappointment. Finally, one day she confided to her mother, "If we could just get here early some morning before they put the names on all of them, I'm sure they'd give us one of those babies to take home!" "Getting to take one home," of course, was actually a process that began approximately nine months before.

Conception

Since primitive times, man has been fascinated by the miracle of birth, but it was not until 1677 that Hamm and Leeuwenhoek first saw a human sperm. "Two camps grew up, one contending that the sperm contained

THE PRENATAL ENDOWMENT FUND: INFLUENCES ON DEVELOPMENT

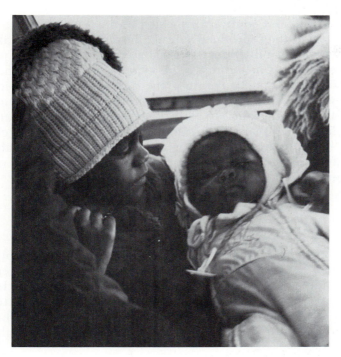

Young children are fascinated with babies, but they may feel a strong sense of rivalry. (*Source:* © *Billy Black/ Envirion*)

the new individual in miniature which was merely nourished by the ovum, the other arguing that the ovum contained a minute body which was in some way stimulated to growth by the seminal fluid" (Corless, 1976, p. 1). Research has since added much to our understanding of how the sperm and ovum combine to form a new and unique individual.

From the onset of puberty, the female usually produces one egg (ovum) each month, about fourteen days prior to the beginning of the next menstrual period. If fertilization does not take place at this time, the female cannot conceive until the next ovulation (generally in about a month). By contrast, the male produces sperms continuously from puberty (thirteen to sixteen years) throughout life. Misunderstanding of this difference in fertilization potential caused one child to remark, "Heidi's in heat, and we're going to have puppies if we can find a daddy dog that's in stud."

When the ovum is produced, it is picked up by hairlike projections (cilia) in the lining of the fallopian tube. The action of these cilia plus the increased muscular contractions which begin prior to ovulation move the ovum through the reproductive tract. Fertilization usually takes place in the fallopian tube and occurs when a sperm penetrates into a particular ovum. Once a sperm has entered the cytoplasm of the ovum, the cell membrane of that ovum changes to prevent penetration by other sperms. The sperm and ovum then shed their separate cell membranes and unite their respective chromosomes to form a new being. Since there are generally 300 to 500 million sperms in each ejaculation, the role of chance in conception of a unique individual is awesome; there is only about one chance in 300 trillion that two identical individuals who are not twins could be conceived (Scheinfeld, 1971).

Heredity

Will Jeremy grow to be six feet tall like his dad? Why does Cynthia have blue eyes when her parents are both brown-eyed? Was King Henry VIII correct in blaming his wives because he had all daughters? Which mental, physical, and personality traits may be affected by heredity? If birth defects have occurred in a family, is there any way to predict the chances of having a normal child? These questions can be answered through a study of heredity.

Review of Genetic Processes

The following section is designed to help you better understand the nature of genetic components and the role they play in heredity.

GENETIC COMPONENTS. All cells contain chromosomes, which are rod-like structures made up of tiny particles strung together like beads. These particles are called genes, and they carry the genetic code that tells the cells which of the parents' characteristics this child is to inherit. The genes dictate that Graciela is to be a little human, not a canary or a Siamese cat. They further specify that she is to have dark hair, brown eyes, narrow shoulders, small feet, and a tendency to be quite bright. The genetic code directs not only the development of the structures that will be evident at birth (two arms, one nose), but also characteristics that will emerge later in life (height range at maturity, tendency for baldness). Since each cell contains about 1 million genes, you can readily imagine how detailed these genetic instructions are.

One of the greatest advances in genetic research occurred in 1953 when Watson and Crick first described DNA (deoxyribonucleic acid), the substance of which the gene is composed (Clark et al., 1980). DNA has the appearance of a double helix or spiral ladder, the rungs of which are chemical bases (see Figure 3.1).

The sequence in which these chemical bases occur directs what the cell is to make. Scientists may now be able to examine and map each of the genes in the human cell. Armed with this knowledge, researchers currently are attempting to splice genes—cutting out defective parts and adding healthy material. Through this process, known as recombinant DNA, many genetic disorders such as hemophilia or sickle-cell anemia may be eliminated.

CELL DEVELOPMENT. Each cell contains forty-six chromosomes arranged in twenty-three pairs. There are two kinds of cells. The first are body

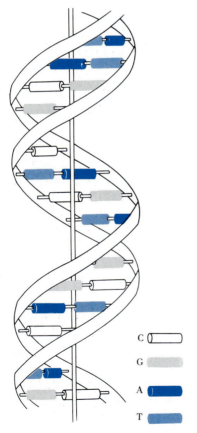

FIGURE 3.1 DNA (the chemical substance of which genes are made) contains the genetic blueprint for the developing person. (*Source: Lucille F. Whaley*, Understanding Inherited Disorders. *St. Louis: The C.V. Mosby Company, 1974, p. 16, in Schiamberg, 1987, p. 112*)

cells, of which bone, muscle, organ, and nerve are made. The second are germ cells, from which the ova of the female and the sperms of the male are derived. The germ cells, before producing sperms and ova, go through a special cell division and reduce their number of chromosomes to twenty-three.

SEX DETERMINATION. Since the female germ cell pattern is XX, all ova are X. When the male germ cell (XY) divides to produce sperms, however, half of the sperms are X and half are Y. Therefore, it is the father who determines the sex of the child.

SEX CHROMOSOME VARIATIONS. Normally the female chromosome pattern is XX and the male pattern is XY. Occasionally, because of mistakes in cell division, a child is born with a different sex chromosome pattern. A girl born with only one X (XO) is known as a Turner's syndrome child. She may be dwarfed in height, have a short or webbed neck, and fail to develop secondary characteristics such as breast enlargement and menstrual cycle (unless induced by hormone therapy). She is generally sterile and sometimes retarded.

The Klinefelter's syndrome child is a male with extra X chromosomes (XXY, XXXY, XXXXY). Because of these additional X components, he will have small testes and secondary sexual characteristics that are female (breast enlargement) rather than male (beard, low voice). He is usually sterile and retarded, and he often exhibits behavior problems.

Other sex chromosome variations have been reported in the literature (e.g., XXX, XYY), but their incidence is rare and descriptions of typical characteristics are thus difficult to establish.

SEX-LINKED CHARACTERISTICS. If, when a female is conceived, a gene on the X chromosome from the mother is defective, a healthy gene on the father's X chromosome may assume the necessary function. The Y chromosome, however, is shorter and contains few genes except those necessary for sexual development. If a male is conceived and the X chromosome from the mother carries a defective gene, there is no component on the Y chromosome to compensate (Apgar and Beck, 1978). For this reason, more males than females are born with birth defects.

DOMINANT AND RECESSIVE GENES. As a result of cell division, an individual does not pass on his or her entire genetic heritage, but merely a random sample. This sample includes both dominant and recessive genes.

BOX 3.1
Dominant and Recessive Genetic Characteristics

Dominant	Recessive
Dark hair	Blond hair
Curly hair	Straight hair
Dark skin	Fair skin
Brown eyes	Blue eyes
Blood type A	Blood type O
Normal color perception	Color blindness (male only)
Extra fingers and/or toes	Ten of each (fingers, toes)
Absence of iris in eye	Presence of iris in eye

A dominant gene, if inherited, will always manifest itself in the appearance or function of the individual (brown eyes instead of blue). A recessive gene, however, will affect development only if no dominant gene for that characteristic is inherited from the other parent (straight hair only if no genes for curly hair were transmitted). Box 3.1 summarizes common traits known to be dominant or recessive.

The chances of inheriting dominant and recessive characteristics can be computed mathematically. For example, if one parent has genes for brown eyes only and the other parent has genes for blue eyes only, the children will have brown eyes, since brown is dominant over blue. Very often, however, either one or both parents inherit genes for both brown and blue eyes. The diagram below illustrates the probabilities for brown-eyed and blue-eyed children in a case in which both parents carry both brown and blue eye color genes.

Please remember that this diagram does not mean that if this couple has four children, three must have brown eyes and one must have blue eyes. It means instead that each time this couple conceives, the odds are 3 to 1 that the child will be brown-eyed.

Early research and formulation of laws governing the inheritance of dominant and recessive characteristics in peas were done by Gregor Mendel, an Austrian monk. Since families don't produce children in the same quantities that Mendel produced peas, predicting individual characteristics for a given child is quite difficult.

In many instances, not one but several genes are involved in producing

	Brown	Blue
Brown	Brown-Brown Brown eyes	Brown-Blue Brown eyes
Blue	Blue-Brown Brown eyes	Blue-Blue Blue eyes

- Brown eyes 25%
  (no genes for blue)
- Brown eyes
  (with genes for blue) 50%
- Blue eyes
  (no genes for brown) 25%

a single characteristic. For this reason, the child sometimes inherits an intermediate expression of a trait, something in between the parental characteristics. If the skin color of the parents is quite different, the child's coloration typically will be a shade between the two. In like manner, the intelligence of the child more often corresponds to the average of the IQs of the biological parents than to that of either parent individually (Faw, 1980).

Heritability

While human development is based on both genetic and environmental factors, certain characteristics are known to be primarily of hereditary origin. Laboratory experiments, family histories, and twin studies all have been important sources for data concerning heritability (Farber, 1981; Schave and Ciciello, 1985).

PHYSICAL TRAITS. From his family tree, John may inherit his father's height, his grandfather's nose, and his Aunt Ada's red hair. Judi may be crushed to learn that no number of visits to the spa will add Dolly Parton–like endowments to the angular frame she inherited.

Functional qualities also may have genetic components. Blood pressure, heartbeat rate, resistance to disease, and longevity are all believed to be linked to genetic elements, though each may be modified by environment.

Some physical disorders are passed from one generation to the next through dominant and recessive genes. Box 3.2 summarizes data concerning some of the more common of these hereditary physical defects.

Many people are very concerned about having children when disorders known to be hereditary are prevalent in their families. In some cases the chance of producing a defective child may be slight; in other instances the risk may be great. How can prospective parents determine these odds? Genetic counseling might provide the answers.

BOX 3.2

Hereditary Physical Defects

DOMINANT INHERITANCE:

The child usually has a parent with the disorder, or there was a change in one parent's reproductive cell at the time of conception. There are about 2,000 confirmed or suspected disorders caused by dominant genes. Some are:

- Achondroplasia—a form of dwarfism
- Chronic simple glaucoma (some forms)—a major cause of blindness if untreated
- Hypercholesterolemia—high blood cholesterol levels, propensity to heart disease
- Polydactyly—extra fingers or toes

RECESSIVE INHERITANCE:

Both parents of an affected child appear essentially normal but, by chance, both carry the same harmful gene although neither may be aware of it. Recessive inherited diseases tend to be severe and often cause death early in life. There are more than 1,000 such confirmed or suspected disorders. Among them are:

- Cystic fibrosis—affects function of mucus and sweat glands
- Galactosemia—inability to metabolize milk sugar
- Phenylketonuria—essential liver enzyme deficiency
- Sickle cell disease—blood disorder primarily affecting blacks
- Tay-Sachs disease—fatal brain damage primarily affecting infants of East European Jewish ancestry

X-LINKED INHERITANCE:

In the most common form, the female sex chromosomes of an apparently normal mother carry one faulty gene and one normal one. Each son has a fifty percent chance of inheriting the disorder, and each daughter has a fifty percent chance of becoming a carrier of it. Among some 250 confirmed or suspected disorders are:

- Agmmaglobulinemia—lack of immunity to infections
- Color blindness—inability to distinguish certain colors
- Hemophilia—defect in blood-clotting mechanisms
- Muscular dystrophy (some forms)—progressive wasting of muscles

MULTIFACTORIAL INHERITANCE:

A large group of genetic disorders result from the interaction of many genes with other genes or with environmental factors. The number of disorders of this type is unknown. Examples are:

- Cleft lip and/or palate
- Clubfoot
- Spina bifida—open spine
- Hydrocephalus (with spina bifida)—water on brain
- Diabetes mellitus—abnormal sugar metabolism

SOURCE: Excerpted from March of Dimes, 1987. Used with permission.

A child often looks very much like the parent. (*Source:* © *1988 Jean Shapiro*)

MENTAL COMPONENTS. Since the parents usually provide both the genetic endowment and the environment in which the child develops, it is difficult to determine the extent to which each of these factors contributes to intelligence. Three types of studies are commonly used to explore the genetic components in mental and personality characteristics. These are the twin method, adoption studies, and family histories (Buss and Plomin, 1984). The methods and assumptions related to each of these types are summarized in Box 3.3. Based on these studies, genetic factors related to intelligence and mental retardation have been suggested.

The heritability of intelligence has been implied in a number of studies involving twins and other family members (Farber, 1981; Schave and Ciciello, 1985). The more closely people are related, the more similar

THE PRENATAL ENDOWMENT FUND: INFLUENCES ON DEVELOPMENT

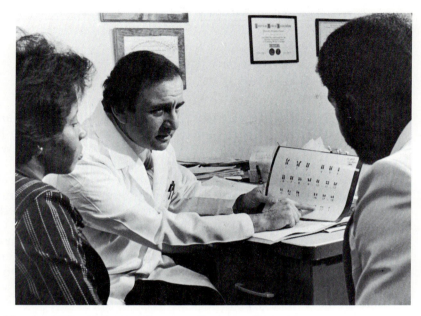

Many couples seek genetic counseling to estimate the possibility of certain birth defects. (*Source: March of Dimes*)

their IQs are apt to be. This correlation is even higher if the individuals were reared together and shared both heredity and environment. Adoption studies also have indicated a genetic factor in intelligence. After an extensive review of research, Musinger found that there is a higher correlation between the IQs of the child and the birth parent than between the child and the adoptive parent (Musinger, 1975).

Although mental retardation may be associated with a family pattern of low intellectual functioning, it also may result from one of the previously mentioned hereditary physical defects (Box 3.2).

PERSONALITY ATTRIBUTES.   Does Linda have tantrums because she inherited the tendency from her father's people? Why is Dennis the Menace in perpetual motion? If Anne's grandmother was schizophrenic, what are the chances that Anne also will be afflicted? Whereas environment plays a vital role in the development of the personality, hereditary factors may make certain behavior characteristics easier for some people to acquire (Farber, 1981; Schave and Ciciello, 1985).

Case Study 3

Genetic Counseling

Sarah's sister died of Tay-Sachs. Debbie and Jeff both have family histories of cystic fibrosis. Hillary's uncle was born with club feet. In Jonathan's family, there have been eight cases of minimal brain damage. What information can genetic counselors offer to these people?

Estimate of risk. These counselors can provide genetic information for those who have already had a defective child or who have a family history of birth defect. They can attempt to determine whether such defects are genetic or the result of a problem in the prenatal environment. Conditions causing damage during pregnancy can sometimes be avoided or corrected. For certain types of disorders, lab tests can determine whether a person is the carrier of a defective gene. Based on this store of data, the counselor can apprise the couple concerning the percentage of risk.

Data on monitoring of pregnancy. If the risk of birth defect is great, the counselor may recommend that prenatal development be monitored by amniocentesis or ultrasound (Seligmann et al., 1980).

Amniocentesis is the analysis of a sample of fluid drawn by needle from the amniotic sac surrounding the baby. From this data, a wide variety of chromosome defects can be detected (e.g., Down's syndrome), oxygen supply can be checked, and even the sex of the baby can be determined. The procedure involves little risk to either mother or child.

Ultrasound provides the opportunity to see the child without the use of potentially harmful X-rays. In this procedure, a quartz crystal is placed on the mother's abdomen, high-frequency sound waves are beamed to the fetus, and a picture is produced. The technique is both reliable and safe.

If birth defects exist, the couple may or may not elect therapeutic abortion. If the pregnancy is continued, the counselor can refer the parents to professionals who can advise them on postnatal treatment for the child's particular disorder.

Differences in temperament appear to be present at birth and persist throughout life (Chess and Thomas, 1984). Some of these differences are activity level, rhythm, distractibility, approach/withdrawal, attention span, intensity of reaction, and quality of mood.

THE PRENATAL ENDOWMENT FUND: INFLUENCES ON DEVELOPMENT 69

BOX 3.3

Methods for Genetic Studies of Mental and Personality Traits

Study Type	Method	Assumptions
Twin method	Compare identical twins (monozygotic—developing from the same ovum) and nonidentical twins (dizygotic—developing from two different ova)	Identical twins will be more alike than nonidentical twins because they have the same heredity.
Adoption studies	Compare the child with: Birth parents	Likeness to birth parents would indicate genetic influence since birth parents provided heredity but not environment.
	Adoptive parents	Likeness to adoptive parents would indicate environmental influence since adoptive parents usually are not genetically related.
Family histories	Study family history to determine: How many times a selected trait occurs What relation (parent, brother, cousin) the person was in whom the trait appeared	The more often the trait appears, the more likely a genetic factor exists. The closer the relationship (e.g., father rather than third cousin), the more likely a genetic factor exists. Caution should be observed in interpreting these findings, since families share both heredity and environment.

It is evident that these behaviors will affect the response the child receives from the environment. Imagine the very active child with a quiet, slow-moving mother. How will the super-salesman react to a son who digs his toe into the carpet when someone speaks to him? What hostility will develop as a mother tries to get her child with a short attention span to practice the piano? Many personality problems can arise from a mismatch between the innate personal qualities of the child and those of the caregiver.

Heredity also may be a factor in certain mental illnesses, although they are not directly inherited. Schizophrenia and depression are two that appear to have genetic components (DSM-III-R, 1987). If a twin becomes schizophrenic, the chances are significantly higher that the other twin will develop the problem if he is identical than if he is nonidentical. There is now some evidence that inherited biochemical processes may account for certain types of depression that appear to "run in families" (DSM-III-R, 1987).

Having a history of mental illness in a family is not a cause for panic, as most family members never develop the disorder. Environmental conditions such as high stress, downward social drift, poverty, and disruptive family interaction patterns may also be contributing factors in the development of mental illness (DSM-III-R).

Periods of Prenatal Development

At the moment of fertilization, a new life is begun. During the next forty weeks, or approximately 270 days, this being will develop from a single-celled organism to a full-term infant. This growth will take place in three major periods: the period of the ovum (first two weeks) from conception to implantation in the uterine wall; the period of the embryo (third to eighth weeks), during which the placenta is formed, the body structure is begun, and the organ systems are laid down; and the period of the fetus (eighth week to birth), a time when existing structures are refined and increased in size.

Period of the Zygote (Conception to Two Weeks)

Conception generally takes place in the fallopian tube. The new cell, the zygote, divides and redivides, forming a mass of cells that continues to travel through the fallopian tube toward the uterus. During this time, the zygote is nourished by the yolk of the ovum. In the early stages, this mass of cells resembles a cluster of grapes. Soon some of these cells form an outer layer from which the placenta, amniotic sac, and umbilical cord will develop. Other cells in this cluster form an inner cell mass which is the beginning of the embryo, or new person. Between the seventh and fourteenth days, the zygote reaches the uterus and attaches to the uterine wall. Through fingerlike projections, it establishes a network of blood vessels and from this time is dependent on the mother for nourishment. Figure 3.2 traces the development and passage of the zygote from conception to implantation.

If two ova are released within a short period of time and both are fertilized, fraternal twins are formed. These children will be no more alike than are any other brothers or sisters, since they were developed from different ova and sperms. Each will develop its own placenta, and the two will grow simultaneously in the womb. If, however, a single ovum divides and forms two zygotes, the resulting individuals will be identical twins and have exactly the same genetic components. In the case of multiple births involving more than two children, the group of offspring produced may include one or more sets of twins and one or more fraternal singles. Since twinning often "runs in families," some people may have an inherited

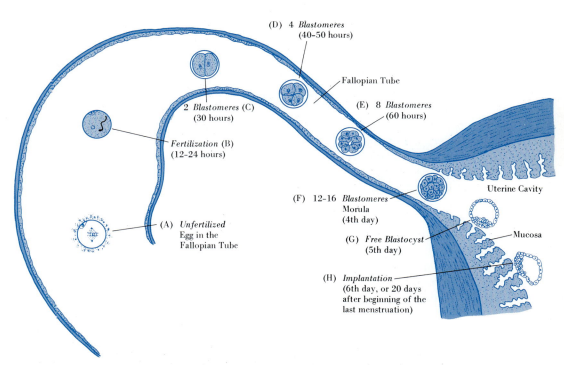

FIGURE 3.2 The ovum (egg) goes through a series of changes from the time it is released into the fallopian tube until it is implanted in the uterus. (*Source: Based on Ruchmann-Duplessis, David, and Haegel, 1972, 1975, in Schiamberg, 1982, p. 128*).

tendency for multiple births. New fertility drugs also may increase the incidence of twins through stimulating ovulation.

Period of the Embryo (Three to Eight Weeks)

The period of the embryo is considered by some authorities to be the most important several weeks of development, since disturbances during this time may result in major malformations (Moore, 1983). Early in the period, folding converts the inner cell mass to a C-shaped embryo. At the same time, the outer layer of cells begins to form a protective cover or sac. This amniotic sac contains a liquid (amniotic fluid) which protects the embryo from sudden jolts and helps to maintain a constant temperature to facilitate development.

Another important structure developed early in the embryonic period is the umbilical cord, which serves as a lifeline between the baby and the mother from this time until birth. This cord and the sac surrounding the baby are attached to the mother's uterine wall by a special layer of cells known as the placenta (see Figure 3.3).

Food and oxygen are filtered from the mother's bloodstream through the placenta and pass by way of the umbilical cord to the embryo. Waste products are excreted from the embryo by the reverse process. Although the bloodstreams of the mother and the embryo are separate, some infections (e.g., German measles, viruses) and harmful substances (e.g., drugs, alcohol) are not screened out and reach the developing embryo, causing malformations.

During the embryonic period, three cell layers are formed for special functions (Oppenheimer, 1984; Mathews, 1986). The outer layer, the ectoderm, develops into the nervous system, sensory structures (ears, nose, eyes), coverings (skin, hair, nails, tooth enamel), and glands (mammary, pituitary). The middle layer, the mesoderm, gives rise to connectives (bones, muscles), circulatory system (heart, blood, lymph vessels), and the urogenital tract (kidneys, sex organs, ducts). The inner layer, the endoderm, provides the linings for a number of body cavities and forms such other structures as the lungs, the liver, and the pancreas.

Since such basic body structures are being laid down during this embryonic period, any disturbance in the growth process is particularly important at this time. Illnesses, particularly viral infections, may interrupt development and cause structural malformations. Use of drugs is also especially dangerous during this time. In fact, any drug or medicine should be taken during pregnancy only at the direction of a physician.

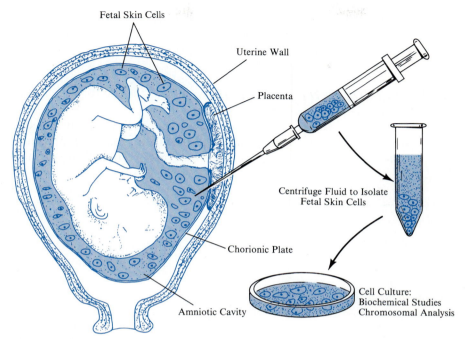

FIGURE 3.3 Amniocentesis is a procedure used to screen for serious hereditary disorders. (*Source: From Schiamberg, 1987, p. 125*)

Period of the Fetus (Eight Weeks to Birth)

Since essentially all of the body parts and major organ systems are begun during the embryonic stage, the period of the fetus is one of growth and refinement (Moore, 1983). Disturbances in the uterine environment during this time are more apt to result in impairment of function, such as mental retardation or a specific learning disability, than in the absence of some vital internal or external structure. The notable exception is that of the brain and nervous system, which are rudimentary at the beginning of the fetal period and undergo major development during the last three months of pregnancy and the first year of life.

As the fetal period progresses, the systems and parts begin to function with ever-increasing precision. During the last two months, the body form is rounded out as fat is added. If birth occurs after twenty-six to twenty-eight weeks, the infant may survive if the environment is specialized to allow for continuation of development. Box 3.4 records the monthly milestones in development from conception to birth.

The Prenatal Environment

Until about forty years ago, most doctors believed that hereditary factors were responsible for most birth defects (Langman, 1975). Since that time, much has been learned about the vital importance of the prenatal environ-

---

BOX 3.4
Monthly Milestones

1	*2*	*3*
• Two cells multiply to thousands of cells—each specialized to develop some body component. • Heart begins to beat, brain has two lobes, and body comprises head, trunk, arm/leg buds.	• Becomes small-scale baby with face, eyes, ears, nose, lips, and tooth buds. Arms have hands, fingers; legs have knees, ankles, toes. • Has complete skeleton of cartilage.	• Muscles and nerves work together making movement possible. • Individual differences can be noted.

4	*5*	*6*
• Has strong heartbeat, some digestive ability, and active muscles. • Skin is transparent. • Head still overlarge. • Eyebrows appear.	• Hair appears on head, eyelashes on eyelids. • Most of skeleton hardens. • Mother is aware of movements.	• Fat deposits form under skin, but fetus very wrinkled. • Eyelids open and close.

7	*8*	*9*
• Underlying fat rounds out appearance. • May suck thumb frequently. • Likely to survive if born late in seventh month.	• May move less because of space limitations. • Valuable growth and maturation occurs.	• Has developed antibodies equal to mother's level (for fighting infection). • Settles head down in the womb.

Seventy-five percent of babies are born 266 days after conception plus or minus eleven days. Frequently they weigh seven to eight pounds and are about twenty inches long.

SOURCES: Summarized from Carnation Company, 1962, and Flanagan, 1987.

ment. This section summarizes the environmental factors now known to be related to development during the prenatal period.

Time of Pregnancy (Apgar and Beck, 1978; Tsai and Stewart, 1983)

AGE OF MOTHER. Mothers younger than sixteen or over forty years of age are significantly more likely to have children with developmental or neurological damage (particularly Down's syndrome for mothers over forty) than are mothers in their twenties and thirties (see Figure 3.4). Age of the mother may also increase the risk of having an autistic child (Tsai and Stewart, 1983). There are several possible explanations for this fact. The teenage mother's body may be underdeveloped and not ready for pregnancy, and the older mother's body may be approaching menopause with its attendant chemical changes. The older mother may also have endured more illnesses and disorders over the years. If, as some researchers believe, all the eggs are present at birth and merely mature

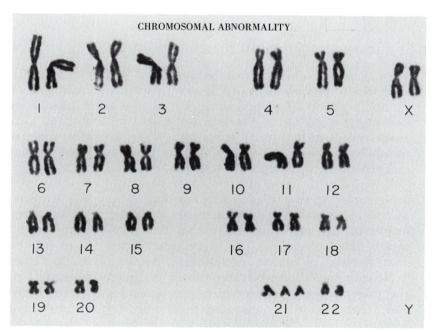

FIGURE 3.4 Down's syndrome occurs when there are three chromosomes instead of two in Number 21. Mothers over 40 are more likely to have such children than are younger women. (*Source: From Schiamberg, 1987, p. 123*)

from adolescence onward, such illnesses or age itself could cause degeneration of the ova of older women.

AGE OF FATHER.   If the father is over forty-five years of age, the chances of stillbirth or malformations are greater regardless of the age of the mother. Research relating to the age of the father as a factor in the child's development is limited. More research is needed in this area.

SPACING OF PREGNANCIES.   A two-year interval between the termination of one pregnancy and the beginning of another is often needed, especially if the mother is quite young. Long-term studies (Apgar and Beck, 1978; Grant, 1985) have indicated that children born a short time after a previous pregnancy are more likely to exhibit significantly lower intelligence than are children spaced at least twenty-four months apart.

NUMBER OF PREGNANCIES.   Women with five or more pregnancies increase the risk of producing children with lower IQs and other birth defects. The most frequently stated research assumption is that the mother's body stores may become depleted and body systems strained from a large number of pregnancies.

Nutrition (Joos, 1983; Shanklin and Hoden, 1979; Pitkin, 1982)

PROBLEMS RELATED TO POOR NUTRITION.   Poor nutrition often contributes to low birthweight. It also may result in a reduction in the total number of brain cells, thus causing irreversible brain damage and retardation in the child. Other functional impairments associated with maternal malnutrition include poor perception, short attention span, listlessness, instability, impaired ability in abstract reasoning, and difficulty in any tasks that involve integrating activities using the senses.

EFFECTS OF NUTRITIONAL ENRICHMENT.   Joos (1983) studied the effects of providing nutritional supplements to mothers during pregnancy and lactation. The results indicated that this enrichment resulted in better motor development for the experimental group than for those in the control group, in which the mothers did not receive supplementation.

No substance should be taken during pregnancy, however, except under the direction of the supervising physician. Large doses of vitamins A, B-6, C, and D and of iodine are potentially harmful to the fetus (Pilkin, 1982).

MATERNAL DIET.   Many women in all social classes exist on unbalanced diets. These eating habits should be corrected prior to pregnancy in order for the body to build the elements necessary for optimal fetal growth. A detailed discussion of diet during pregnancy is found in Chapter 5.

Maternal Diseases and Disorders (Apgar and Beck, 1978; Fitzgerald, 1978; Volpe, 1984)

GERMAN MEASLES (RUBELLA). Cataracts on eyes, heart disease, and deafness often result from measles infection during the first three months of pregnancy. These three handicaps are often referred to as "rubella syndrome" since the probability of their occurrence is so high if the mother has German measles during this period.

VIRUSES. Several viruses may cause defects during the prenatal period. Cytomegalovirus is relatively harmless to adults and older children, but it can cause a miscarriage if contracted during early pregnancy. If the unborn child becomes infected with cytomegalovirus, such problems as brain damage, epilepsy, or blindness may result. Smallpox, chickenpox, mumps, and polio often result in miscarriage. Prior to becoming pregnant, the prospective mother should check with her doctor concerning the advisibility of getting vaccinations for some of these diseases. Once pregnancy has occurred, she should exert utmost care to avoid exposure to communicable diseases.

TOXOPLASMOSIS. Toxoplasmosis is another infection that may be transmitted to the unborn child during pregnancy. It is an organism common to many birds and animals and is often found in cat feces. A woman should be very careful in her contacts with cats during pregnancy.

DIABETES. Diabetic mothers produce three times as many children with malformations as do nondiabetic women. These include skeletal differences and unusually large infants.

RH BLOOD FACTOR INCOMPATIBILITY. Rh is one of many factors within the blood. It may have positive or negative characteristics. If an Rh-negative mother is carrying an Rh-positive baby, her body will produce antibodies that destroy the red blood cells of the fetus. Damage to first children is rare, since most antibodies build up after delivery. A vaccine, administered to the mother within seventy-two hours after delivery, prevents antibodies from forming. Therefore, there is no concentration of antibodies within the Rh-negative mother to harm or abort the next child when the mother again becomes pregnant. If the mother is Rh-positive and the father is Rh-negative, there is no problem, since Rh-positive persons do not produce these antibodies. If both parents are Rh-negative, there is no blood factor incompatibility.

Harmful Substances

MEDICATIONS AND DRUGS (FITZGERALD, 1978; VOLPE, 1984). Many medications used to treat physical disorders should not be taken during pregnancy. Dilantin and phenobarbital (two anticonvulsants) and warfarin (used to prevent blood clots) have been linked to specific developmental deficiencies. Several years ago, an epidemic of children born with flippers instead of arms and legs occurred when expectant mothers took thalidomide to combat nausea and insomnia. Of even greater danger are the drugs capable of causing chromosome damage, which may be passed on to future generations as a genetic mutation.

Extreme caution also should be exercised in the use of drugs for pregnancy complications. Diethylstillbesterol (DES), prescribed to mothers to prevent miscarriage during pregnancy, has been identified as causing vaginal cancer in the female offspring at the time they reach maturity, and children of both sexes whose mothers received this hormone during pregnancy showed lower assertiveness and athletic abilities when tested at age six. Appetite suppressants and antibiotics have also been linked to fetal damage.

ALCOHOL (ROSETT, 1984; VOLPE, 1984; IOSUB, 1985; PLANT, 1985). A history of chronic alcoholism prior to or during pregnancy has been associated with mental retardation, skull and facial malformations, arrested growth, and abnormalities of the central nervous system. In a recent congressional report, the recommendation was made that intake of hard liquor not exceed 2.3 ounces per day.

SMOKING (GARN ET AL., 1982; LONGO, 1982). Babies of smoking mothers are usually smaller, weigh less, and are apt to show overall retardation in growth and development. Since nicotine is known to pass through the placenta, it is believed that elevated levels of carbon monoxide reduce the amount of oxygen available to the fetus. The more a mother smokes, the greater the danger of damage.

Radiation (Langman, 1975; Sells and Bennett, 1977)

Radiation during early pregnancy is related to microcephaly (unusually small head) and mental retardation. The extent of damage depends on the amount of radiation received and the stage of embryonic development occurring at that time. Extensive X-ray exposure of the abdominal area prior to conception also has been implicated. Efforts should be made to limit use of X-ray throughout the childbearing years, as radiation of sex organs may result in permanent chromosome changes that may be passed on to future generations. Even necessary dental work, if possible, should be scheduled prior to becoming pregnant to avoid the necessity even of dental X-rays during pregnancy.

Maternal Emotions (Apgar and Beck, 1978; Chess and Thomas, 1984)

Being frightened by a snake will not produce a child with a sneaky disposition, nor will reading poetry guarantee an academic bent. However, the mother's anxiety may cause biochemical changes that may adversely affect the unborn child (e.g., may cause constriction of blood vessels resulting in reduced oxygen for the fetus and possible brain damage). Emotional problems also may affect the mother's ability to cooperate in the delivery process. If this happens, the delivery may be slowed, and the chances of mental and/or physical damage to the infant may be increased. To be harmful, stress must be prolonged (e.g., throughout most of the pregnancy) or intense (e.g., sufficiently shocking to create chemical changes in the mother's system).

Birth

Grandmother says to stay in bed for two weeks after delivery. Susie and Shane have read a new book, and they are going to have their baby at home. Bill, Jr., is already asking if we can send the baby back. As a couple faces the birth process, they have many options to explore.

Trends in Hospital Services

PARENTING CLASSES. In the early 1970s, only about 10 percent of the hospitals offered classes designed to prepare mothers and fathers for childbirth; now most do (Seligmann et al., 1980). These classes generally begin with an orientation to the hospital and its facilities. One major emphasis is the teaching of breathing exercises used to foster relaxation and reduce labor pains. In most instances, the father is encouraged to assist his wife during labor. He also may be given the opportunity to be present during the actual delivery. Other information included in parenting classes relates to the mother's physical and emotional health and to preparation for helping both parents care for the child after birth.

The most widely used prepared childbirth approaches are the Lamaze and the Leboyer methods. Many hospitals offer courses in one or the other of these methods, and books are available for those who want detailed, step-by-step instructions for exercises and procedures to be used by prospective mothers and fathers who want to work together to prepare for the delivery process.

Gloger-Tippelt (1983) has developed a special course for first-time mothers. The course deals with both biological and psychological factors and is presented in four sections: (1) life disruption and changes caused by pregnancy, (2) readjustments during pregnancy, (3) focus on the developing baby, and (4) preparation for birth and child care.

Sometimes social agency personnel team with university professors to offer child-care training for teenage mothers (Bell 1983). Such courses

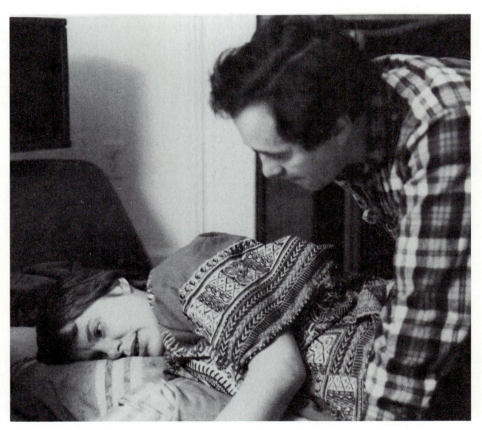

Fathers become actively involved in the birth process before actual delivery. *(Source: © 1988 Jean Shapiro)*

help both mothers and babies and provide excellent field training for students interested in social work.

EXPLAINING BIRTH TO SIBLINGS. One man quipped that trying to get a small child to welcome a new brother or sister was like expecting your mate to respond with enthusiasm if you told her you are going to bring home a new wife next week. Hospitals have tried to lessen possible family tensions by offering sessions for the other children in the family. "There is enough love to go around," "Here's how you can help take care of it," and "Someday Matthew/Carolyn will make a good playmate" are some of the standard themes.

When the preschooler asks where the baby is coming from, what are you going to say? The "birds and bees" story is a little abstract for preschoolers, and if you resort to the cabbage patch line, you deserve to have your garden dismantled by the child who attempts to find the baby there ahead of time. The best is a simple, factual, and perhaps well-rehearsed version of the truth. Avoid explanations that are too long or too detailed.

"Bet I know what babies like about being born. They can stretch."

(*Source: Reprinted with special permission of Cowles Syndicate, Inc. © BilKeane*)

It is best to answer one question at a time, preferably in a sentence or two (e.g., "Where is the baby?" "Inside mother.") Try to avoid exhibiting embarrassment. Generally children will ask what they are ready to understand. Some children will ask several questions in rapid-fire succession; others will ask one question at a time over a period of weeks or months. The pitfalls of sex education for preschoolers is exemplified by the story of the father who spent ten minutes responding to his son's question about where children come from, only to have the child reply, "Wow, and the new kid down the street only came from Detroit!"

Variety of Delivery Settings

When that "blessed event" finally transpires about 270 days after conception, the parents may choose from among several delivery settings. The health and welfare of both mother and child should be the prime considerations in making this decision.

INVOLVER 3

A New Baby Is Coming!

Almost everyone, sooner or later, faces the need to tell a young child that a new baby is coming. Many people have great difficulty deciding what to say. A number of new books related to this topic have been designed to share with youngsters. First, scan several of these (available at libraries or local bookstores). Using a two-column format, record what you like about each of these explanations and/or illustrations and what you found to be inane or offensive. Next, design your own material (to be used with a child at present or saved for future reference). Finally, show your presentation to another adult and note the response.

THINKING IT OVER

- What information did you elect to put in your material, and what did you leave out?
- Why did you make these choices?
- How does your explanation compare with what you were told as a child?
- What reactions and suggestions did you receive from the adult with whom you shared your ideas?
- What questions do you anticipate the child will ask next?
- In what ways has this activity made you feel more confident in explaining sex to a child?

HOSPITAL DELIVERIES. Many authorities encourage hospital deliveries (Apgar and Beck, 1978; Guttmacher, 1984). Emergency problems can occur suddenly, and it is often crucial to the welfare of mother and child that the best medical facilities are immediately available. In a traditional hospital setting, the mother generally remains with her husband in a labor room until birth is imminent. Then she is taken to a delivery room, while her husband engages in the traditional floor pacing in a waiting room.

Standard procedure for first handling of the newborn usually involves spanking him or tapping his feet to induce crying and thus clear the child's lungs. Contrast in your mind this "welcome to the world" with the Leboyer method, in which the child is placed in a warm bath of water (reminiscent of the amniotic fluid) to make him feel at home in his new surroundings.

Many hospitals are now designing special "birthing rooms." These em-

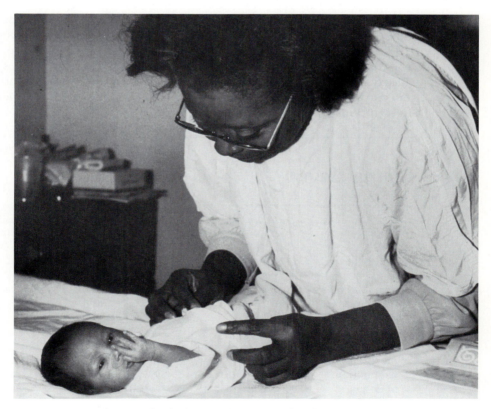

Newborns are given a physical screening soon after birth. *(Source: © Dwight Ellefsen)*

body a homelike atmosphere—easy chairs, curtains, and decorator wallpaper. Here the father, and sometimes the siblings, assist in monitoring delivery. This arrangement makes birth a family affair and allows for close and immediate contact between the arriving infant and the other family members.

HOME DELIVERIES. There has been a recent increase in the number of babies born at home. Family closeness and decreased cost are often heralded as the advantages. The delivery may be the work of a doctor, a nurse, a midwife, or a husband. If there are no complications, the facilities may be adequate. Such arrangements can be more hazardous, however, if an unexpected problem arises, which occurs in approximately 10 percent of the cases.

Evaluation of the Newborn

Immediately after birth, newborn infants are given a physical screening. The most widely used instrument is the Apgar Scale (Apgar and Beck, 1978). The child is rated from 0 to 2 on each of five vital signs: appearance (or coloring), pulse, grimace (reflex irritability), activity, and respiration. Based on the child's score, the doctor determines whether other tests need to be run. Box 3.5 contains the Apgar rating scale with some additional descriptions and details relating to the Apgar score.

BOX 3.5
Apgar Scoring System

	2	1	0
A (appearance, color)	Completely pink	Body pink, arms and legs bluish	Body entirely blue
P (pulse, heart rate)	Higher than 100 per minute	Less than 100 per minute	Absent
G (grimace, reflex responsiveness with light tap on soles of feet)	Cries vigorously	Grimace or slight cry	No response
A (activity or muscle tone)	Active motions	Some movement of arms or legs	Limp, motionless
R (respiration, breathing)	Strong efforts to breathe, vigorous crying	Slow, irregular breathing	No respiration

SOURCE: Based on Apgar and Beck, 1978.

Nature and Nurture: Forces Interacting to Shape Development

As the newborn child ventures forward in life, there are a number of forces, some inborn and some environmental, that will shape development. These are studied in depth throughout the remainder of the book. Briefly summarized, these forces include individual characteristics, environmental stimulation, family and peer relations, and societal and ethnic affiliations. As you read this section, remember that elements of these forces interact with each other to affect the individual's development and behavior.

Individual Characteristics

Several individual characteristics seem to affect direction of development (Chess and Thomas, 1984). One is activity level. The child who constantly seeks new encounters will make more contacts with his world. This initiative may be rewarded with praise or condemned as brattishness. The child who is extremely active may have difficulty focusing his attention on the task at hand. His distractibility may result in poor work habits and constant conflicts with others. By contrast, a low-activity child will tend to be quiet and still. He may be a conscientious and thorough worker, or he may be one who sits much and does little.

A second characteristic is the child's rhythm—the regularity by which he patterns his behavior. Some children seem to possess an inborn clock that causes their behavior to be very predictable. They awaken each morning at about the same hour, they get hungry at mealtimes, they nap in the afternoon, and they go to sleep on schedule even if the family is away from home and they have to curl up on a couch. These children accomplish such tasks as toilet training with ease, since their needs can readily be anticipated. They are easily liked and accepted children. By contrast, some children seem to "wake up in a new world every morning." They are forever running late, their mittens are always lost, and they liked spinach yesterday but not today. Some adults have great difficulty dealing with such children.

Intensity of reaction and quality of mood also vary from child to child. Some children require constant sameness and react violently to any change in routine. Others show few signs of disturbance even in the most hectic environments. Some children have fluctuating moods; they are happy one minute and sad the next. For some youngsters, these moods may be very intense. They become very frightened, excited, happy, or depressed. Other children are more even-tempered.

Children vary in level of activity and penchant for exploring.

Special talents and/or handicaps are also characteristics that affect development. They may extend or limit the child's choice of activities and affect the response he receives from his environment.

Finally, the child's self-concept, or feeling of competency and self-worth, will affect him in many ways. This characteristic is not inherited, but rather is developed as a result of interactions with others. A child's self-concept may determine the tasks he will select to try, his chances of success, his relations with his peers, and his satisfaction with himself.

Environmental Stimulation

Some children do not receive enough environmental stimulation and, as a result, fail to develop necessary skills. Others are reared in confused, disorganized, and overstimulating settings and have difficulty developing adequate attention spans. Insufficient stimulation may hinder the development of concepts, as the child may not have noticed enough detail to compare and contrast, to classify things into categories, or to perceive likenesses and differences.

It is also necessary to provide a wide range of activities, so the child's development is not limited to a few basic skills. A child cannot become interested in an area to which he is not exposed. Many children with special talents never blossom, because they are never given the opportunity to explore the area of their giftedness.

Finally, the caregiver's response is in itself stimulating. Approving fosters continued effort; ignoring or rejecting may dampen enthusiasm. Often there is little relationship between ability and motivation. The underachiever may have been discouraged by significant others and, as a result, internalized defeat. Erikson (1963) states that if a child is encouraged to believe he can successfully do for himself, he will develop autonomy which will serve as a foundation for initiative. The most enthusiastic child may not be the most talented. He may merely be the one who has been encouraged to believe he can do anything.

Family and Peer Relations

The answers to the following questions about the child's family and friends may greatly affect both the direction and the extent of his development:

Does the family view the world as a good or a bad place?

Was the child wanted (at all, at this time, of this sex)?

Do the parents encourage the child to try new things, do they restrict him from all decision making and risk taking, or do they simply let him "do as he pleases"?

Is the parenting style encouraging, restricting, or laissez-faire?

How does this child rate compared with brothers and sisters?

Does this child have personality traits and/or special talents that are valued by his social group?

The child cannot exist in a vacuum. All the people with whom he interacts will affect his interests and feelings.

Societal and Ethnic Affiliations

Societal and ethnic affiliations often affect development in two basic ways. First, poverty and discrimination may limit an individual's opportunity to participate in many experiences, whereas affluence and social favor may open many doors. Second, the degree of social acceptance a person experiences may become a part of his self-concept. When this occurs, both motivation and direction of endeavors are affected. Additional information concerning the impact of the socioculture on the child's development is found in Chapter 12.

Summary

- Conception occurs when the sperm from the male penetrates the ovum from the female and their chromosomes unite. This event usually transpires in the fallopian tube about fourteen days after ovulation.
- Hereditary characteristics are carried by genes that are located on rodlike structures called chromosomes. Each cell contains twenty-three pairs of these chromosomes. The normal chromosome pattern for a female is XX; for the male, XY. If the inherited gene is dominant, the characteristic it controls will always appear in the individual; if the gene is recessive, the characteristic will be manifest only if no dominant gene is inherited. In many disorders, a recessive gene must be inherited from each parent in order for the characteristics to be manifested. Often, more than one gene is involved in the inheritance. Skin color and intelligence are examples of this principle.
- Physical traits that can be inherited include those related to physical appearance (color of hair, shape of nose), bodily function (blood pressure, longevity), and physical disorders (diabetes, hemophilia). Intelligence is the result of the interaction between inherited factors and experience. Personality attributes believed to be related to heredity include differences in temperament and a predisposition for certain types of mental illnesses, particularly schizophrenia and depression.
- Prenatal development occurs during three periods: the zygote, the embryo, and the fetus. During the zygotic period, the new being travels from the fallopian tube (where conception occurred) to the uterus (where it becomes implanted). During the embryonic period, basic structural systems are begun. The fetal period involves growth and refinement of the unborn child.
- A number of factors in the prenatal environment have been found to be related to the development of a healthy child. Pregnancies that are timed to occur when both mother and father are in their twenties or thirties are less likely to involve complications and/or result in birth defects. A two-year interval between pregnancies is advisable. Adequate nutrition should be maintained both prior to and during pregnancy, as malnutrition has been related to a variety of physical and mental

disorders. Many maternal disorders and diseases such as German measles, viruses, diabetes, and Rh blood factor incompatibility are known to harm the developing fetus. Many substances regularly used by the mother when she is not pregnant may be harmful during the prenatal period. These include medications, drugs, alcohol, and smoking. Any use of radiation should be avoided at this time. The expectant mother's emotional health is also important, as stress or shock may change her body chemistry and thus affect her unborn child.

- Hospital services and delivery settings now include many innovations. Classes are available both for parents-in-waiting and for young brothers and sisters. Parents often may choose between a traditional labor/delivery setting or a more homelike "birthing room." The incidence of home deliveries is on the rise, but this arrangement can involve greater risks to both mother and child.
- Newborns are most frequently checked by use of the Apgar Scale for appearance, pulse, grimace, activity, and respiration.
- Both nature and nurture—both inborn characteristics and environmental factors—help to shape the child's development. Among these forces are individual characteristics, environmental stimulation, family and peer relations, and societal and ethnic affiliations.

Selected Readings

APGAR, V., AND BECK, J. *Is My Baby All Right?* New York: Pocket Books, 1978, and Beck, J. *Best Beginnings: Giving Your Child a Head Start in Life.* New York: Putnam, 1983.
Written in nontechnical language for the lay reader, these books deal with conception, a month-by-month description of prenatal development, and a thorough treatment of birth defects—causes, prevention, and genetic counseling.

FARBER, S. L. *Identical Twins Reared Apart: A Reanalysis.* New York: Basic Books, 1981.
This book about twins summarizes the findings from many studies and explores the genetic components related to physical appearance, diseases and disorders, psychosis, intelligence, and personality traits.

GUTTMACHER, A. F. *Pregnancy, Birth, and Family Planning.* New York: Viking Press, 1984.
Each of the three areas indicated in the title is discussed in detail by a leading obstetrician.

HARRISON, R. F. *In Vitro Fertilization, Embryo Transfer and Pregnancy.* London: Kluwer Academic, 1984.

In vitro fertilization is one of the most exciting new topics in prenatal development. This work summarizes current knowledge and practice.

Moore, K. L. *Before We Are Born: Basic Embryology and Birth Defects* (2nd ed.). Philadelphia: Saunders, 1983.

The entire process of development from the male and female reproductive systems to the birth of the child are detailed in a clear and concise manner.

Nilsson, L. A. *A Child Is Born.* New York: Dell (Delacorte Press), 1977.

This book is a spectacular photographic achievement. The entire process from the earliest beginnings to birth itself are captured on film. The pictures are interspersed with a very interesting commentary.

PART III

Early Child Development

CHAPTER 4

Physical Development

CHAPTER OUTLINE

Principles Governing Growth and Development
Physical Characteristics and Needs
    Maturation of the Body
    Factors Related to Physical Development
    Child Health Care
    Child Safety
Motor Development
    Importance of Motor Development
    Readiness Factors Related to Motor Development
    Sequence of Basic Motor Skills
    Facilitating Motor Development through Movement Exploration
    Facilitating Motor Development through Instruction
Perceptual Development
    Vision
    Hearing
    Touch
    Taste and Smell
Coordination of Physical, Motor, and Sensory Development
Summary
Selected Readings

As you enter Saint Michael's Child Care Center, you witness a flurry of activity. One child with athletic build and assertive manner is organizing three other children for a game. Another child, tall, slender, and shy, stands on the fringe of the group and looks on. A small but active youngster flits from one area to another with the perpetual motion of a hummingbird. Mandy and Sarah skip happily down the side of the room, while Linda trails behind, stumbling in her efforts to match their fancy footwork. At the writing table, Jerri forms her letters with neat precision and scorns the efforts of David, whose writing, according to her evaluation, is "messy and ugly."

    The physical characteristics of each of these children is unique. What principles of growth and development help us understand these individual differences? How does maturation in various areas of body structure lead to increases in physical ability? How is precision in large and small motor skills attained? How do the perceptual areas of vision, hearing, and touch mature and develop? These are the questions to be answered in this chapter.

Principles Governing Growth and Development

Several principles of growth and development should be kept in mind as you read this chapter.

Growth proceeds in an orderly fashion. The child learns to grasp objects before she can coordinate finger muscles for writing; she walks before she runs.

Growth does not occur at a constant rate. The child sometimes experiences growth spurts of rapid development. At other times, she appears to be consolidating previous gains.

There is no absolute timetable for the acquisition of a particular skill. Although average ages for the emergence of certain abilities have been computed, a child should not be considered slow because she does not meet some preset deadline.

Critical periods appear to exist for certain aspects of development. For example, beginning attachments need to be formed during the first two years of life. In like manner, adequate nutrition during infancy is necessary for brain development.

Physical Characteristics and Needs

A comprehensive survey of the physical development and welfare of children needs to include a study of the growth and maturation of body parts and systems, identification of some of the factors that affect these changes, and consideration of issues related to the health and safety of these youngsters. The physical changes that occur in children are governed partly by the inborn characteristics of the individual and partly by conditions within the environment. Children generally experience rapid growth during the first two or three years, then slower growth for the remainder of the childhood period (Rallison, 1986).

Maturation of the Body

How does the child evolve from a wiggling, kicking infant in the crib to a competent and confident schoolchild? Changes that occur in the structure of the brain, the endocrine system, the bones, and the muscles enable children to develop many new and increasingly complex skills and abilities.

BRAIN AND CENTRAL NERVOUS SYSTEM. The first year of life is crucial for the completion of brain structure, since the brain of the newborn contains only two-thirds the number of neurons found in that of an adult. At birth, the midbrain, which controls more simple functions such as sleeping and waking, elimination, and attention, is fairly well developed. The cortex, located above the midbrain, is present but limited in function (Leve, 1980; Ornstein and Thompson, 1984). As the cortex develops, more complex body movements and more advanced responses are possible.

Impulses sent through the nervous system of the newborn are not precise because the myelin which insulates or covers the nerves has not yet fully developed. As this myelination becomes complete during the early childhood years, brain messages are transmitted more quickly and accurately. This enables the child to think and act more effectively.

ENDOCRINE SYSTEM. The endocrine system comprises a group of glands that secrete chemical substances called hormones. These hormones help to direct growth and function within the body. They may cause increases in height, stimulate development of body parts, or aid in digestion. Insufficient or absent production of vital hormones can result in a variety of disorders.

BONES. The bones of the infant are soft, because they have limited mineral content. For this reason, undue pressure or twisting can cause permanent deformity. X-rays of child abuse victims often show evidence of such maltreatment.

You may have wondered how an infant can put her foot in her mouth. (An adult can do this only when talking.) The infant's bones are separated by large spaces at the joints. As the bones lengthen and the spaces narrow, this ability is lost (Cratty, 1986).

By toddlerhood, the bones have begun to harden. As children begin to walk, they need a good supply of Vitamin D to strengthen bones and prevent a deficiency disease called rickets, which could cause permanent bowing of legs and spine. During this period, some small bones and parts of the skeletal frame that were made of cartilage turn to bone. By school age, the long bones in the arms and legs will have grown sufficiently to give the child adult-like proportions. During the school years, bone growth is slow and relatively steady (Rallison, 1986).

MUSCLES. All the muscles an individual will ever have are present at birth. With age, they change in length and thickness. Control and use of large muscles develop first. Coordination of small muscles for fine motor activities such as writing, use of small hand tools, and sports develops later as a result of maturity and practice.

PHYSICAL DEVELOPMENT 97

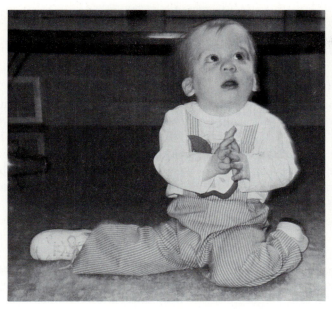

The infant often appears double-jointed because bones are separated by large spaces which will narrow as he gets older.

A concise summary of physical development in childhood appears in Box 4.1.

One special task associated with physical development that may result in problems is that of *toilet training*. Although some caregivers feel pressured to train the child early, success is strongly rooted in the biological capabilities of the individual child. The development of the nerves that govern control of urination are not complete until between two and four years of age, and the age at which a child develops anal muscle control is not known (Havighurst, 1979). Postponing toilet training until age two or after may lessen psychological strain and elimination mishaps for many children.

Several clues, some physical and some psychological, may indicate the child is ready for training. When the child can stay unsoiled for several hours, when she can walk with ease but doesn't mind sitting still for a few minutes, when she is not in a negative stage (saying "no! no!" and running away at adult suggestions), when she is beginning to imitate adults and other children, and when she shows an interest in such training, she may achieve success with relative ease (Brazelton, 1976). The process should be gradual and the patience unlimited. If possible, the

BOX 4.1
Physical Growth and Development during Childhood

Early Childhood (2 to 6 years)
- The child gains about two inches in height and about five pounds in weight each year.
- Boys and girls have similar physiques, but boys have more muscle and bone mass than do girls.
- Body proportions change as the chest becomes bigger and the stomach flatter.
- Myelination of the brain is mostly complete; therefore, complex movement patterns are possible.
- Sensory equipment changes during the preschool period. The eyeball does not reach adult size until about twelve years of age. The eustachian tube between the throat and the inner ear is shorter in the young child.

Later Childhood (6 to 12 years)
- Steady growth continues at about the same rate as in early childhood.
- Changes that occur in body build are slight.
- Great advances in coordination and integration of sensory and motor skills occur.
- Boys and girls can participate in games and sports together because of body similarities.
- Girls twelve to fourteen years of age are taller and heavier than boys because they enter adolescence earlier.
- Instruction and practice for development of sensory motor skills are very important for development of potential.

SOURCE. Summarized from Gallahue, 1982, pp. 112–117.

---

child should have a special, comfortable chair. Both explanations about what is expected and modeling by others are helpful. To minimize accidents, the child should be encouraged to go after meals and on first arising from sleep. The caregiver should praise success but not punish failure.

Among children, toilet training is often a highly valued social accomplishment. One child in a nursery school class had been teased by age-mates for repeated accidents. On discovering that he had "puddled" again on the floor, he quickly snatched up a stuffed dog, threw it on the spot, then snatched it up and began to paddle it saying, "Bad doggy, bad doggy!" Not one of his peers recognized the deception.

Factors Related to Physical Development

"Nobody else in the world like me!" is a very true line from a children's song. Factors related to differences in physical development include body type, sex, ethnic affiliation, and nutrition.

BODY TYPE. Sheldon (1940), after extensive research, concluded that there are three basic body types: the endomorph, the mesomorph, and the ectomorph. The *endomorph* tends to be soft, rounded, and often fat. The *mesomorph* is hard and firm with well-developed bone and muscle structure. The *ectomorph,* by contrast, is tall and thin with long arms and legs and little muscle. Although no one matches one of these body types exclusively, each person is predominantly one of the three (see Figure 4.1).

Sheldon believed these physical differences were accompanied by distinctive personality characteristics. The endomorph is described as a relaxed lover of food and friends, the mesomorph as an exercise and activity buff, and the ectomorph as a shy, withdrawn, and secretive individual. Research has failed to establish positive correlations between body type and personality. What has been found, however, is that people often are treated differently because of physique.

Dill (1978) reported a study in which children from ages six to ten

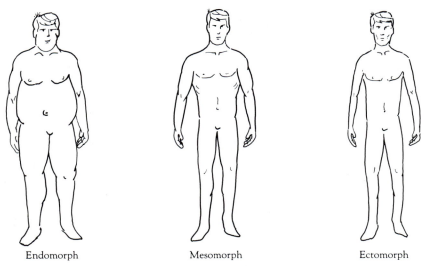

Endomorph   Mesomorph   Ectomorph

FIGURE 4.1 Some research has indicated that mesomorphs are better accepted by peers.

were asked to match descriptions to the three body types. The endomorphs were described as dirty, lazy, untrustworthy, sloppy, and ugly. The mesomorphs were rated as best-looking, healthiest, neatest, smartest, and strongest. The ectomorphs were viewed as frightened, worrisome, sad, sneaky, and weak. In three more recent studies, Eisenberg (1984) found that mothers of preschoolers expect more advanced cognitive and social behavior from taller children. Preschool males also prefer taller peers as playmates. A health spa attendant raised an interesting question. Since most of her customers needed to reduce from the waist to the knees, she asked, "What personality pattern would Sheldon have predicted for the individual who is an ectomorph on top and an endomorph on bottom?"

SEX.   Unless their clothes give us a clue, it is often difficult to determine the sex of a young child. Each of us has had the embarrassing experience of saying, "What a cute little girl!" only to have the mother reply in icy tones, "It's a boy!" While physical appearance may be very similar, important developmental differences exist that may affect degree of success in certain activities.

During the early childhood years, girls mature physically several months ahead of boys. Two important areas of acceleration are coordination and bone hardening. As a result of these maturational differences, girls exceed boys in paper-and-pencil activities and are six months to a year ahead of boys in hopping on one foot, jumping and landing on both feet, throwing a beanbag overhand, and catching a beanbag (Ames et. al., 1979). Girls also grow at a more regular rate with fewer spurts. No differences, however, have been noted in strength and speed. Child-care workers should individualize learning experiences involving physical skills so that boys are not discouraged by being unfavorably compared with female age-mates.

During the elementary school years, the skeletal growth patterns for both boys and girls are similar until the beginning of the adolescent growth spurt. For girls, this adolescent acceleration usually begins between the ages of ten and twelve; for boys, the age is about fourteen or fifteen (Richey and Taper, 1983). Much rivalry and social shyness are precipitated by this fact that the girls are taller and more maturely developed in upper elementary grades than the boys are. The early maturing children of both sexes, when compared with later bloomers, are often accorded greater social status and positions of leadership. Parents and teachers often need to reassure the later maturing children that they will ultimately achieve comparable maturational features.

ETHNIC AFFILIATION.   Ethnic affiliation is related to acceleration in physical development for some groups. Black children, when compared to their white counterparts, are superior in gross motor development in infancy (Cratty, 1986). Part of this developmental difference may result from early training, as many African groups make special efforts to teach their children to sit, stand, and walk (Hennesee and Dixon, 1984). Although the differences in height and weight between white and black children are not significant after age six, body proportions do vary. Black children have longer arms and legs, and their chests and hips tend to be more narrow (Meredith, 1968). Findings from worldwide studies indicate that body size is related to ethnic or racial affiliation even when the children are equally well nourished (Meredith, 1970; Cratty, 1986). As a general rule, however, the largest children are found in areas where nutritious food is plentiful and where diseases that might stunt growth have been controlled.

NUTRITION. Adequate nourishment is vital to optimal physical development. Consider the following key problems which may occur as a result of malnutrition: (1) loss of four to six inches in height at maturity (Winick, 1976), (2) delay of one to two years in skeletal development (Reisenger et al. 1972), and (3) significantly lowered scores on intelligence tests (Winick, 1976). Although malnutrition may be related to poverty, this condition may be found in all socioeconomic groups. Many overstuffed children are starving for needed body nutrients because of poor eating habits. Many children in the United States fall into this overweight category. What constitutes adequate nutrition? What problems may result from faulty eating habits? How can the food choices of children be improved? These and many other nutrition questions are discussed in Chapter 5.

Child Health Care

What constitutes good health care for children? Seeing that the child is properly nourished is one basic component for normal development. Another important factor is the use of preventive measures in an attempt to keep the child from becoming ill. These include daily health care routines, vaccinations against commonly occurring childhood diseases, and early recognition of illnesses when they do occur. The caregiver also should know how to care for a sick child.

DAILY CARE. One of the primary goals of daily care is to involve the child so that healthful habits become an automatic part of her daily routine. Both personal cleanliness (e.g., bathing, brushing teeth, cleaning nails, washing hands before meals) and care of the environment (e.g., picking up possessions, wiping counters, emptying wastebaskets) should be introduced and made a part of the child's activities. Learning to dress appropriately for the weather and for the activity is another healthy habit that

Good brushing habits may prevent tooth decay.

the preschooler needs to establish. Nose blowing instead of sniffling, keeping hands out of mouth, and reporting symptoms of illness also should be included.

Another important aspect of daily care is to see that the child gets needed rest. Although individual sleep needs may vary, an eighteen-month-old needs about sixteen hours. From two to five years, the child's sleep needs decrease from about twelve to eleven hours (Bergman, 1987). These estimates include both nap (for younger children) and night rest. Some children fall asleep with ease; others need encouragement and assistance. Much stress, both for the caregiver and for the child, can be avoided by the establishment of a routine, so the child will know what to expect and when.

The caregiver should anticipate the child's needs—water, kiss, toilet, or a story or individual quiet activity. These are a comfort to the child, who is giving up the excitement of her surroundings. When time for nap or retiring comes, the caregiver should be kind but firm. Mother may look forward to the child's naptime with relish, but she must remember that too long a nap may interfere with the youngster's nighttime rest.

Some children give up naps by age two or three; others still nap at six. The important consideration is to see that the child's total amount of sleep is sufficient for growth and energy.

Although the bedtime routines for school age children will differ from those of the younger child, they are of equal importance. Planned relaxation before sleep may include reading, listening to soft music, or talking to a sympathetic adult. Whatever the choice, a feeling of peacefulness and well-being is the desired outcome.

IMMUNIZATIONS AND CUMULATIVE HEALTH RECORDS. Many childhood illnesses can now be prevented through vaccinations. Since a number of health problems in later life have been traced to some of these early diseases (e.g., measles and visual difficulties, rheumatic fever and heart malfunctions), prevention is now deemed quite important. Box 4.2 contains a suggested schedule for the vaccinations that are most commonly administered.

A cumulative health record should be kept for each child. In addition to a list of immunizations, this record should include the child's name, date of birth, address, and telephone number; the home and business addresses and telphone numbers for each of the parents; emergency instructions (what to do and whom to call in case of accident or sudden illness); a list of all previous accidents and illnesses; and a record of all

---

BOX 4.2

Suggested Immunization Schedule

Age	Disease	Immunizing Agent
2 months, 4 months, and 6 months	• diphtheria • tetanus (lockjaw) • pertussis (whooping cough) • poliomyelitis	• DPT • poliovirus vaccine—live, oral, trivalent
12–15 months*		• tuberculin test
15 months	• measles • mumps (3) • rubella (German measles)	• measles, mumps, and rubella virus vaccines—live
18 months	• same as 2, 4, 6 months	• same as 2, 4, 6 months
4–6 years	• same as 2, 4, 6 months	• same as 2, 4, 6 months

* Not an immunization, but a necessary procedure
Individual schedule should be established by physician. Age intervals are flexible and are often modified.
SOURCE. Bergman, 1987b.

growth measurements and physical examinations (Reinisch and Minear, 1978). The moment of crisis is not the time to discover what needed bits of information you do not have.

EARLY DETECTION OF ILLNESS AND CARE OF THE SICK CHILD. Observation is the chief method of detecting a child's illness in the early stages. The caregiver should learn to notice facial expressions (bright-eyed and happy or fatigued and in pain), movement (spry or slow-moving and perhaps limping), skin (clear or blemished by rashes, bruises, or infection), eyes, ears, and nose (clear or crusty and discharging) (Reinisch and Minear, 1978). It is equally important to learn how to care for a sick child. Box 4.3 contains suggested procedures for dealing with some of the illnesses common to children.

BOX 4.3

Early Detection of Illness: Care of the Sick Child

Illness	Causes	Suggested Care
Vomiting	• Something eaten • Epidemic illness	• Reassure child; keep still and quiet • Give ice chips or sips of water (food might cause further vomiting) • If vomiting persists, have child sent home
Diarrhea	• Infections	• Give plenty of fluids to avoid dehydration • If diarrhea occurs more than twice in one day, notify parent at pickup time or send child home early
Fever	• Common "first sign" of illness • Often indicates infection	• Isolation, rest, and sips of water until child can be picked up • Always send feverish child home
Sore throat	• Associated with many illnesses • May be "strep throat" (streptococcal infection)	• Isolate, keep comfortable • Always send home
Cough	• Choking from swallowing foreign object • Infection in throat	• Check for foreign object in throat • Give sips of water or honey with lemon juice • Send child home if coughing persists

PHYSICAL DEVELOPMENT

BOX 4.3 (cont.)

Illness	Causes	Suggested Care
Earache	• Often associated with colds, sore throat, allergy, mumps, tooth decay • Accumulation of ear wax	• NEVER dig in child's ear • Look for fluid in ear (infection) • If earache persists, notify parent and suggest that doctor examine (eardrum could burst)
Pinkeye	• Infection on surface of eyes (eyes may have discharge, crusty lashes, pink or red on whites of eyes)	• Highly contagious • Remove child from center immediately • Wash all items that have been handled by the child to prevent spread of disease
Skin rashes (many varieties; some contagious, some not)	• Allergies • Contagious diseases such as measles, chickenpox, scarlet fever • Pinworms, lice, mites, ringworm • Insect bites	• Check medical record for special recurring conditions (allergies, eczema) • Any rash present more than one day should be examined by a medical authority

SOURCE. Summarized from Reinisch and Minear, 1978, pp. 132–144.

Child Safety

"Every year 17 million children in this country are injured accidently, almost 12,000 fatally. This means that accidents, not disease, pose the greatest threat to your child's health" (Gerber, 1980, p. 1). Children are naturally active and curious. The following suggestions are designed to promote safety as a way of life for the child. The material relating to home hazards is from Gerber (1980, p. 2); the remainder is from Hutchins (*Child Nutrition and Health,* pp. 20–21, Hutchins, B. © 1979, McGraw-Hill, adapted with permission).

HOME HAZARDS

Install safety plugs in wall sockets.

Don't use tablecloths that hang within easy reach.

Remove lamps that can be easily overturned and sharp-edged furniture.

Avoid leaving small objects within the reach of young children; they may choke on them.

FALLS

Reduce the number of obstructions that might cause falls (e.g., throw rugs, litter in walkways).

Safety education becomes a family affair as parents and children ride together.

- Teach children how to play safely on such devices as swings, jungle gyms, platforms, stairs, and escalators.
- Encourage children not to run on slick surfaces or on stairs.
- Never lift a child to a high play area to which she could not climb. (She probably can't get down unassisted and may panic.)

POISONS
- Keep household chemicals and medicines in locked cabinets. ("Out of reach" is often accessible to the preschool climbing expert.)
- Don't use anything with lead content around children (e.g., lead paint).
- Don't allow children to sample-taste things found growing in the wild. Many such plants are very poisonous, and what the child may decide to sample while you're not around is anybody's guess.

FIRE
- Keep sources of fire away from children (e.g., matches, cigarette lighters).
- Teach children not to play with fire or with electrical outlets. (Adapted from Hutchins, © McGraw-Hill, 1979)

PHYSICAL DEVELOPMENT

WATER
- Don't leave children alone near water (even if shallow; may land face down).
- Don't leave a child under two alone in the bathtub for even a minute.
- Always have a sufficient number of adults to supervise any waterplay.

ACCIDENTS WITH AUTOMOBILES
- Don't allow children to stand in seats or hang out windows.
- Use safety belts, infant and child care seats.
- Teach children when, where, and how to cross streets safely.
- Teach children to exert great caution when chasing a ball or other toy that rolls into the street.
- Provide appropriate adult supervision.
(Adapted from Hutchins, © McGraw-Hill, 1979)

Motor Development

Motor skills do not come to children automatically with maturation. They will occur only if necessary developmental experiences are provided.

Importance of Motor Development

Motor development is vital to the total functioning of the individual. It is related to many cognitive, emotional, and social functions. McClenaghan and Gallahue (1978) identified the following benefits that accrue to children through motor development:

- Enables children to explore the world and develop cognitive concepts. (Adult responses to these adventures will affect children's inclinations to assume initiative in the future.)
- Makes children capable of performing daily tasks such as dressing, eating, cleaning (or restoring order after making a mess).
- Contributes to general health and physical well-being through the development of muscle strength, physical endurance, and heart and lung capacity.
- Facilitates participation in activities with peers (helps children to be good enough to be chosen rather than having to be added to the team at teacher suggestion or insistence).
- Affords one avenue for prestige with peers as skill increases.

- Bolsters self-concepts, as children feel successful in their endeavors and receive favorable feedback from peers (although some children feel competent and are well-accepted with limited skill development).
- Encourages voluntary performance of motor skills alone, with a partner, or with a team. As children begin to use these skills for recreation, they acquire lifelong value. Voluntary use of motor proficiencies is increasingly important, as more recreation time is now available in our modern society.

Readiness Factors Related to Motor Development

A number of factors appear to be related to a child's motor skill potential. Hereditary characteristics such as size, body proportion, sensitivity, and response patterns may predispose some children to do better in one activity and some in another. The birth process may affect motor development potential, since difficulties during delivery may have limited the capabilities of certain youngsters. The previous experiences children have had—both in variety and in amount in a given area—will affect their readiness levels. Interest is another crucial variable. If a child really wants to do something, many weaknesses can be overcome. Finally, the child's state of maturation at the time of learning opportunity may be a deciding factor.

What are the major physical components of this state of maturation or readiness for motor development? Stallings (1982) lists four important factors to be considered: (1) *Strength* is an obvious requirement. This includes muscle strength for such tasks as pushing and pulling; muscle force for sprinting, gripping, and other drive activities; and muscle endurance for repetitious actions such as push-ups and long distance runs. (2) *Flexibility*, or the range of movement each joint can make, will sometimes determine which activities are best suited to a given child (e.g., "How many ways can you move your foot, move your body?"). (3) *Balance* is very important while in motion or standing still. Does the child fall over her feet at play; can she move backward as well as forward; can she move with her eyes closed? These are indicators of the child's degree of balance proficiency. (4) *Coordination,* or the child's ability to synchronize the movements of different parts of the body in a single activity, is a final requisite. Many activities require that a child use hands, feet, and other body parts simultaneously to succeed at the motor task.

Sequence of Basic Motor Skills

Two of the most basic motor skills are locomotion (moving from one place to another) and manipulation (effective use of the hands). Since these abilities develop sequentially, it is important to identify which tasks the child has already mastered in order to know what she can do next (see Figure 4.2).

LOCOMOTION. Crawling, creeping, and walking are the rudiments of all locomotion. The sequence of these forms of locomotion is described by Arnheim and Pestolesi (1977) and Gallahue (1982). In the beginning, the infant's movements consist of random wiggling and arm and leg waving. The first major achievement is that of turning over, which occurs at about three months. At about the same time, *precrawling* begins. While keeping the body in contact with the surface for support, the child (1) first wiggles legs, then arms, (2) moves an arm and a leg on one side of the body, then on the other, and (3) finally succeeds in *cross-pattern crawling*, alternating one arm with the opposite leg. *Creeping*, moving on all fours with body raised, occurs when the child's muscles are ready (at about eight or nine months) and follows the same sequence as did crawling.

Walking, which usually occurs after the first year, progresses in the following sequence: pulling up to objects (beware of lamp cords and tablecloths in this stage), toddling along holding onto something, stumbling onward with legs widespread and arms up for balance, and finally, independent locomotion.

As walking speed increases, the child begins to *run* (McClenaghan and Gallahue, 1978; Gallahue, 1982). Initially, the child runs in a rather stiff-legged manner, with feet wide apart for support. In the elementary stage, the length of the stride increases, the child lands more on the toes instead of the flat foot, and the arms swing in opposition to the legs. Mature running is characterized by smooth, refined movements with more time spent in propulsion than on the supporting ground surface. Timing on the 50-yard dash improves for girls until about age fourteen, but boys continue to increase in running speed until about age seventeen (Williams, 1983).

Jumping is the form of locomotion that propels the child through space. Essential segments of the action are preparatory crouch, take-off, flight, and landing (McClenaghan and Gallahue, 1978; Gallahue, 1982). Early jumping is unstable and usually up-and-down rather than forward. With practice, the feet begin to work together on take-off and landing and mature jumping is achieved. Jumping (both vertical and broad) improves with age from five to fourteen years. Boys tend to outjump girls at all ages (Williams, 1983).

The child combines and varies the motor patterns she has learned to develop other forms of locomotion (Gallahue, 1982). *Hopping* is a type of jumping in which the child takes off and lands on one foot instead of two. Girls usually hop faster than boys and are superior to them in all hopping-related footwork (Williams, 1983). *Skipping* is an advanced form

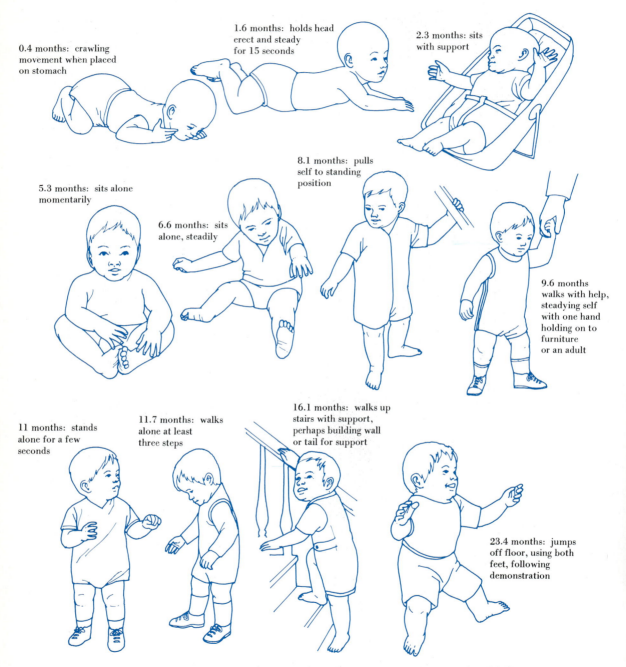

FIGURE 4.2   (*Source: From Bayleg, 1969, in Schiamberg, 1987, p. 237*)

of hopping in which the child combines a step and a hop and alternates feet (with an even rhythm after she acquires the skill). *Leaping* is advanced running. The child goes higher into the air and travels farther on each alternating bound. *Climbing* is a crawling variation in which the body is pulled upward, and it usually involves the use of both arms and legs. Much to the dismay of some parents, climbing often occurs even before walking.

A number of factors affect a child's motor performance (Pissanos et al., 1983). Age, body size (height and weight), and skeletal maturity all contribute to increased skill. Sex differences, however, are not as great during the school years as they were during preschool times. When boys and girls in grades one through three were compared in terms of power, balance, agility, speed, strength/endurance, flexibility, and cardiovascular function, differences between the sexes were slight. The researchers conclude that there was no valid physical basis for separating boys and girls in these age groups for physical education activities.

MANIPULATION. *Grasping* is a reflex present at birth that serves as the basis for future hand skills (Arnheim and Pestolesi, 1977). The tendency of the infant to grasp and not let go (remember those hair pullings) is based on the fact that her grasping muscles (flexors) are stronger than her releasing muscles (extensors). A further refinement of grasping, the ability to move the thumb in opposition to the hand, is vital since it enables the child to pick up objects and perform such advanced skills as writing. A child usually has this opposable thumb ability at about sixteen months, but not until two years is she likely to be able to use this skill with both hands simultaneously.

Many caregivers are concerned about whether a child is right or left handed. *Handedness* appears to be based primarily on genetic factors. No concentrated effort should be made to change a child's natural preference, since such attempts may create tension and continuing clumsiness. During the preschool years, the child usually explores manipulation with both hands, and not until the early school years does a preference for one hand over the other become established (Tan, 1982).

Further basic extensions of manipulation are throwing, catching, and kicking (McClenaghan and Gallahue, 1978; Gallahue, 1982). In *throwing*, the child first pushes the object forward with her whole body (and often loses her balance in the process). With practice and experience, the arm moves back, the trunk rotates away from the target, the weight falls on the rear foot, the ball is released, and the body shifts appropriately to follow through. The child's first reactions to *catching* involve closing her eyes, stiffening, and turning away from the approaching object. Next the child uses the "basket catch"—arms extended and curved to "scoop

---

Case Study 4

The "Y" programs (YMCA/YWCA) provide a wide variety of developmental and physical activities for children. The following is a partial inventory of their offerings:

- Discovery camps—designed to introduce preschool children to outdoor activities; small group settings used.
- Progressive swim classes—develop increasing levels of swim skills beginning with aquatots (six months to three years) and continuing to adulthood.
- Gymnastics and tumbling—starts with movement exploration for ages three to four and continues through a developmental series of tumbling and gymnastic skills.
- Summer day camp—organized for boys and girls six to twelve years of age; includes informal physical activities (hiking, games, overnight campouts) and structured skill training in a variety of sports.
- Week-long camps—offers six sessions per summer for boys and girls ages nine to sixteen; development through such activities as swimming, horseback riding, water skiing, canoeing, archery, and sailing.

---

in" the ball. Eventually the youngster follows the object visually from release to catch and moves her body in space as necessary to be in the right place at the right time. *Kicking* initially involves little backswing. The child's foot may miss the ball or slide over the top of it, and she may lose her balance. Eventually the child can kick with sufficient force and accuracy to direct the ball to the desired destination.

Facilitating Motor Development through Movement Exploration

Every child needs many opportunities to explore both the movements her body can make and the characteristics of objects in her environment. Hours of free play with a wide variety of play equipment and manipulatives can provide this foundation. As the child experiments, she is both teacher and learner. She discovers the parts of the body and their potentials, gaining a more accurate and complete body image. This internalized body

PHYSICAL DEVELOPMENT   *113*

Motor skills are refined through movement exploration. (*Source: Courtesy, National Science Teachers Association*)

image is a necessary prerequisite for the refinement of motor skills, hand preference, and laterality. As she manipulates objects, she learns how to relate to them with ever-increasing skill. "The big ball is easier to catch than the little one is." "I can't skip yet, but I can hop." These are the bits of self-knowledge that can serve as a background for future motor development. A list of common items that can be used to develop motor skills through explorative play is found in Box 4.4.

Facilitating Motor Development through Instruction

Instruction should never be used as a substitute for movement exploration. It can be an enhancing experience, however, if both readiness level and interest indicate that the child will experience a degree of success. Cratty (1986), a prominent authority in motor development, suggests that the following instructional sequence be used during the childhood period.

BOX 4.4
Inexpensive Equipment for Enhancing Fundamental Movement

Equipment	Materials	Approximate Cost
1. Ropes of various lengths	200 feet of rope, tape for both ends	$14
2. Hoops of various sizes	½- to ¾-inch plastic pipe, wooden dowels, tape	65¢ per hoop
3. Carpet squares (for hopping games)	Extra carpet or samples	Free
4. Beanbags of various sizes and shapes	Cloth, thread, popcorn, or filter	15¢ per bag
5. Yarn balls	Skein of yarn	85¢ per skein
6. Bamboo poles	Centers of carpet rolls	Free
7. Bouncing tubes	Auto inner tubes	Free
8. Stretch tubes	Bicycle inner tubes or cut auto tubes	Free
9. Wands (Lumi sticks)	Wooden dowels or cut broom handles	75¢ per 3-foot dowel
10. Can stilts	Tin cans, rope, tape, or plastic lid	Free
11. Balance boards	¾-inch plywood, 2-foot × 4-foot blocks	$10
12. Barrels	Old barrels, cleaned	$5
13. Bowling pins	Small plastic bottles	Free
14. Catching scoops	Large plastic bottles, tape	Free
15. Hockey set	Old brooms, paper ball	Free

SOURCE. Appendix B, p. 203, from *Fundamental Movement: A Developmental and Remedial Approach* by Bruce A. McClenagham and D. L. Gallahue, copyright © 1978 by W. B. Saunders, a division of Holt, Rinehart and Winston, Inc., reprinted by permission of the publisher.

TASK PREPARATION. In presenting a new skill to the child, visual, verbal, and manual modalities should be used. The child needs to see the task correctly being performed, so she can internalize a mental image of the act. These visual presentations can include teacher demonstrations, exhibitions by other children who already have mastered the skill, or videotapes of other performers. Verbalization may expand understanding by giving reasons for what is being seen. Tactile (hands-on) experience helps the child "get the feel" of the action in a way that sight and sound cannot convey. Demonstrations should be precise and correct; never show children how *not* to do something.

GUIDANCE PHASE. The guidance phase involves the actual performance of the task by the child. As the child performs, the teacher may make verbal corrections ("Keep your eyes on the ball."), add quick demonstrations ("See, I step, then hop like this to skip."), or give manual assistance by actually moving the child's arms, legs, or hands. Two cautions need to be observed. Don't talk too much, as this may distract from concentration and self-correction. Don't be too exact, as too much attention to detail may detract from the "wholeness" of the movement, and criticism may discourage or defeat the child.

KNOWLEDGE OF RESULTS. Give the child immediate feedback while she can still remember what she did. Help the child analyze "internal cues," feelings she had while she was moving ("I felt I was going to topple over." "I was afraid I'd not be able to stop if I ran so fast."). If the teacher and child compare notes—the teacher sharing what she saw and the child explaining what she felt and observed—plans for improved performance can be made. In this way, practice and repetition become meaningful, since each trial involves changes based on feedback.

INVOLVER 4

Beanbag Accuracy Throw

Accurate bean bag throwing can be used to assess a child's eye-hand coordination and involves the maturation and development of many body parts and systems. Select two children of the same sex, one about three years of age and one about six, for the following game-test situation.

Using masking tape or chalk, make four lines two feet apart. Place a small plastic hoop just beyond the lines. Have the child try to throw a beanbag from each of the lines. Record (1) the distance(s) from which each child can successfully land a bag in the hoop, (2) how the child held the bag, and (3) whether child threw overhanded or underhanded (game idea from Arnheim and Pestolesi, 1977).

THINKING IT OVER

• What differences did you note in the distance of the throw, the way the

> **INVOLVER 4** (*cont.*)
>
> beanbag was held (palming or use of fingers), and the way it was thrown (overhand, underhand, or just pushed forward)?
> - What differences were there in understanding and ability to follow instructions? Success of motor skill development is often based on the ability of the caregiver to communicate with children at different developmental levels.
> - If you wish to expand this activity, try using a boy and a girl of the same age. If differences are noted, how can you explain them?
> - Another interesting related activity would be to attempt to increase the skill of one of the children through using the instructional skill sequence (task preparation, guidance phase, knowledge) in the section "Facilitating Motor Development through Instruction."

Perceptual Development

We automatically analyze and organize the cues we receive through our senses. Generally these perceptual systems do not work alone; several of them combine to give us more information about our experiences. Flowers and ship channels, football games and fat stock shows, ice cream cones and stroganoff all become familiar to us through the avenues of sight, sound, touch, taste, and smell.

What meaning we derive from any given encounter is based on our needs and expectations, past experiences, current physical and mental health, and details involved in the happening itself. The non-English-speaking child literally may not hear certain vowel and consonant sounds. The fearful child may, in her own mind, see a bear in the corner of a dark room. The child who has had little opportunity to hear stories may have very limited recall.

The importance of the senses in helping us assimilate and process information led Piaget to refer to the first two years of life as the sensorimotor period, that time during which the child uses her senses and emerging motor abilities to explore her new world (Piaget, 1969). How does each of the perceptual areas—vision, hearing, touch, taste, and smell—develop? What can be done to increase the child's ability to receive input through each of these systems?

PHYSICAL DEVELOPMENT *117*

Vision

It has been estimated that about 80 percent of all the information we receive comes through sight (Taylor, 1985). Although most children are born with the capacity to see, they develop a variety of visual skills as a result of maturation and experience. These have been described in detail by Arnheim and Pestolesi (1977) and Williams (1983). Much of the information contained in this section on vision is based on their work.

Visual acuity is the ability to see details clearly. While outside, this skill enables the child to accurately observe the world around her and also to participate in a variety of games and other activities. Within the classroom, sharpness of farpoint vision helps the child see the chalkboard and other learning displays from across the room.

Visual coordination is the training of the eyes to work as a team for fixation, tracking, and convergence. *Fixation* involves focusing the eyes on a particular point. As the child matures, she is able to make rapid

Much learning is based on looking.

and accurate shifts between nearpoint and farpoint. This enables her to examine closely the materials at the science table, glance across the room, and return her gaze to the activity at hand. Through *visual tracking,* the child learns to follow objects moving in space. The baby who continues to drop an object and have you pick it up is not being brattish; she is developing this very necessary skill of visual pursuit. (Just figure that you are contributing to her becoming a good tennis player someday.) This tracking ability is crucial to many individual games and sports. Not only does visual tracking enable the individual to follow an object moving in space, it also helps her determine the speed at which the object is moving. As this skill becomes better developed, the child can accurately judge the speed of an approaching automobile and learn to safely cross the street alone. *Convergence* is the turning of the eyes inward toward the nose to see objects at different distances (more inward for closer objects). One of the reasons most preschoolers tend to be farsighted is that their smaller head size makes the child's eyes closer together than those of an adult. Since this convergence skill is not fully developed during the preschool years, the caregiver should remember not to plan too many "closework" activities that might strain the child's eyes.

Visual discrimination, or the ability to detect small differences among similar configurations, is a much-used skill. At a very early age, the child learns to differentiate the face of her major caregiver from that of a stranger. As this ability to see differences develops, the child recognizes an ever-increasing number of persons, places, and things. The child learns to distinguish among various shapes and symbols. This facilitates matching activities and reading (including the ability to visually discriminate between such look-alikes as "dog" and "bag"). The child also learns *figure-ground discrimination*—the ability to focus on a particular thing without being confused by the background. Figure-ground development leads to skill in scanning—glancing over a room to find a lost object or looking over a page in a book for all the words beginning with "b."

Visual memory is the ability to call to mind things that have been seen previously. An early use of this skill is that of mapping—being able to draw a diagram of one's room from memory. Later, visual memory is used for spelling (getting all those letters in order), reading (recognizing previously studied words), and game sequences (first you do this; then you do that).

An important aspect of visual memory is *form constancy,* the ability to recognize a given shape wherever one sees it. Learning letters in reading, putting parts together in assembly tasks, and recognizing shapes of surfaces in mathematics and science are important applications of form constancy.

Position in space and *spatial relationships* are important in activities in which location is critical. "Is the 'e' before 'i' in 'receive'?" "Is the car I see in the distance far enough away for me to cross the street safely?" "Am I running to the right spot to hit the tennis ball back across the net?" These visual determinations are being made constantly throughout the day.

A final visual skill to be considered is that of *visual-motor coordination.* One frequently used application is that of locomotion—first walking, then running. Another is the coordination of sight with fine-motor activities. Eyes and hands work together for writing, sports, and a variety of other everyday and creative tasks. Hands and feet work together in fine coordination for dancing and for many intricate game strategies.

Since these skills develop over a period of time rather than being present at birth, approximately when can the caregiver anticipate that each may appear? Many child development specialists have researched the developmental sequence of vision. Williams (1983) has analyzed the findings of a number of studies. A summary of these findings is presented in Box 4.5.

BOX 4.5

Age and Sex Differences for Selected Visual Skills

Visual Acuity (ability to see likenesses, differences, and details clearly)

Static visual acuity (involving still objects)
- Rapid development 5–7 years; little change 7–9 years; second developmental spurt 9–10 years; mature ability achieved 10–12 years.
- Boys superior to girls at all ages.

Dynamic visual acuity (involving moving objects)
- Ability depends on speed (ability to judge slow speeds about the same as static visual acuity).
- Ability to judge fast speeds 5–6 years; little change 6–9 years; further refinement 9–12 years; mature ability achieved 11–12 years.

Eye movement control (Ability to scan)
- More visual fixations used to determine likenesses and differences as children get older.
- Children will vary number of fixations according to material by 6½–9 years.
- Identical materials take most fixations for comparisons; objects with only one difference next; things not similar the least number of fixations.

Figure-Ground (ability to distinguish object from its background)
- Gradual improvement with age until about 8; little change from that age on.
- Girls slightly more advanced than boys by age 6.

BOX 4.5 (cont.)

Form Constancy (reliable perception of shape)
- Girls slightly ahead of boys in development of form constancy.
- Both sexes achieve mature level at about 10 years.

Position in Space and Spatial Relations (relative locating of objects)
- Boys and girls develop at about the same rate.
- Depth perception develops rapidly through early childhood; fine development and maturity reached about age 12.

Perception of Movement (accurate estimation of speed)
- Children aged 6, 7, and 8 recognize that an object is moving rapidly but have difficulty directing their own body movements in relation to the moving object.
- Perception of movement continues refinement until about age 12.

SOURCE. Harriet G. Williams, *Perceptual and Motor Development*, © 1983, Chapter 4. Adapted by permission of Prentice Hall, Inc. Englewood Cliffs, New Jersey.

Hearing

Gibson (1983) described several basic functions of hearing that are related to daily living and to the growth of intelligent thinking. First, the fact that we have two ears placed on opposite sides of the head helps us locate the *direction* from which the sound is coming. By turning toward the sound, we often can use our other senses to enlarge upon the informational input; we may see, feel, taste, or smell the thing that has been brought to our attention. Locating the direction of a sound also may be a safety feature. The blare of a horn or the clatter of a falling object may alert the child to danger. A second important use of hearing is for *identification* of things in the environment by the sounds they make. Even without looking, the child can recognize familiar sounds such as the voice of a friend or the thud of a canned drink falling in a coin machine. The third vital function served by hearing is to *gain information* from meaningful sounds. As the child comes to understand words, verbal instruction can be used to explain the things she sees and tell her about things she has never seen. Words can give her feedback on performance and comfort her when she is troubled. Sounds other than words can give information, too. A buzzer can tell us that some process is complete and a "funny noise" often alerts us to the fact that something is malfunctioning.

Three important auditory skills are acuity, discrimination, and memory (Arnheim and Pestolesi, 1977). As children develop *auditory acuity,* or sharp-

PHYSICAL DEVELOPMENT

The soft sound of the shell is in sharp contrast to the noises of children at play.

ness of hearing perception, they are able to discern the direction from which a sound is coming, how loud or soft the volume is, and how high or low the pitch is. This ability develops early, and there is little change during early and middle childhood (Williams, 1983). Through *auditory discrimination* children distinguish other likenesses and differences among sounds; they can determine which sounds match each other and which do not. This skill can help children stay on pitch or match rhythm patterns while singing or playing musical instruments. It can also help in reading (hearing the "t" sound at beginning, middle, or ending position in a word). One of the great difficulties faced by bilingual children is that they have not had sufficient opportunities to hear certain sounds that do not occur in their native language. Research studies have indicated that the child of eight years is significantly better at auditory discrimination than is the child of five or six (Williams, 1983). Reading success might be greatly enhanced if phonics training were delayed until the child's hearing is more developmentally advanced.

Auditory memory, or retaining what has been said, is a vital learning tool. It enables children to follow spoken directions and to remember the stories, songs, finger plays, and poetry they have heard. The child's ability for auditory memory increases sharply between the ages of five and eight years. Refinement of this skill continues through about the age of fifteen.

Children are born with the capacity to receive and process sounds, and this potential is transformed into the auditory skills just discussed through interaction with the environment. In fact, prenatal research has indicated that children can hear as early as five weeks after conception and can demonstrate this sensitivity to sound by movement and change in fetal heart rate (Arnheim and Pestolesi, 1977). By three or four months of age, youngsters have developed considerable skill in locating the origins of sounds (Piaget, 1969; White, 1984). They also are fascinated by their own noises and will entertain themselves for hours with their cooing and gurgling. This preoccupation with listening to the sounds made by themselves and by others continues through the eighth month and serves as a prelude to speaking. Many opportunities for hearing a wide variety of sounds should be afforded during this period. Language expansion during the preschool and school years is based largely on the child's opportunity to hear words used frequently and in a wide variety of contexts. The relationship of hearing to speaking will be discussed in greater detail in Chapter 7.

Skills are not generally used in isolation. Almost all activities require the integration of input from two or more senses. Auditory-visual integration is used so frequently in problem solving and in daily living; this combination of sensory processes is illustrated in Box 4.6. This information was drawn from the work of Williams.

BOX 4.6

Development of Auditory-Visual Integration

1. From birth, children explore objects and events using several senses.
2. Auditory-visual integration usually improves with age.
3. The ability to use auditory and visual information at the same time (as in learning to read) increases significantly between the ages of five and seven years.
4. Visual-integration abilities develop in advance of auditory integration abilities until about the age of seven years after which both integration abilities are apt to be at about the same level.
5. Auditory and visual integration abilities improve significantly between eight and ten years and continue to improve somewhat to the age of twelve.
6. Presenting material by sight first generally improves intersensory auditory-visual integration for all ages.

SOURCE. Harriet G. Williams, *Perceptual and Motor Development*, © 1983, p. 147. Adapted by permission of Prentice Hall, Inc., Englewood Cliffs, New Jersey.

Touch

The feelings derived from the sense of touch are valuable in many ways. Children use this sense to explore the characteristics of things in the environment (thorns are prickly and hurt, mud feels good squishing between the toes). From infancy, youngsters learn how comforting it is to be cuddled and stroked. Feelings also aid in movement as the body feeds back to the mind such information as "I'm off balance and about to fall!"

Like the other senses, touch develops as the child matures and gains experience. During the first three to four months of life, the child's hands remain tight-fisted most of the time. Her exploring by touch consists of "gumming" everything that gets near her mouth (White, 1984). Sometime between the third and fifth months, the infant learns to use the hand as a "reaching tool" directed by the eye. Now the child will use both hand and mouth to learn about the hardness, shape, and texture of everything within reach. My cousin fondly dubbed her infant crawler "the vacuum sweeper" because he would go all over the floor popping everything he found into his mouth. By sixteen months of age, the child is aware of the third dimension and realizes that all objects are not flat (Arnheim and Pestolesi, 1977). The two-year-old learns to perceive differences in

Through touch, children gain both cognitive knowledge and warm feelings.

surfaces (rough/smooth, wet/dry, hot/cold) and enjoys "feeling" shapes (tracing their outlines with a finger). By about the age of four, many children can identify shapes and objects by touch alone.

Related to touch and feeling is kinesthesis, an awareness of body position and movement (Arnheim and Pestolesi, 1977). This sense is based on internal feedback from such body structures as muscles, joints, and the inner ear. This perception helps the child with balance, precision of movement, and spatial orientation.

Taste and Smell

It is difficult to separate taste from smell since the two often work together (Taylor, 1985). Much of what we call taste is actually smell, and some smells are really feelings (sniffing ammonia yields pain plus smell). This combination of senses occurs because the receptors for taste, smell, and feelings are located so close together in the adjoining mouth and nasal area. A kindergarten teacher added more confusion than light when she tried to explain that smells often cause taste. When she later asked, "Can we sometimes taste with our noses," one child prudently answered, "No, 'cause our noses don't have any teeth" (Taylor, 1978).

Contrary to this youngster's guess, our taste buds are not located on the teeth but rather on the tongue, along the sides of the cheeks, and in the throat. As these buds are stimulated by the chemical substances in foods and drinks, we taste sweet, bitter, salt, or sour. Several factors may affect the taste we perceive: temperature, odor, surface texture (smooth or rough), fluid content (dry or moist), consistency (hard, soft, or sticky), and size of pieces. One teacher demonstrated the relationship of taste to sight by showing the children that when blindfolded they could not tell the difference between eating onions and apples. Everyone can visualize the taste and smell connection by remembering how tasteless food is when the nose is congested from a bad cold.

Some ability to taste and to smell is present at birth. Infants can distinguish between sweetened and plain water and like the sugary taste best. They often react to odors by moving away from the source or by changing breathing patterns.

Coordination of Physical, Motor, and Sensory Development

Children never learn skills in isolation. They constantly recombine bits and pieces of various capabilities in order to accomplish new tasks. Consider some of the possible physical-sensorimotor coordinations in the following example:

PHYSICAL DEVELOPMENT *125*

Task: Cutting with Scissors

PHYSICAL
- Maturation of nervous system for coordination and steadiness of hand
- Development of small muscles

SENSORY
- Seeing the cutting outline; seeing that the scissors are perpendicular to the paper; seeing the separation of severed parts
- Hearing instructions; hearing the scissors snip
- Feeling the pressure of the scissors against the paper while cutting

MOTOR
- Controlling small muscles
- Moving the scissors forward while cutting
- Matching hand movement to cutting line

In facilitating skill development in children, it is always necessary to consider the physical, motor, and perceptual components in the task. From this analysis, the caregiver can help the child master the necessary subcomponents required for success in that particular activity.

Summary

- Growth follows a predictable direction: from head to toe and from the center of the body to the extremities. Whole-body movements develop first, followed by fine-motor movements. Although the rate of growth varies from one person to another, growth proceeds in an orderly fashion and appears to involve critical periods.
- As the body matures, developmental changes in the brain and central nervous system make more-complex body movements possible. The endocrine system stimulates growth of body parts, bones harden to give upright stability, and maturation of muscles increases motor control.
- Several factors relate to physical development. Body type (endomorph, mesomorph, or ectomorph) may affect physical/motor interests and proficiencies. Sex differences, including an earlier maturation rate for girls, should be considered in planning activities for children. Research studies of ethnic affiliation indicate that even when nutrition and disease control are held constant, some groups grow larger and mature earlier

than do others. Adequate nutrition is necessary for optimal physical development; however, malnutrition may occur as a result of economic poverty or from a lack of knowledge and/or concern for proper eating habits.
- Health care for children should include helping children establish daily routines that will contribute to their well-being, having them vaccinated for common childhood diseases, and maintaining cumulative health records for them. The caregiver also should become knowledgeable in early detection of illness and care of the sick child.
- More children are hurt through accidents than through disease. The environment should be carefully screened for hazards, children should be taught basic safety rules, and adults should provide appropriate supervision.
- Motor development does not come automatically through maturation. Experiences for building motor skills are vitally important, since they relate to many physical, emotional, social, and cognitive functions. Major readiness factors related to motor development have been identified as hereditary characteristics, events during the birth process, previous experiences, interests, and state of physical maturation. Children develop abilities in locomotion (movement of the body through space) and manipulation (use of hands) through a series of stages. Both movement exploration and instruction are necessary for optimal motor development.
- Children are born with the capacity to receive input from the environment through the senses of vision, hearing, touch, taste, and smell, but skill in the use of the senses comes through experience. Necessary components of vision are visual acuity (ability to see details clearly), visual coordination (teaming of the eyes to see objects both near and far, moving or stationary), and visual discrimination (detection of small differences in similar configurations). Hearing helps us locate the direction from which a sound is coming, identify things in the environment by the sounds they make, and gain information from meaningful sounds. We are able to do this through the auditory acuity, discrimination, and memory that develop as we interact with the environment. Touch is used to determine the characteristics of objects (rough/smooth, hot/cold), to receive comfort from others, and to aid in movement. Taste and smell, used both for identification and for pleasure, are closely related, since the receptors for both are located in close proximity in the body and both are stimulated by chemical substances.
- Physical, motor, and sensory capabilities work together to make experience possible and meaningful.

Selected Readings

CRATTY, B. J. *Perceptual and Motor Development in Infants and Children* (3rd ed.). Englewood Cliffs, NJ: Prentice-Hall, 1986.
    This comprehensive work summarizes research related to neurological, physical, and motor development and their relationship to the acquisition of skills.

GALLAHUE, D. L. *Understanding Motor Development in Children.* New York: Wiley, 1982.
    This text presents the sequential development of motor skills. It summarizes fundamental patterns for locomotion (walking, running, jumping) and manipulation (overhand throwing, catching, and kicking). Numerous activities and instructions for teaching motor skills are also given.

REINISCH, E. H., AND MINEAR, R. E. *Health of the Preschool Child.* New York: Wiley, 1978.
    The child health topics discussed in this work include preschool health programs, nutrition, infection, behavior problems, first aid, and safety education. Many sample materials and forms are included.

WHITE, B. L. *The First Three Years of Life.* New York: Avon Books, 1984.
    This report of extensive research includes a very detailed analysis of development during these early years and includes practical suggestions for enriching the child's environment and experience.

WILLIAMS, H. G. *Perceptual and Motor Development.* Englewood Cliffs, NJ: Prentice-Hall, 1983.
    This book contains in-depth discussions as to how and when various perceptual and motor sequences and skills develop.

CHAPTER 5

Nutrition and Development

(Source: © 1988 Jean Shapiro)

CHAPTER OUTLINE

    Nutritional Status of Children
    Analysis of Needed Nutrients
        Major Nutrients
        How Food Digests
        Four Basic Food Groups
        Special Dietary Needs of Children
    Problems of the Malnourished
        Physical
        Cognitive
        Behavioral
    Programs for Fostering Better Nutrition
    Summary
    Selected Readings

Every Thursday at 4:00 P.M. a parade of youngsters arrive at the special Obesity Center for Children at North Shore University Hospital in Manhasset, New York. Most are 20 to 50 percent overweight, and it is the goal of the clinic to stop their gains and allow their height to catch up with their weight. Many myths contribute to the high incidence of obesity in children. Physician-in-charge Dr. Ruth Waldbaum decries the belief that chubby children are healthier and that youngsters will outgrow weight problems. Since fad diets and very restrictive eating plans are particularly dangerous for growing children, the thrust of the clinic's work is to teach healthy food habits to both the children and their parents. In fact, children are not enrolled in the program unless family cooperation and participation are ensured. With family support, these obese children may establish better nutrition practices, achieve appropriate weight levels, and avoid the problems associated with lifelong obesity (Galton, 1978).

    How well nourished are the young children of the United States? What constitutes an adequate diet for youngsters? What physical, cognitive, and behavioral complications may result from malnutrition? Can programs be designed to foster better eating habits? These are the concerns to be addressed in this chapter.

Nutritional Status of Children

Several national surveys have been conducted to investigate the nutritional status of children in the United States. The findings indicate that although there is little overt starvation in this country, malnutrition frequently occurs. Two major factors involved are economic poverty and lack of nutritional knowledge. Persons in lower socioeconomic groups tend to be smaller in size and less mature in skeletal development. These differences may result from the limited quality and quantity of food available to those subsisting on severely restricted incomes.

Malnutrition is not limited to the poor, however. Even in affluent areas, the diets of many children are substantially deficient in vital nutrients. These children apparently suffer from "poverty of knowledge"—their parents simply do not know what constitutes a healthy diet.

In one comprehensive survey, including both low and middle socioeconomic groups, the following deficiency profile emerged (Watson, 1974):

PREGNANT AND/OR NURSING TEENAGE MOTHERS

- One of three ate less than half the recommended daily allowance (RDA) for calories, calcium, iron, and Vitamin A.
- One in five ate less than half the RDA for protein, Vitamin C, and niacin.

CHILDREN UNDER AGE FOUR

- One out of two had less than the RDA for Vitamin C.
- One in six had inadequate blood levels for Vitamin C.
- Over 30 percent had inadequate blood levels of Vitamin A.
- Twenty to 25 percent ate less than half the RDA for calories, calcium, Vitamin A, and niacin.
- Seventy percent received less than half the RDA for iron.
- Ten to 20 percent were anemic (low level of hemoglobin in the blood).
- One in three was a significant nutritional risk.

Several factors are believed to be affecting eating habits in America (Richey and Taper, 1983). First is food advertising. Eighty percent of all commercials designed for children involve food. Many of these advocate the eating of heavily sugared, salted, or fried foods. Second, more mothers are now working. Children are now more likely to prepare their own food or snacks with limited knowledge of nutrients. Third, fast-food restaurants have proliferated. The foods they serve are frequently high in fat; are low in vitamins A and C, calcium, and fiber; and include few fresh vegetables. Fourth, snacking is common. These snacks may be high in sugar, salt, and fat. They may also contribute to obesity when they are "forgotten" (not counted into the total daily intake). Fifth, much of our food now comes from vending machines. The selection of nutritious food here is often limited. All of these factors tend to increase the risk of poor nutrition.

# Analysis of Needed Nutrients

What nutrients are needed to constitute a healthy diet, and how do they affect body functions? What are the special dietary needs of youngsters from infancy through childhood? How are good eating habits established? These questions frequently are posed by those who are caregivers for young children.

Major Nutrients

Nutrients are the elements in food that help build and repair the body's tissues and regulate its functions. About fifty nutrients have been identified as beneficial to health. The most important of these have been analyzed in Box 5.1 (Hutchins, 1979; Richey and Taper, 1983; Commission on Nutrition, 1985; Spencer, 1986; Watson and Leonard, 1986; Science and Education Foundation, 1987).

A careful reading of Box 5.1 should impress you with the necessity of

---

BOX 5.1
Nutrients and Their Functions

Nutrients	Common Sources	Major Functions
Proteins	Meat, fish, poultry, eggs, milk, dried beans and peas, peanut butter	• Builds body cells • Makes blood element that carries oxygen • Fights infection • Can give energy
Carbohydrates (starch, sugar, fibers)	Bread, cereal, potatoes, corn, beans, fruit	• Provides energy so protein can be used for body repair • Provides fiber necessary for elimination
Fats	Cooking oil, butter and margarine, nuts, some meats	• Gives twice the energy per unit as carbohydrates or proteins • Is structural part of every cell • Cushions vital organs • Carries fat-soluble vitamins A, D, E, and K

BOX 5.1 (cont.)

Nutrients	Common Sources	Major Functions
Calcium	Milk, cheese, dark-green leafy vegetables	• Gives hardness of bones and teeth • Helps blood to clot
Iron	Organ meats, red meat, dried beans and peas	• Helps prevent anemia (iron-poor blood) • Makes blood element that carries oxygen • Helps cells get energy from food
Magnesium	Green leafy vegetables, beans and peas, whole-grain products, nuts	• Helps prevent nervous problems • Helps prevent tremors and shaking • Promotes normal muscle action in the heart
Vitamin A	Dark green and yellow fruits and vegetables, (e.g., carrots, greens, sweet potatoes)	• builds healthy skin and body linings • Helps night vision • Helps prevent certain types of cancer
Vitamin B1 (Thiamine)	Lean pork, liver, meats, whole grains, enriched cereal, nuts, beans and peas, potatoes	• Promotes good appetite and digestion • Combats tiredness • Helps prevent constipation
Vitamin B2 (Riboflavin)	Liver, milk, meat, eggs, enriched cereal, green leafy vegetables	• Helps bright vision • Reduces eye sensitivity • Helps prevent cracks at corners of mouth
Niacin	Liver, poultry, meat, fish, whole grains, enriched cereals, beans and peas, mushrooms	• Helps prevent gum disease • Promotes healthy skin • Fights nervousness and depression • Helps prevent diarrhea
Vitamin C (ascorbic acid)	Citrus fruits, tomatoes, strawberries, cantaloupe, broccoli, brussel sprouts, cabbage, parsley, turnip greens	• Strengthens blood vessel walls • Helps wounds heal • Helps fight infection • Helps prevent sore mouth and sore, bleeding gums • Helps prevent certain types of cancer

NUTRITION AND DEVELOPMENT

BOX 5.1 (cont.)

Nutrients	Common Sources	Major Functions
Vitamin D	Milk (with D added), butter, egg yolk, liver, sardines, salmon, tuna, sunlight	• Helps build strong bones and good teeth
Cholesterol	Some manufactured in the body, other from organ meats, egg yolk, shellfish	• Essential constituent of blood and tissues • Affects body chemistry
Water	Intake of fluids, some vegetables and fruits	• Holds particles to be digested and transports them to the bloodstream • Carries away wastes • Regulates body temperature • Helps maintain health of all cells.

eating a wide variety of foods. Many fad diets involve omitting whole categories of foods. Several problems have occurred as a result. A lack of protein results in mood and energy swings. Proteins digest slowly and give sustained energy. By contrast, carbohydrates metabolize quickly. "Junk foods" tend to give the body a quick spurt of energy and an equally fast letdown. This causes the body chemistry to fluctuate up and down like a roller coaster with alternating feelings of hypertension and fatigue. Diets that omit or severely restrict carbohydrates are equally dangerous. Without these elements, extreme energy loss and depression often occur. Another problem related to a diet that is low in fiber is that a lack of roughage causes wastes to move much more slowly through the intestine. Persons with fiber-poor diets are more prone to cancer of the colon.

Special diets or poor eating habits that cause a person to select a very limited number of foods will result in a body that cannot function, sustain, and repair itself with maximum efficiency. For many persons in the United States today, improper nutrition results in tension, irritability, listlessness, and a variety of disorders and diseases. Watson and Leonard (1986) estimate that cancer is related to diet in 30 to 40 percent of the cases involving men and 60 percent of those involving women.

Since nutrients are vital to good health, should everyone take a variety of daily supplements to ensure that no shortages exist? This can be very dangerous for several reasons:

1. The chemical balance within the body is most important, since this balance affects the use the body makes of nutrients.
   - An excess of one vitamin or mineral may prevent the body from making some important hormone or enzyme.
   - This imbalance also could prevent some substance from carrying out its proper function.
   - Body needs for different nutrients vary. (Calcium and phosphorus are needed in large amounts; iron, iodine, and zinc in very small amounts.)
   - Taking more than the recommended daily allowance (RDA) of many substances is apt to throw the system out of balance.
2. Excesses of many vitamins and minerals can poison a person.
   - Since elements are much less concentrated in food than in pills, the chances of gross overdose (sufficient to poison) is less likely from eating than from taking supplements.
   - A parent should not attempt to substitute daily supplements for the establishment of good eating habits in children.
3. Many substances, when taken to excess, are stored in the body.
   - Many people believe any excess will be excreted from the body and is therefore harmless. This may be true of "water-soluble" vitamins such as Vitamins C, B1, and B2 and niacin.
   - Vitamins A and D and many minerals are "fat soluble"—they are stored in the body tissues. Research studies have indicated that these excesses can cause damage to tissues and organs.
4. Food contains traces of nutrients that have not yet been identified but may be very necessary in body metabolism.
5. The excess strength of supplements may cause allergic reactions.
   - An individual may have a low tolerance for a certain substance (be slightly allergic to it) and not be affected by foods containing small amounts of this element.
   - The increased amount of a given substance in a high-potency pill may be more than the body can tolerate and may trigger an allergic reaction).

Shall we then say that we should never take dietary supplements? No, supplements can be valuable, sometimes even vital, but precautions should

NUTRITION AND DEVELOPMENT

be observed. A chemical analysis of the individual's particular system should be made by a physician to determine supplementary needs. If possible, any deficiencies should be arrested by proper diet. When supplements are taken, the person's body chemistry should be regularly monitored to determine effects and possible dosage revisions. None of the people who have written nutrition books have ever examined your particular body system and don't know your exact needs; many people who sell supplements are not medical experts and can't determine the effects overdosage will have on your body; and many studies cited to justify treatments have not been conducted with sufficient controls to justify the claims being made. The body is a delicate chemical system. It can function properly only if the correct amounts of needed nutrients are supplied.

How Food Digests

How does the body transform the food that is ingested into body energy and tissue? Box 5.2 illustrates and briefly summarizes this process.

BOX 5.2

How Food Digests

Mouth
- Teeth break food into small particles.
- Glands produce saliva to soften food and mix it with a substance that begins to turn the starch to sugar.

Esophagus
- A tube about twelve inches long serves as the passageway to the stomach.
- Food is moved through this tube by muscle contractions.

Stomach
- Gastric juices and the churning action from stomach muscles break down the food into a substance called clyme.
- Proteins and fats take longer to break down than liquids and carbohydrates do. They prevent hunger for a longer time.

Pylorus
- This small muscle separates the stomach and small intestine.
- It acts as a gatekeeper, turning back pieces of food that are not sufficiently broken down and may cause indigestion.

Small intestine
- In this coiled, twenty-foot tube, food is completely broken down into its nutrient parts: carbohydrates, sugar, fats, fatty acids, glycerol, proteins, and amino acids.
- Tiny projections (villi) line the walls of the small intestine and absorb the

BOX 5.2 (cont.)

nutrients and move them to the blood vessels

Liver
- The liver is one of the largest and most important organs of the body.
- It manufactures, changes, and stores nutrients and chemicals needed by the body.

- It sends these through the bloodstream to the body cells.

Large intestine (colon)
- About 10 percent of the food eaten is excreted as waste.

SOURCE. Excerpted and adapted with permission of Glencoe Publishing Company, a Division of Macmillan, Inc., from *Discovering Nutrition*, 2nd ed., by Helen Kowtaluk. Copyright © 1986 by Helen Kowtaluk.

Although recommended daily allowances (RDAs) have been established for many nutrients and this information often appears in cookbooks and on packaged foods, most people find it difficult to determine how much of each food to eat each day in order to be properly nourished. For this reason, nutritionists working in conjunction with the U.S. Department of Agriculture have organized foods into four basic food groups based on their similarity of nutritional content.

Four Basic Food Groups

The four basic food groups are milk, meat, vegetables and fruits, breads and cereals. Despite the fact that Lindsay would prefer hamburgers three times a day and Blair chokes on "the trees" (known to adults as broccoli), family eating patterns can be improved by planning a diet based on the recommended portions from each of these groups. Box 5.3 contains the data relevant to these four groups.

The variety of food listed in the four groups makes it possible to plan meals to suit a wide range of personal tastes. For instance, lunch might be peanut butter on bread (meat, cereal), an apple, and a glass of milk; or it might be beans in a flour tortilla (meat, cereal), lettuce and tomato, and cheese. Many times our concept of "good diet" is limited to the familiar foods of our own culture. When working with children in a multi-ethnic setting, the caregiver needs to become familiar with the food patterns of various groups in order to assist the children in developing good eating habits related to the basic foods of their own cultures. Box 5.4 presents some of the foods that frequently may be eaten by children in several cultural groups.

Two other factors need to be mentioned. This chart is by no means

NUTRITION AND DEVELOPMENT

BOX 5.3
Four Food Groups

Milk group (number of servings varies with age condition); 8 ounces = 1 cup	• 2 to 3 cups (children under nine) • 3 or more cups (children 9–12) • 4 or more cups (teenagers) • 2 or more cups (adults) • 3 or more cups (pregnant women) • 4 or more cups (nursing mothers)	Various types of cheeses may be counted in the milk group (1 slice = approx. 1 serving)
Meat group (2 or more servings)	• serving size—about 3 ounces of cooked lean meat	Sample alternatives to meat: eggs (2), cooked dried peas or beans (1 cup), peanut butter (4 tablespoons)
Fruit-vegetable group (4 or more servings)	• serving size—½ cup cooked or raw	Be sure to include 1 citrus choice (orange, tomato, strawberries) and 1 deep green vegetable each day
Bread-cereal group (4 or more servings)	• serving size—1 slice of bread, 1 ounce of dry cereal, ½ to ¾ cup of cooked cereal	Sample alternatives to bread-cereal: rice, grits, pasta products (e.g., macaroni, spaghetti)

SOURCE. Rallison, 1986; U.S. Department of Agriculture.

complete; the diet of any group is more rich and varied than a brief summary can reflect. Many other culture groups could be added to this list. Caution should always be observed in statements concerning culture-related foods, however, since some people feel that derogatory reflections have been cast on some ethnic groups about the food they eat. The caregiver, in conversations with children, should continually add knowledge concerning foods commonly eaten by any given group. Second, much "food acculturation" is continually taking place in the United States. The

The balanced diet planned by Mother may be sabotaged by food trading at nursery school.

Anglo child may have a passion for pizza, the Chinese child a real love for steak and potatoes, and the Mexican-American child a yen for egg rolls. The important consideration from a nutritional standpoint is that of helping children to evaluate the nutritive content of whatever they choose to eat.

As long as you are eating whole foods, be they carrots or eggs or rib eye steaks, you can tell what you are eating. Difficulty often arises, however, when you try to determine the nutritive content of processed foods. The government has tried to help by requiring that the contents be specified on the label. The label pictured in Box 5.5 was taken from a can of tomatoes.

Check the label carefully for several bits of information. What is actually in this package or can? The processor is required to list the major ingredient first. When I checked the label of a widely distributed "protein" bar from a health food distributor, I discovered that the main ingredient was sugar. To meet the requirements of a special diet, check to see if prohibited items are included (most processed foods contain salt and sugar). Finally, compare the vitamin and mineral content. Some brands may be enriched with needed nutrients although others are not.

BOX 5.4
Sample Foods from Various Cultures

Culture	General Characteristics	Sample Foods
Southwest Native-American (American Indian)	Diet varies greatly with tribe and region	• Mutton—mature sheep and goat meat (eaten by Navajos, who are herders) • Tortillas—flat corn breads (eaten by Southwest Indians) • Jerky—dried meat from herds raised by Indians • Pemmican—dried meat mixed with wild berries, fat, and sugar • Wajapi—dried wild berries or raisins ground and cooked with sugar and cornstarch to make a pudding
Chinese	• Food is cooked quickly so that natural flavors and textures are retained • Rice is a staple and is eaten with most meals • Soy sauce is a frequent seasoning • Tea is a major drink	• Egg roll—thin dough filled with meat and vegetables and deep fried • Egg foo yong—omelet of egg and meat • Sweet and sour pork—deep fried, battered pork seasoned with pineapple, vinegar, and sugar • Stir-fried vegetables and meat
Jewish	Observance of dietary laws varies with groups within the religion	• Matzo—flat, unleavened bread • Gefilte fish—balls of seasoned fish cooked in broth • Bagel—doughnut-shaped hard roll • Blintzes—thin pancakes (usually with a filling) • Latkes—potato pancakes
Mexican	Blend of Spanish and native-Indian influences	• Pasole—lime treated with whole-grain corn • Refried beans—twice-cooked beans • Chile con carne—beans cooked with beef and chili peppers • Tortillas—thin corn pancakes

SOURCE. Adapted from Hutchins, B., *Child Nutrition and Health*, pp. 59–62, © 1979, McGraw-Hill, adapted with permission.

BOX 5.5
Sample Tomato Can Label: Contents and Nutrients

- *Ingredients:* Sliced tomatoes, tomato juice, sugar, salt, onions, celery, peppers, artificial firming agents, citric acid, and natural flavorings.

	Nutritional Information per Serving		*Percentage of U.S. Recommended Daily Allowances*		
Serving size	1 cup	Vitamin A	10%	Niacin	4%
Calories	35	Vitamin C	25%	Calcium	4%
Protein	1 g	Thiamine	4%	Iron	2%
Carbohydrate	9 g	Riboflavin	2%	Magnesium	4%
Fat	0 g				
Sodium	355 mg				

The following additional considerations need to be recognized in meal planning:

- Meat contains amino acids recognized as essential (complete protein); other foods in the meat group have one or more of these important elements missing (incomplete protein). When using nonmeat sources for protein, certain combinations of foods will yield more complete nourishment—peanut butter and bread, cereal and milk.
- Each day's eating plan should include one fruit high in Vitamin C such as an orange, a grapefruit, a tomato, or a few strawberries, and one serving of a dark green or yellow vegetable.
- To protect the nutritive value of meats and vegetables, avoid prolonged storage.
- When vegetables are cooked, use a minimum amount of water, cook for a short period of time, and serve immediately.
- In deciding whether to eat more than the minimum number of servings, one should consider age, activity level, body structure, and the maintainance of desirable weight.

Special Dietary Needs of Children

Good nutrition for the child begins with the physical health of the mother. This includes her general state of well-being prior to becoming pregnant as well as her eating habits during the nine months she is carrying the child. Proper nutrition from adolescence will increase the probability that pregnant women's body systems will be functioning with maximum efficiency. Iffy states that approximately 90 percent of the health problems in the unborn child are related to the mother's physical condition prior to pregnancy (Witherspoon, 1980). Although other authorities might not rank the percentage this high, there is unanimous agreement that good maternal health at the onset of pregnancy is vital.

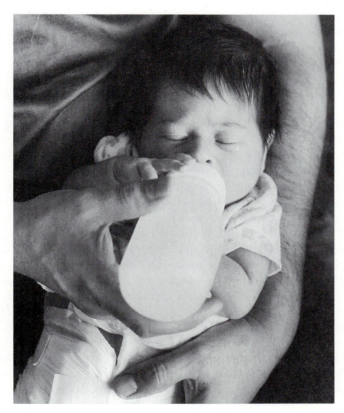

Whether bottle feeding is an adequate substitute for breast feeding has been widely debated. *(Source: © 1988 Jean Shapiro)*

The old adage that the expectant mother is "eating for two" should refer to choice of food, not to quantity. Although good eating habits cannot be established overnight, the mother should be very conscientious concerning her choice of foods while pregnant. During this time the child should be able to store vitamins, minerals, and proteins as "internal supplements" on which its body can draw during the nursing period (Rechcigl, 1982).

Whether breast or bottle feeding provides superior nutrition has not been established (Himes, 1979); there are many factors to be considered. Breast milk may be richer and contain antibodies that could provide the baby with a natural immunity to many things. On the other hand, bottled formulas can be made to provide for special nutritional needs. If the child is allergic to substances found in breast milk, these can be omitted in the formula preparation. The choice between bottle and breast feeding also depends on whether the mother is sufficiently healthy for nursing (Fomon, 1986). The wisdom of the choice between breast and bottle feeding may also be affected by geographic location. In some developing countries, even when nutrition is marginal, breast feeding may be better, because bottle contents may be more inadequate in nutrients than breast milk would be (Stini et al., 1980). The formula may also be made from contaminated water, which may cause dehydration and possible death.

Perhaps the greatest gains to be garnered from breast feeding are not nutritional but emotional and are related to the holding and cuddling that usually accompany this form of nursing. This contact comfort, however, could also be given by the mother during bottle feeding.

Two other cautions should be observed. First, from the very beginning infants should be allowed to stop eating when they are full rather than encouraging them to consume some preset amount. Second, the caregiver should read baby food labels carefully to avoid foods containing hidden empty calories such as sugars. Many children fight a lifelong "battle of the bulge" because they were overstuffed from infancy. Such persons are less likely to be able to lose weight or to control future gains than are those who become obese during adulthood (Drahman et al., 1979).

Between three and six months of age, iron-enriched cereal should be added to the infant's milk diet (Fomon et al., 1979; Guthrie, 1983). Gradually fruits, vegetables, egg yolk, cottage cheese, and meat should be included, but no more than two new foods per week should be introduced. The cup is generally first presented at about eight months, although the bottle is not usually relinquished until about age two. Strained foods should be used until the first teeth arrive, then foods that are finely chopped should be offered (Briggs and Calloway, 1984). A very excited kindergartener proudly announced concerning her one-year-old brother, "Guess what? Our baby is eating table scraps now!"

NUTRITION AND DEVELOPMENT

During toddlerhood and early childhood, the child establishes his attitudes toward food. Favored foods (Guthrie, 1983; Briggs and Calloway, 1984) are apt to be:

- "finger foods" since they are easy to handle and the child enjoys feeling the foods
- lukewarm rather than hot or cold, since the tendency of a child to play with ice cream until it is mushy shows his dislike for very cold foods (Guthrie, 1983). (He may also be fascinated by the texture or by the melting process.)
- familiar tasting since children notice slight differences in flavor
- preferred in small amounts, the average serving being about one bite or teaspoon for each year of age

Eating patterns that emerge during the upper elementary years are of particular importance, since children have increasingly more control over their food choices. Friends with poor eating habits may provide negative influences on a child's nutrition at this time. However, consistently providing a healthy diet, a wide variety of food choices, and a relaxed family eating environment should help the child establish habits that will result in sound nutrition.

A pleasant emotional climate at mealtime is essential. Eating should not be associated with punishment (eating it all to get dessert) or coaxing (just one more bite). Children tend to lose their appetites at about one year because of rapid growth. During this eating lag, parents should not form a habit of urging that may later result in overfeeding. Throughout childhood, morning and afternoon snacks are not apt to result in poor eating habits if these snacks are limited to milk, juice, fruit, or raw vegetables rather than sweets or salted chips. When the preadolescent spurt occurs, snacking can present a particular problem, since the child always seems hungry and frequently snacks away from home. At this time junk food could become a habit.

What are some of the major factors associated with eating disorders in chidren? Satter (1986a) finds that most of these problems are related to family dynamics. Conflict between parents may create tension that spoils the child's appetite. The caregiver may be rigid and constantly urge the child to eat even when he is not hungry or in need of food. The family may be withdrawn from outside social contacts and may overeat as compensation. The parent may be overly permissive and fail to set reasonable food limits (allowing the child to refrain from eating or to eat to excess). A parent who is dissatisfied with the child's inborn body type may starve or stuff the child in an attempt to make him conform to some preset notion about desirable appearance.

Satter (1986b) offers the following age-related suggestions:

- In toddlerhood, set reasonable limits and consider the child's food preferences.
- During preschool and elementary years, (1) establish a pleasant social context for eating times, (2) promote acceptance of a wide variety of food, and (3) provide nutrition education reinforced by daily family eating patterns.

Can changes in diet produce physical differences in children who are born with certain developmental problems? Many research studies are being conducted in an attempt to answer this question. Case Study 5 presents one such study.

Case Study 5

The "miracle of Dolly" is the story of a child born with Down's syndrome who is now an active and attractive eight-year-old who lacks many of the usual characteristics of this disorder. A special nutrition program was begun when Dolly was four months of age. It involved the use of a glandless cottonseed protein called a TAMUNUT (for Texas A & M University), a product developed by Texas A & M University. This bland-tasting substance is available in both kernels and flour and mixes easily with all types of food.

Dolly's food intake was closely monitored, and almost immediately her bone density and muscle tone began to improve. In addition to nutrition supplements, Dolly was provided with a stimulating environment. In evaluating the treatment, nutritionist Dr. Alford wrote:

> Dolly's growth is not just due to cottonseed protein . . . but to a total pattern of medical, nutritional and developmental support. This is an ideal case study of what can happen when a child with limited potential is put in an optimum environment.

Dr. Alford was cautious in predicting whether or not this treatment would prove successful with all Down's syndrome children. Although more research is needed, this study illustrates that carefully planned nutrition can help individuals maximize whatever their potential may be.

SOURCE. Johnson, 1979.

Problems of the Malnourished

Inadequate nutrition contributes to physical, cognitive, and behavioral malfunctions. Many research studies are being conducted to explore these relationships.

Physical Problems

The most severe forms of protein-calorie malnutrition—kwashiorkor (red patches, bleeding lesions on the body) and marasumus (lethargy, shriveled look)—are not often seen in this country (Van Heerden, 1984). Major physical problems that do exist in the United States include chronic undernutrition, deficiency disorders, dental caries, obesity, and ill health resulting from food fads.

Poor nutrition results in a variety of physical disorders. (*Source: UNICEF Photo by M. & E. Bernheim*)

UNDERNUTRITION AND DEFICIENCY DISORDERS. Children who are undernourished are likely to fall below age-level standards for height and weight (Guthrie, 1983). They are also likely to develop anemia, an iron deficiency blood disorder characterized by a decrease in hemoglobin, a smaller number of red blood cells, and general weakness and failure to thrive (Rallison, 1986). In addition to being related to postnatal malnutrition, anemia frequently is found in children whose mothers suffered from an iron deficiency during pregnancy.

Vitamin deficiencies also may create health problems (Passmore et al., 1974; Rallison, 1986). One of the most common vitamin deficiencies for children in this country is a severe shortage of Vitamin A, which can cause the cells that line body cavities to flatten and lump together. When this occurs in the cornea of the eye, impaired vision and/or night blindness may occur. A lack of Vitamin C may be associated with gums that bleed easily, swollen joints, slow healing of wounds, and a tendency to bruise easily. A deficiency in Vitamin D is often associated with rickets, a bone disorder that causes a bowing of the bones in the legs and chest (Rallison, 1986). Even the incidence of appendicitis may be linked to diet. Brender (1985) found that substantial amounts of whole-grain cereals and bread may significantly decrease the risk of appendicitis.

OBSERVABLE CHARACTERISTICS RELATED TO POOR NUTRITION. Caregivers should be alert to signs of poor nutrition that may appear among the children with whom they work. The following abnormalities are frequently noted (Reinisch and Minear, 1978):

- skin irritations
- bleeding gums
- bleeding under the skin (not associated with bruises)
- sluggishness, tiredness
- puffiness of face, arms, and legs
- sore, cracked, or burning tongue
- cracks in the skin at the corners of the mouth
- decayed teeth (dental caries)

DENTAL CARIES. Tooth decay is one of the most common diseases in childhood. By the age of ten, 80 percent of the children in the United States have at least one cavity in their permanent teeth (Fomon, 1974). The following "tooth facts" should help the reader understand the importance of diet and oral hygiene (Fomon, 1974):

- When teeth are first cut, the enamel is immature and especially subject to decay.
- Primary (baby) teeth must not be lost too early, since they are necessary for chewing, correct speech, and social development.
- Premature loss of primary teeth may shorten the dental arch and cause the teeth to lap the wrong way.
- Abscesses in primary teeth may damage the enamel of the developing permanent teeth.
- Permanent teeth begin to form soon after birth.

In early times, a toothache was believed to be caused by a "tooth worm" that lived inside the tooth and would stop hurting only if the priests appeased the angry gods. Today we recognize that one of the major causes of tooth decay is the presence of sugar in the mouth (White-Graves and Schiller, 1986). Such foods as apples, celery, and carrots, when used as snacks, not only reduce this amount of sugar but also are less apt to stick to the teeth. Sugary drinks and mints are especially dangerous to dental health.

OBESITY. According to data from the National Center for Health Statistics, weight averages for Americans have increased 5 to 7 percent over the past many years (Bray, 1979). Ten percent of all ten-to-fourteen-year-old children are more than 20 percent overweight (Epstein et al., 1986). "The syndrome of the pale, flabby child who spends his summers in an air-conditioned house, immobilized in front of a television set and drinking calorie-laden carbonated beverages to keep cool is frequently observed and is a cause for concern" (Guthrie, 1983, pp. 407–408).

Overweight may be associated with several factors (Rechcigl, 1982; Guthrie, 1983):

PHYSICAL

- lack of exercise and activity
- faulty metabolism, causing decrease in rate at which calories are burned
- hereditary factors

PSYCHOLOGICAL

- eating as compensation for unhappiness in some other area of life
- use of food as a reward
- eating in response to stress (excess weight may cause additional pressures)

ENVIRONMENTAL
- family eating patterns
- economic ability to purchase balanced diet
- knowledge of nutrients

Whatever the cause, research findings now indicate that overeating makes the individual more susceptible to heart disease, stroke, hypertension, diabetes, gallstones, cancer (of the breast, large colon, or uterus) and dental caries (Connor, 1979).

These findings are especially alarming when combined with data indicating that

1. the percentage of overweight children who become overweight adults accelerates the longer the child remains overweight (14 percent for infants, 40 percent for age seven, 70 percent for ages ten through fourteen), and
2. an individual who is overweight as a child is unlikely to attain or maintain normal weight as an adult. (Epstein et al., 1986)

Cognitive Problems

Three factors relating to nutrition may affect development: (1) Malnutrition may alter the structure and function of the brain, (2) energy loss may render the child unreceptive to his environment, and (3) environments in which physical nourishment is not available also frequently lack opportunities for mental enrichment.

CHANGES IN BRAIN STRUCTURE AND FUNCTION. There are critical stages during which brain development is accelerated (Winick, 1977; Perry, 1985). During the last three months of the prenatal period, the number of brain cells increases rapidly. From birth to about eighteen months, this increase in number continues, and the cells also increase in size. During this time, nerve cell connections vital to relaying the brain's messages are developed. After about eighteen months, no more new brain cells are formed. Since malnutrition slows the rate of growth, infants who experienced both low birthweight and malnutrition during the first year of life showed a 60 percent reduction in their total number of brain cells (Lowenberg et al., 1979). They also frequently exhibit a slower developmental rate in cognition and psychomotor skills (Richey and Taper, 1983). Although the exact relationship between number of brain cells and ability to think has not been clearly established, the findings from a number of studies have indicated that severe malnutrition is associated with irreversible mental retardation (Cravioto and DeLicardie, 1973; Perkins, 1978). The earlier in life the malnutrition occurs and the longer the deprivation continues, the greater the chance that cognitive deficits and low school achievement will occur (Pollitt, 1984).

LACK OF RESPONSIVENESS TO THE ENVIRONMENT. In addition to possible brain growth retardation, early malnutrition may affect cognitive development indirectly by causing the child to be less active, less likely to explore and experiment, and less responsive to stimulation from the environment. When children become anemic, Read (1979) has found that they exhibit shorter attention spans and reduced persistence to learning tasks. During the period when the malnourished child is not alert to his surroundings, he also suffers a loss of learning time. Other children move ahead in their skill development, and this may cause the child to develop a negative self-concept, to see himself as the "dumb" one. Since much evidence exists to indicate that some tasks can be learned more easily at certain ages, the child who fails to respond during one of these "critical periods" may find learning at a later time much more difficult.

MATERNAL NURTURANCE. In determining the role of nutrition in cognitive development, it is important to realize that many physically malnourished children come from environments that are also lacking in stimulation. Havighurst states that the development of intelligence is based on two interacting and mutually dependent elements, the biological base and the social-psychological environment (Perkins, 1978). Mothers of malnourished children have been found to lead more chronically disrupted lives, to exist in more impoverished environments, to have fewer social contacts, and to be victims of depression (Kerr, 1978).

Behavioral Problems

How does nutrition affect a child's activity level? Can deficits in certain substances produce changes in behavior? May nutrition be related to hyperkinesis? Much research has been designed to determine the relationship of nutrition to behavior.

GENERAL CHARACTERISTICS. Improper nutrition affects the activity level of children. Some become sluggish, drowsy, easily fatigued, and lacking in energy. Others react by being unusually irritable and overactive (Winick, 1977). Morris and Lubin (1985) found that snacks or small meals high in protein enhanced alertness, whereas those high in carbohydrates diminished concentration. In another study, a seven-day analysis of food intake indicated that a high sucrose (sugar) level was associated with lower attentional performance and a low sucrose level with better attention. Lowenberg and his colleagues (1979) reported that a 20 percent weight loss resulted in disorderly and quarrelsome behavior, and a 50 percent loss resulted in such a reduction in activity level that there was almost no behavior at all.

Specific nutritional deficiencies may be related to particular behavior problems. The following were reported by Leverton (Peugh, 1976).

1. Lack of thiamine causes anxiety, irritability, depression, and increased sensitivity to noise and pain.
2. Insufficient iron results in lowered hemoglobin levels, which reduces the capacity of the blood to carry oxygen needed for normal functioning of the brain.
3. Inadequate amounts of niacin result in lassitude, apprehension, and depression.
4. Lack of Vitamin B12 produces mental confusion.
5. Too little iodine results in a low basal metabolic rate and physical and mental languor.

ATTENTION DEFICIT DISORDER (SOMETIMES CALLED HYPERACTIVITY). The most common child behavioral disorder seen by psychiatrists is some form of attention deficit disorder (DSM-III-R, 1985). Characteristics of this condition are extreme inattention and excessive activity. Although these manifestations can be caused by organic, genetic, and/or psychological factors, diet has been investigated as a possible contributing factor.

Dr. B. F. Feingold, an allergy specialist in San Francisco, has researched this area. He believes some children are hyperactive because they are allergic to certain chemicals, particularly those found in some artificial colors and flavors (Feingold, 1973, 1985). He recommends a diet that eliminates all artificial food colors and flavors and certain foods containing natural salicylates. Some researchers agree that some children are helped by the diet (Powers and Presley, 1978). Many other professionals feel, however, that the behavior changes that occur with diet modification may result from the extra attention the child receives or from favorable changes in family patterns that may occur at this time.

Programs for Fostering Better Nutrition

A small child who was being taught to say "grace" surveyed the table, dutifully bowed her head, and proclaimed in a firm voice, "No, no, Jesus! Don't want any! Amen." Not wanting to eat the foods necessary for a healthy diet is a basic problem involved in poor nutrition. Programs designed to foster better eating habits may focus on the general public, on the parents, or on the child. The examples that follow were selected to illustrate these possibilities.

PUBLIC AWARENESS PROJECTS. Each year, the American Dietetic Association sponsors National Nutrition Month. During this month, nutrition publicity is promoted by allied health services, food industry associations, and the media. As a result, thousands of column-inches of complimentary newspaper space are donated for stressing the need to improve eating habits. The American Medical Association also sponsors a variety of endeavors. These include courses, conferences, and research scholarships for medical personnel; booklets for the general public; consultant services to media and government agencies; and speakers for local community groups. Other groups involved in public awareness programs and trade materials include the American Dental Association, the National Dairy Association, Kellogg, and Gerber (Richey and Taper, 1983).

GOVERNMENT-SPONSORED PROGRAMS. The government sponsors a wide variety of programs related to nutrition. Some of these are designed to provide breakfast, lunch, or milk supplements for schoolchildren (Richey and Taper, 1983). Others are designed to help pregnant mothers and preschool children. The Special Supplemental Food Program for Women, Infants, and Children (WIC), began in 1982, is such a venture. Its purpose is to enhance the nutritrional status of low-income pregnant women and their infants and young children. Research studies have indicated that participation in this program for more than six months has resulted in higher infant birthweights and fewer premature deliveries than has occurred in control groups (Kotelchuck, 1984; Stockbauer, 1986).

PARENT PROGRAMS. In the Family Development Research Project in Syracuse, New York, a home visitor was the key figure in presenting nutrition education to low-income families (Snowman and Dibble, 1979). The specialist worked with parents from the last three months of pregnancy through the first six months of the infant's life. Information concerning nutrition and early cognitive stimulation were provided. At six months of age, infants in this program scored higher on the Cattell Infant Intelligence Scale than did children in the control group.

Many programs are designed for pregnant high school girls. To aid in developing parenting skills related to nutrition, instruction is given in such areas as breast and bottle feeding; food buying, storing, and preparing; daily nutritional requirements for young children; and special topics such as caring for the sick or handicapped child. Many of these endeavors are sponsored by local school districts.

152 EARLY CHILD DEVELOPMENT

PROGRAMS FOR CHILDREN. In an attempt to interest children in nutrition, many colorful materials and interesting activities have been designed. Puppets are used to give information about nutrition and to discuss with children their attitudes about food. Projects often include research related to nutritive content of food, where it comes from, and how it is processed. Worksheets are used to record food intake and to reinforce data about nutrition. (One program even has intermediate-grade children enter data

School nutrition programs stress both knowledge and attitudes for responsible eating. (*Source: Courtesy, National Science Teachers Association*)

NUTRITION AND DEVELOPMENT

153

into a computer and receive spread sheets.) In menu planning, children learn to combine foods for a balanced diet. Actual food preparation may be one of the most important nutrition activities, since so many children are responsible for preparing many of their own meals.

How effective are these various nutrition programs? Lee (1984) found that even at the preschool level, children can learn concepts about the nutritive content of foods, how nutrition functions in the body, and the relationship of nutrition practices to health. Unfortunately, knowledge and practice are not the same. In two studies involving older children (ten to thirteen years), results indicated that nutrition concepts were learned, but eating habits remained unchanged (Lindholm, 1984; Peterson, 1984).

Two factors should be considered in relation to nutrition programs for children. One is that children often have limited control over the

---

INVOLVER 5

Eating Log

One of the best ways to improve eating habits is to become conscious of what is being consumed and when. Select three upper elementary students (grades 4 to 6). Explain to each one individually that you are studying what people eat. (Do not mention nutrition at this point.) Give each of them two-column data sheets with the following designations:

What I Ate	When I Ate

Ask the child to keep a complete record of everything that he eats for a two-day period.

Meet with each child and help him fit what has been eaten into the four food categories (Box 5.3).

Then discuss with the child the answers to the following questions:

1. In which food groups are you eating adequately, and which ones are being slighted?

2. Are you eating many high-calorie, nonnutritious snacks?

3. Why do you eat as you do?

THINKING IT OVER

- What similarities and differences did you see among the three children's eating patterns?

- What kinds of programs might help these children improve their eating habits?

contents of their diets. They cannot eat what parents do not provide. Second, eating habits are established very early. The preschooler who becomes aware of good nutrition may influence the parent in food selection before that young person has developed a taste for junk food. More research is needed to indicate the ages at which particular types of nutrition programs for children are most effective for diet changes.

A large number of food-allied industries publish materials for teaching children through worksheets and kits. Many of these are very colorful, contain materials for both teacher and student use, and include suggestions both for teaching nutrition and for relating it to other areas of the curriculum.

Since many children make their own meals and snacks at home, it is important to involve them in food preparation. Ideas and experiences should include "no-cook cooking" such as salad and sandwich making. Efforts should be made to introduce foods with which the children may not be familiar. Children should learn that any given food can be prepared in several different ways, since they may detest the only way they have tried a particular food. Pleasant group food preparation and eating experiences are important in helping the child form a happy attitude toward foods and eating. After many such activities, most preschoolers will even try "the trees" (broccoli).

Since nutrition is of critical importance, the American Dietary Association offers the following guidelines (JADA, 1986, pp. 107–108):

1. Eat a variety of foods.
2. Maintain desirable weight.
3. Avoid too much fat, saturated fat, and cholesterol.
4. Eat foods with adequate starch and fiber.
5. Avoid too much sugar.
6. Avoid too much sodium.

If these guidelines are established as daily practices during childhood, the quality of health in adulthood will be enhanced.

Summary

- The findings of national nutrition surveys indicate that malnutrition in this country is most often based either on economic poverty or on poverty of nutritional knowledge. Obesity is the most prominent dietary health problem in the United States today.

NUTRITION AND DEVELOPMENT

- The most commonly needed nutrients are proteins, carbohydrates, fats, calcium, iron, and Vitamins A, B, C, and D. Together they give energy, repair body tissue, regulate body processes, and fight infection. To assist the public in the selection of a nutritious diet, foods have been divided into four basic groups: milk, meat, vegetables and fruit, and breads and cereal. A specified number of servings from each of these groups should be eaten each day.
- The caregiver should become familiar with the preferred foods from various cultural groups. By learning the nutritive content of these foods, this individual can help children achieve nutritious and balanced diets based on selections from their own cultures.
- Food labels should be examined carefully to determine the major ingredients and to check for any additives that might conflict with individual needs.
- Good nutrition begins prenatally. Throughout childhood, careful attention should be given to developing the child's taste for nutritious foods and to establishing an emotional climate related to eating that involves neither punishment nor coaxing.
- Physical problems that may result from poor nutrition include height and weight that fall below age-level norms and disorders related to specific nutritional deficits.
- Tooth decay is a problem that affects 80 percent of the children in the United States. Another major problem, obesity, may be associated with physical, psychological, or environmental factors.
- Cognitive problems related to malnutrition include retardation in the development of the brain, inattentiveness to the environment because of severe loss of energy, and lack of stimulation from parents who themselves are likely to be malnourished.
- Behavior problems may result when, because of improper nutrition, the child becomes underactive, overactive, or inattentive. Some substances in food are now believed to affect behavior. In treating hyperkinesis (extreme overactivity), foods containing artificial dyes and flavors and natural salicylates are often eliminated in an effort to bring behavior under control.
- Many programs have been designed to foster better nutrition. Some focus on public awareness, some on parent education, and some on child training.
- The cultivation of sound eating habits through a greater knowledge of the principles of nutrition can improve both health and length of life for the peoples of the world. This is the goal of nutrition education.

Selected Readings

BRIGGS, G. M., AND CALLOWAY, D. H. *Bogart's Nutrition and Physical Fitness* (11th ed.). New York: Holt, Rinehart & Winston, 1984.
This very readable survey includes sections on nutrients and their functions, food intake and utilization, and applied nutrition.

GRANT, J. P. *The State of the World's Children in 1985.* Oxford: Oxford University Press, 1985.
This work contains summaries of research issues related to the welfare of children. A partial list of topics includes effects of poverty, health practices and service, nutrition, education, and prenatal/postnatal child development.

GUTHRIE, H. *Introductory Nutrition (5th Ed.).* Saint Louis: Mosby, 1983.
In this book all terms are well explained for lay reading. Part I contains a comprehensive analysis of the basic principles of nutrition. Part II deals with applied nutrition and includes diet selection and nutrition during pregnancy, infancy, and childhood.

Journal of the American Dietetic Association.
This journal can furnish the reader with a continuing source of current information on a wide variety of topics related to nutrition.

RECHCIGL, M., JR. *Man, Food, and Nutrition.* Melbourne, FL: Krieger, 1982.
This work is a good reference for readers who are interested in the world food problem and strategies related to correcting this condition.

CHAPTER 6

Cognitive Development and Learning

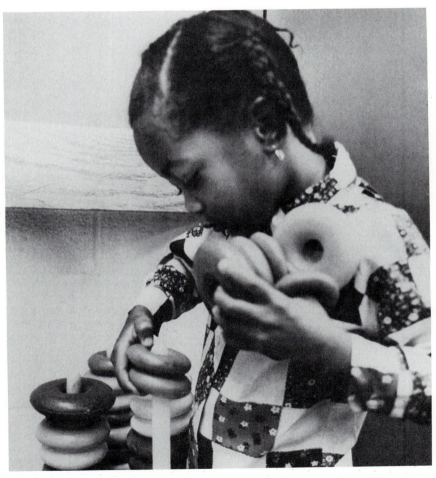

(Source: National Science Teachers Association)

CHAPTER OUTLINE

Mental Development: Intelligence and Cognition
Construction of Knowledge
A Sequence of Cognitive Development
    Sensorimotor Period
    Preoperational Period
    Concrete Operational Period
    Formal Operational Period
Cognition as an Information Processing System
    Perception
    Attention
    Memory
    Problem-Solving
Cognitive Learning Styles
    Impulsiveness or Reflectiveness
    Field-Dependence or Field-Independence
    Broad Categories or Narrow Categories
    Susceptibility or Resistance to Distraction
Evaluation of Cognitive Development
    Stanford-Binet Intelligence Scale
    Wechsler Preschool and Primary Scale of Intelligence
    Wechsler Intelligence Scale for Children-Revised
    Issues Related to Cognitive Development
Summary
Selected Readings

Two children who had received Easter animals were anxious to share them with the other kindergartners. I tried to plan the session in such a way as to maximize cognitive development. As the poor rabbit was passed lovingly around the circle from one eager set of little hands to another, we stroked the fur and talked about its softness. As the baby chick was presented, I explained that although it was soft and downy today, it would soon lose the down and grow feathers. Thinking that I would check to see if any of the children had reached the stage at which they could classify, I said, "Since the chicken will have feathers, what kind of animal is it?" One advanced youngster promptly replied, "A bird!" Just as I was getting ready to have him tell us more about how he knew it was a bird, a small voice from the other side of the circle asked, "Angels have feathers, too. Are they birds, Mrs. Webb?"

  One of the most refreshing aspects of working with children is the opportunity to observe the way their minds work. They make a new observation, fit it into what they already know about that subject (which often isn't very much), and come up with a unique but distorted idea that strikes the adult mind as hilarious. The study of how children develop their mental powers and how their cognitive abilities change during the early childhood years is the focus of Chapter 6.

Mental Development: Intelligence and Cognition

Defining intelligence evokes much controversy. Just what is intelligence? Is it fixed at birth, or does it change as a result of age or experience? Is it a single factor or a composite of many traits? How do intelligence and cognition differ, and what role does each play in the development of an individual's mental powers? Rather than to be like the old codger who said, "Don't bother me with the facts, I done made up my mind," let's look at some findings from research for the answers.

Intelligence

Intelligence has been variously defined. Burt described it as a mental potential set at the moment of conception that does not change in amount as a result of maturation or environment (Lewis, 1983). By contrast, Piaget (1952) wrote that intelligence develops through constant restructuring of thinking as the individual integrates internal capacities and external experiences. (The processes involved in this development of intelligence are discussed in Chapter 1 and later in this chapter under "A Sequence of Cognitive Development" and "Construction of Knowledge.") Although some authorities stress the role of genetic inheritance as most important and others put more emphasis on the impact of environment, all tend to agree that an intelligent person is one who can cope successfully in new situations.

Is intelligence a single or a multiple unit? One early pioneer in the study of intelligence was Charles Spearman (Eysenck and Kamin, 1981; Wagner and Sternberg, 1984). He observed that some people did better than others in all types of learning related tasks. He therefore decided that there must be a general component that undergirds all intellectual activity. He labeled that component the "g (general intelligence) factor." He contended that a person with a high level of g factor would exceed one with lower g measure in all cognitive endeavors. For example, an individual possessing a high level of general intelligence might be able to see many more factors related to a given problem or situation, to generate more solutions, and/or to work or learn with greater speed because of a variety of capabilities associated with high intellectual functioning.

He further felt that intelligence could be correctly described by a single number such as an IQ score.

Dr. Thurstone of the University of Chicago had a different concept (Eysenck and Kamin, 1981; Wagner and Sternberg, 1984). He felt that intelligence comprised a number of primary mental abilities such as verbal, numerical, spatial, and visual aptitudes. Instead of reporting a single number, such as IQ, a test of intelligence should report a profile showing strengths and weaknesses in functional abilities. Perhaps the most detailed factor analysis of intelligence was designed by Guilford (Guilford and Hoepfner, 1971). He designed a three-dimensional model through which 120 mental abilities could be classified and analyzed for interrelationships. A major importance of the Guilford model is this demonstration of how various components of intelligence relate to each other.

Cognition

How does cognition differ from intelligence? Whereas intelligence is the ability to perform mental functions, cognition is the process of knowing. Neisser has defined cognition as "all processes by which the sensory information is transformed, reduced, elaborated, stored, recovered and used" (Mook, 1982, p. 365). Several of these processes—perception, attention, memory, problem solving, and metacognition—are described in more detail later in this chapter.

Construction of Knowledge

Piaget viewed the child as an active constructor of knowledge (Piaget, 1930, 1954; Inhelder and Piaget, 1958). The freedom to explore, examine, manipulate, and initiate action is the key factor in the child's ability to construct knowledge and extend cognitive understandings. What kinds of knowledge does the child construct? Why and how do these constructions take place? What are the implications of the child's construction of knowledge for facilitating cognitive development? The answers to these questions will help the reader better understand the kinds of interaction between children and the environment that lead to cognitive expansion.

KINDS OF KNOWLEDGE CONSTRUCTION. The child is constantly involved in the construction of three kinds of knowledge: physical, logico-mathematical, and social. Physical knowledge is the child's discovery of the properties of objects. (Oranges are round; bananas are long. Round things roll; square things don't. Some things float; others sink.) Logico-mathematical knowledge refers to the relationships among objects and/or processes. (I

COGNITIVE DEVELOPMENT AND LEARNING

The construction of knowledge is based on the freedom to explore.

can separate the beads into groups by color. I can arrange objects in sequence—first, second, third. If the glass isn't too full and I carry it carefully, the water won't spill.) Social knowledge is based on the child's observations of social interactions. (We can share and take turns. If I hit, others are likely to hit back.)

IMPETUS FOR CONSTRUCTION. As a child has the opportunity to freely explore the environment, she is confronted with problems to be solved (Piaget, 1985). How are things alike and different? What causes things to change, and what can be done to make them stay the same or be restored to a previous state? Sometimes chance encounters in the environment lead to discoveries. At other times, the child initiates actions as an experiment to check some idea she is formulating. As she tries to overcome a limitation (how to stack blocks so they won't fall) or notices special ways to tell things apart (lemons are yellow, limes are green), she constructs strategies for refining knowledge.

FACILITATING CONSTRUCTION OF KNOWLEDGE. Piaget did not believe that basic mental tasks could or should be taught, since the results are often heavily weighted with rote memory. An individual can be taught to divide a given set of pictures into correct categories, but she may not be able to generalize the basic classification principle to other situations. She may also be unable to explain fully the relationships among the major and subcategories involved.

Piaget advocated an enriched learning environment filled with many opportunities for "hands-on" exploration of the properties of objects and situations. The individual may then experiment, observe results, think about causality and relationships, and solicit ideas and feedback from caregivers and peers. In this way, the child gradually sharpens her perceptions and refines her concepts in a given area of knowledge. These mental constructs and their everchanging qualities were key points of interest in Piaget's research. The major focus of current research is on how the child constructs knowledge at each stage (sensorimotor, preoperational, concrete, formal) rather than on identifying an operational period.

A Sequence of Cognitive Development

How does the child progress from a newborn infant to a talkative, mentally active elementary school student? Answers to this question are important, since they can provide ideas for facilitating cognitive growth in children. Piaget, a foremost research authority in this area, has investigated the cognitive changes that make this transition possible and has identified three periods of cognitive development that occur during this time. Some children may enter a fourth stage at about age eleven. These periods were briefly mentioned in Chapter 1; they are considered in greater detail here. The reader should remember throughout this discussion that changes in a child's thinking take place very gradually over an extended period of time. In addition, development may be uneven. The child may be able to function at a higher level in certain types of situations than in others.

Sensorimotor Period

During the sensorimotor period, from birth to about age two, children use their senses and emerging motor abilities to explore the world around them (Piaget, 1952; 1963; 1969; 1973). This period has been divided into six stages based on the cognitive advances developed in each one.

Stage 1:   Use of reflexes, birth to one month. Children are born with the ability to perform certain body actions. From birth, they can suck objects placed in or near the mouth, grasp things within reach, cry and make vocal sounds, and move arms, legs, head, and trunk. For the first month, children strengthen many of these reflexes through repeated use. Later these reflex abilities will be combined with other skills, and the child will become more capable of adapting to the environment.

Stage 2:   Primary circular reactions, one to four months. This stage is called primary because it involves the child's own body. It is called circular because the child performs actions over and over again. For instance, the child discovers that she can kick, and she gurgles with delight as she repeatedly wiggles her legs. She uses sucking to explore anything that can be placed in the mouth. Time is now (she doesn't remember past events), and objects have no permanence (if out of sight, the child assumes that they no longer exist).

Stage 3:   Secondary circular reactions, four to eight months. These circular reactions are called secondary since they involve interactions with objects in the environment. When the child masters the hand-to-mouth sequence, exploration of everything within reach becomes a pleasant possibility. During this stage, caregivers should provide a stimulus-rich environment with many opportunities to be actively involved with objects.

Stage 4:   Coordination of secondary schemas, eight to twelve months. The child now learns to combine two schemas for use in a new situation. "I saw that ball somewhere; I'll feel around the crib for it" (looking and searching). "If I flop my legs down on the bed, I can see the butterflies over the crib flutter" (self-action and anticipated result). Being able to combine even two schemas greatly expands the child's repertoire of skills.

Stage 5:   Tertiary circular reactions, twelve to eighteen months. At this stage the child coordinates existing schemas for experimentation. She may delight (?) her caregivers by dropping objects from her highchair, varying such factors as choice of item, height of drop, and force expended. Forgive the splatters and console yourself that Lydia is not being messy; she is just practicing her pre-tennis coordination and visual tracking skills!

Through a series of stages, the child refines cognitive abilities and skills. (*Source: Courtesy, United States Department of Health and Human Services. Photo by Arnold Zann*)

Stage 6: Invention of new means, eighteen months to two years. Finally, the child can use memory in problem solving. Piaget related an incident in which his daughter Jacqueline rolled a ball under the sofa and went around to the other side to look for it. She had mentally followed the path of the ball and knew where it was even though it was out of sight. With sharpened sensorimotor skills and internalized memories, the child is ready to enter the preoperational period.

COGNITIVE DEVELOPMENT AND LEARNING   *165*

Preoperational Period

Piaget describes the preoperational period as a time when the child relies heavily on the immediately perceived surface characteristics of a situation for understanding and decision making. The approximate age span for this period is from about two to seven years. Extensive experience and language expansion during this period will be needed to enable the child to move toward more mature thinking abilities.

DEVELOPMENT OF PREOPERATIONAL THOUGHT.   A major task of the preoperational period is the development of preoperational thought (Piaget, 1950). During the sensorimotor period, particularly in the last stages, the child gradually learns to associate representations with actions, objects, and events. For example, the child may pretend to be asleep (imitating

Imitation aids in the development of representational thought.   (*Source:* © *1988 Tom Kelly*)

an absent situation) or put the doll to bed (reenacting an often-repeated sequence of events). Two types of representation described by Piaget are symbols and signs. Piaget describes a symbol as something that, to a particular individual, resembles and stands for an object or event. (A child playing house may use pebbles for bits of food.) By contrast, signs are representations that have been agreed on by the members of one's culture. (Words and gestures are two examples of signs.)

Imitation is an important avenue by which a child develops representational thought. Such imitations are frequently expressed through play. Alone or in the company of others, the child experiments with actions, objects, and words as she develops the symbols and signs that become a part of her thinking.

CHARACTERISTICS OF PREOPERATIONAL THINKING. The limited logic typical of the preoperational period results in four basic problems in thinking: egocentrism, centering, inability to follow transformations, and inability to perform reversals (Piaget, 1952; Wadsworth, 1979; Beard, 1983). Each of these characteristics affects both learning and human relations.

The young child's thinking is typically egocentric (self-centered). From birth, she has been able to see the world only from her own point of view. Therefore, she "logically" concludes that everyone sees things as she does. To observe a child's response to being presented with different perspectives, Piaget used a scale model involving three mountains (Piaget and Inhelder, 1969). The model was placed in the center of a table and chairs with dolls in them were placed on three sides. The child was seated in the fourth chair and was then shown four photographs. She was asked to identify the picture that "shows how the mountains look" to the doll in each of the other chairs. The preoperational child believed the mountain configuration looked the same to each of the dolls from its vantage point as it did to her from where she was sitting.

This lack of ability to anticipate what someone else feels may create behavior difficulties. Biting and hair pulling are common during this period, since the child does not realize how much these actions hurt until another child returns the attack. This constant feedback from others who will not tolerate these self-centered, aggressive acts helps the child modify behavior in a more social direction.

The child evidences problems with centering when she focuses on one set of characteristics and ignores all others. If the child sees small candies scattered over a tabletop and watches as you scoop them all into a plastic bag, the preoperational child will still insist there were more candies on the table than are now in the bag. The child is focusing on the large size of the table top compared with the small size of the bag rather than on the number of candies involved. My first grader described her new teacher as "an elderly woman." At a PTA meeting I discovered that she was tall, slender, and about ten years my junior. When I asked Joy how she knew that the teacher was elderly, she explained, "Because she's grown so tall, Mother!" Only after much experience and caregiver feedback will the child learn to look at more than one dimension at a time.

The preoperational child cannot follow transformations and understand how one thing can become something that looks so very different. This occurs because the young child focuses on the original state and the final state of the object or occurrence and fails to see the small, successive changes in between. When big brother puts on a sheet to go "trick or treating" for Halloween, the preoperational child is likely to be terrified. Even if she watched the dress-up process, once brother looks like a ghost, he *is* a ghost in her thinking until he removes the costume and again looks like her brother. This inability to follow transformations accounts for many of the fears children have of the dark. If, in the dark, the chair in the corner looks like a lion, it *is* one until the light is on again, and, until this period has passed, a night light is worth a great deal more than anyone's reassurances!

The ability to do reversals involves being able to picture mentally how something changes and returns to its original order or state. In order to understand reversals, the child must be able to (1) see that an operation that has been done can be undone or (2) reason that one action or condition can counterbalance another (Kamii, 1985).

To illustrate doing and undoing, consider Piaget's experiment using a line of counters (Piaget, 1928). The experimenter places two lines of counters side by side in one-to-one correspondence. After the child has agreed that the two lines contain the same number of counters, the counters in one line are moved farther apart. A preoperational child will contend that the second line contains more counters, because it is visually longer. An older child will immediately state that the amounts are the same and point out that the counters can be moved back to their original positions.

To demonstrate how an understanding of equivalence affects ability to do reversals, Piaget used a tall, thin beaker and a shorter, wider one. Water was poured from one to the other in the presence of the child. When asked which beaker contained more water, the preoperational child selected the taller beaker. She centered on height, ignoring that it was the same water with nothing added or taken away. By contrast, the older child explained that the width of the shorter vial compensated for the height of the taller one. Therefore, they both contained the same amount of water (see Figure 6.1).

For a simple but practical illustration of reversibility, read the instructions

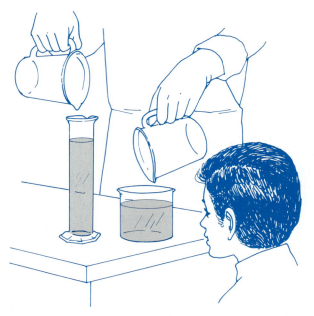

FIGURE 6.1 A preoperational child will center on beaker height and will contend that the tall beaker has more water. The older child will recognize that since equal amounts of water were poured in, the beakers contain the same amount of liquid even though they look different. (*Source: From Schiamberg, 1987, p. 375*)

for Involver 6 carefully. When you try this experiment with a young preoperational child (three years old) and compare his or her comments with those given by an older child (seven years old), you will see the growth in thinking that comes during the preoperational period.

The preoperational child also has great difficulty understanding which actions can be reversed and which cannot. When my student Gretchen was in this period, she was playing "dress-up" with a friend. Since the other child was supposed to be Daddy, they cut her hair even with the nape of her neck. (The child's hair had been growing uncut from birth!) After the play session, they took the long strands and pressed and pressed, trying to get them to stick back. (When they had worked with clay the day before, all the clay scribbles stuck back together.) Cutting a favorite bird out of the middle of the bedspread or drawing graffiti on the walls is likely to be done by a young child who has limited knowledge of reversal processes.

INVOLVER 6

Conservation is the understanding that if nothing has been taken away and nothing has been added, an amount stays the same. Children under the age of about seven years are constantly confused by a change of appearance not accompanied by a change in amount, because they are not able to make reversals. In Involver 6 you will investigate such a task.

PROCEDURE

1. Select two children, one between three and four years of age and one about age eight. (Each child is to be tested separately.) After making friendly conversation to establish rapport, begin the experiment.
2. Place five pennies fairly close together in a row in front of the child and another row in front of you (: : : : :). Explain, "These are your pennies and these are my pennies. Do you have more pennies, do I have more pennies, or do we both have the same number?"
3. After the child has agreed that both rows have the same number of pennies, move the child's pennies into a longer row (· ·.·.·. ·), repeating the questions used in Step 2.
4. The younger child will likely insist that she has more pennies, because she can't realize that by moving the pieces back closer together she can make the lines of pennies look the same again. The older child will not only solve the problem but is likely to move the pennies to their original position to demonstrate. Ask each child to explain his or her answer.

THINKING IT OVER

- Compare the answers given by the children with the information about concept development that you have read in this chapter.
- Compile a list of other situations in which the younger child is likely to make errors because of this lack of reversal ability.

PREOPERATIONAL LANGUAGE. Early in the preoperational period, the child gains understanding through "action thinking" (Beard, 1983). The child acts out the thoughts and new learnings that are occurring. She then begins to attach words to these actions, and rapid language expansion transpires. Caregivers should remember that the child's language provides insights into her level of thinking. The child who verbally observes in play, "When I pour it in it's full; when I pour it out it's empty," is mentally trying to conceptualize the reversal process. She may also be attaching mental pictures to the words "full" and "empty." For fuller details of language development, see Chapter 7.

Concrete Operational Period

The concrete operational period extends from the age of about seven to eleven years. It is so named because it is the time during which the child becomes capable of constructing "operational groupings of thought concerning objects that can be manipulated or known through the senses" (Piaget, 1950, p. 123). The availability of concrete objects for examination and reference is very important. Chief mental milestones of this period are conservation, classification, seriation, and numbering (Piaget and Inhelder, 1969; Beard, 1983; Wadsworth, 1984).

CONSERVATION.   Conservation is the concept that if nothing is taken away and nothing is added, an amount remains the same even if different physical arrangements cause the amount to look different. Consider the questions and diagrams in Figure 6.2 in order to visualize conservation in several situations.

These examples show the relationship between conservation and reversals. If the child could mentally move the pennies, rearrange the stones, reroll the sausage into a ball, or know that shape does not affect weight,

Question and Type of Conservation	Sample	Average Age of Attainment
Which line has more pennies? (number)	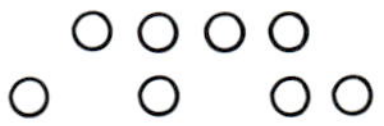	6–7 years
Which stones cover more grass? (area)		7–8 years
Which has more clay in it, the ball or the sausage? (substance)		7–8 years
Which is heavier, the ball or the sausage? (weight)		9–10 years

FIGURE 6.2

she could answer the conservation questions correctly after just a glance at the pairs in the samples. The child must have many experiences over a period of months or years to fully comprehend the principle of conservation as it applies to different elements.

SERIATION. Seriation is the ability to arrange items in a sequence based on a single criterion such as length (longest to shortest), size (largest to smallest), or height (tallest to shortest). The very young child uses much trial and error. An older child comes to understand that she is to start with the longest or the shortest and then select the next in length sequence. Ultimately the child will learn to use seriation words such as "first," "second," "third," "then," or "next." Early in the concrete period, children tend to confuse criteria. They may start sequencing by length and switch to width before the series is complete.

CLASSIFICATION. When the young child first begins to place items into groups, she often switches criteria as she goes along. For instance, she will place the blue ball and the red one in a group, because they are both balls. Next, she may add a red cap since it matches the color of the second ball. Furthermore, she is likely to arrange all the chosen items into the likeness of some figure (e.g., a square or a circle). For this reason, Piaget calls these beginning classifications "figural collections." By about five or six years of age, the child will appear to classify by a system based on a chosen criterion (Piaget and Inhelder, 1969). Piaget refers to this stage as "nonfigural collections." Given a set of picture cards, the child can put all the dogs into one group and all the cats into another. She can even make subcategories. If the cards showed six collies, one beagle, and two poodles, she probably would group the collies together. If you question her, however, you may discover that she has difficulty keeping an abstract category in mind. If asked, "Do you have more dogs, or do you have more collies?" she is likely to mentally lose the major dog category when confronted with the visual distraction of seeing more collies than any other kind of dog. She is likely to insist she has more collies than dogs. The relationship of major classes and subcategories becomes clear at about the age of eight, at which time the child will be capable of true classification. Later she will even be able to do double classifications. Given six cubes (three green and three yellow) and six balls (three green and three yellow), she can ultimately make four groups.

NUMBERING. Closely related to seriation is numbering. Do not assume that because a child can "say her numbers" she can count. Numbering involves a synthesis of two important concepts: (1) learning a one-to-one relationship between a number name and an object being counted and

(2) class inclusion (Kamii, 1985). Kamii's explanation of the numbering process follows.

An understanding of one-to-one relationships among numbers is indicated as the child points to, moves, or mentally considers one item for each numeral spoken. Initially young children tend to recite a string of numerals with no attempt at matching numerals stated to objects counted. One reason for this situation is that these children are not physically or mentally ordering the objects so they can determine which have been counted and which have not.

The second vital concept in numbering, class inclusion, involves the understanding that each item becomes part of the whole group indicated by the next number. Consider the following illustration: A young child counts a row of five objects. If asked then to show the five, the child is likely to point to the fifth one rather than to indicate all of the group. Such a child is still naming individual objects as she would if they were independent people (Maria, Josh, Cindi). She does not understand that in numbering a group, one becomes part of two, one and two a part of three, and so on. When the child is able to synthesize these one-to-one and class inclusion concepts, an understanding of numbering is achieved. Many opportunities to experiment with objects, both alone and in the company of others, will facilitate the development of these concepts.

Formal Operational Period

Some children may reach the period of formal operations during the eleventh or twelfth year. Many individuals, however, never reach this level of mental functioning. The term "formal operations" indicates that a person can perform thinking tasks through abstract thinking. The individual can solve problems related to past, present, and future. Hypothetical "what ifs" can be analyzed mentally without actual experience. Thinking may be "speeded up," since a whole series of ideas or events can be run through the mind at a rate much faster than these things could occur. Judgment and behavior may be improved, since problems can first be solved mentally and the best solution used.

An individual may be at the concrete level in some areas of thinking and the formal operations level in others. Patterns of experience appear to account for these differences. For example, if the child comes from a very verbal background and has read extensively, she may be able to perform formal operations in areas such as history and literature but not in mathematics or science if her experiences have been much more limited in these areas.

Cognition as an Information Processing System

Another way to consider cognition is to view it as an information processing system. When we use this approach, we investigate how various components of cognition work in sequence to help us organize and understand the environment. In this section, we consider four of these cognitive elements—perception, attention, memory, and problem solving. Language, as it is used in conjunction with these cognitive processes, is considered separately in Chapter 7.

Perception

Perception has been defined as "deriving meaning from sensation" (Kirk and Chalfont, 1984, p. 110). When we first receive a sensation through one of our senses, it enters our cognitive system through a sensory register. (We have one for each of the five senses.) It is held there for one to three seconds (Biehler and Snowman, 1982). During this time, pattern recognition occurs. We perceive a relationship between the sensation we have just received and knowledge we already have stored in the mind. Thus we develop and constantly refine "a system of interdependent relations" based on the perceptual data we receive (Piaget, 1950, p. 67). Research with young children has indicated that by the age of four years, a child can automatically picture the meaning of a word she sees (Simpson and Lorsback, 1983). Ethnic affiliation may also affect what is perceived. Because of differences in value systems, children from different cultures may vary in what they notice and the importance they attach to the things available to be perceived.

The brief time a sensation is held in the sensory register can create learning difficulties. When the child who speaks limited English says, "Zee ball is red" and you model the desired pronunciation, "The ball is red," the child is apt to continue to make the same mistake for some time. "The" doesn't match the "zee" already in her memory, and she may not be able to hold the new sound in the sensory register long enough to hear the difference and make the correction. Only after she has heard "the" many times and it has registered in her memory will she be able to match her sound to the correct pronunciation.

Perception is a function of age and experience. The upper elementary child may notice more, because familiarity may increase her ability to perceive finer levels of detail. She may also take in more perceptions as a result of a wider variety of interests.

Attention

After we have perceived something, we often focus on it or "give it our attention." One authority compared this selective attention to a filter that sieves out all sensations except the one selected for further processing (Klatzky, 1980). Let's consider the answers to questions that are frequently asked with reference to attention.

What sorts of things catch an individual's attention? The following list was compiled from several research studies (Berlyne, 1960; Calvert et al., 1982; Greer et al., 1982):

• movement	• novelty	• visual change	• lively music
• intensity	• contrast	• action	• sound effects
• change	• fast pace	• characters	• visual effects

What are some of the possible uses and misuses of this information? The short-term goal of getting the child to pay attention to the teacher in the immediate learning situation is limited to whatever the child happens to incorporate into her thinking at that time. The creation of a life-long learner should be the focus of education. The teacher might wish to determine how the elements mentioned in these research studies can be used in planning developmental materials and learning environments. For example, a well-designed playground might offer the child an unlimited number of opportunities to explore different kinds of movement, to initiate change, to plan actions, to create characters (both alone and with friends), to produce sound and visual effects, and to explore novelties (already present and/or self-initiated). A creative teacher or parent can look at these items and think of many more ways to incorporate them into activities for young children.

How may cultural affiliation affect attention? Children from different cultural groups may vary in the things that capture their attention. If

(*Source: Reprinted by permission of United Feature Syndicate, Inc.*)

the characters being presented are seldom from their own ethnic group, they may not identify with the material or they may be offended at the lack of respect evidenced by such character selection. Wide variety in music, sounds, and visuals can also enhance attention in two ways: (1) Each child can receive some familiar sights and sounds on which she has a readiness to build, and (2) each is enriched as she is exposed to elements of other cultures.

Which types of learning situations hold the child's attention? First, the material and experiences should be personally related to the child's needs and interests. Second, an appropriate cognitive match between the child's present level of ability and the requirements of the activity should be planned. (This match should be at the cutting edge. An activity that is too easy may be boring; one that is too difficult can be frustrating.) Third, the child should have some choices in learning activities. When a child choses to do something, she will likely be motivated to give it sustained attention. Another important and related benefit of choice is that the child learns to plan from among alternatives.

How can I help children be more attentive while I am talking? A cardinal principle is "Don't talk too often or too long." The larger portion of the child's time should be in active doing rather than in sitting still and listening. The following guidelines, however, should increase the effectiveness of "teacher talk." Use objects or pictures, if possible, when explaining things, since children are more attentive if comments are related to something that can be directly observed rather than to something in the past or at some other location (Anderson et al., 1981). Set a purpose at the beginning of an activity. For example, a story might be prefaced with a comment such as "I want you to listen carefully to find out why Chicken Little thought the sky was falling." If you are trying to hold the attention of a group of young children, try weaving different children's names into your comments ("Jason will especially like what we are going to do next."). Children will listen intently for the sound of their own names (Rinne, 1982). Finally, consider the fact that adults talk too much. They should learn to listen and talk more in response to the interests and concerns expressed by the children with whom they work.

After considering factors related to children's attention, we should better understand how they remember. In the next section, the focus is on the processes involved in retaining information.

Memory

Once a perception has been identified, it is placed in short-term memory. Without further processing, this information will be forgotten in about twenty seconds (Biehler and Snowman, 1982). Rehearsal is a technique designed to help a person hold information in short-term memory for an extended period of time. The type of rehearsal used most frequently by young children is that of repeating the data over and over again. This system is often employed when the child needs to memorize number facts, learn letters in sequence for spelling, or master individual words by the sight or flash card method. Children from some cultures are more likely to rehearse visually by repeatedly picturing a sequence of events. Others have been conditioned to use more-formal, structured language as a basic tool for rehearsal. The most important reason for using a rehearsal strategy is that the longer information is held in short-term memory, the more likely it is to be transferred to long-term memory.

WHAT IS LONG-TERM MEMORY? It has been described as a complex storage that may contain everything we have ever learned (Klatzky, 1980). There are two types of long-term memory—episodic and semantic. An episodic memory is the record of an event and its details. A semantic memory (or meaning memory) is one compiled from all the experiences one has had related to a particular meaning. (Your semantic memory for "red" will be an amalgam of all the shades of red you have ever seen.) Because semantic memory contains a summary of many individual experiences, it is more comprehensive than episodic memory is, and it can be used for a variety of mental tasks such as problem solving and decision making.

Until they are about seven years of age, children have more episodic memories than they have semantic ones (Calvert et al., 1982). This finding helps us understand why a young child often remembers so many details and misses the main idea. Incidental content is more readily understood than is the main idea. Incidents are usually very concrete. They may also be very appealing to the child if they are highly exciting. Main ideas require more mental "piecing together" of many bits of information and are therefore more abstract and more difficult to understand (Calvert et al., 1982). Television is often criticized because young children "miss the moral" and remember the gore. Practice in looking for the main idea and discussions as to how to find it do help, but time and experience seem to be necessary for the attainment of this mental skill.

Age is an important factor in rehearsal strategy use in both short- and long-term memory. A number of interesting studies have been designed to compare the rehearsal strategies of young children with those of older ones. These were reviewed by Kail (1984), and the following are some of the significant findings:

- By four or five years of age, many children use rehearsal strategies automatically.

- Words, ideas, or objects are frequently clustered into categories by age ten or eleven.
- With age, children can think of more cues to facilitate storage. (When asked for ways to remember an upcoming party, ten-year-olds generated about twice as many ideas as did kindergartners.)
- By age eight, children often use categories to retrieve items from memory. By eleven years, children tend to stay with one category until all they can remember has been recalled, then move on to the next category.
- Older children can create retrieval strategies for solving hypothetical problems. (When asked, "How can you help a child remember which Christmas he got a dog that is now several years old," almost half the kindergartners could think of no suggestions, whereas all the fifth graders furnished ideas.)

Problem Solving

A primary goal of education is helping the child become an autonomous decision maker, a person who can think for herself. The development of problem-solving skills is essential to the attainment of this self-sufficiency. How does the child construct knowledge through problem solving? What role can adults play in nurturing the child's inventiveness? These are important issues to be discussed.

CONSTRUCTION OF KNOWLEDGE THROUGH PROBLEM SOLVING. First, the child should be surrounded by an abundance of open-ended things with which she can interact—objects that can be used in many different ways. (Blocks can be used to discover how to stack and what formations will fall. Wheel toys can be used to discover the relationship between how many times the child pedals and how fast she goes.) A second important consideration is that the number of ready-made answers should be minimized. As you can visualize, learning through a series of actions and observation of results is the opposite of trying to remember what one has been told. Advantages of the experience approach are that the child can (1) use more than one sense at a time (sight, hearing, touch), (2) see why something does or does not work in a particular way, and (3) repeat the process as many times as desired for comprehension and/or pleasure.

ADULT ROLE IN ENCOURAGING CHILD PROBLEM SOLVING. There are many points of view as to how an adult can help the child develop skill in problem solving. Here I shall include both directive and nondirective approaches.

The work of Kirk and Chalfant can be used as an example of direct adult involvement in presenting a systematic problem-solving technique to children (Kirk and Chalfant, 1984, p. 134). Each stage offers possibilities for cognitive development. With help, even young children can follow this sequence.

Stage 1: Recognize that a problem exists. Get the child herself to state the problem as she sees it; you probably already know what it is. Her description will give you an opportunity to see her level of understanding and to give corrective/supplemental feedback.

Stage 2: Decide to solve the problem. This requires personal commitment from the child. Knowing you are there to help may give the added courage to start.

Stage 3: Analyze the problem. The child may plan several possible solutions, or she may decide not to tackle the problem at this time. If success is developmentally out of reach, help the child feel good about delegating the job to someone else for the present.

Stage 4: Formulate alternative solutions. Since the young child is apt to be egocentric, helping her see several points of view can be beneficially mind stretching. Older children usually can generate several possible solutions. Before the period of formal operations, however, children need help in estimating possible outcomes of behavior.

Stage 5: Test alternative approaches. Remember that the child needs to have concrete experiences whenever practical. Role playing (acting out solutions) is an excellent avenue for gaining the feeling of reality.

Stage 6: Problem is resolved/not resolved. If the problem is solved, the child will have the personal satisfaction and feeling of power that comes from knowing that the resolution came at her direction. She may further enjoy the praise and approval of others. Unresolved problems should never be interpreted as failures—rather, as unfinished business. When feasible, let the child make the decision as to when she is ready to tackle the problem again.

A nondirective approach to nurturing problem-solving skills in children is more child-centered. Here the child is the leader and the adult is a resource person (if help is solicited by the child). Most importantly, the adult should not overshadow the child by talking too much. The child's concentration should not be interrupted while she is implementing a plan. Adults can help by learning to answer the child's questions with related questions (Kamii, 1985). For example, when the child adds 2 + 3 and gets 6, the adult might say "How did you get 6" rather than "No, it's 5." Letting the child explain the process helps the young learner to rethink and self-correct. "What would happen if . . . ?" and "How could you change that so this will happen?" are the kinds of questions that elicit problem solving rather than dictate answers to be learned. The adult's most important role is that of affording the child a stimulating environment in which she is encouraged to explore and invent.

Many exciting learning materials are being developed to give children concrete experience in problem solving. They may help the child organize data, summarize material, make assumptions based on facts, hypothesize about results, and make decisions. Creative computer toys are also being marketed. TORTIS (Toddler's Own Recursive Turtle Interpretive System) is a foot-long turtle whose actions can be programmed by preschoolers (Zeiser and Hoffman, 1983). Another programmable toy is Big Trak, a robot truck that moves in accordance with the young child's instructions (Keller and Shanahan, 1983).

Case Study 6

Community Programs for Cognitive Development

The community may offer many programs related to cognitive development. Consider these three examples:

- *Library programs.* Most libraries offer story time on a weekly basis for young children. The library may also sponsor many exhibits that give children concrete referents for the things about which they have been reading. Expanded lending services, including the opportunity to check out paintings and recordings as well as books, further expand the child's horizons.
- *Museum programs.* Trained guides help both individual children and groups understand what is to be seen. They not only expand the young person's knowledge through answering questions, but they also frequently explain the process—how a picture was painted or how an antique churn worked. Museums also frequently sponsor workshops for "hands-on" experiences by children.
- *Zoo programs.* Any visit to the zoo can introduce the child to animals that can be named and classified. Signs also give information about origins and living habits. Some zoos sponsor a "zooniversity," a summer program in which trained zoo professionals use the animals to teach children about the world around them.

Cognitive Learning Styles

Cognitive learning styles are relatively constant personal characteristics that affect behavior in a learning situation. They are not related to intelligence. They tend to forecast how the individual will approach a learning task, not whether she will succeed or fail (Garger and Guild, 1984).

Each of these styles should be considered as opposite ends of a continuum. Consider the following example involving children A, B, and C:

C B	A
Impulsiveness	*Reflectiveness*

Children B and C are highly impulsive; child A is reflective, but only moderately so. A knowledge of cognitive learning styles can have a very important impact on the planning of learning experiences for children (Partridge, 1983). Although many dimensions have been investigated, we shall consider four that are closely related to working with young children: impulsiveness or reflectiveness, field-dependence or field-independence, broad categories or narrow categories, and susceptibility or resistance to distraction.

Impulsiveness or Reflectiveness

The impulsive child takes instant action, and the reflective one thinks before responding. Therefore, the reflective child will make fewer errors on recognition, recall, discrimination, and reasoning tasks. She will also be able to analyze her mental processes, gather information systematically, and evaluate the quality of solutions (Borkowski, 1983). By contrast, the impulsive child will make more mistakes, since she will not consider all the related information in her present store of knowledge. Impulsiveness is not all negative, however. Impulsive people often get more done than their more reflective counterparts. Children tend to become less impulsive with age. They may also learn to control some of their impulsiveness through planned learning experiences and through self-monitoring.

Field-Dependence or Field-Independence

Field-dependence or field-independence refers to the degree to which a person can separate an item from its background (Kogan, 1976). A field-dependent person thinks globally (considers the background as a part of

COGNITIVE DEVELOPMENT AND LEARNING

Some children are better able to concentrate and resist distraction than are others. (*Source: Monkmeyer Press Photo Service*)

everything she views), whereas the field-independent person is analytic (isolates a part from the background for special attention). Witkin, who did the original work in this area, used a technique called the embedded figures test to determine field dependence or independence. Many children's magazines use this technique in the form of a picture containing hidden objects.

The effects of field orientation are of primary importance to educators. Box 6.1 contains a summary of the characteristics associated with field-dependent and field-independent learning styles.

Many research authorities believe that cultural background is one factor in the degree to which a person is field dependent or independent (Hale, 1982; Garcia, 1983), and that field style is based on whether the left or right hemisphere of the brain is predominantly used for problem solving and human relations. The suggestion is made that all people, in order to be fully functioning, should make an effort to fully develop both the right hemisphere of the brain (which specializes in relational data)

BOX 6.1
Cognitive Learning Styles

Field-Dependent (Relational)	*Field-Independent (Analytical)*
• Thinks globally (concentrates on whole rather than parts)	• Thinks analytically (examines parts)
• Is interested in general ideas	• Concentrates on specifics
• Interprets ideas in terms of immediate context	• Identifies basic concepts as having meaning within themselves
• Has a social orientation	• Has a stimulus-centered orientation
• Seeks concepts that have special, personal relevance	• Is interested in new concepts for their own sake
• Sees cognitive relationships as tentative and inferred	• Sees cognitive relationships as more established principles
• Uses language meanings that are highly affected by context and nonverbal cues	• Uses language based more on established verbal meanings
• Uses more direct observation for concept attainment	• Uses more hypothesis testing to attain concepts

SOURCES. Adapted from Hale, 1982, pp. 32–33; Garger and Guild, 1984, p. 10.

and the left hemisphere of the brain (which processes information analytically).

The relationship between field-dependence and field-independence and such factors as interpersonal relations, teaching styles, and motivation are also of interest to educators. There should be no implication that one style is "better" than the other. Each orientation helps the individual excel in different ways and areas. Findings in these areas should be valuable in planning activities for children.

Broad Categories or Narrow Categories

Another dimension of cognitive learning style is that of category breadth. Does the individual usually form large categories including many items, or does she elect to divide things into many narrow groups with few items (Partridge, 1983)? Younger children, regardless of learning style, make smaller categories, because their concepts do not include much information and, therefore, are very specific. This creates problems in their ability to see and understand relationships among things. As the caregiver arranges more experience and discussions related to selected concepts, the child's understanding of those things enlarges. When the child is able to see more relationships, more items can be included in a given category. Care should be taken, however, to understand clearly the criteria for any particular grouping. Putting too many things that are not sufficiently related into a group results in vague and unclear thinking.

Susceptibility or Resistance to Distraction

A final dimension to be considered in this section is that of susceptibility or resistance to distraction. Can the individual control her attention in a wide variety of settings, or must she be in a relatively distraction-free environment in order to concentrate? Some children can learn to "tune out" distractions; others need to be in a quiet area or a study carrel (a partially enclosed space) in order to work effectively. Caregivers need to observe study behaviors and help each student determine which study environment is best for herself. Respecting individual differences in distractibility and modifying the learning environment to accommodate them can maximize cognitive growth and development.

Evaluation of Cognitive Development

No one instrument has ever been devised that adequately measures all cognitive functions, because they are so varied. Three tests, however, are most widely used to evaluate those cognitive elements we label as intelligence. These tests are the Stanford-Binet Intelligence Scale and two forms of the Wechsler, the Wechsler Preschool and Primary Scale of Intelligence (WPPSI) and the Wechsler Intelligence Scale for Children–Revised (WISC–R). Observational material presented in Chapter 2 should be useful with children for whom standardized tests may not give a valid evaluation (e.g., those who are ethnically or culturally different from the norming sample). In this section, we first consider descriptions of each of these instruments. Then we discuss some of the broader issues related to the measurement of intelligence.

Stanford-Binet Intelligence Scale

The Stanford-Binet Intelligence Scale estimates general intelligence through the use of test items that are sequenced in order of increasing difficulty. Goldman and her colleagues (1983) have provided excellent descriptions and evaluations of this instrument.

Items are arranged into groups according to age levels rather than into subtests based on special abilities. There are six items and one alternate for each age level. To the age of five years, there is a separate level for each half-year. After age five, each level represents one year. Sample items for the two-year-old include placing shapes correctly into a form board, naming body parts, and building a tower with blocks. At age six, the child is checked for vocabulary and number concepts, maze completion, and true-false responses to pictures.

If a six-year-old child passes all the six-year items, some of the seven-year items, and none of the eight-year items, she is said to have a mental age of six years and some months depending on the number of seven-year items she has answered correctly. This mental age is then converted to an IQ by using a table in the testing manual. Since an IQ of 100 is average for each age level, this child will have an IQ above 100 and will be considered mentally advanced for her age.

Two advantages of the Stanford-Binet over other available instruments are its game format and the short time in which it can be administered. The major disadvantage is that separate verbal and performance scores are not easily computed from the scoring data.

Wechsler Preschool and Primary Scale of Intelligence (WPPSI)

One of the most widely used intelligence tests for young children is the Wechsler Preschool and Primary Scale of Intelligence (WPPSI). It is designed for use with children from four to six and one-half years (see Figure 6.3). Examine Box 6.2 carefully for descriptions and examples of each of the WPPSI's eleven subtests.

The individual subtests are functionally grouped into a verbal scale that checks verbal comprehension and a performance scale that measures perceptual-motor competence. By combining subtest scores for each scale and using a conversion table in the testing manual, three IQ scores can be derived: verbal, performance, and full scale.

The differentiation between verbal and performance competence often is important. A wide difference between verbal IQ and performance IQ may indicate some type of problem related to cognitive functioning. Analysis of scales and their component subtests frequently are used to gain further information concerning learning disabilities, language impairment, brain damage, developmental immaturity, and reading difficulties (Sattler, 1982).

COGNITIVE DEVELOPMENT AND LEARNING 185

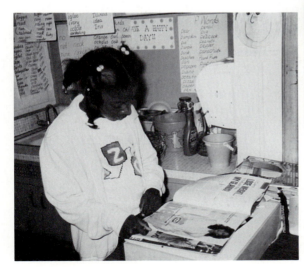

Cognitions are formed through many activities.

BOX 6.2
Descriptions of Items Like Those on the WPPSI

Information (23 questions)
- Show me your eyes. Touch them. How many legs does a cat have? In what kind of store do we buy meat? What is the color of an emerald?

Vocabulary (22 words)
- boot
- book
- nice
- annoy

Arithmetic (20 problems)
- Card with squares of different sizes. Card is placed in front of child. Examiner says, "Here are some squares. Which one is the biggest? Point to it."
- Bill had one penny and his mother gave him one more. How many pennies does he now have? Judy had four books. She lost one. How many books does she have left?
- Jimmy had seven bananas and he bought eight more. How many bananas does he have altogether?

Similarities (16 questions)
- You can read a book and you can also read a
- Apple pie and ice cream are both good to
- In what way are a quarter and a dollar alike?
- In what way are a cow and a pig alike?

Comprehension (15 questions)
- Why do you need to take a bath?
- Why do we have farms?
- What makes a sailboat move?

Sentences (10 sentences)
The task is to repeat sentences given orally by the examiner.

- Mother loves me.
- Ted likes to eat apples.
- Martha likes to visit the museum. She will go there today.

Animal House
The task is to place appropriate-colored cylinders in the corresponding holes on a board. The colored cylinders are matched with four different animals.

Picture Completion (23 items)
The task is to identify the essential missing part of the picture.

- A picture of a tricycle without handlebars.
- A picture of a doll without a leg.
- A picture of a swing without a seat.

Mazes (10 mazes)
The task is to complete a series of mazes.

Geometric Design (10 designs)
The task is to copy geometric designs that are shown on printed cards. The designs include a circle, square, triangle, and diamond.

Block Design (10 designs)
The task is to reproduce the stimulus designs using three or four blocks.

Note. The questions resemble those that appear on the WPPSI but are not actually from the test.

SOURCE. Sattler, J. M. *Assessment of Children's Intelligence and Special Abilities*, 2nd ed., pp. 206–207, © Allyn and Bacon, Boston, 1982.

Wechsler Intelligence Scale for Children–Revised

The Wechsler Intelligence Scale for Children–Revised (WISC–R) is used for testing children from six to sixteen years of age (Sattler, 1982). Eight of the subtests (information, similarities, arithmetic, vocabulary, comprehension, picture completion, block design, and mazes) also appear in the WPPSI, which we have just discussed. Digit span, coding, picture arrangement, and object assembly are added.

The methods for computing verbal, performance, and total IQs are the same for the WISC–R as for the WPPSI. The WISC–R is also used for diagnosis of learning problems and for evaluation of special strengths.

Issues Related to Cognitive Development

There are several questions that are frequently asked with reference to intelligence and cognitive development. These are posed in this section and answered on the basis of current research (Jordan et al., 1975; Hale, 1982; Phinillos, 1982; Sattler, 1982; McCall, 1983).

Does an intelligence test measure a person's cognitive ability? Intelligence tests such as the Stanford-Binet and the Wechsler were designed to predict an individual's ability to succeed in schoolwork. There are many other cognitive functions that are not measured by these tests (e.g., creative and divergent thinking).

Why should observational data be used in conjunction with intelligence tests in order to accurately measure cognitive ability? Standardized tests of all varieties (e.g., intelligence, achievement, reading proficiency) have been criticized as favoring the middle-class, white, Anglo-Saxon culture for several reasons: (1) The sample populations on which many tests are standardized do not include sufficient numbers of minority persons, (2) most of these tests rely heavily on either reading or listening to verbal instructions, which may cause a child from a less verbal or different language background to score lower, (3) the test items or materials are culturally biased (more familiar to persons from the majority culture), and (4) the teacher's own cognitive style and ethnicity may affect a child's learning and her success on tests in which various learnings are reflected. Many of the observational techniques described in Chapter 2 can be used to gain clearer insights into the cognitive working of children's minds.

What personal and social factors are associated with high IQ scores? High IQ scores have been found to correlate with such factors as high family intelligence, social class of middle level or above, small family size, birth order (oldest child in the family), stimulating environment, and parental nurturance.

How are the child's wrong answers often a sign of intellectual reasoning?

Whether an answer is actually wrong is often impossible to determine without explanatory feedback from the child. In response to the instruction, "Point to the animal that goes in the truck," thirty-seven out of forty of the children I tested pointed to the lion. About half of them volunteered that his name was Clarence and that he was cross-eyed. (Clarence was the pet lion of a game warden in the then-current television series "Daktari.") One major problem in standardized testing is that scoring instructions seldom allow for the unique but valid observations of young minds.

Are infant intelligence tests strong predictors of later-measured intelligence levels? Although infant tests are valuable in determining how the child is functioning in sensorimotor activities, these early measures do not correlate highly with later intelligence scores. Most tests used from about age four have a strong language component and, therefore, evaluate different abilities from those measured in infant tests. On such tests, the child from a strong language background would score higher than would the child who has been exposed to less verbalization.

Can the IQ be raised? Since the IQ is a score on a given test, learning information and processes related to the various subtests may affect a score. Many authorities believe that enriched home environments and increased early educational experiences can be particularly helpful to children who come from disadvantaged backgrounds. In some programs, mothers have been trained to work with their children (home start programs). In others, children have been placed in special learning environments in public schools, community facilities, or college-based developmental arrangements. Many related research studies have indicated that the IQs of participating children have been raised. Other findings raise questions concerning whether large, permanent gains can result from training or coaching. Some authorities believe that gains are more likely to occur when intelligence has been depressed by deficits in the environment and less likely to occur in cases involving genetic limitations.

Summary

- Some authorities view intelligence as a quantity of mental potential set at conception, and others believe it is a capacity that develops over time as a result of both inheritance and environment. Intelligence may be considered a general component (g factor) or a composite of many factors. Intelligence is the capacity to know; cognition is the process of knowing.
- According to Piaget, the child progresses through a sequence of cognitive development. During the sensorimotor period, children use their senses

and motor abilities to explore and begin to understand the world. While in the preoperational period, egocentricism, centering, inability to follow transformations, and inability to perform reversals distort thinking. Extensive experience and language expansion help children refine their understandings. The major cognitive accomplishments of the concrete period are conservation, seriation, classification, and numbering. Comprehension of each of these mental operations helps children to move toward the ability to do abstract thinking.

- Cognition, the process of knowing, comprises many elements. Chief among these are perception (the induction of stimuli into the sensory registry), attention (selective focus on a thing of interest), memory (a mental storage with both short-term and long-term capacities), problem solving (a process involving recognition, analysis, and solution of problems), and metacognition (a knowledge of cognitive processes and conscious control over them).

- Cognitive learning styles are characteristic personal behaviors that affect response to the environment. The individual may be impulsive (quick to act) or reflective (more thoughtful); she may be field-dependent (considering things globally) or field-independent (analytical in thinking). The person may group things into broad or narrow categories, and she may or may not be particularly susceptible to distractions.

- The cognitive development of young children is evaluated through the use of several test batteries. The Stanford-Binet Intelligence Scale uses a series of test items at increasing levels of difficulty. Mental age is computed on the basis of level successfully completed and is converted to an IQ score by means of a table in the testing manual. The Wechsler Preschool and Primary Scale of Intelligence (WPPSI), used for ages four to six and a half, comprises eleven subtests grouped into a verbal scale and a performance scale. This test yields three IQ scores—verbal, performance, and total. The Wechsler Intelligence Scale for Children–Revised (WISC–R) has many of the same subtests as the WPPSI, but it has additional tests that make it applicable for use from age six to sixteen years. The WISC–R also furnishes three IQ scores.

- Research findings have indicated that intelligence tests measure school-related tasks rather than creative thinking or special talents. Other observational techniques should be used for estimating intelligence for the culturally different and other special populations. Many factors related to family structure and quality of home-enrichment opportunities affect the IQ score. Children's "wrong" answers can give many valuable cues to cognitive processes. Infant intelligence tests are not strong predictors of later IQ level, because they focus on sensorimotor skills, whereas later tests focus on verbal ability. Although the IQ score can be raised by coaching, many authorities question whether intelligence itself has actually been modified or whether the individual has simply reached a previously unrecognized potential.

Selected Readings

BIEHLER, R. F., AND SNOWMAN, J. *Psychology Applied to Teaching* (4th ed.). Boston: Houghton-Mifflin, 1982, Chapters 4, 5, and 6.
    These chapters contain concise information relating to behavioral theories, cognitive strategies, and information processing. Many examples for using this information with students in the classroom are included.

FLAVELL, J. H. *Cognitive Development.* Englewood Cliffs, NJ: Prentice-Hall, 1977.
    In this classic work, the author describes the development of cognition from infancy through adolescence with particular emphasis on perception, communication, and memory.

GOLDMAN, J.; STEIN, C. E.; AND GUERRY, S. *Psychological Methods of Child Assessment.* New York: Bruner/Mazel, 1983.
    This book contains a very comprehensive treatment of child assessment including principles for conducting tests, using interview techniques, and interpreting findings. Also included are descriptions of intelligence and achievement tests, developmental instruments, and behaviorally-based measures.

KAMII, C. *Young Children Reinvent Arithmetic.* New York: Columbia University Press, 1985.
    In this work the author describes the cognitive processes through which the child develops an understanding of number concepts.

MEADOWS, S. (ED.). *Developing Thinking.* New York: Methuen, 1983.
    This books contains articles on a wide variety of topics related to thinking and language.

PIAGET, J., AND INHELDER, B. *The Psychology of the Child.* New York: Basic Books, 1969.
    This work presents an overview of Piaget's periods of cognitive development and includes many first-hand illustrations.

REYNOLDS, C. R., AND BROWN, R. T. (EDS.) *Perspectives on Bias in Mental Testing.* New York: Plenum Press, 1984.
    This book contains eleven readings highlighting various issues related to test bias. Each author makes suggestions for ameliorating such problems.

WADSWORTH, B. J. *Piaget's Theory of Cognitive and Affective Development* (3rd ed.). New York: Longman, 1984.
    This is an excellent "first" book for those who wish to understand Piaget's ideas. It is written in lay terms and contains many interesting pictographs.

WAGNER, R. K., AND STERNBERG, R. J. "Alternative Conceptions of Intelligence and Their Implications for Education." *Review of Educational Research* 54(2), 1984, 179–223.

This article presents three basic views of information processing. The authors consider these complementary rather than conflicting. The educational implications of each position are explored. This article is clearly written and provides an excellent summary of an important topic.

CHAPTER 7

Language Development

CHAPTER OUTLINE

Components and Functions of Language
Theories of Language Development
    Behaviorist
    Innate (Nativist)
    Cognitive
Sequence of Language Development
    Prelanguage Sounds
    Beginnings of Language Understanding
    First Words
    Two-Word Sentences
    Period of Rapid Language Expansion
    Language Refinement during the Elementary School Years
Relationship of Language Development to Other Factors
    Cognitive Development
    Motor Development
    Personal Factors
Summary
Selected Readings

At recess, a child came dashing up to tell me that Jerry and Doug were slugging it out. I hastened to intervene, and, as I pulled them apart, I asked about the problem. With tears streaming down his face, Jerry assured me that he had done nothing. I turned to Doug for clarification, and he heatedly insisted Jerry had insulted him. Since we were operating in a neighborhood in which children frequently made rude remarks about each other's ancestors, I asked Jerry to tell me exactly what he had said. "I just said I was a Christian, that's all," he sobbed. I knew something was wrong with that report, so I turned again to Doug. "You tell me what it was he said that made you so mad," I instructed. "Well," Doug explained, "We were talking about going to Sunday School, and I said, 'I'm a Baptist, what are you,' and Jerry said, 'I'm a Christian,' just like us Baptists aren't Christians, and I'm going to beat _____ out of him!" Jerry, a member of the Disciples of Christ, wailed, "I'm just a Christian, and I don't know any other way to say it."

    Despite our best intentions, our words are not always understood by others. The development of language is, therefore, one of the most important tasks of childhood. What are the components and functions of language? Why do we develop language? What universal sequence does language development appear to follow? What is the relationship of language development to other factors such as cognition, motor skills, and personal attributes or conditions? These are the questions we strive to answer in this chapter.

Components and Functions of Language

Through an awareness of the components and functions of language, we may become effective in the expression of our thoughts through words. First we become aware of various sounds and combinations of these sounds into words. Then we associate these words with meanings and note the ways by which the sequence of words can also affect the message. Awareness involves the lifelong process of monitoring the speech one hears to note the variety of ways that thoughts can be expressed. It also involves a recognition of nonconventional pronunciations and sentence structures that can make meanings unclear.

Language involves three basic components: phonology, syntax, and semantics. Through our knowledge of these, we are able to use language for many purposes. The study of such language functions is called pragmatics. In the following section we consider details related to phonology, semantics, syntax, and pragmatics. Both comprehension (our understanding of what is being said) and production (our ability to say things) are included. As you read this section, remember that development in these component areas is overlapping. For instance, you may analyze phonetic elements to distinguish semantic meanings between two different words with similar spellings such as "internal" and "infernal." You may consider syntactical word order in determining meaning ("The boy with the broken leg saw the dog." "The boy saw the dog with the broken leg").

Phonology

Phonology is the study of the sound system of a language. A *phoneme* is the smallest unit of sound. From all the possible sounds a human is capable of making, each language uses certain phonemes. In English there is not a one-to-one correspondence of sounds to letters. Several letters make the same sound (*c, k*). Other sounds are represented by more than one letter (*ch* in character).

At birth, the child is able to make the sounds for all languages. As a result of listening and imitating, he establishes his command of those sounds that are used in his particular language. Often when he attempts to speak another language when he is older, he has difficulty making sounds that are not a part of his native sound system.

Awareness of phonemes appears to be closely related to the development of reading skills. Lundberg and his colleagues (1980) found that the ability to segment words into phonemes was the most accurate predictor of future

LANGUAGE DEVELOPMENT

success in both reading and spelling. The findings of another study indicated that poor readers do not code the phonetic properties of words as well as good readers do (Olson et al., 1984).

Syntax

Syntax refers to the form of language. It involves the systematic arrangement of words in sentences. Through sequence, the relationship of various elements of the sentence are indicated. Consider the word order of sentences in English. In declarative sentences, the subject comes first, then the predicate. (The book is here.) In questions, the order is reversed. (Where is the book?)

Each language has its own syntax. For example, in English words that describe are placed before the name of the thing described (red taxi). By contrast, in Spanish the descriptors follow (taximetro rojo). In learning another language, one must learn both vocabulary (new words) and syntax (conventional word arrangement).

Where does a child get syntax? One possible explanation is that the child's inborn structures predispose him to generate orderly communications. Another point of view is that he learns the syntax through observa-

Awareness of phonemes appears to be related to success in both reading and spelling.

tion. Both innate and observational learning may be related to the child's acquisition of the language syntax of his particular culture.

Semantics

Semantics involves both the meanings of individual words and the meanings that result from the arrangement of groups of words. Initially, the number of words in the child's vocabulary is quite limited. Therefore, he tends to overgeneralize. For example, he may learn the word "ball" and use it to denote round objects from an orange to a full moon.

The development of language and the construction of knowledge are interactive. As the child notices more details through constant observation and experimentation, he develops more precise concepts. At the same time, he learns new words that help him express his thoughts more exactly.

Pragmatics

Pragmatics is the study of the various forms of language that we use to express our intents, and it stresses the social functions of language. Piaget (1952) discussed several of these functions. The following list is based on his work:

Questions: to gain knowledge from others
Answers: to give requested information

Sharing information is an important function of language.

Information sharing: to volunteer known information; to express preferences
Requests: to seek help; to encourage social interaction
Commands, threats: to direct; to insist

These functions appear very early when the child first begins to use sound and movement to convey meaning to others. Not all skills are developed equally by everyone. Some people may concentrate more on information gathering, whereas others are more involved with social initiation. Pragmatic skills are constantly refined throughout a lifetime. Some people develop them to a much higher degree than others do.

Theories of Language Development

Language development is a very complex process, and there are many explanations as to why we acquire this ability to think and to communicate in verbal symbols. In this section, we consider three basic points of view—the behaviorist, the innate, and the cognitive—since each of these highlights some important factors related to language acquisition.

Behaviorist Theory

The prominent behaviorist B. F. Skinner believes language is one of many behaviors we acquire through conditioning (Skinner, 1957). In this section, we consider a number of factors that Skinner believes are related to language acquisition.

POSITIVE REINFORCEMENT OF LANGUAGE.   As you will recall from previous chapters, reinforcement is an important determinant of behavior. Behaviorists believe a person will increase the frequency of a behavior that is followed by something he enjoys. When the newborn infant cries, comfort in the form of food or assistance is forthcoming. Therefore, the child learns early to vocalize for desired results. When he learns to babble, he discovers, to his delight, that the adults at his house will lean over the crib and babble back. Studies have indicated that smiling at and talking to the child when he babbles will increase his verbal production significantly. Thus the child and the caregiver reinforce each other through verbal exchanges that enhance the language development of the child.

STIMULUS-RICH ENVIRONMENT.   Skinner believes the stimulus quality of the environment is another important factor in language acquisition. From toddlerhood, the sheer number of interesting objects and events in the environment affects the inclination to speak. Toys such as dolls and model cities/farms/trains encourage the child to use speech even when playing alone. Stimulation is not, however, limited to things; people and their actions also provide much material for conversation.

QUALITY OF MODELS.   Since Skinner believes language is learned by observation and listening, the quality of speech heard by the child is very important to the acquisition of correct pronunciation. Many people speak "motherese" to children. This language form includes smiles, gestures, more frequent repetition of short words, shorter sentences, and frequent explanations (Shatz, 1984; Cox, 1986). This interactive language form is constructive for language development, because it is tailored to the needs and acquisition rate of the individual child. Motherese encourages verbal exchanges and increases meaningful vocal output. It provides a measure of corrective feedback with a minimum of stress. Motherese should not be confused with "baby talk," which comprises such elements as mispronunciations and poor sentence structure. This form of speech places the child who is learning to talk at a distinct disadvantage. Since he is learning the language, he needs the best verbal model possible; therefore, baby talk might best be reserved for the family poodle (when the child is not present).

SUCCESSIVE APPROXIMATIONS AND SHAPING.   Since the child does not master the production of all sounds at the same time, his first words are likely to be abbreviated or distorted. Caregivers can greatly improve the quality of the child's speech by echoing back his words in corrected form. For example, if the child says, "Bing it to me," the adult can respond, "Yes, I'll be happy to bring it to you." When corrected forms of speech are echoed back to the child, he can correct his speech through successive approximations (in successive attempts to get closer to the model). Pressure and shame should never be used in this shaping process. With consistent corrective feedback, the child will self-correct according to his own private schedule of language development.

DISCOURAGEMENT OF SPEECH.   Skinner believes several environmental conditions tend to inhibit language development. The most obvious is the "Children should be seen but not heard" concept. Some children are directly discouraged from engaging in extended conversations and from asking questions. They may be told to "be quiet" so often that they come to feel that any attempts at conversation will be classified by their caregiver as interruptions. Constant criticism of the child's speech and ideas or excessive corrections of words he has difficulty saying may also retard language acquisition. Lack of availability of someone to listen also

LANGUAGE DEVELOPMENT

discourages speech. Finally, an excessively noisy environment can cause the child to tune out so many sounds that few verbalizations are left to be used for modeling.

Innate Theory (Nativist)

Chomsky (1957, 1972) was one of the earliest proponents of the innate theory—the idea that the human brain is programmed to develop language. His theory was a reaction and an alternative to the behaviorist position, which was a dominant language theory at that time. Subsequent research studies related to his ideas have focused on evidence concerning this inborn language acquisition device on findings germane to a set of universal language characteristics, and on the question of a critical period for language development.

The child's pointing and eye contact show a desire to communicate even before the child has command of words.

Language Acquisition Device.   Chomsky believed the physical design and structure of the brain caused it to record and analyze input from the senses and to produce language. He called this the *language acquisition device* (LAD). He pointed out that language involves both deep structure and surface structure. When we wish to communicate, we must sequence our words in an order that is conventional to the members of our particular language group. This grammatical order, as well as the words, gives the sentence its meaning. "Deep structure" refers to the basic idea we are trying to convey. We can change, or transform, the word structure in many ways without changing this essential meaning. "Surface structures" are the transformations in word order that can be made to convey a given idea. Through our knowledge of the word-order rules of our language, we can construct an endless number of surface structures that accurately represent our deep structure meanings.

For a better understanding of deep structure, surface structure, and transformations, consider the material in Box 7.1.

From about three to seven years, children extend their ability to construct sentence transformations. Samples of transformations they may use are (Samuels, 1984):

• Passive	Dennis got wet.
• Reflexive	She hurt herself.
• Use of word "there"	There must be some good reason.
• Movement of element	He threw it away.

McNeill (1970, p. 1087) studied this mental language acquisition device extensively and concluded that "LAD is so constructed that it can develop a theory of regularities that underlie the speech to which it has been exposed." Because of LAD, an individual can combine all the words he has learned with the grammar structure he has internalized and create an endless number of utterances he has never heard before. His LAD helps him determine how to construct these sentences so they will match the regular grammar patterns of the language of his culture group. Although the concept of some innate predisposition for language is considered valid by many theorists, the particular details of LAD have been widely questioned rather than accepted.

Universal Language Characteristics.   Extensive cross-cultural research has been conducted to determine the extent to which all people develop language. The findings of these studies have validated the following worldwide similarities (Chomsky, 1957; McNeill, 1970; Slobin, 1972; Cruttenden, 1979).

BOX 7.1
Deep Structure and Surface Structure

Deep structure refers to the basic meaning of the sentence. Surface structure refers to any one of several ways that such meaning can be expressed by changing the word order of the sentence. Chomsky called these changes transformations.

The surface structure of sentences may affect the deep-structure meaning in three ways (Chomsky, 1965):

1. Sentences with different surface structures may mean the same.
   - *Juan ate the apple.*   *The apple was eaten by Juan.*

   (In both cases, Juan is the eater, and the apple is the eaten.)

2. Sentences with similar surface structures may have very different meanings.
   - *The puppy is easy to love.*   *The puppy is eager to love.*

   (First the puppy is the object of love; second the puppy is doing the loving.)

3. A single sentence may have two very different meanings.
   - *The truck hit the car with the protruding trailer hitch.*

   (Because of ambiguous word order, the reader may have difficulty determining whether the trailer hitch was on the car or on the truck.)

- The rate of language acquisition is approximately the same for people of all cultures that have been studied.
- Every language comprises some type of consonant-vowel combination and has words that can be divided into syllables.
- The grammar structure of each language is based on a subject and predicate relationship.
- All groups of people create and understand a variety of sentence types whether or not they have heard them before.

The proponents of the innate theory do not deny the importance of environmental stimulation. They believe exposure to language through hearing the utterances of other people activates this inborn LAD and causes the individual to develop language.

Have any beings other than man shown this capacity for acquiring language? A number of interesting studies have been conducted with primates, particularly with chimpanzees. Although they do not have the necessary vocal structure to produce human speech, they can sometimes learn to communicate with people through sign language or computers.

Box 7.2 presents some interesting information concerning one of these research projects.

CRITICAL PERIOD FOR LANGUAGE LEARNING. A subject of great debate is whether or not there is a critical period during which language can be acquired and after which language progress will be retarded or absent. Many data have been collected and analyzed in an effort to answer this question.

Studies related to the development of vocalization in other animals have shown positive evidence of critical periods. A sparrow seems to be innately disposed to develop certain song patterns (Goldin-Meadow, 1982).

BOX 7.2

Speech in Other Primates

SON OF WASHOE LEARNS TO TALK

In 1966, scientists began teaching a female chimpanzee named Washoe the American Sign Language hand gestures used by the deaf. An apt pupil, Washoe is now teaching the gestures to Loulis, an eleven-month-old chimp she has adopted as her own.

Dr. Roger Fouts, a psychologist who trained Washoe from infancy, has a National Science Foundation grant to study how Loulis acquires signs from his adoptive mother. "This will be the first case of cultural transmission of a language between generations," says Fouts, "and it's going better than I expected."

Eight days after baby Loulis arrived, he made his first sign: slapping his head with his hand in imitation of Washoe's gesture for "George"—trainer George Kimball. Loulis has since used the signs for "food," "drink," "hot," "fruit," and "give me." Earlier this month, he became enraged and began screaming and slapping Washoe's hand away. A few minutes later, his temper tantrum over, he repeatedly crossed his arms over his chest—the sign for "hug"—until Washoe forgave him.

"Dirty": Washoe knows more than 200 signs, and often strings three or four together to form the equivalent of meaningful human sentences. She has also made some abstract associations. "We taught her the sign for 'dirty' to indicate feces," says Fouts, "and now she uses it for people who don't do what she wants them to do."

Washoe makes signs with her trainers as well as with Ally—the chimp who fathered her second offspring. But she reserves most of her long conversations for Fouts. "They're very close," explains Kimball, "and they have a lot to talk about."

SOURCE. From *Newsweek,* May 28 and © 1979, Newsweek, Inc., All rights reserved. Reprinted by permission.

If he does not hear the warblings of other sparrows during a critical period, his song will be distorted. In fact, if he is exposed only at the beginning or end of his critical period, he will learn some of the song patterns but not others. Resilient elements are those that can be learned more easily or over a longer period of time. Fragile elements are those that must be learned during a critical period or not be learned at all. This concept of resilient and fragile language elements has been of great interest in observations related to human language learning.

Many findings indicate that a critical period for language development in humans may also be a valid concept. The following are some of the most conclusive of these (Cruttenden, 1979; Wood, 1981):

1. A child receiving a head injury to the left hemisphere of the brain (where verbal language and sequential functions are usually processed) will relearn language by using the right hemisphere (generally specialized for visual and spatial input) if the injury occurs before the age of about thirteen. After that age, language learning will be slow and incomplete.
2. Retarded children seldom acquire new language skills after puberty even though their verbal proficiency at this time is quite limited.
3. Persons who become bilingual in childhood speak each language with the native accents of that language; older persons who learn a second language usually speak with the accent of their original tongue.
4. Severely deprived children who are identified before adolescence usually learn to speak rapidly and correctly; those found later tend to acquire only bare rudiments of language.

Very seldom do we have the opportunity to observe a child who has suffered severe isolation throughout childhood. Such a case, discovered in 1970, is described by Curtiss (1977) in *Genie: A Psycholinguistic Study of a Modern-Day "Wild Child."* A brief account, based on this book, is found in Case Study 7.

From the case study you will note that although Genie learned some of the more resilient elements of language, many of the more fragile attributes of speech communication seem impossible to develop after the usual time for language acquisition had passed.

Cognitive Theory

Piaget (1952) believed the major functions of language were to consolidate cognitive gains and to facilitate social interaction. He contended that concepts were formed first, then language was acquired for the purpose of

Case Study 7

Genie

Genie was born into a family in which both parents were severely mentally disturbed. The father was physically abusive to the family members, and the mother was abnormally compliant with his bizarre behavior. Genie was confined to a small room, and at all times she was either tied to a potty chair or caged in a crib covered with wire mesh. Feeding was irregular, she was beaten for making sounds, and the only auditory input Genie had was in the form of dog-like barking and growling sounds made by the father to frighten and control her.

When Genie was 13:7 years, her mother fled with her, and ultimately Genie was admitted to a hospital in Los Angeles. She could not speak, understand language, stand, or chew food. A multi-disciplinary team worked with her for several years. In three years she attained a speech level similar to that of a two- or three-year-old child. Although she continued to make significant progress, she was not able to attain fully developed, fluent speech.

---

describing these concepts. Piaget wrote that as the child's development progresses, he uses speech for different purposes. Each of these may continue in some form throughout life but is most typical of a particular time. These uses include echolalia, monologues, collective monologues, and socialized speech.

ECHOLALIA. Echolalia, which begins with babbling, is characterized by repetition of sounds for the sheer joy of hearing them. Older children evidence delight in such repetitions and in the repeated refrains in some children's stories and in the poems that become favorites ("Little pig, little pig, let me come in. Not by the hair of my chiny, chin, chin."). In certain types of speech disabilities, the child repeats sounds inappropriately. Suggestions for working with such children may be found in Chapter 13.

MONOLOGUES. Young children frequently talk to themselves about what they are doing or thinking. They are not speaking to communicate; there is no audience intended. Piaget (1952) suggested that the monologue

LANGUAGE DEVELOPMENT

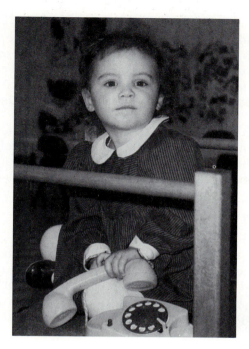

When a young child talks to herself, she focuses on her own thinking rather than on communication with others.

helps young children focus their attention on the task at hand. Thought is also facilitated, as children have the opportunity to verbalize problems that are being analyzed. A small child setting the table might say, "First I put a place mat for everyone; one for me, one for Mother, one for Tim [placing one at the mention of each name]. Then I put the plates . . . , the glasses . . . , and the silver."

COLLECTIVE MONOLOGUES. One of the most amusing incidents to observe in an early childhood facility is that of a collective monologue. Two children playing side-by-side will be speaking alternatively with no recognition of each other. The "conversation" will sound something like this:

"I'm taking off into space—zoom!"
"And I have two cows and one horse in the barn."
"My men are getting out to walk on the moon."
"There's a cat in the barn, too."

SOCIALIZED SPEECH. Gradually, from playing in close proximity to each other, children begin short verbal exchanges that involve speaking to and answering each other. Their own thoughts, however, are apt to take precedence over those of others. They will frequently interrupt, and they will change the subject without consideration for responding to the remarks of others. (Some adults do this, too.) In analyzing the content of young children's speech, Piaget found that they use socialized speech for adapting the information of others into their own schemes; for making comments and criticisms; for commands, requests, and threats; for questions; and for answers.

From the foregoing descriptions of Piaget's observations, you can see the ways in which the child uses language for cognitive development and social interaction. These cognitive and social needs, according to Piaget, serve as the impetus for the individual's acquisition of language.

Sequence of Language Development

The newborn comes with a lusty cry, the preschooler bombards us with a million questions, and the young elementary school student uses words to interact with others and to extend her knowledge of the world. How the child progresses from that first burst of sound to a fluent command of whatever language is spoken in his environment is the focus of this section.

Prelanguage Sounds

To the novice all crying sounds the same, but to the experienced caregiver there are definite meanings associated with different cries. Wolff (1973) described four different cries commonly used by infants. The first is the uncomfortable cry, which involves an alternation between a half-second of crying and a half-second of breath catching. Much more intense are the cries of pain—sharp, four-second bursts of alarm. A display of anger can be detected in the mad cry, which involves half-second on and off alternations of rage-sounding protests. After about two weeks of tender loving care, most children develop a fourth crying pattern, the fake cry, which consists of a series of fretful noises. This signal means, "There's really no problem, but I'd surely like a smiley face and some attention."

During the second month or the beginning of the third, the child begins to emit a series of language sounds called babbling. The onset of babbling can be attributed to several causes (Cruttenden, 1979; Oksaar, 1983): (1) The child has reached the age at which he is physically able to make many consonant and vowel sounds, (2) he has heard a large number of sounds from his caregivers, and (3) he has discovered that sound making is fun and has used his vocal abilities for self-amusement. This use of babbling for personal enjoyment is frequently observed by caregivers; a

LANGUAGE DEVELOPMENT

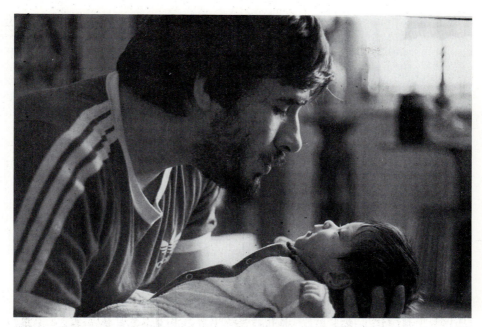

Through babbling, the child imitates the sounds of his or her own language. (*Source:* © *1988 Jean Shapiro*)

baby left alone will babble for extended periods of time, smiling and waving his arms and legs in delight.

The child also uses this form of vocalization for practice in learning to match particular sounds he utters to those made by the people in his environment. He may work on one sound over and over, try another sound, then come back to the first for further improvement. During the babbling stage, the child uses all the sounds of all languages. Gradually the child ceases to use those sounds not reinforced by the environment in which he is developing.

This effect of reinforcement on babbling is also evident in deaf children. Initially they babble just as all children do. Since they cannot hear themselves and others, however, they stop babbling. This cessation of babbling is one of the early clues to a diagnosis of hearing loss in children.

Beginnings of Language Understanding

During the first year of life, the child begins to build understandings of his world. As he makes sounds and observes the responses he gets from others and as he hears the words his people use as they do things with him, he begins to associate those words with actions and objects. He soon makes the wonderful discovery that he, too, can make sounds that communicate. Even at the babbling stage, some children attach meaning to certain combinations of sounds. One child in our family regularly said, "Um blaum blaum blaum," in a loud and angry voice whenever she was displeased. We were happy not to know the exact interpretation of this phrase, though we definitely understood her meaning!

Phonology, as you will recall, is the study of the sound system of the language. The first stage in acquiring this sound system occurs during this babbling time when the child consciously uses certain sounds in an attempt to communicate meaning (Locke, 1983).

The child shows that he understands words before he uses them spontaneously by his ability to respond to statements such as "Where is _____?" or "Touch your nose" (Oksaar, 1983). By the end of the first year, the child's language understanding has developed to a level at which he is ready to use his first words.

First Words

At about the age of one year, the child says his first word. How can the caregiver distinguish this first word from the combinations of sounds the child makes in babbling? Dale (1976) listed three criteria for a "true" word: (1) It is some form of a recognizable word in that child's language, (2) the child makes spontaneous and consistent use of the word, and (3) the context in which the child uses the word indicates that he understands its meaning.

The words learned first reflect the child's environment. "Dada" and "mama" are frequent choices, since these have been repeated to the child so many times. This repetition of syllables ("Dada," "go-go") is also reminiscent of the repetition of babbling. Frequently the first words added to the vocabulary as the child extends his repertoire include things from his immediate environment—names of people and pets, body parts, and frequently used objects. The child is said to have reached the cognitive stage of phonological (sound system) development when he begins to produce these nonadult forms of words he has heard (Locke, 1983).

Children show individual differences in their choices of first word categories (De Villiers and De Villiers, 1979; Peters, 1983). Some children emphasize referential words that point out or label things in the environment. They want to talk about things and therefore need to know as many labels as possible in order to communicate. They constantly ask "What's that?" and their utterances tend to be short, often using just one word. By contrast, some children are more concerned with expressive words related to social interaction. They collect social phrases ("hi," "bye-bye," "thank you," "good girl"), and they use more multiword utterances ("I want," "Let's go").

An interesting phenomenon that frequently occurs in children's early speech is the practice of overgeneralization. Examples of this word use are the child's inclination to call all men "Daddy" and to refer to all round objects as "ball." Overgeneralization is typical in the speech of children from about one to two and one-half years. In some cases, the child overgeneralizes because he has a limited vocabulary and doesn't know the names of all the things he wants to discuss (Hoek, 1986). In other cases, the mistake may be related to the fact that he doesn't know enough about the characteristics of the objects to be able to distinguish between them (e.g., the difference between an apple and an orange).

Although overgeneralization involves some mistakes in naming objects and persons, it also accounts for some of the most delightful and picturesque examples of children's speech. The following examples were taken from Oksaar (1983, p. 176):

- a cow in the field—"the elephant"
- a stone lion in front of the museum—"lamby" (the child's stuffed lamb also sits on all fours)
- a full moon—"a yellow ball" (the child ran toward it to catch it)
- a baby carriage—"Nana's car" (the nursemaid pushed it just as Daddy drove the car)

As new words are learned and correct word forms are modeled by caregivers, these inaccuracies are usually corrected.

Which do children learn first, specific names or names of categories? This sequence depends on common usage (Cruttenden, 1979). Children tend to learn specific words such as "dime" and "penny" before the word "coin" because they handle money frequently. In other cases, children learn the common category word first ("car" before "Ford"). Sometimes a child may learn the specific and the category as a pair. One child in our family referred to all automobiles as "Linc cars," because his grandfather had a Lincoln Continental. The child is not grouping things into categories at this time; he is simply repeating either a specific name or a category name as he has heard it.

Children use these first single-word utterances as whole sentences. These are called "holophrases." The meaning of the sentence is understood through context. The single word "Mommy" may mean "There's Mommy," "I want Mommy," or "Where is Mommy?" As the caregiver expands on these one-word sentences either by stating in full the intent of the child's statement as indicated above or by using the holophrase as a part of a two-way conversation, the child is encouraged to say more.

Two-Word Sentences

At about the age of two, the child begins to use two-word sentences. To explain the structure of these sentences, specialists in language development have identified two kinds of words—pivot words and open words (Dale, 1976; Cruttenden, 1979). A pivot word is a high-frequency word to which many other words may be attached. It may be used first ("See baby," "See Daddy," "See doggy"), or it may be in second place ("Daddy gone," "Mama gone," "Baby gone"). Open words are all other words that are not used as pivots. These open words can also be used to form two-word sentences ("Baby car," "Doggy eat"). Generally, children form two-word sentences in the following order (Dale, 1976): (1) A pivot word in the first position plus an open word, (2) an open word followed by a pivot word, and (3) two open words.

BOX 7.3

Content of Two-Word Sentences

Reason for Speaking	Sentence Pattern	Example
1. Pointing out	That + name	That ball, that dog
2. Speaking to	Hi + name	Hi mama, hi shoe (young child speaks to both people and things)
3. Asking for (recurrence)	More + name	More milk, more gum
4. Declaring it missing	Gone + name	Gone toy, mama gone
5. Describing	Adjective + name	Big boy, good kitty
6. Showing possession	Name + name	Daddy car (daddy's car), baby ball (baby's ball)
7. Showing	Name + name	Ginny chair (Ginny is sitting in the chair), book table (The book is on the table.)
8. Showing location	Action + name	Come Polo, Baby here

SOURCES. Adapted from Brown, R., *Psycholinguistics*, p. 220, © Free Press, Macmillan Publishing Company, New York, 1970 and adapted from page 24 in *Language Development: Structure and Function*, Second Edition, by P. S. Dale, copyright © 1976 by Holt, Rinehart and Winston, Inc., reprinted by permission of the publishers.

The content of two-word sentences has been carefully researched. If you will study the examples contained in Box 7.3, you will better understand the communication powers of the child at the two-sentence stage.

What are some of the factors related to a child's move from one- to two-word utterances? Through research, Donahue (1986) identified five:

1. the number of single words the child knows
2. the physiological ability to say two consecutive words
3. the ability to see relationships among words to be put together
4. a knowledge of syntax for word order in using more than one word
5. the ability to plan longer units of sound

With the advent of the two-word sentence, the child begins to evidence his knowledge of syntax—the correct word order used in the language system of his environment. Although the use of syntax develops with age, many studies indicate that the ability to acquire syntax is inborn (Valian, 1986). By school age, most children have mastered the basic syntax of their native language.

Period of Rapid Language Expansion

The child's language undergoes rapid expansion between the ages of two and six. The magnitude of this accomplishment is summarized in a quotation from Templin (Clark, 1983, p. 69):

1. By the age of 6 the average child is estimated to have learned some 14,000 words;
2. If that child begins to acquire vocabulary at the age of 18 months, he must learn at least 9 new words a day;
3. At the same time, that child is mastering the sound system, . . . the syntax rules for combining words, [and] the conventions of use for words and for word combinations.

In addition to this rapid vocabulary expansion, the child further develops his language expertise during this period through modifications in word formations, by the development of relational meanings, and as a result of caregiver answers to his ceaseless "why" questions.

MODIFICATIONS IN WORD FORMATIONS.   Many sounds that most children can make with ease at age six are difficult for three-year-olds. Younger children, therefore, have characteristic ways of simplifying their language. De Villiers and De Villiers (1979) have identified three of these practices. First, children frequently shorten a word by dropping part of it ("Dar"

(*Source: Reprinted by permission of United Feature Syndicate, Inc.*)

for "Darlene," "nana" for "banana"). They also shorten and simplify by omitting blends that are hard for them to make before about age four or five years ("bing," for "bring," "back" for "black"). Second, they frequently use only one consonant throughout a word ("goggy" or "doddy" for "doggy"). Finally, they substitute sounds they can make with ease for those that are difficult ("bie" for "pie," "doe" for "toe," "boff" for "both"). Once a child begins to use a simplified word form, he will continue even after he can make the necessary sounds with ease. If the caregiver echoes back the word to him in corrected form, without scolding, the child will improve pronunciation as he is able. Unfortunately, some of these mispronunciations are so funny that caregivers model the child's word form rather than vice versa.

Children also form new words to fill in the gaps in their emerging conversational needs. Clark (1983) listed several categories of such creations which will be shared in the following paragraphs.

The child may mispronounce words, not because he can't make the sounds, but because he misunderstands what is said. One of our children said "lickstick" for "lipstick" because it was applied to the mouth, and she thought we were licking it on.

Another common way to form new words is by adding a new ending to a word already known. In this case "sleepers" is used for pajamas, and the phrase "broomed the porch" is used to describe sweeping. Sometimes such restructuring of words leads to interesting distortions. Consider the transformation that occurs with reference to the word "went." At first, as a result of imitation, the child learns to use a past tense word such as "went" correctly. Then he observes that we add "ed" to make past tense. At this point, he follows the newly discovered rule and says "goed." Only after much more listening is he able to know which words follow the rule and which are exceptions.

Young children also extend their vocabularies by using nouns, adjectives, and prepositions already in their word repertoire as verbs. Examples of the results are as follows (Clark, 1983):

- noun—"to key it"—to open with a key
- adjective—"to bright a room"—to open drapes and let sunlight in
- preposition—"to up me"—to lift me up

Finally, the child may combine two known words in a new situation for which he has no word. My daughter identified the backyard smoker as "the stroller-oven," since it had handles like a baby's stroller and was used as an oven. Children also say "store-man" for clerk and "letter-man" for postman, perhaps as a result of following the example of "fire-man."

DEVELOPMENT OF RELATIONAL MEANINGS. During this period of rapid vocabulary expansion between the ages of two and six years, meanings slowly become refined (Cromer, 1983). Each incident in which a word is used may furnish new ideas about precise or extended word meanings. The following information concerning relational meanings is based on Cruttenden's (1979) research:

- "Big" and "little," which refer to three dimensions of an object, are learned before "long" and "short," which refer to only one dimension.
- When words appear in pairs such as "good/bad" or "first/last," language specialists call the first word the positive term and the other the negative term. Children generally acquire the use of the positive term before the use of its negative term.
- When children first begin to use words to indicate time, such words as "before" and "after" are confused. As indicated in the previous discussion on word pairs, "before" is learned first. A young child often uses the word "before" to indicate both previous and later action and thus confuses his listener.
- "Up/down" and "on/under" are some of the first pairs of words used to describe spatial relations. "Front" and "back" are learned before "side," probably because of usage frequency. "Front," "back," "side," "left," and "right" are learned first in terms of the child's own body. "Left" and "right" in relation to situations or things other than the body generally are not learned until about age nine.

WHYS. Anyone who has worked with young children has, at times, been bombarded with "whys." These questions appear at about age three and continue to be an important part of conversation through the early elementary years (Piaget, 1952). Early questions often involve name and location ("What is it?" "Where is _____?"). Later questions are apt to focus on

Children investigate the whys of things they see.

cause and time ("What caused babies?" "When will it be Christmas again?"). Children often pose a question, then answer it themselves. In such cases, they seem to be using the question merely to announce a topic of thought. Although questions often seem to come at inopportune times, the caregiver's response is very important in two ways: (1) The child needs answers for expansion of understanding, and (2) he needs to be encouraged to keep asking questions, since knowledge, values, and attachment are all involved in these caregiver-child exchanges.

NORMAL NONFLUENCY AND STUTTERING. From the onset of talking, children sometimes hesitate when speaking. The child may pause, then begin again repeating his last words. He may continue to speak and appear to be stuck like the needle on a phonograph, repeating one or more words several times before continuing his expression of thought. This phenomenon is referred to as normal nonfluency. It often happens because the child's thoughts are occurring at a faster rate than his verbal proficiency permits—his ideas are outrunning his words. As he becomes more adept in the use of language, these repetitions will become less frequent. The child should not be scolded, nor should he be asked to repeat his utterance without these repetitions. Negative procedures are likely to create tension,

LANGUAGE DEVELOPMENT

215

which could lead to stuttering. (Stuttering and practices related to dealing with this problem are discussed in detail in Chapter 13.)

A brief summary of speech development during these early years is capsulated in Box 7.4.

BOX 7.4

Summary of Early Normal Speech and Oral Language Developmental Stages

Age	General Characteristics	Usable Speaking Vocabulary (Number of Words)	Adequate Speech Sound Production
Months			
1–3	Undifferentiated crying. Random vocalizations and cooing.		
4–6	Babbling. Specific vocalizations. Verbalizes in response to speech of others. Immediate responses approximate human intonational patterns.		
7–11	Tongue moves with vocalizations (lalling). Vocalizes recognition. Reduplicates sounds. Echolalia (automatic repetition of words and phrases).		
12	First word.	1–3	All vowels
18	One-word sentence stage. Well-established jargon. Uses nouns primarily.	18–22	
Years			
2	Two-word sentence stage. Sentences functionally complete. Uses more pronouns and verbs.	270–300	
2.5	Three-word sentence stage. Telegraphic speech.	450	h, w, hw
3	Complete simple-active sentence structure used. Uses sentences to tell stories that are understood by others.	900	p, b, m
3.5	Expanded grammatical forms. Concepts expressed with words. Speech disfluency is typical. Sentence length is 4–5 words.	1,200	t, d, n

BOX 7.4 (cont.)

Age	General Characteristics	Usable Speaking Vocabulary (Number of Words)	Adequate Speech Sound Production
Years			
4	Excessive verbalizations. Imaginary speech.	1,500	k, g, ng, j
5	Well-developed and complex syntax. Uses more complex forms to tell stories. Uses negation and inflexional form of verbs.	2,000	f, v
6–8	Sophisticated speech. Skilled use of grammatical rules. Learns to read. Acceptable articulation by 8 years for males and females.	2,600+	l, r, y, s, z, sh, ch, zh, th, consonant blends

SOURCE. "Summary of Early Normal Speech and Oral Language Developmental Stages" from *Exceptional Children in the Schools: Special Education in Transition,* Second Edition, by Lloyd M. Dunn, et al., copyright © 1974 by Holt, Rinehart and Winston, Inc., reprinted by permission of the publisher.

Language Refinement during the Elementary School Years

Between the ages of six and twelve years, children refine their use of language. Representative of the areas in which these changes transpire are vocabulary, syntax, conversation, and storytelling. In each of these areas, memory plays an important role, since it helps the child organize, store, and retrieve sounds and ideas from the environment (Leventhal and Dawson, 1984).

VOCABULARY. The elementary child's vocabulary becomes more precise in several ways (Samuels, 1984). First, because he now has many contacts outside the home, he learns a large number of new words (some of which his caregivers may not like). This increase in synonyms gives him the opportunity to select the word that most nearly expresses his meaning. ("He *accepted* the idea/he *was enthusiastic about* the idea."). Second, after about age eight, most children for whom English is a first language can hear and accurately pronounce most words. (Cultural and regional differences may perpetuate pronunciations that vary from dictionary designations but are clearly understood by associates.) Third, elementary age children recognize and enjoy words with multiple meanings ("the drill *bored* a hole in the wall," "speaker *bored* audience"). All of these vocabulary changes increase the child's verbal fluency.

LANGUAGE DEVELOPMENT

At school, the child has many opportunities to expand conversational skills. (*Source: From Armstrong*)

CONVERSATIONAL SKILLS.   In order to communicate effectively, the child must not only have an adequate vocabulary at his command, but also be able to put words together for effective conversation. To be easily understood, a statement must have clear references; it must not be something that can have several different meanings. Young children will accept and attempt to act on unclear communications; upper elementary young people will seek more information (Robinson, 1983). By the sixth-grade level, children can usually judge whether the messages used in connection with a game are clear or unclear (Patterson and Kister, 1981).

Most children between the ages of eight and twelve years have considerable skill in conversation (Cooper and Cooper, 1984). They can make statements to get attention and modify content if they need to be more specific to be understood. They can verbally plan and monitor activities, serve both as effective teacher and as listener/doer, and use words to redirect attention in case of disruption. They can also use appropriate verbalizations for negotiations with both adults and peers.

NONVERBAL COMMUNICATIONS.   The use and understanding of nonverbal cues are of vital importance in communication. Studies in which nonverbal cues were eliminated from conversations have indicated that without

> **INVOLVER 7**
>
> Children vary in both the amount and the complexity of their verbal expression. Two major factors in this variance are individual differences and age. In this involver, you will tell the same story to two preschoolers (age three to four) and two primary-grade children (age seven to eight) and get them to tell the story back to you. From this experience, you will be able to analyze both within-age and between-age differences in verbal fluency.
>
> *Procedure.* Review the details of a short fairy tale (e.g., *Three Bears, Three Little Pigs, Billy Goats Gruff*). After practice, record your version of the story using a tape recorder. Talk to each child for a few minutes to establish rapport, then play the tape. After the child has heard the story, ask him or her to tell the story into the tape for you. After you have made the four recordings, consider the thought questions in the following section:
>
> *THINKING IT OVER*
>
> - What individual differences in language fluency did you note between children of the same age?
> - How did the length of story, amount of detail remembered, complexity of sentences, and other language differences vary between the older and younger children?
> - What other differences did you note, and how do you account for these differences?

these aids, the message is significantly less accurate (Allen, 1981). By the sixth-grade level, most children could reproduce voice tones and inflections for communication in the groups to which they belonged.

STORYTELLING. By upper elementary grade levels, children have refined the storytelling abilities they developed much earlier (Kemper, 1984). They can include a wide variety of characters, roles, themes, and symbols. They can relate individual episodes clearly, coordinate several episodes in a story sequence, and embed subordinate episodes into main ones. They can also word stories so as to indicate motive or cause rather than simple fact.

Relationship of Language Development to Other Factors

Language development is a process that is related to a number of other factors. Three of these relationships have received extensive attention in research literature: language and cognition, language and physical development, and language and personal attributes or conditions. A better understanding of these relationships is needed since, in many instances, modifications can be made in the environment that will help the child reach his maximum potential language development.

Language and Cognition

Language and cognition so frequently occur together that there have been great debates concerning what each contributes to the other. We shall consider four hypotheses that have been advanced.

Hypothesis 1: Cognition and language are the same. J. B. Watson, the father of American behaviorism, contended that speaking is simply thinking aloud (Mosenthal, 1975; Slobin, 1979). As evidence to support his theory, he pointed out the fact that so many of us recite lists of things to be remembered and talk to ourselves as we try to solve problems. Most authorities today, however, feel that the relationship is more complex than this.

Hypothesis 2: Cognition and language are separate, and cognition precedes language acquisition. Piaget is one of many authorities who believe an individual first understands something as a concept and then finds words to explain it (Piaget, 1952; Slobin, 1979; Rice, 1983). A very interesting description of this process is found in the writings of the great scientist Albert Einstein (Ghiselin, 1955, p. 43):

> The words of the language, as they are written or spoken do not seem to play any role in the mechanism of thought. . . . elements in thought are certain signs and more or less clear images which can be "voluntarily" reproduced and combined. . . .
>
> Conventional words or other signs have to be sought for laboriously only in a secondary stage, when the mentioned associative play is sufficiently established and can be reproduced at will.

Apparently Einstein was one who conceptualized first and then spoke.

Hypothesis 3: Cognition is dependent on language for refinement, perhaps even for content. Bruner (1964) and Schlesinger (1977) both believe that language is necessary for improvements in analytical thinking and attention to detail. Bruner found that children who could verbalize accurately as they performed transposition tasks were more likely to accomplish them correctly than those children who could not put their thinking into words. Thus Bruner believes that precision and specificity come with language development rather than by abstract thought alone. A different but fascinating theory concerning the ascendency of language over cognition has been postulated by Whorf (Mosenthal, 1975). Whorf hypothesized that the words in a language control the subjects about which a person in that culture can think. In other words, he believed that if hate, greed, or war was absent from the vocabulary of a people, they could not perceive these things. Several studies have been conducted to investigate this idea, and the findings have indicated that although the members of such a group could think about these things, "speakers of languages lacking such words will have more difficulty in recalling the concepts because they will have less efficient means for coding and storing them" (Mosenthal, 1975, pp. 207–208).

Ecolinguists study the effects of computer use on language development. (*Source: Courtesy, National Science Teachers Association, photograph by William E. Mills, Montgomery County Public Schools*)

Hypothesis 4: Cognition and language are very closely related and interdependent, and either the word or the thought may come first (Slobin, 1979; Rice, 1983). Vygotsky compared thought to "a cloud shedding a shower of words" (Mosenthal, 1975, p. 101). The cloud is a collection of moisture from the earth; by the same token, much of the moisture of the earth comes from the clouds. Adherents of this theory feel the two (cognition and language) are so interrelated that it is futile to quibble over which comes first. The individual uses both together, and each is strengthened by the other.

One of the most exciting trends in current research in language development is the combination of efforts by psychologists and linguists. In 1951, a joint conference for psychologists and linguists was held at Cornell University. From this beginning, much research, labeled "psycholinguistic," has been generated.

Psycholinguistic studies do not reflect a single point of view as to why or how language develops. Some psycholinguists emphasize the construction of thought processes and relate their findings to cognitive theory. Others, sometimes called ecolinguists, study the context in which language occurs. They examine things in the environment that they believe may stimulate language growth and expression. Their findings are often interpreted from a behaviorist point of view. Neurolinguists study brain structure and its relevance to the development of language. They often stress innate factors and contribute to our understanding of universal aspects of communication through language. As professionals from various fields share their expertise, a more comprehensive understanding of language development is emerging.

Language and Motor Development

Lenneberg (1967) found that both motor and language development are closely tied to brain maturation. During the first two years of life, the brain grows about 350 percent heavier than it was at birth. At about the age of two years, two things occur that appear to be related to the expansion of speech and motor development (Wood, 1981). First, there is a significant growth spurt of the cerebral cortex, an area of the brain identified as related to language processing. Second, the growth of myelin sheaths (coverings) on the nerves within the brain is sufficiently complete to permit the quality of nerve impulse transmission necessary for both talking and walking.

Lenneberg made an extensive study of the relationship between motor development and language acquisition. He found that the child

- babbles at about the time he sits alone and pulls himself to a standing position

- says first words when he can stand alone and has control of the grasping reflex
- expands vocabulary to two- and three-word sentences when he can run and go up and down stairs

Lenneberg was so emphatic about the relationship between physical maturation and language that he wrote, "Since language is an aspect of a fundamental, biologically determined process, it is not scientifically profitable to look for a cause of language development in the growing child just as we do not look for a cause for the development of his ears" (Lenneberg, 1967, p. 376).

Language Development and Personal Factors

A relatively large number of personal factors have been found to be related to language development in children. We discuss some of these and consider how caregivers can modify the environment to maximize the child's opportunities for language growth.

INTELLIGENCE. Language development appears to be enhanced by intelligence. A brighter child is apt to notice more in his surroundings, ask more questions, remember more answers, and require fewer repetitions to absorb both vocabulary and comprehension in language. Many bright children, however, may be language-learning disabled. A large discrepancy between the verbal and nonverbal IQ on a standard intelligence test is indicative of such a condition. Details about this learning disability are discussed in Chapter 13.

SEX OF THE CHILD. After an extensive review of the literature, Sarafino and Armstrong (1980) concluded that during the preschool years girls exceed boys on most measures of language acquisition and skill, but that at the later elementary level both sexes have comparable levels of ability. This advanced proficiency in girls at the preschool level may be related to the finding that the left hemisphere of the brain, which is responsible for language functions in most persons, matures earlier in girls. By later childhood, boys are generally equal in verbal performance. Differences in parent behavior may also be a factor. Some research studies indicate that mothers talk more to their girls during the preschool period.

ORDINAL POSITION IN THE FAMILY. First children and only children have more verbal fluency than do their later-born siblings (Hurlock, 1980; Oksaar, 1983). They talk more and make longer and more complex sentences. Two reasons for this difference are frequently cited: (1) First and only children are apt to have more contact with the parents than do later children, who have more interactions with the other siblings in the family, and (2) adults are better models for correct speech.

FAMILY SIZE.   Family size is also a factor in language development. In both black and white families, the larger the family, the lower the verbal fluency level of the children (Steelman and Doby, 1983). One factor that could affect the validity of these findings is that many large families are of low socioeconomic status. Whether family size or level of affluence accounted for these differences cannot be positively determined. As with ordinal position, the fact that in large families children tend to talk to each other and have less verbal contact with adults could possibly lead to imitation of less mature models.

MULTIPLE BIRTHS.   What effect do multiple births have on language acquisition? Research has indicated that twins have less advanced verbal development than do single children of the same age (Oksaar, 1983). If the multiple birth involves more than two children, the depression of speech development increases with the number of multiples involved. According to Savic (1980), twins generally speak later, use shorter utterances, and are delayed in the development of articulation, in all types of sentence construction, in the use of parts of speech, and in most types of socialized speech. These speech delays probably result from the fact that the togetherness of twins enables them to communicate without language and therefore to have less incentive to speak. These differences in language development lessen after the twins have spent some time in school (Oksaar, 1983).

SOCIOECONOMIC CLASS.   In a classic study, the British psychologist Bernstein (1977) described two different language codes used by middle- and working-class families. The language pattern used in the middle class was designated as the "elaborated code." It was characterized by longer, more complex sentences and was rich in detail and explanation. By contrast, the typical working-class language pattern, referred to as the "restricted code," involved short utterances, frequent incomplete sentences, and a reliance on gestures for conveyance of meaning. The existence of language code differences has been verified through many research observations (Oksaar, 1983).

Many authorities consider the term "restricted code" a misnomer (Hale, 1982). This language style is used by many groups. It is rich in gesture, vocal inflection, symbolism, and creative vocabulary. It tends to be characteristic of persons who use a relational, field-dependent style of thinking and communicating (see "Cognitive Learning Styles" in Chapter 6). Very precise and fine shades of meaning can be conveyed through this combination of words, tones, gestures, and other situational factors. The restriction of meaning related to this code is basically that the speaker of the "elaborated" code may not understand the multiplicity of cues used in this more global manner of speaking.

Social class may still be a factor in language development. According to Barbieri and Devescovi (1982), middle-class parents, when compared with their working-class counterparts, read more to their young children, use more explanations and analogies as they read, and adjust these comments to current understanding levels. The question now being raised concerns the effects of television on these social class language patterns. Since all socioeconomic groups spend so much time watching the same language input through televiewing, these differences may be significantly modified.

HOME ENVIRONMENT. Many research persons believe we should concentrate on the environment of the individual home rather than making assumptions based on socioeconomic status, since there are great differences in language enrichment within both middle- and working-class homes. Another advantage of such a focus is that regardless of socioeconomic status, elements of language enrichment can be added to any home. Elardo, Bradley, and Caldwell (1977) examined specific aspects of home environment and their impact on children using the Home Observation for Measurement of the Environment (HOME). After testing children at ages six months and twenty-four months, they found that "emotional and verbal responsivity of the mother, provision of appropriate play materials, and maternal involvement with the child" all correlated significantly with the advancement of a child's auditory reception, auditory association, visual association and grammatical closure (Elardo et al., 1977, p. 599). Many research authorities now recognize that the qualitative elements of the home environment are a decisive factor in language development.

Summary

- Three of the major theories concerning the reason for language development are the innate, the behaviorist, and the cognitive. Adherents to the innate theory believe the individual's brain is programmed with a language acquisition device (LAD), and they point out that people in all cultures develop language skills that are basically similar at about the same age. They also believe language must be developed during a critical period prior to puberty if normal language fluency is to be attained. Proponents of the behaviorist theory believe language development results from exposure to a stimulus-rich environment, positive reinforcement from caregivers, language models who speak the language correctly, and language shaping through successive approximations from early babbling to later articulate and fluent speech. The cognitivists feel that language is developed to explain concepts that are already formed. Piaget describes early language acquisition already formed as egocentric speech involving echolalia (practice in perfecting sounds that have been internalized), monologues (conversations with oneself concerning ideas that have been acquired), and collective monologues (verbalizations made in the presence of others but not directed toward them). Later speech is characterized by Piaget as socialized speech for the purpose of communicating thoughts to others.

- The sequence of language development begins with prelanguage sounds such as crying and babbling, which involve all the sounds basic to all languages. These sounds may be made for self-amusement or as rudimentary attempts to communicate with caregivers. Even before first words at about one year, children evidence understanding of language by being able to respond to verbal instructions. Children's first words may be referential (referring to things) or social (referring to interactions). Overgeneralization of a word to many other things that are in some way similar is common at this stage. First words are called holophrases, because they represent a whole sentence whose meaning is determined by the context of the situation. Two-word sentences appear at about the age of two years. They are based on two kinds of words, a pivot word to which other words may be attached ("See baby," "See Daddy") or an open word (all other words not used as pivots). From about age three throughout the remainder of early childhood, the child goes through a period of rapid expansion. During this time children greatly expand vocabularies, modify word formations, develop relational meanings, and bombard caregivers with endless "whys."

- Language development has been found to be related to a number of other factors, particularly to cognition, physical development, and personal attributes. Some authorities have considered language and cognition the same, whereas others have seen them as separate entities and have questioned whether cognition develops before language or whether language develops and refines cognition. Many authorities describe language and cognition as interdependent processes, either of which may be developed first. The effects of maturation on both language and motor development have been studied extensively. During the first two years of life, brain growth and development are greatly accelerated. For this reason, there are significant parallels between the acquisition of language and motor skills. Recent investigations concerning the relationship of language development to personal factors have indicated the following: Degree of intelligence is positively related to language ability; girls exceed boys in language skills during the preschool years because of earlier brain maturation; first and only children, children from small families, and single-birth children compared with those from multiple births are more advanced in language development than their respective counterparts, because they have greater exposure to adult models. Although social class may have some effect on language development, extensive exposure to television may lessen these differences. The emphasis present in individual home environments appears to affect language development more than does socioeconomic status.

Selected Readings

CHOMSKY, N. *Language and the Mind.* New York: Harcourt, Brace & World, 1972.
In this work, Chomsky explains his theory concerning innate mental structures and their impact on language development.

DALE, P. S. *Language Development: Structure and Function.* New York: Holt, Rinehart & Winston, 1976.
This work contains clear and concise explanations of language structure and uses.

LENNEBERG, E. G. *Biological Foundations of Language.* New York: Wiley, 1967.
This classic work served as a basis for many later research studies.

OKSAAR, E. *Language Acquisition in the Early Years.* (Trans. Turfler, K.) New York: St. Martin's Press, 1983.
The author traces the sequence of language development and discusses related factors.

PIAGET, J. *Language and Thought of the Child.* London: Routledge and Kegan Paul, 1952.
Piaget discusses his research findings concerning the relationship between the development of language and thought.

SKINNER, B. F. *Verbal Behavior.* New York: Appleton-Century-Crofts, 1957.
Skinner explains the behaviorist position concerning the acquisition of language.

CHAPTER 8

Personality Development

CHAPTER OUTLINE

What Is Personality?
The Mosaic of Self: Personality Development from Basic Elements
    Inborn Temperament
    Physical Appearance
    Sexual Identity
    Ethnic Affiliation
    Birth Order
    Early Experience
The Process of Becoming
    Self-Awareness, Self-Concept, Self-Esteem, Self-Confidence
    Coping Ability: Locus of Control and Initiative
    Industry
    Sense of Humor
Negative Roadblocks
    Tension
    Anxiety
    Frustration
    Fear
Facilitating Personality Growth
Summary
Selected Readings

A little league player proudly announced to his grandmother, "I'm the best pitcher in all of Dallas County." A bit abashed by his modesty (?), the grandmother countered, "How do you know that." "Oh," the child happily replied, "my coach says I'm the best pitcher on the team, and our team won city, so that makes me the best pitcher in all of Dallas County."

Unfortunately, not all children feel so positively about themselves. A child in my class kept breaking his pencil lead and was forever grinding away at the pencil sharpener. When I questioned him, he said sadly, "When I'm bad, Mother and Daddy say they're going to move off and leave me. I can see the top of our trailer from this window (we were on the second floor), and I know they haven't left me yet."

How children feel about themselves greatly affects their emotional development, and this, in turn, has a tremendous impact on their relationships with others. What is personality? From what components is the self derived? How does the child develop self-confidence, coping ability, industry, and a sense of humor? How can negative emotions block healthy development, and what can caregivers do to facilitate this process of becoming? These are the questions to be discussed in this chapter.

What Is Personality?

Since the individual is so complex, any attempt to define personality will involve descriptions of many facets and functions. Our basic personality is considered to be those enduring qualities we repeatedly display under a variety of conditions even though our behavior may also be affected by daily circumstances (Allport, 1955). It is made up of many parts. We assign greater importance to some areas of our personality and lesser importance to other parts according to our own value system. Our personality patterns are formed as a result of interaction between our own inborn tendencies and elements in our environment, particularly those involving other people. The personality serves as a standard by which we make such choices as how we will behave in given situations and in what direction we will focus our life and energies. Our personality structure may change somewhat over a period of time. The degree of this change varies from one individual to another. Some people are quite flexible, and others are very rigid. Through our particular personality, each of us affects others and in turn is affected by our environment.

The Mosaic of Self: Self-Personality Development from Basic Elements

A mosaic is an art form in which small pieces of various colors are arranged to form a pattern or picture. In like manner, the self is composed of many elements, each contributing to the uniqueness of the whole person. Some of these, such as temperament, sex, and physical appearance, are strongly affected by inheritance; others, such as ethnic affiliation, birth order, and early experience, are influenced more directly by the environment in which the individual develops. In this section each factor is considered separately in an effort to understand the contribution it makes to the total emerging self.

Inborn Temperament

When Jennifer hangs her head and digs her toe into the carpet when she is being introduced to great-aunt Matilda and Robert cavorts in perpetual motion twenty-four hours a day, are they "showing their rearing" or

Each child has his or her own unique temperament   (*Source:* © *1988 Tom Kelly*)

were they born that way? Much recent research has indicated that children are born with certain innate predispositions that make some behaviors easier for them to learn than are others (Chess and Thomas, 1984; Plomin and Dunn, 1986). Thomas, Chess, and their colleagues followed the development of 141 children from infancy to adulthood. A number of qualities of temperament that were discernible at birth persisted as permanent characteristics of the personality. These factors and their descriptions are found in Box 8.1.

One of the most important aspects of the study was the way in which the child's behavior affected the caregiver. By combining the characteristics of temperament into clusters, most of the children could be classified into one of three groups: easy, difficult, and slow to warm up. *Easy children* "quickly establish regular sleeping and feeding schedules, are generally cheerful and adapt quickly to new routines, new foods and new people." By contrast, *difficult children* "are irregular in bodily functions, are usually intense in their reactions, tend to withdraw in the face of new stimuli, are slow to adapt to changes in the environment and are generally negative in mood." *Slow-to-warm-up children* usually have "a low activity level, tend to withdraw in their first exposure to new stimuli, are slow to adapt, are

BOX 8.1

Persistent Dimensions of Temperament

Activity level	• Amount of time spent active or inactive
Rhythm	• Regularity of eating, elimination, sleep/wakefulness
Distractibility	• Amount of stimulation from environment necessary to disrupt child's behavior
Approach/withdrawal	• Reaction to new situation or person
Adaptability	• Ease with which child adapts to changes
Attention span/Persistence	• Amount of time child can stay on task and resist distraction
Intensity of reaction	• How energetically child responds to a new situation
Threshold of responsiveness	• How much stimulation is necessary to cause child to respond
Quality of mood	• Amount of happy, friendly behavior compared with unpleasant, hostile behavior

SOURCE. Thomas et al., 1970

somewhat negative in mood and respond to situations with a low intensity of reaction" (Thomas et al., 1970, p. 105). Caregivers naturally become frustrated when they compare difficult or slow-to-warm-up children with their more easily managed peers, and this tension is often internalized by that child as rejection. Should the parent fatalistically accept undesirable behavior because it "comes naturally"? Let's hope not. For suggestions on behavior management of difficult children, see Chapters 10 and 14.

Physical Appearance

As previously discussed in Chapter 4, physical attractiveness affects the way a child is accepted by others. Television is a potent force in promoting the notion that beauty is good and ugly is bad through both its commercials and its programming. In like manner, children's literature is replete with examples such as pretty Cinderella who is sought by a prince, unsightly stepsisters who are wicked and mean, and the ugly duckling who meets with repeated rejection because he looks different. Research indicates that teachers tend to rate attractive children as smarter and better adjusted than plain children, and in the case of misbehavior, ugly children are more apt to be labeled as dishonest or unpleasant than are their prettier counterparts (Langlois and Downs, 1979). This desirability or rejection based on physical appearance is often noted by children and incorporated into their feelings about their own worthiness. The effects of such feelings may be lifelong. Noles (1985) found that adult depressives viewed themselves as less attractive and were more dissatisfied with their bodies than were nondepressives.

Sexual Identity

Since people in our society are generally clothed, knowledge of body parts is often not the basis of early identification. Willerman (1979) found that when children were shown drawings in which hair and dress were the only clues, most of the children in the sample could correctly identify sex. When sketches included only genital clues, however, accurate identification could be made by only 23 percent at age five, 52 percent by age seven, and 79 percent by age nine. A teacher reported that when some preschoolers went to see a litter of puppies, a child lovingly inquired as to whether the one he was holding was a boy or a girl. The mother flipped the puppy over and announced that it was a boy. The child observed with a smile, "Isn't it wonderful how my mother can tell the boys from the girls just by looking at their little paws?" The presence of siblings in a family may accelerate the learning of sexual differences. A young child, when teased by older brothers about "the part that got left off her," went sobbing to her mother to inquire as to whether God might come down and finish her someday.

SEX-ROLE IDENTITY. Youngsters need to be involved in many activities with the same-sex parent for identification and imitation and the opposite-sex parent for a better understanding of role differences (Willerman, 1979). Ideally they should have ample opportunities to interact with several adults of each sex in order to better understand the full range of behaviors that may be included. If the parents view their own sex roles positively, the children are apt to like theirs. If, however, these caregivers are unhappy with themselves or perhaps wanted a child of a different sex, they may fail to reward same-sex behavior and inappropriately reinforce opposite-sex tendencies. Such actions may create role-preference distortions. In our society, girls appear to have more flexibility in sex roles than do boys. By twenty months, girls show more cross-sex interests and, through age ten, often prefer boys' activities and dress. Such behavior would be taboo for boys. Girls often receive trucks, but boys seldom receive dolls. Sex roles are no longer as stereotyped as they were in the past, however. Individuals are becoming increasingly free to use their strengths and pursue their interests irrespective of sex.

BOX 8.2

Sex Differences Related to Children

Significant Differences	No Significant Differences	Inconclusive Data
• Brains differ in hemisphere characteristics and in the organization and processing of information • Aggression levels of boys exceed those of girls • Word recognition levels of girls exceed those of boys (in reading)	• Self-esteem • Imitative behavior • Curiosity • Social responsiveness • Motivation • Learning ability • Analytic thinking • Interest in computer software • Auditory and visual skills • Achievement in reading, spelling, and math	• Activity level • Competition • Dominance • Nurturance • Shyness, worry, fear • Sensitivity of touch

SOURCES. Maccoby and Jacklin, 1974; Gerhard, 1985; Harty and Beall, 1985; Naour, 1985; Powell and Batters, 1985; Sherman, 1985; Whorton, 1985; Yore and Ollila, 1985.

SEX DIFFERENCES. What sex differences actually exist between young boys and girls? When Maccoby and Jacklin (1974) did an extensive survey of the literature, they discovered that many of the ideas we hold about the relative behaviors of boys and girls are not supported by facts. Many research studies have been conducted since this time. Box 8.2 summarizes data concerning sexual differences that are currently believed to exist.

Some of these sex differences are affected by biological factors; others result from environmental opportunities and nurturance. For example, two studies illustrate sex differences in treatment of children in school. One indicated that teachers were more attracted to girls than to boys (Oettingen, 1985); the other found that in case of misbehavior, teachers advocated more severe punishment for boys (Woolridge and Richmann, 1985). Because of sex-linked differences in treatment and flaws in research studies designed to measure sex differences, our findings must be considered tentative.

Ethnic Affiliation

A person's ethnic affiliation is a basic part of that individual's self. In an effort to avoid stereotyped thinking, let's consider various factors related to any ethnic group that could affect the self-esteem of a child growing up in that setting.

First is the *prestige* of the group. If its members are highly valued by other persons in the mainstream of that society, the child will benefit from esteem by association. Second is the *average economic status* of the group. Generally, more affluent groups are treated with preference. Some groups, however, are rejected for other reasons regardless of monetary status. Third is the *existence of conflict between groups.* New immigrants, be they Irish or Indochinese, are apt to meet with initial reserve from the members of the mainstream. Differences in color, language, or religion may also elicit rejection. Fourth is the *status within the ethnic group* of that particular child's family. Some families are "looked up to" by the other members of their group, and others are considered of low status even by their own people. Fifth is the *attitude of the parents* about their ethnic group membership. If they are proud of their identities, the child will come to model this pride. Finally, the *appearance of the individual child* is a factor. Regardless of ethnic affiliation, some children are considered prettier than others. Langlois and Downs (1979) found that the physical attractiveness of the individual child was more important than race in determining social acceptance.

How and at what age do children develop racial attitudes? Goodman made an extensive study of existing data and delineated a three-stage sequence (Milner, 1983). First the child develops *racial awareness.* The child notices racial differences among people and can correctly identify her own racial group. This awareness occurs between the ages of three and five years. In an overlapping timespan, the child develops a *racial orientation;* she absorbs feelings of like or dislike for various groups and comes to prefer some groups over others. This racial orientation begins with racial awareness at about age three and is fairly well established in the six-year-old. The final stage of the sequence is *racial attitude,* which occurs between the ages of six and eight years. The child's racial attitude includes her beliefs concerning the relative status, ability level, character, and desirability of people from various ethnic groups.

What can caregivers do to foster better relations among children of various ethnic groups? They can

- model acceptance of all children in their care
- discourage negative ethnic remarks or behaviors by the children
- use persons from various ethnic groups as speakers or classroom helpers
- discuss storybook and television characters from different ethnic backgrounds

PERSONALITY DEVELOPMENT

- tell the children about the accomplishments of talented people from all groups so that each child will have models with whom she can identify with pride

One kindergarten was doing such an excellent job of instilling ethnic pride in conjunction with a Cinco de Mayo celebration that one youngster, when asked what he wanted to be when he grew up, immediately replied with glowing tone, "A Mexican-American." (One small problem existed—he wasn't of that ethnic group.)

Birth Order

How does the position of a child within the family affect personality? Historically, firstborn males were treated with great deference since they were to inherit the family wealth and perpetuate the family tradition (be it tailor or king). Little was expected (or done) for the youngest, since barring another sweep of the great plague, his older siblings would have everything anyway (remember all those youngest sons in fairy tales who always had to go out and find their own fortunes?). The possible effects of such practices on self-concept are obvious. Ernst and Angst (1983) found evidence relating birth order to biological differences, IQ, school achievement, occupational status, and mental health.

First-borns have been described in research as independent, dominant, self-sufficient, and academically superior (Baskitt, 1984). They are more apt than later-born children to seek adult attention. Generally, middle-born children tend to be less conventional, more eager for action, more people-oriented, and less dependent on adults. Youngest children are often more sociable, more popular, less obedient, and less conforming than other children in the family (Baskitt, 1984, 1985; Steelman and Powell, 1985). They may also be more dependent and less mature than their siblings.

The most frequently cited reason for personality variations related to birth order is difference in treatment and/or family situation. Birth order correlates significantly with the amount of interaction between mother and children, the organization of the home environment, and the availability of play equipment (Bradley and Caldwell, 1984). Steelman and Powell (1985) found other factors that must be considered:

- family size
- spacing of children
- socioeconomic status
- maternal age
- sex of children
- marriage harmony or disruption

One of the fascinating questions yet to be answered is, "Do personality differences related to birth order persist throughout life, or are they only apparent in childhood?"

Early Experience

A final component in the mosaic of self is that of experience. Because the young child is relatively helpless, early occurrences are of special importance. These may be classified into two categories—those eliciting emotional responses between the child and caregivers and those involving stimulation from objects or activities in the environment. Very early the child comes to feel that her world is warm and safe or cold and hostile as a result of interactions with primary caregivers. Montagu (1971) stresses the importance of close physical contact since, as he points out, the skin is the body's largest organ. His phrase "mind of the skin" is used to

At first children are apt to be shy in a group, but confidence may build with experience.

stress the fact that touching experiences are relayed through the skin to the mind where they are stored and this information relayed back to affect an individual's behavior. Visual experiences of smiles, auditory memories of gentle speech, and even olfactory sensations from the smell of freshly baked cookies may also contribute to the child's sense of well-being. The importance of environmental stimulation cannot be overstressed.

The availability of activities and the awareness that these things are important to the child's caregivers are crucial in the development of motivation and competence (Deci, 1980). The effects of both emotionality of caregivers and variety of activity will be explored further in the following sections dealing with the development of positive and negative personality characteristics.

The Process of Becoming

"Each to each a looking-glass
Reflects the other that does pass."

Cooley, in his "looking-glass" theory, emphasizes the role of interaction between child and others in the development of the self (Staub, 1980, p. 85). Research has identified a number of personality characteristics that are related to the happiness and well-being of the individual. In this section, we consider the emergence of five of these: self-confidence, coping ability, initiative, industry, and sense of humor.

Self-Awareness > Self-Concept > Self-Esteem > Self-Confidence

All that a person comes to describe as "I" or "Me" is a part of that person's self (Calhoun and Morse, 1977). This identity is developed through a series of four stages:

1. Self-awareness (recognition of me as a separate person)
2. Self-concept (beliefs about what I am and what I can do)
3. Self-esteem (positive or negative feelings about my perception of me)
4. Self-confidence (anticipation of success or failure based on my self-appraisals)

The importance of early attention to this self-development is stressed by Allport (1955). He believes that until the age of four or five, the child's personal identity is unstable. Beginning at that age, however, it becomes the most powerful force in the child's existence, since the child uses self-opinions to determine how she will react to events and which experiences she will volunteer to undertake.

SELF-AWARENESS. Children become aware of themselves first as they explore their own body parts and how each of these function (e.g., reaching, walking, vocalizing). As they extend their activities, they become aware that they can *cause* things to happen. They also discover self-will ("I *will* scream and say 'No' to you, too!"; or "I *won't* potty on cue if I don't want to!"). If the caregiver can somehow muster the patience (and it takes a lot at this point) to enforce rules without attaching personal labels (bad child, monster), the child may become reasonably civilized without negative self-connotations. Another pitfall at this point may be called smother love (as opposed to mother love). Smothering parents are so concerned that the child do everything right that they do everything for the youngster, thus denying her self-awareness of her own capabilities.

SELF-CONCEPT. The self-concept has been described as "the total collection of attitudes, judgments, and values which an individual holds with respect to his behavior, his ability, his body, his worth as a person—in short how he perceives and evaluates himself" (Byrne and Kelley, 1981, p. 271). Each of us has organized our early experiences as "good-me," "bad-me," and "not-me" (Epstein, 1980). A good-me is an experience that was rewarded by a significant caregiver. A bad-me is an event for which a moderate level of disapproval was expressed. These concepts of what is bad may become the basis for our conscience. When we did something for which disapproval was very intense, we may have become so engulfed by anxiety and remorse that we denied even to ourselves that we ever committed such an act, and it became a not-me. Throughout life, when events trigger memories of not-me experiences, we may again be overcome by great anxiety.

Children are quite accurate in estimating how their parents feel about them, and there is a high positive correlation between what their parents think of them and how they see themselves (Byrne, 1981). If the parent's appraisals are not accurate, however, many problems may arise. Children may feel good while acting atrocious, they may feel bad without reason, or they may set standards for themselves that are too high or too low in terms of their abilities.

If parents or principal caregivers disagree on standards of behavior, even more confusion will ensue. Children in such situations will have great difficulty figuring out what is right and wrong, and they are apt to

PERSONALITY DEVELOPMENT

239

be less motivated to try to please, since one parent is going to be unhappy no matter what they do.

SELF-ESTEEM. The child's self-esteem, or feeling of self-worth, may go all the way from zero to infinity depending on the responses of caregivers, siblings, and peers. Parents of high-esteem children are attentive and accepting of the child, but also demand a high level of desirable behavior. They set clearly defined and enforced limits, but respect the child's need to take independent actions in areas warranted by maturity. These people themselves have high self-esteem and can serve as confident models (Coopersmith, 1981).

(*Source:* Reprinted by permission of United Feature Syndicate, Inc.)

The importance of peers in the development of self-esteem is drawing increasing attention, since they affect the behavior of a youngster at a much earlier age than was previously thought (Kerchner and Vondrack, 1975; Fogel and Melson, 1986). In the Kerchner study, the three-to-five-year-olds were asked, "Who likes you?" to determine the sources of esteem that were important to these young children. The findings are summarized in Box 8.3.

Several implications may be drawn from this study. Since other children have such an important impact at such an early age, helping a child get along in group settings appears to be important from toddlerhood. Childcare responsibilities need to be more evenly divided so that both fathers and mothers spend time with the children and the father is not viewed merely as the disciplinarian. This time and attention from the father is particularly crucial if the child is living with the mother only. In our culture, girls generally receive more affectionate treatment than boys do; emotional development might be better for all children if these expressions were more evenly divided between boys and girls.

BOX 8.3

"Who Likes Me?": Sources of Esteem for Preschoolers

Source	Finding
Peers and siblings	Mentioned far more often than were parents and caregivers.
Mothers	Mentioned more frequently than were fathers.
Fathers	Mentioned much less frequently in mother-only one-parent families than in two-parent families.
Age of responder	Not significant—there was no relationship between the age of the child and the number of people she felt liked her.
Size of family	Not significant—even though more people were present in home, children from larger families did not name more people than did those from small families.
Sex	Girls named more sources of esteem than did boys.

SOURCE. Kerchner and Vondrack, 1975.

SELF-CONFIDENCE. After children see themselves as separate persons, discover who they are and what they can do, and like what they perceive about themselves, they can tackle life's problems with self-confidence. Children whose basic self-orientations are positive can even absorb daily setbacks. The child can say to herself, "If someone in the carpool kicks me or if the teacher lets someone else pass out art paper, I won't scramble someone else's puzzle or sit by myself and sulk." By contrast, a negatively oriented child has no way to balance failure. As things go wrong, events merely confirm what she already suspected—"It's a rotten world!" Many success experiences may have to be contrived before this child even begins to react with confidence.

Coping Ability

The ability to successfully cope with life's challenges depends on two closely related factors: (1) the belief that the individual can control the events that affect her life and (2) the inclination to tackle problems and/or projects. How does a child develop each of these characteristics?

LOCUS OF CONTROL: INTERNAL OR EXTERNAL. Locus of control refers to what we believe causes our experiences. Those who believe in internal locus of control feel that what happens depends on their own actions, good or bad. Proponents of external locus of control feel that life is controlled by luck, fate, other people, or things about oneself that cannot be readily changed such as physical attributes or intelligence. The initiative we assert or fail to assert is related closely to whether we perceive locus of control as internal or external.

EMERGENCE OF INITIATIVE. Initiative is based on internal motivation. Its foundations are laid in infancy as the child discovers that she can exert control on the environment and make things happen. Box 8.4 outlines stages, ages, and descriptions of this process.

To study the effects of arranged environment on this development, Watson designed games by which happenings occurred in response to the child's voluntary efforts (Lefcourt, 1980). He found that infants made more motor responses and laughed and cooed with delight at the results of deliberate acts.

LOCUS OF CONTROL, INITIATIVE, AND INTERACTION WITH SIGNIFICANT OTHERS. The effects of even drastic adverse conditions can be offset by positive guidance. Both Supreme Court Justice William O. Douglas and President Franklin Delano Roosevelt overcame the debilities of polio because of encouragement and independence training provided by their families (Lefcourt, 1980). To develop an internal locus of control, the child must be taught "I can even if things go wrong, and I have to plan around certain difficulties." Neglected or overindulged children, however,

---

BOX 8.4

Beginnings of Internal Motivation

Stage	Age	Description
1	0–5 months	Child responds to stimulation, both internal and external; child learns to keep attending to stimulation.
2	4–9 months	Child wants to maintain pleasurable stimulation; when stimulation stops, child attempts to restore it even if she doesn't understand cause and effect. (Piaget noted all-over body movement in attempt to restore tickling.)
3	9 months +	Child deliberately seeks out novel situations.

SOURCE. Deci, 1980, pp. 59–60.

A child is proud of what she can do if "significant others" show an interest.

often do not develop the concept that they can control events. They frequently fail to explore and discover relationships between cause and effect. When dependency continues in areas that are not appropriate for the age, the child misses the opportunity to test her own abilities.

Persons who are not rewarded equally, sufficiently, and consistently for their efforts tend to develop a belief in external locus of control, because rewards are dispensed by some agent beyond their power. Many members of low socioeconomic and minority groups fall prey to such discouragement. Children from nonliterate homes often fail to exert maximum efforts in "book learning," as they have never known anyone who got ahead that way. Some individuals, however, because of their commitment to internal locus of control (and perhaps some good breaks), battle the odds and move from very humble beginnings to positions of prominence in their chosen areas of interest and talent.

In summarizing the effects of parenting patterns and early environment on the development of locus of control, Lefcourt (1980, pp. 222–223) wrote:

> The ideal home atmosphere for producing children that will grow up with an internal locus of control is one that changes with the child's needs; warm

PERSONALITY DEVELOPMENT

and nurturant when the child is helpless, but increasingly challenging and encouraging of independent pursuits as the child becomes of age to test his developing power. Accelerating demands for competence as the child's abilities mature may be a necessary ingredient that supplements the security created by the initially supportive, dependency-gratifying home.

Industry

The feelings of control and initiative developed in early childhood begin to blossom into industry during the elementary school years. Erikson, whose theories were briefly discussed in Chapter 1, has described the development of industry in some detail (Erikson, 1963, pp. 258–261).

Through industry the child learns to win recognition by producing things. The joy of completing tasks gradually becomes more than the excitement of merely starting projects. Children take pride in their abilities and in the tools or equipment earmarked as "theirs" (their desk, their crayons, their room).

All societies provide some type of systematic instruction of skills basic to the needs of that group. As we have previously discussed, even at a very early age peers as well as caregivers are an important part of this teaching team. In a complex society, children must be given very general and basic training to prepare them for the largest possible number of careers. For this reason, tasks are often unrelated to the immediate needs

Industry is working diligently when no one is looking.

and interests of the children and, therefore, may not automatically stimulate the desire to "work hard."

The danger at this time is that children will develop a sense of inadequacy and inferiority. This may occur if the child's abilities are limited, her status with peers is low, or her preparation for expected roles has been insufficient. The structure and demands of the public school often conflict with the background experiences of children from less verbal and less regimented homes. A lack of industry will have both personal and social implications. If I cannot perform as well as my peers, I feel bad about myself. At the same time, my friends come to see me as incompetent, and they "include me out" of many activities.

Sense of Humor

"A merry heart doeth good like a medicine," observed one ancient writer (Proverbs 17:32). Since humor is such a refreshing and essential part of the child, it has been studied in considerable depth (McGhee, 1979; McGhee and Chapman, 1980). In this section we consider the answers contributed by these two research authorities to these questions: What is humor? How does it develop? What are some of the individual differences in response to humor? How is humor used in the child's everyday life?

What is humor? The word "humor" originally meant fluid or moisture. Doctors in early times believed the body contained four humors that affected the person's feelings and behaviors: yellow bile (upsets, anger), black bile (sadness, depression), blood (confidence, cheerfulness), and phlegm (sluggishness and apathy). An individual was said to be in "good humor" when there was a proper balance of the humors in the body. Currently we use the word "humor" to connote words, ideas, events, or situations in which the element we expected has been replaced by something that is absurd, unexpected, inappropriate, or out of context. Graduate students often refer to "statistics" as "sadistics," because this subject is often hard for them. The roadrunner and the coyote have achieved cartoon fame as a result of the many unexpected ways the coyote plans to "do in" the roadrunner and the way these ideas always backfire.

How does humor develop? At four months, infants will laugh at tactile and auditory stimulation. By eight to twelve months, children have a better understanding of what is likely to happen in a given situation and can detect incongruities (events different from what is expected). Youngsters between twelve and eighteen months begin to use objects as if they were something else. Awareness of expected use enables children to detect incongruencies that, in turn, lead to humor.

Being able to share a funny situation with friends often greatly enhances its mirthfulness. Many times when youngsters perceive something as potentially funny, they will first begin a shy giggle, watch the reaction of peers, and, if encouraged, burst into gales of laughter.

What are some of the individual differences in response to humor? Reflective children show greater understanding of jokes, but impulsive children laugh more. Some youngsters like jokes that require their best thinking to understand; others prefer easy, obvious jokes that don't strain the brain. Having the prerequisite knowledge to understand the concept doesn't guarantee the child will "get the joke," and comprehension doesn't guarantee appreciation (jokes may involve slurs of some "out" group). Children should be taught to avoid humor that is cruel and hurtful of others. A young child reported to her mother, "A little girl fell down at school today, and everybody laughed but me." Before the proud mother could brag about her child's empathy, the child added, "See my skinned knee!"

How is humor used? Humor is valuable for a variety of reasons (McGhee, 1979). Many children use humor to release fear and anxiety. (How can you be afraid of a monster you laugh at?) Understanding humor shows mastery. (It convinces youngsters that they are big folks who know how things are supposed to be; they can "catch on" because they know things that the little kids don't know.) Through the use of humor, children can reassure themselves that the world is orderly. (They can choose to change the rule, but order still exists.) Humor can make children socially attractive. (The jokester/prankster is often loved.) Finally, humor can help to stimulate joy, smiling, and laughter, and it can take the edge off what might otherwise be a rather somber experience.

Negative Roadblocks

From the very earliest years of the child's life, negative emotions arise which, if they become habitual, will block healthy personality development. Among these are tension, anxiety, frustration, and fear.

Tension and Stress

Tension and stress are two problems often experienced by children. Factors related to these emotional states have been investigated in many studies. Tension has been the subject of extensive research by the Gesell Institute (Ilg and Ames, 1980). Although tension is often associated with a specific situation, it also appears to be characteristic of certain ages. Two-and-a-half, three-and-a-half, and five-and-a-half to six years seem to be times of particular stress. The build-up of tension at these ages may be related to other developmental tasks that require adjustments and put pressure on the child. At two-and-a-half the child may still be in the throes of potty training, at three-and-a-half the environment may be expanding to include adjustments to persons outside the home and immediate family, and by five-and-a-half to six the pressures of "doing well in school" may be introduced.

In response to tension, young children may resort to tantrums, biting, hair pulling, thumb sucking, nail biting, whining, stuttering, or tics (unconscious, repetitive movements of face or body). Ilg and Ames (1980) suggest two guidelines for dealing with tension: (1) Make a special effort to be understanding and to arrange the environment in ways that will reduce tension and (2) recognize these age-related times of tension as normal periods of stress, and don't worry too much. Tension is contagious, and calm caregivers will provide less stressful models.

The older child is particularly susceptible to stress because of basic self-concerns (Humphrey, 1984). She may question her own worth and be troubled that she may not be "good enough." (She may be concerned about certain habits or traits she feels are undesirable.)

Home conditions such as discord among family members and unmet needs related to poverty can contribute to tension and stress (Medeiros et al., 1983; Humphrey, 1984). Stress related to divorce may include such problems as loss of security, change of neighborhood, pressure to take sides between parents, and partial or complete loss of one parent's presence. Poverty contains many elements that may make family members stress-prone. Difficulty in managing necessities while still having some resources for wants can create frustration in both parents and children. A downward change in financial status, which is particularly troubling, is experienced by many children as a result of parental job loss, divorce, or death of a parent.

School anxieties can exist at all grade levels (Medeiros et al., 1983; Humphreys, 1984). Teacher-pupil conflicts, subjects that are hard for particular children, and test anxiety are all sources for an acute state sometimes called "school phobia."

How do older children deal with stress differently from younger ones? Maccoby (1983) studied the effects of developmental maturity on responses to stress. She makes the following observations about older children:

- Their behavior is less likely to become severely disorganized in times of stress because (1) they know more coping strategies, and (2) they are less dependent on their primary attachment figure.
- They use their obedience to adult authority as a means of reducing stress. (When peers pressure them to do things that are frightening or that they know are forbidden, they take comfort in saying, "My folks won't let me.")

- When they don't make friends or lose the ones they have, they are more hurt by the loss of emotional support than by the missing of activities.
- They become very aware of the reactions of others to themselves, and they increasingly evaluate their performance in terms of social comparisons.
- With age, they become aware of and attempt to use a wider range of solutions to stressful problems.

Anxiety

Anxiety is an apprehensive feeling that something is wrong when an apparent problem may or may not exist. Anxiety may be a temporary condition (the child whines with worry when the caregiver is late for a pickup), or it may be a chronic trait (the child is usually fretful and clinging). This emotion may be mild (consisting of apprehensive looks and fidgeting), or it may be extreme (expressed by hysterical, uncontrollable crying). In older children, anxiety may be expressed through avoiding difficult tasks, running away, weeping, wetting (long after continence has been previously attained), and vomiting (Varma, 1984).

Several theorists have postulated on the origins of anxiety. Freud believed that when we suppress natural desires, the feelings of need do not go away. Instead, they are converted into anxiety, a vague but intense feeling of urgency. Over a period of time we may accumulate a large store of this anxiousness. Since the causes are not directly connected to anything in the immediate environment, anxiety is very difficult to eradicate (Zurcher, 1977; Bavelas, 1978; Dickstein, 1978).

Horney contended that individuals meet needs by moving toward people, away from people, or against people. If childhood socialization experiences are too painful, the individual develops anxiety as a basic component of her personality. This basic anxiety can be avoided if child-rearing practices focus on love, trust, tolerance, and security (Zurcher, 1977; Bavelas, 1978; Dickstein, 1978).

Lewin pointed out that anxiety often results when we can't decide between two things we want to do (approach/approach conflict) or between two things we don't want to do (avoidance/avoidance conflict). Have you ever seen a child take forever to decide whether she wants rocky road or peppermint delight ice cream (approach/approach conflict)? Or perhaps you remember the child who shuffled papers all morning because she didn't want to do either her math or her history (avoidance/avoidance decision). In either case, anxiety shows both in the facial expression and in the slowness of activity.

Which children are more likely to be anxious? In a comprehensive cross-cultural review of research, Lokare (1984) found that

- Anxiety is found in children of all cultures.
- Girls tend to score higher than boys on all types of anxiety measures (perhaps more willing to admit anxiety because culture allows them to be more helpless).
- Many studies show an increase of anxiety with age (perhaps can perceive more dangers).
- Anxiety level is not more prevalent in one race or culture than another, but does occur more often at low socioeconomic levels than at higher ones.

Frustration

Frustration is an emotion that is often expressed when a person has difficulty gaining success or control in a particular situation. Coopersmith (1981) states that the degree of frustration experienced by the child depends not so much on whether failure actually occurs, but rather on whether the child thinks it did. Young children frequently react to frustration by withdrawal, aimless wandering, whining, thumb sucking, and aggressive screaming and struggling. Among very young children, the temper tantrum is an oft-selected recourse.

Ilg and Ames (1980) make four suggestions for handling temper tantrums: (1) Walk away from the distraught child. (Loss of your physical presence is frightening to child and she will seek to restore contact.) (2) Try to determine the cause of the tantrums (fatigue, need for attention, getting her way). (If tantrums are frequent, keep a log of what is going on just before the onset of each tantrum to help determine the origin of the misbehavior.) (3) Plan around these sensitive times (snack to break afternoon fatigue, avoidance of long shopping sprees with child). (4) Never reward tantrum behavior by giving the child something special to stop an ongoing tantrum.

Older children may develop a variety of responses to frustration. These may include general irritability, pounding heart, accident-proneness, trembling, startle reactions, teeth grinding, stuttering, insomnia, indigestion, and nightmares (Medeiros et al., 1983).

Fear

Young children have many fears. Some of these result from unpleasant or harmful experiences; others are engendered by the youngsters' relative state of helplessness. Their limited knowledge of the environment makes

PERSONALITY DEVELOPMENT 249

"IT'S NOT THE **DARK** I'M AFRAID OF...IT'S THE STUFF IN IT I CAN'T **SEE**!"

(Source: DENNIS THE MENACE® used by permission of Hank Ketcham and © by North America Syndicate)

many commonplace things appear frightful, and their misunderstandings of cause and effect make potential harm difficult for them to predict. They also mirror many of the fears of others in their lifespace. As children grow older, their fears may include both their expanded knowledge of harmful things and their sensitivity to the approval of others.

UNPLEASANT EXPERIENCES. For the very young child, loud noises, a sudden pain, or the ferocious barking and jumping of a friendly but frisky dog may strike terror to the heart. For the older child who places great value on peer relations, fear of being left out, of being ridiculed, or of failing may be a source of great distress. Most children also have some genuinely hurtful experiences—a trip to the dentist, a stay in the hospital, a bad fall. Any or all of these may fuel the child's imagination. ("Next time I go to the hospital, I'll probably die—Poppa did.") In this way, concrete mishaps become the basis for both real and fanciful fears.

STATE OF HELPLESSNESS. The child's relative state of helplessness gives rise to many fears. Relative size alone is awesome, as big people tower over little people ("What if they aren't friendly?" "What if I get stepped on?"). According to Eme and Schmidt (1978), the child's three most common fears are (1) injury or harm to the body from falling or some other accident, (2) robbers, kidnappers, or dying, and (3) vicious animals that bite. The fear of intrusion was further confirmed in a national survey of seven- to eleven-year-olds; two-thirds of these children were afraid someone was going to break into the house (Zill, 1977). The bigness of older children and of adults also enables them to coerce small youngsters. Actual abuse and threats of abuse may make life very frightening. A fuller discussion of child abuse may be found in Chapter 9.

Many children are afraid of the dark. Because younger children have difficulty distinguishing fantasy from reality, everyday objects can become frightening monsters when the lights go out. Shaming and ridicule are both unkind and ineffective in dealing with this fear. Pleasant experiences such as bedtime stories in a darkened room, reality checks that involve turning the lights on and off to verify that the shadows are harmless, and use of a nightlight to prevent total darkness are techniques that have been found to be helpful in helping young children to deal with this problem. Older children may also need reassurance without negative remarks. Both the daily news and horror fantasy stories may prolong fear of the dark for some young people.

LACK OF EXPERIENCE. The young child's lack of experience causes many things to look strange, if not outright threatening. A long hall with many closed doors may terrify a shy young child who can imagine all sorts of monsters lurking just out of sight. The child has no store of knowledge to use as a basis for deciding whether a stranger she has just met is friendly or harmful, and the signals she gets from caregivers may be mixed. Mother says, "Don't talk to strangers; they might hurt you!" Then she insists, "Don't scream at Uncle Bobby; he just wants to hold you. He's never seen you before." Although many specific fear referents could not actually harm the child, strangeness based on limited comprehension creates many pressures for the youngster that do not exist for older persons.

Older children have fears related to lack of experience in social and skill areas. Many of them want to be included in peer groups but fear rejection. National organizations (e.g., YMCA/YWCA, Boy/Girl Scouts of America) and local churches or synagogues provide opportunities for social growth and success that may help allay these fears. Children in upper elementary grades may also want to shine as participants in sports, drama, or musical activities. If previous opportunities to develop beginning skills in these areas have been limited, these children may be afraid to try because of possible ridicule.

MISUNDERSTANDINGS OF CAUSE AND EFFECT.   Many children's fears are rooted in their inability to understand cause and effect. Because of their egocentric belief that everything is related to them, younger children fear that any loud noise is some unnamed terror that is after them. They also have difficulty determining what will happen next. Will the thundering stampede of elephants come crashing through the television to chase them down? Will they go down the drain with the bath water? The world can be a very frightening place if they can't understand what causes what. Fortunately, if reassurance is given and teasing is not allowed, the child's fears will lessen with age and with the construction of knowledge.

Misunderstanding of cause and effect plagues older children, too. When they become so eager to please their peers, they imagine all sorts of bad effects from many causes. Having to wear glasses or getting braces on their teeth, having to take younger children with them to the movies, not having the latest fad, not being allowed by parents to "do what everyone else is doing"—all these things may strike terror of rejection into the heart of a socially sensitive upper elementary child. (They fail to realize that some of the most popular children have these same problems.)

IMITATION.   Many children's fears are "caught" from fearful peers and adults. In addition to copying the fears of others directly, children generalize these apprehensions to create new fears. Although some fears are needed to protect the child ("Keep your fingers away from the electric plug!" "Don't run into the street!"), children must learn to distinguish between necessary and unnecessary fears. Older children absorb the fears of their peers concerning any deviations from standards. They may fail to realize that fear is causing their friends to be so rigid in their conformity.

Facilitating Personality Growth

One of the caregiver's most important functions is that of helping to develop happy, healthy personalities in the children with whom they work. The following suggestions may help to facilitate this goal.

HELP EACH CHILD ACHIEVE SELF-ACCEPTANCE.

- Make each child aware of something that is "especially nice" about herself (bright smile, helpfulness, kindness).

Positive self-feelings develop as children interact in a warm and accepting environment   (*Source: Courtesy, National Science Teachers Association*)

- Help each child realize that both boys and girls can do a wide variety of interesting activities.
- Stress the accomplishments and contributions of all ethnic groups. (Watch for current heroes, since children are more interested in the present than the past.)
- Provide many developmental materials and experiences so that each child can achieve some success each day and thus feel capable.

HELP THE CHILD OVERCOME NEGATIVE TENDENCIES.
- Set up daily routines to lessen the anxiety of unexpected happenings.
- Let the child help plan procedures to be followed in unpleasant situations (when lost, at the doctor's office, when meeting new friends).
- Use children's stories, role playing, and discussions to help the child explore her fears. (Understanding, not ridicule, alleviates fears.)

INVOLVER 8

The interview is a valuable technique for becoming more knowledgeable about children's self-concepts. In this involver you will compare the child's perception of herself with her opinion of what her peers and caregivers think of her.

Procedure. Select a target child and take a full-length Polaroid picture of her. In three separate sessions (to avoid repetitious chaining of comments), ask the child to finish the sentences you start. In the first interview, show the picture and ask the child to tell you what she thinks about herself. In the second interview, show the picture and ask the child to finish the sentences by saying what another child in this group would say about her. In the third interview, show the picture and ask the child to finish the sentences by saying what the teacher would say about her. At the close of each session, be sure to smile and to thank and pat the child.

COMPLETION STATEMENTS:

1. "I think I'm good at . . ."
2. "I worry about . . ."
3. "When something is hard for me to do, I . . ."
4. "I'm not happy when . . ."
5. "When I work on things . . ."
6. "I'm afraid when . . ."
7. "It's very funny when . . ."

THINKING IT OVER

- Review the findings related to emotional development and compare them with the results of your interviews.
- Repeat the interview by showing the picture to another child in the group and by asking the same questions about the target child. Compare the answers. How accurate were the target child's self-perceptions when compared with the opinions of a peer?

HELP EACH CHILD TO DEVELOP A HAPPY ATTITUDE TOWARD DAILY LIVING.

- Teach a wide variety of coping skills such as planning work, having patience, and being optimistic that something good will happen each day.
- Foster industry by scaling each child's tasks to her ability level.
- Teach the child to laugh (by example, please).

Summary

- Personality refers to all the relatively enduring qualities the individual displays under a variety of circumstances.

- Factors that contribute to a person's psychological uniqueness include inborn temperament, physical appearance, sexual identity, ethnic affiliation, birth order, and early experience. Some of the qualities that are present at birth and remain consistent throughout childhood are activity level, rhythm, distractability, approach/withdrawal, adaptability, attention span, intensity of reaction, threshold of responsiveness, and quality of mood. Both self-acceptance and social responses from others are affected by physical appearance. Sexual identity does not come automatically with birth. It involves recognition of sex differences and sex roles, development of a preference for one's biologically assigned role, and adoption of that role. Research has dispelled many myths concerning sex differences in potential. The effects of ethnic affiliation on the personality are impacted by a host of other sociological, economic, and personal factors. Birth order often entails differences in treatment from family members which, in turn, affects personality characteristics. Both the emotional responses and the experiential activities provided by early caregivers interact with inborn characteristics to provide a foundation for the development of the personality.
- Four elements that are important in the process of becoming are self-confidence, coping ability, industry, and humor. After a person recognizes herself as a separate person (self-awareness), she develops beliefs about who she is and what she can do (self-concept). The positive or negative feelings about this perception (self-esteem) determine the degree of self-confidence. What we believe about ourselves will most likely be closely related to the appraisals others have mirrored to us. The ability to cope successfully with life's problems is based on the belief that our success depends on our own efforts and not on fate. This faith gives rise to the initiative needed to accomplish the problem solving. Whereas initiative gets things started, industry completes them. If tasks are realistically related to ability level, if self-confidence has been built through previous successes, and if preparation for the present task has been adequate, the child usually will be industrious. A sense of humor is also helpful, since it releases fear and anxiety, shows mastery of concepts, reassures children that the world is orderly, and makes children a pleasure both to themselves and to others.
- Negative roadblocks include tension, stress, anxiety, frustration, and fear. Tension, or the "tied in knots" syndrome, is characteristic of certain ages at which children are having to make major adjustments. It is also often related to self concerns, home conditions, and school experiences. Anxiety, or a vague feeling of uneasiness, may be caused by suppression of major goals, painful experiences, difficult decision making, or misunderstandings about cause and effect. When children have difficulty in succeeding or gaining control in a situation, frustration may result.

Withdrawal, whining, and aggression are some of the means used by children to express this emotion. Like other negative emotions, fear may result from unpleasant experiences, state of helplessness, limited knowledge of the environment, misunderstandings of cause and effect, and direct imitation.
- Caregivers help orchestrate the personality development of children. They encourage young people to like and accept both themselves and others. They help relieve negative emotions by increasing children's understanding of the world around them. Finally, through planning for success, they help move children from uncertainty to self-confidence and enthusiastic participation in life's activities.

Selected Readings

BAVELAS, J. B. *Personality: Current Theory and Research.* Monterrey, CA: Brooks/Cole, 1978.
: This work includes a comprehensive but easily read treatment of eleven different theories of personality. Included are both a summary of each theory and a research analysis of its status. The author designates the works of Freud, Allport, Cattell, Sheldon, Murray, Rogers, and Kelley as individual personality theories and the contributions of Lewin, Dollard Miller, Skinner, and Sandura as social personality theories.

Child Development.
: This journal contains current studies related to all areas of child development.

HUMPHREY, J. H. (ed.) *Stress in Childhood.* New York: AMS Press, 1984.
: This is a particularly useful resource book. Part I describes factors related to stress in childhood, and Part II contains materials related to analyzing stress and helping the child deal with it.

MCGHEE, P. E. *Humor: Its Origin and Development.* San Francisco: Freeman, 1979.
: In this well-written book, many facets of humor are explored. The author includes such topics as types of humor, its developmental sequence in childhood, individual differences in response to humor, and uses of humor for personal growth and socialization.

MORRIS, R. J., AND KRATOCHWILL, T. R. *Treating Children's Fears and Phobias.* New York: Pergamon Press, 1983.
: This highly readable book includes many points of view, is heavily based in research, and outlines many concrete behavior techniques for dealing with children's fears.

PLOMIN, R., AND DEFRIES, J. C. *Origins of Individual Differences in Infancy.* New York: Academic Press, 1985.
: This book contains comprehensive discussions concerning the effects of genetic endowment on cognition, language, personality and temperament,

physical/motor development, and behavioral problems. Interactions between heredity and environment are stressed.

Staub, E. (ed.). *Personality: Basic Aspects and Current Research.* Englewood Cliffs, NJ: Prentice-Hall, 1980.
In this collection, each author writes in his or her own area of special expertise. The result is a very comprehensive description of many aspects of personality development and an account of the research on which these assumptions are based.

CHAPTER 9

Social Development

CHAPTER OUTLINE

    From "I" to "We": Foundations of Socialization
        Forming Attachments
        From Dependency to Autonomy
        Modeling and Identification
    Agents of Socialization
        Parents
        Siblings
        Peers
        Television
    Social Pluses and Minuses
        Developmental Sequence of Prosocial Behavior
        Antisocial Behavior
    Summary
    Selected Readings

One balmy afternoon, two preschoolers were playing in the park. A Catholic Sister, who had brought a small group of her charges to the area, approached the pair. One child flew in fright to her caregiver and reported between pants, "When that thing with the covers on her head came and sat down by us, I ran." The caregiver noted in amusement that the other child was now seated on a park bench craning her little neck to look up under the mantle for the Sister's hair.

How can we account for the differences in social behavior between these two young children? Why are early attachments so important, and how are they formed? In what way is early dependency related to later independence (autonomy)? Who is likely to become the child's model, and why? How do early interactions between the child and his "significant others" (family, age-mates, and caregivers) help him to progress from "I" as the center of the universe to a concern for the welfare of "we"? What special impact does television have on the child's socialization? Which factors facilitate friendly positive interactions with others and which contribute to troubled socialization as evidenced by jealousy and aggression? These are some of the questions we explore in this chapter.

From "I" to "WE": Foundations of Socialization

During the first few months of life, the newborn begins to register his impressions of the world in which he has landed. He notices whether it is warm and friendly or cold and hostile, whether his needs are promptly and cheerfully met or neglected and ignored. Erikson (1963) believes

SOCIAL DEVELOPMENT

these early interactions lay the foundations for later socialization. Nurturant early attachments, age-appropriate levels of dependency, and well-socialized models are key factors in the development of a child who likes people and enjoys their company.

Forming Attachments

Attachments are not inborn characteristics, but are enduring emotional bonds that result from interactions between the infant and his caregivers. At birth, the child possesses a variety of signaling powers such as gazing, visual tracking, crying, and cooing (Ainsworth et al., 1978). The infant actively uses these powers to reach out to his environment and to prolong contact with the people in it. Forming attachments is not a one-sided

Early interactions form the foundation for attachments.
(*Source:* © *1988 Tom Kelly*)

proposition; both the child and the caregiver must be responsive to signals from the other and initiate mutually enjoyable exchanges. Contrary to popular opinion, the mother is not always the primary object of the infant's attachment. The child's social network also includes father, grandparents, adult caregivers, and children with whom the infant is in frequent contact (Fogel & Melson, 1986). The child may form warm, satisfying emotional ties with any or all of these persons.

Several factors have been found to be related to the formation of attachments (Rutter, 1972, pp. 17–22; Lamb et al., 1985):

> The child needs to maintain contact with the same person over an extended period of time so that each can learn to satisfy the other's needs.
>
> As many as three or four caregivers may be included in the child's daily network without diminishing his ability to attach, provided the child has one person with whom he can relate on a long-term basis.
>
> The attachment will be stronger if responses are quick and dependable than if they are slow or haphazard.
>
> Strong attachments will be formed with anyone who is present during times of stress and anxiety. For this reason, children often become attached even to abusive caregivers.
>
> Strength of attachment is not based on the particular activity the child and caregiver do together but rather on whether it is mutually enjoyable.
>
> The quality, intensity, and enjoyment of the interaction, not the actual amount of time spent together determines the extent of attachment.

Just as some conditions facilitate the forming of attachments, so are others detrimental to the process. A baby's excessive crying, resistance to cuddling, ill health, or inability to sleep through the night are often mentioned as characteristics that may incline a caregiver toward rejecting the infant. Differences in personality, as discussed in Chapter 8, also may be a pivotal factor in poor attachments.

Knowing what behaviors to expect as typical of an infant and becoming familiar with a particular child's unique characteristics are both very helpful in establishing a relationship with a new baby. Dr. Barry Brazelton, an eminent child-care authority, designed a measure for this purpose (Brazelton, 1984). Although the babies in the experimental and control groups were not significantly different at one week of age, the infants whose parents used the Brazelton instrument to become better acquainted with them were significantly more alert and more positively rated by their parents than were the children whose parents had no guide for fostering interaction and the formation of attachments. More research involving the use of various instruments and procedures should be conducted to determine which means are most effective.

SOCIAL DEVELOPMENT

These early interactions between children and the significant people in their worlds is of crucial importance. They color the child's attitudes, expectations, hopes, and fears. These early encounters are likely to exert great influence on whether the child moves toward people, away from people, or against people as he grows older.

From Dependency to Autonomy

Because of the premium our culture places on independence, caregivers are often confused as to which dependent and independent behaviors are desirable at given ages. Many people also fail to recognize that satisfying dependency needs is a necessary prerequisite to later independent (autonomous) behavior. Initially the child has many physical and emotional needs that must be met by others. Some behaviors that indicate a need for dependency include attention seeking, bids for reassurance ("Is this the way you want it?"), touching, hand holding, and following or standing near a valued person. If these dependency needs are respected and met promptly and cheerfully, the infant develops a sense of security. Gradually the child moves toward the ability and desire to "do it for myself." If the caregiver is patient in demonstrating various tasks, helpful in guiding the child to select activities that he is likely to be able to perform at a given age, positive and supportive in helping the child correct his mistakes, and lavish with praise for jobs well done, then the youngster can forge ahead toward independence. There should never be a sharp line between dependence and independence; much guided practice should precede any requirement for independent action.

Modeling and Identification

Modeling is copying the behavior of another person. Five-year-old Susie is dabbing her mouth with lipstick, Terry is trying to walk with the swaggering gait of his older teen-aged brother, and Demeris is shaking her finger in the cat's face and speaking in a stern tone. Each is imitating a behavior that to that child seems important. Some children, like Susie, copy things they feel will make them more physically attractive. Others, like Terry, imitate the antics of their peers in the hope of being "one of the crowd." Demeris's confrontation with the cat illustrates the child's need for power; she wants to straighten out someone else just as "big people" have "bossed" her.

The following questions are frequently raised: "How can such a good child come from such a bad home?" "How can such a troubled child come from such good parents?" These queries can be answered in part by considering the selective way in which the child chooses his models.

Children repeat many interactions that they have seen and "try on" new behaviors. (*Source: © 1988 Tom Kelly*)

He does not copy every action he sees. He carefully decides what is important to him. He then copies the behaviors of those persons in his environment who have these characteristics or possessions. Anyone in his lifespace is a potential model. Some of the factors that determine whether a particular person actually becomes a model to the youngster are (Winch and Gordon, 1974):

- The amount of interaction available between the model and the child
- The amount of affection extended by the model with whom the child wishes to identify

SOCIAL DEVELOPMENT

- The match or mismatch of temperament between the child and the model
- The attitude of other influential people toward the model
- The consistency or clarity of behavior demonstrated by the model
- The ability of the child to imitate the model's characteristics
- The extent to which modeling of that person will meet the immediate needs of the child

The sense of pride that a child feels as a result of identification with an accomplished parent is reflected in the pioneer child's report, "WE killed a bear; Paw shot it." For more information on modeling, see Chapter 10.

Since a young child has difficulty understanding cause and effect, he may copy a behavior that is typical of his model but in no way related to his goal. For example, little boys who want positions of group leadership often imitate the pushing, shoving, and sharp words of their peer idols without realizing that the chosen models actually have group status because they have well-developed skills and talents, not because they are aggressive. Children who slavishly copy the dress and mannerisms of the "popular kids" apparently believe such imitations will confer favor. After the child has "tried out" many behaviors, some actions will seem to warrant permanent repetition—he will make them a regular part of his everyday life. We call this permanent modeling *identification*.

BOX 9.1

Children Learn What They Live

If a child lives with criticism
He learns to condemn.
If a child lives with hostility
He learns to fight.
If a child lives with ridicule
He learns to be shy.
If a child lives with shame
He learns to feel guilty.
If a child lives with tolerance
He learns to be patient.
If a child lives with encouragement
He learns confidence.
If a child lives with praise
He learns to appreciate.
If a child lives with fairness
He learns justice.
If a child lives with security
He learns to have faith.
If a child lives with approval
He learns to like himself.
If a child lives with acceptance and friendship
He learns to find love in the world.

SOURCE. Nolte, Dorothy Law. "Children Learn What They Live." Original publisher unknown.

The child frequently selects one individual and, for an extended period of time, identifies and models a number of his characteristics. Then, as the young person's needs and interests change, he will add other models, often keeping some established behaviors he finds particularly useful. By the time an individual reaches maturity, his social habits are a complex combination of the actions of many people with whom he has identified along the way. The effects of modeling and identification on a child's socialization are very well stated in "Children Learn What They Live."

Agents of Socialization

The term "significant others" is often used to denote all those people in the child's environment who contribute significantly to his social development. Parents play a key role, since they frequently are the child's first caregivers. Brothers and sisters may be friends or foes (depending on which day it is), and other children outside the family introduce new ideas and ways of doing things (some of which mother feels she can do without nicely). Television "friends" expand the child's vistas even further. All of these are important agents of socialization.

Parents

Parents have always been considered to be primary socializers of children. Erikson (1963) has discussed in great detail the contribution parents make to young children during the first four stages of psychosocial development. In this section we consider the parents' role in the establishment of the positive aspects of Erikson's stages. Later in the chapter we investigate the role of parents and significant others in socialization problems.

TRUST VERSUS MISTRUST. As we have previously discussed in the section on foundations of socialization, the forming of attachments is a crucial first step in the establishment of trust (Brazelton, 1983; Lamb et al., 1985). The quality of mothering during infancy helps the young child develop a psychological mechanism called *introjection*. This mechanism is a sort of mental set or habit that causes a person to "feel or act as if outer goodness has become an inner certainty" (Erikson, 1963, p. 249). This mothering quality is not based primarily on quantity of food or demonstrations of affection. It involves three basic factors concerning the infant's social environment: (1) the sensitivity of a caring human being to the child's individual needs, (2) the dependable sameness with which someone meets needs promptly and regularly, and (3) the infant's eventual realization that whatever is given is good for him and whatever is denied is withheld for his best interest. If the infant internalizes these three concepts, he is likely to trust the people in his environment and view the world as a nurturant place.

AUTONOMY VERSUS SHAME AND DOUBT. With the physical maturity of the typical two-year-old comes the glorious power to control two basic processes—holding in and letting go. Regardless of the opinions or wishes of the caregiver, the child always makes the ultimate decision as to when and where to eliminate. The parent can make this a cooperative learning experience or an all-out war. If the parent respects the individual time schedule of the child and waits to begin training until the child is physically able to hold and is psychologically ready to enjoy cooperating, the child will feel reassured that he is loved, accepted, and capable of making wise decisions. He will feel that his autonomy and control are not threatened by his caregivers. If his being autonomous is not respected, he is likely to come to view the significant others in his life as threatening and domineering. If such feelings develop, he may continue throughout life to use anything over which he has control for manipulation of others. (If he can have his way, he will share; if not, he will withhold.) The parents' greatest responsibility during this stage is to gradually guide the child toward self-control and cooperative behavior without crushing his self-esteem.

INITIATIVE VERSUS GUILT. The preschooler is a bundle of energy—constantly planning new projects, starting things, tackling new situations. No stage is better for learning quickly and eagerly. The crisis of this stage is not being able to finish what is started. Parents must help provide a balance. The child's exuberance must not be squelched, but he must be guided into projects at which he can succeed in order not to feel guilty of poor performance.

At this stage the child will feel intense rivalry toward older, more capable siblings and peers (Fogel & Melson, 1986). Parents should never hold an older child up as an ideal model; equality of accomplishment with an older child is an unattainable and very frustrating goal. Time and attention should be devoted to helping preschoolers set developmentally realistic standards. Parents can also foster good feelings among children by getting older siblings to help younger children, to show an interest in what they are doing, and to refrain from teasing and laughing (even good-naturedly) at the things the younger child has attempted.

INDUSTRY VERSUS INFERIORITY. During the elementary school years, the child focuses on becoming a good worker. The first important parental

(Source: DENNIS THE MENACE® used by permission of Hank Ketcham and © by North America Syndicate)

responsibility is to be sure the child is "ready" for school. Such readiness should include a variety of experiences in the community, communication proficiency from parent-child verbal interactions, hands-on opportunities to use many kinds of materials, and opportunities to socialize with other children. Once the child is in school, the parents should realize that all teaching responsibilities cannot be delegated to the classroom; developing industry is a child-parent-teacher team effort (Hartup and Rubin, 1986). The complexity of modern society makes instruction of the child more difficult. In times past, a farmer knew exactly how to teach his son to farm. Now the parent must develop the widest possible range of skills in the child, since no one can predict what he will want to do or need to become.

SOCIAL DEVELOPMENT

NURTURANT FATHERS. For years, the concept of father as breadwinner was so entrenched in public thinking that many people questioned whether a male could meet the social and emotional needs of small children. In my first year of college teaching, one metropolitan school system refused to assign male student teachers below the fourth grade because of this bias. Since fathers can be much more responsive than many people in our culture have realized, I should like to include data related specifically to the father's role in the child's development.

In a series of studies based on observations of two-to-four-day-old infants in a hospital setting, no significant differences in nurturing behaviors by mothers or fathers were noted when either was alone with the infant (Parke, 1975). When the three (mother, father, and infant) were together, however, three interesting interactions were noted: (1) The father held the baby twice as often as the mother did, (2) he vocalized and touched more than she did, and (3) he appeared to affect the mother's behavior. When the father was present, the mother smiled at and explored with

A father can be seen as a helper and a friend. (*Source: Courtesy, National Science Teachers Association*)

the baby more. This interaction of mother, father, and child together may have profound implications for some of the problems noted in single parenting.

The father frequently loses contact with the infant shortly after birth. He is often not given the benefit of the training in child care offered by the hospital and misses the repeated parent-infant contacts that occur between mother and child during these first few days of the baby's life. The problem may be compounded by the fact that the infant is often asleep both when the father goes to work and when he returns.

By the preschool years, children have more contact with the father at mealtime, in conversation, and through play activities. In a study by Lynn (1974), children between the ages of two and four were asked which parent they wanted to play games with. Both boys and girls in the two- and three-year-old range showed a significant preference for playing with their fathers rather than their mothers. In the four-year-old sample, however, the boys picked their fathers and the girls preferred their mothers by a three-to-one margin. Findings of extensive research have indicated that children with attentive fathers felt better about themselves and related more effectively with other children (Lamb, 1986). What happens to the child's socialization if the father is absent from the home? Children who had no father in the home rated significantly lower on social characteristics such as leadership and responsibility (Rapoport, 1985).

Not all one-parent families are father-absent. As the male's potential for nurturant behavior has received more credibility, more men are becoming involved in a new phenomenon—single fathering. Single fathers are now rearing an ever-increasing number of minor children. They attempt to manage supervision by trying to synchronize home responsibilities with their work schedules. In order to fulfill these dual responsibilities, they seek help from a variety of sources. One study indicated that 73 percent of the fathers interviewed solicited child-rearing advice from a network of both nonrelated friends and kin (Riley and Cochran, 1985). They often hire outside help to work in the home, but they are plagued with high turnover of personnel. Most men eventually enroll the child in some out-of-home child-care facility. With or without help, these fathers cook, shop, clean, and care for the children without feeling threatened concerning their masculinity.

The changing role of the father in child care is summarized in the following statement (Rapoport and Rapoport, 1980, pp. 56, 57):

> The era of the hands-off father is ending and it's high time. . . . Forget all those stereotypes of the fumbling father trying to look after the baby. Father knows more than he thinks . . . and letting that relationship thrive and grow in a warm and loving environment can only enhance it.

BOX 9.2
Suggestions for Rearing Socially Responsible Children

1. The adult should model behavior that is both socially responsible and self-assertive, especially if the adult is seen as powerful by the child and as eager to use resources over which he has control for the child's benefit.
2. Firm enforcement policies and reinforcement techniques should be used to reward socially responsible behavior, and both demands and prohibitions should be accompanied by reasons consistent with principles the parent practices as well as preaches.
3. Parental attitudes should be nonrejecting, and neither overprotective nor passive. The parent's interest in the child should be continuous and intense, but approval should be conditional on the child's behavior.
4. The parent should make high demands for achievement and for conformity with the parent's policy. This should be accompanied by receptiveness to the child's needs and a willingness to offer the child numerous opportunities to use independent judgment.
5. The parent should provide the child with a complex and stimulating environment that offers challenge and excitement as well as security and rest—where creativity as well as conformity is encouraged.

SOURCE. Summarized from Baumrind, D., 1981, p. 177.

The impact of parents as agents of socialization is tremendous. The parenting styles employed, the individual interactions with the children by both mother and father, the degree to which the parents can cooperate with each other, and the attention they give to the physical, emotional, and mental needs of their children will set the tone for their children's future social relations with others. Box 9.2 summarizes suggestions made by Baumrind (1981), a noted specialist in parenting research, concerning the rearing of socially responsible children.

Siblings

Brothers and sisters are often the first playmates a young child meets (Dunn, 1985). At times they are a source of great comfort; on other days the harried mother may wonder if they are going to be able to live on the same planet! The intensity of possible negative feelings was well-illustrated by the little boy who told the following story about Joseph to his Sunday school teacher, "And Joseph's brothers took his new coat away from him, and they put him in a deep hole, and then they sold him at their next garage sale."

Growing up as a sibling has some definite advantages. Nadelman and Begin (1982) point out that through sibling status the child learns to cooperate, practices negotiation skills, competes and establishes territoriality, and learns that others have needs and feelings that are important to them, too.

Many speculations have been made concerning the effects of birth order on socialization. The findings from cross-cultural studies indicate that older children in a family are more helpful and nurturant (Dunn, 1985). Conversely, younger children, through having to negotiate with the often bossy "olders," develop more social skills and are apt to be better liked (Rubin, 1980). The plight of the middle child is expressed by the child who wailed, "Anytime Mother wants anything done, she either says, 'This is a good job for my two big boys' or 'This is a job for my two little boys,' and I get stuck either way!"

Is the "lonely only" a myth or a valid concept? Although findings vary, much research indicates that the more siblings a child has, the less he is likely to seek interaction with his peers (Falbo, 1982). Since the only child has no siblings, he is often more outgoing than is a child who can depend on brother/sister companionship. Many factors other than singleness affect the only child's development. These include single or dual parentship, attitudes of the parent toward the child, and socialization opportunities—the entire context in which the child develops.

Just how much "company" are siblings to each other? Although some are very close, many are hostile during childhood and grow apart in adulthood. Several factors affect the social closeness or distance between siblings. First is sibling rivalry, "the intense competition that children feel because of their need to share the love and attention of their parents" (Rubin, 1980, p. 122). If the parents show partiality, hold one child up as an example to another, or interact with one more because of age, sex, or similar interest, this rivalry is more apt to be lasting. Another factor is the personality of the individual child. Sometimes opposites attract and the quiet child is fascinated by the exuberance of the noisy, lively one; or the less-talented child glows with pride in the accomplishments of an especially talented brother or sister. More often, however, even siblings are drawn to the people with whom they "have more in common." In larger families, it is interesting to note clusters of friendships among siblings based on these likenesses. A final factor in the degree of companionship among siblings is the attitude of our society. Both children and adults generally associate with people in their same age range. This limited cross-age interaction may help account for a lack of closeness between siblings

SOCIAL DEVELOPMENT

of widely different ages. The following is a poignant but typical story (Lipstein, 1980, pp. 122–123):

> I was the older sister and the way I remember it, there was not much reinforcement given to my younger sister when she wanted to be included in my play with my same-age friends. When she was included, it was usually out of obligation to my younger sister. She was put in the role of "baby" or "tag-along," and my friends and I must have made her feel fairly unwanted and out of place. Because of my role as "the big one," I felt it was an imposition to have to accommodate my younger sister in my play relationships. As I look back, I remember feeling that it was just more "natural" for children to be playing with other children their own age.

The child who, as he grows older, has brothers and sisters who are also good friends is very fortunate.

Peers

Once the child begins to associate outside the family, other children (peers) become very important. What characteristics do children seek in friends? Why are peers important? Of what value are cross-age associations? These questions highlight important issues in peer relations.

WHICH CHILDREN ARE DESIRED AS FRIENDS? Unfortunately, making friends does not come automatically for all children. Much research has been devoted to determining which characteristics tend to help young children to be desired and which may contribute to their being rejected. The following is a summary of descriptions given by young children for liking other age-mates (Elkind and Weiner, 1978; Hayes, 1978; and Rubin, 1980):

Reasons for Liking	*Reasons for Disliking*
• Is helpful, friendly, cooperative, and adaptable	• Is aggressive or hostile
• Is able to give desired kinds of attention and approval	• Takes things away from others
	• Violates rules or does forbidden activities
• Shares common interests	• Disrupts ongoing activities
• Possesses desirable material goods	• Ridicules peers
• Lives close by	• Ignores others or withdraws
• Is able to manage conflicts successfully	• Exhibits behavior that is considered by the group as "strange"

Many children need help in developing "entry skills." The following scenario occurs all too frequently:

> A "Hi" may be ignored, a "What ya doing?" responded to with "We're making cupcakes and you're not," and a direct "Can I play?" answered with an equally direct "No." (Rubin, 1980, p. 49)

Repeated social failures can easily result in withdrawal and shyness. Direct intervention in the form of social skills training is needed. Young children should be encouraged to notice strategies used by other children in various social encounters. Parents and other child-care workers should plan informal training sessions in which specific social skills needed by the child are demonstrated. These observations should be accompanied by many opportunities to practice these selected skills and to receive warm, supportive feedback with suggestions for improvement (Rubin, 1980).

WHY ARE FRIENDS IMPORTANT? Successful peer relations fulfill many important needs in the life of a child (Leventhal and Dawson, 1984; Oden et al., 1984). Knowing that other children like him gives the youngster

Everybody needs a special friend.

SOCIAL DEVELOPMENT

feelings of pride, worthiness, and self-esteem. Approval by friends also provides the child with a sense of identity and status—who he is and his place of importance in the group. Friends become a source of standards and values that supplements and eventually may even exceed the importance of principles held by the child's family. Friends also provide valuable training opportunities. Not only may a child learn how to relate to others by watching his peers, he may also learn how to perform many basic life skills through peer tutelage.

Elementary children consider "best friends" a necessity. In kindergarten, these pairings may last only a few weeks. In upper elementary grades, friendships may be made that will last for years. Close friends contribute to the child's ability to become sensitive to the feelings of others and to put himself in another person's place. Through friendship, the child develops the desire to please someone else, to be helpful, to cooperate, and to be a dependable source of companionship and nurturance.

As children reach upper elementary levels, peers become even more important. They serve as models, counselors, critics, and companions. Through these social exchanges, children learn the important "give and take" skills they will use throughout life. Successful peers are those who learn the social skills necessary for group participation without sacrificing their own individuality.

How Do Cross-Age Friendships Affect Social Behavior? When older children play with younger ones, they often display leadership abilities, whereas their younger companions engage in more receptive roles (Dunn, 1985). This situation can be mutually beneficial. The older child gains experience in directing activities and, in some cases, enjoys greater status among younger children than he does with friends his own age. Even older children with limited social skills often blossom when placed with younger children. The advantages to the younger child are twofold: (1) He can often understand the explanations of another child more easily than those of an adult, and (2) he is more likely to want to imitate the actions and ideas of a child who is slightly older more than he is than those of an age-mate or a younger child.

Another important fact to consider is that older children are not always more advanced than younger ones. Cross-age friendships provide the faster younger child with an opportunity to practice skills not yet acquired by age-mates and gives the slower older child less critical company as he engages in levels of performance and in activities that might be considered "babyish" by his peers (Rubin, 1980).

Many benefits may be accrued from cross-age pairings, but the child's friendships should not be limited to those of other ages. Playing with older or younger children does not necessarily increase play or friendships

> ### INVOLVER 9
>
> It is interesting to note the similarities and differences in children's understandings of friendship. Select two preschool children of approximately the same age and two upper elementary children of approximately the same age.
>
> Talk or play with each child separately for a length of time sufficient to establish trust and rapport. Then ask the child the following questions:
>
> 1. Who are your best friends?
> 2. What is a friend?
> 3. What does a good friend do?
> 4. What do the people you don't like do?
> 5. How do you get new friends?
>
> *THINKING IT OVER*
>
> How does the child's concept of friendship compare with your feelings about your friends? What differences did you note among these children at each age level concerning what they like and dislike about their peers? What do you think may have caused these differences? Which ideas expressed about making friends do you think would actually work and which would not? What suggestions would you make and what activities would you plan to help children become more effective in making friends?

with age-mates. For maximum social development, the child needs the opportunity to interact with older, younger, and same-age peers.

Involver 9 is designed to help you see friendships from a child's point of view. The comments made by the children you interview should give you some additional insights into the importance of friends in the development of the child.

Television

Although parents, siblings, and peers are primary socializers, the impact of television and its effects on behavior must not be overlooked. Home television sets in the United States are turned on an average of six and one-half hours a day, and the preschoolers in these households watch approximately thirty hours per week (Moody, 1980). The startling truth is that many children spend more time having their ideas and values shaped by television than they do receiving social guidance from any other single source. "By the time the child finishes high school, he will have spent 18,000 hours with the TV curriculum and only 12,000 hours

SOCIAL DEVELOPMENT

The effects of television on social behavior are widely studied and debated. (*Source: United States Department of Health and Human Services*)

with the school curriculum" (Moody, 1980, p. 5). How does a child use observational learning to internalize these visual images, and what good and bad effects may they have on his behavior?

INTERNALIZING TELEVISION CONTENT. Liebert and Poulos (1976) discuss the following three stages of observational learning and their application to televiewing: exposure, acquisition, and acceptance. *Exposure* occurs when the child views the act. Merely seeing a behavior does not guarantee that the child will repeat it. He may not be paying attention. He may not be interested and thus not store the act effectively in his memory. The act may remind him of something else and set up a train of daydreaming that takes him away for a time from the action being portrayed. A host of factors might keep the exposure from registering. Many times, however, the child does make a mental note of the action, and acquisition takes place.

Two primary reasons for acquisition are value and novelty. When the child views something he feels will be useful to him, he mentally files it away for future reference. The novelty of seeing something exciting but out of the usual realm of the child's experience also frequently results in acquisition. When a distraught mother was trying to determine how her locked car had been stolen during the ten minutes she was in the grocery store, her six- and seven-year-olds explained to her in detail how the heist could be accomplished in three minutes flat. They had seen this on television. Liebert and his colleagues (1982) report that viewing an exciting action one time is sufficient for many children to be able to repeat the sequence in detail even six or eight months later. Fortunately, not all ideas acquired through observational learning result in acceptance and thus become a guide for the child's own behavior. *Acceptance,* for the child, is based partly on previous training and partly on the current situation. The child who has been taught consideration for others and has witnessed nurturant behavior in his life setting is more apt to copy the prosocial rather than the violent actions he sees on television.

TELEVISION AND BEHAVIOR. Because of the vast amount of time children spend televiewing, many research studies have been conducted to determine the media's effects. (See Selected Readings at the end of the chapter for a sampling.) Major areas of concern relate to aggressive behavior, emotional and social well-being, physical development, and learning ability.

Authorities disagree as to whether watching violence on television promotes aggressive behavior (Barlow & Hill, 1985; Winn, 1985). Some feel that viewing violence is cathartic—that it provides a harmless release of the tensions within the individual. The social learning theorists, however, disagree. They believe that repeated exposure to violence may make one less sensitive to the suffering of others and may cause the individual to "think violent" in times of stress. The findings of several research studies support the thesis that violence breeds violence (Liebert and Poulos, 1976). In one study, playground observation showed significantly higher levels of aggression for a group of young children who were shown violent cartoons when compared with another group who were shown prosocial stories. In another investigation, preschoolers who had watched aggressive cartoons for eleven days showed an increase of 200–300 percent in active, overt aggression such as kicking and hitting.

Bandura's classic studies indicate that children are less apt to copy aggression if the violent model is punished (Bandura et al., 1961). Unfortunately, stories on television are so complex that young children are able to correctly identify the motive and the consequence only about one-third of the time (Liebert and Poulos, 1976). The level of aggression the youngsters in these studies exhibited was directly related to the amount of violence they had just witnessed rather than to motivation or consequence.

Although many studies have centered on possible encouragement of aggression, investigators also have been concerned about the effects of television on other emotional and social aspects of children's behavior (Berry and Mitchell-Kernan, 1982; Durkin, 1985). The high level of excitement in the programming may produce intense fears in children, particularly in situations that relate to real-life fears or those in which a favorite character is threatened. Stereotypes, especially those dealing with the roles of women and minority persons, may cause children to feel that some groups are inferior in ability, judgment, and initiative (Berry and Mitchell-Kernan, 1982; Durkin, 1985). Even the hard-sell advertisement of toys may lower the self-concept of children whose families cannot afford these items.

Television is not without its emotional and social pluses, however. Research has indicated that regular watching of shows especially designed for teaching children is related to increases in self-control, cooperation, and positive feelings toward minority groups (Cullingford, 1984).

TELEVISION AND PHYSICAL FUNCTIONING. A second important area of television research deals with the physical effects of excessive televiewing. The young child's eyes are not sufficiently mature for sustained use on small figures or small movements, and prolonged television watching may result in eyestrain (Winn, 1985). Impaired eye movement ability also may occur. This condition will cause the child to have difficulty with such a task as following lines of print in reading (Moody, 1980). In addition to these lags in small-muscle development, the child who sits in front of the television by the hour may miss the exercise necessary for the acquisition of large-muscle strength and coordination.

TELEVISION AND LEARNING. A third group of television studies have been designed to answer the question, "Is television a help or a hindrance in learning?" (Liebert et al., 1982; Winn, 1985). On the positive side, television has vastly enlarged the child's world. People, places, and things far removed from everyday experience have been vividly pictured to televiewers. Constant exposure to language also has enabled children from verbally limited backgrounds to enlarge their vocabularies. Several problems may exist, however (Moody, 1980). Since children's concepts are developed by doing, lack of first-hand experience with materials may retard understanding in some areas. The fact that young children tend to center on one aspect of a situation and ignore other factors may cause excessive television watchers to tune out either sound or vision and miss much of what is presented in the classroom at school. Television addicts also are apt to have difficulties in reading. Television comprises short segments, fast action, and quick cuts. By contrast, reading requires continuous thought and line-by-line attention. Conditioning to the excitement of television may make reading seem dull to some children. The National Association of Librarians has noted a significant drop in the circulation of children's books which may be due, in part, to the time spent watching television (Moody, 1980).

Whether television is a positive or a negative influence in the lives of children depends partly on which programs they watch and partly on the variety of other activities in which they are encouraged to participate. Television is not a substitute for conscientious caregiving and must not become the ultimate babysitter!

Social Pluses and Minuses

Developmental Sequence of Prosocial Behavior

The socially competent child is one who can relate effectively and diplomatically with both peers and adults. Many studies have traced the early beginnings of these behaviors in children (Holte, 1984; Eisenberg, 1985). These investigations may be grouped into the following categories: recognizing the feelings of others, seeing another person's point of view, sharing, distinguishing between intentional and accidental actions, and determining fairness (equity).

RECOGNIZING THE FEELINGS OF OTHERS. At first the child is egocentric; the fact that others do not share his feelings never occurs to him. Nursery workers have reapeatedly reported that during the first weeks of life, infants cry "in chorus" because they can't distinguish between themselves and others. They merely imitate the sights and sounds that surround them. The beginnings of sympathetic feelings for another person usually occur between twelve and eighteen months. During observation of children's play, the following examples of this budding empathy were noted (Hoffman, 1976).

> An eleven-month-old saw another child fall and begin to cry. She looked on the verge of tears herself, then sought comfort by popping her thumb in her mouth and burying her face against her mother. Another toddler took her own mother to soothe a crying child even though the child's mother was present.

Research indicates that several conditions facilitate the development of prosocial feelings for others (Zahn-Waxler et al., 1979). Among these are

- kind and thoughtful caregiving to the child
- parental model of sharing, helping, and comforting others
- explanations concerning the feelings of others whether they are happy or hurt
- use of discipline that concentrates on how the injured party feels when the child has aggressed

SEEING ANOTHER PERSON'S POINT OF VIEW. Sharing, generosity, patience, and many other prosocial attributes are based on the ability to put oneself in another person's place and to see the world from that point of view. In one research study, children between the ages of three and seven years were involved in a variety of tasks related to anticipating the desires of others (e.g., choosing a gift for a family member, selecting a game that a friend would enjoy). Even at age three, such perceptions were found to be possible (Zahn-Waxler et al., 1977).

Case Study 9 illustrates the ability of young children to place themselves in another child's position and to use this information to guide their behavior.

Case Study 9

Marcy, aged 20 months, was in the playroom of her home and wanted a toy with which her sister Sara was playing. She asked Sara for it, but Sara refused vehemently. Marcy then paused, as if reflecting on what to do, and then began rocking Sara's favorite rocking horse (which Sara never allowed anyone to touch), yelling "Nice horsey! Nice horsey!" and keeping her eyes on Sara all the time. Sara came running angrily, whereupon Marcy immediately ran around Sara directly to the toy and grabbed it. One can infer from her actions that she had deliberately lured her sister away from the toy. Though not yet 2 years of age, Marcy was capable of being aware of another person's inner states that were different from her own. . . .

Michael was struggling with his friend, Paul, over a toy. Paul started to cry. Michael appeared concerned and let go of the toy so that Paul could have it, but Paul kept crying. Michael paused, then gave his teddy bear to Paul, but the crying continued. Michael paused again, then ran to the next room, returned with Paul's security blanket, and offered it to Paul, who then stopped crying. Several aspects of this incident deserve comment. First, it does seem clear that Michael assumed that his own teddy, which often comforts him, would also comfort his friend. Second, its failure to do this served as corrective feedback, which led Michael to consider alternatives. . . . Michael, as young as he was, could somehow reason by analogy that Paul would be comforted by something that he loved in the same way that Michael loved his own teddy.

SOURCE. Hoffman, Excerpt from pp. 129–130 in *Moral Development and Behavior: Theory, Research, and Social Issues* by Thomas Lickona, copyright © 1976 by Holt, Rinehart and Winston, Inc., reprinted by permission of the publisher.

The ability to understand and assume the role of another person is a very important social skill. This role-taking ability will not occur automatically, however. Children must have many opportunities to interact with others and to see and hear their responses.

SHARING.   Sharing has been noted in children as young as two years of age. Sharing increases as children are able to note the needs of others and consider these desires in their decision making. Several factors appear to be related to children's inclination to share (Eisenberg-Berg et al., 1979). First, sex appears to be a factor; boys are more likely to assert themselves and exploit others by dividing things unequally in favor of themselves. Second, sharing with one's friends and withholding from the "outgroup" occurs as early as children are able to categorize their peers into friends and nonfriends. Third, helping is often seen by the child as a way to "get close" to some high-status peer. Finally, adult pressure encourages sharing. The older child who does not share may feel so guilty that he may construct elaborate explanations to justify his behavior.

A distinction should be recognized between taking turns and sharing one's own possessions. A young child can be taught that he must "take turns" in a group care setting where the play materials belong to the establishment. (The caregiver can explain repeatedly that these things belong to all of the children and that each has the right to some playtime with the object of his choice.) Another point to be considered is that children whose autonomy is respected may find it easier to share. "Let Tammy know when you are finished with the truck" lets Mary control

Sharing can be learned through observation in a warm and caring atmosphere.

the situation and often results in a shorter turn. This behavior represents actual sharing rather than merely obedience to the adult who says, "Your five minutes are up. Give the truck to Tammy."

By contrast, three- and four-year-olds may not be maturationally ready to share personal possessions. Each child needs to feel the pride and responsibility of ownership. First his own right to enjoy his possessions and to be assured that they will not be destroyed must be respected. Then, as he moves from egocentrism to socialization and group membership, he may be willing to share his own things with others.

As children grow older, their focus changes from "what I want" to "what others think of my behavior." In a study with fourth graders, the children were given two opportunities to share (Holte, 1984). After the first occasion, those who shared were praised and their behavior was discussed very positively. When the next opportunity for sharing occurred, the incidence of sharing increased significantly.

DISTINGUISHING BETWEEN INTENTIONAL AND ACCIDENTAL ACTIONS. To determine the difference between what is done "on purpose" (intentionally) and what is done accidentally, the child must know three things (Smith, 1976): (1) Does the actor know what effect will be produced? (A baby doesn't know that the lamp will fall if the cord is pulled.) (2) Is there a motive? (The child doesn't like the classmate on whose picture he "accidentally" spilled water.) (3) Is the act one that can be either accidental or intentional, or is it one that is always intentional? (You may accidentally bump into people or drop something on them, but can you accidentally punch or bite them?) Inability to understand intention has caused many young children to spank a door that closed suddenly or scold the blocks that fell on them. Between the ages of three and five years, children begin to consider motive in evaluating the right or wrong of an act (Berndt and Berndt, 1975). By five or six years of age, many children can determine whether an injury has resulted from an intentional or accidental act (Berndt and Berndt, 1975; Smith, 1976). Until about age seven or eight, however, children still consider what was done as more important than why it happened (Lyon, 1978). Children must have many opportunities to learn rules if they are to correctly label "good" and "bad" behaviors and accurately evaluate motives and intentions (Berndt and Berndt, 1975). Children who are punished in terms of damage level rather than with reference to motive and those who do not understand the reason for a punishment will have trouble learning the importance of intent in determining right and wrong.

DETERMINING FAIRNESS (EQUITY). Initially, the young child believes that what is fair is what he can take or what he can get by with. When he is frustrated or when he perceives that he has been wronged by another person, the preschooler is apt to react aggressively even if the injury (real or imagined) was not intentional on the part of the other individual.

What is fair also includes concepts concerning rewards. Three- and four-year-olds will reward all work equally even when it varies greatly in quality. This practice may result from the child's modeling of supportive caregivers, who rightly reward the child's efforts even if the results aren't perfect. Another possible explanation is that the child's inability to understand intent prevents him from evaluating differences in effort among children. At about school age, the policy of responding to aggression eye-for-eye and the necessity of returning favors in like kind becomes translated into common practice (Berndt, 1979).

The upper elementary child, when compared with the preschooler, thinks of fairness more in terms of exchange (doing for each other) than in considering only one's own personal pleasure. Eisenberg (1985) found a progressive shift in thinking from self to others and an increasing interest in humaneness for all involved in a situation. Further information concerning stages of moral development and feelings of responsibility toward others is included in Chapter 10.

Antisocial Behavior

ERIKSON'S THEORY AND NEGATIVE SOCIALIZATION. Erikson (1963) described a developmental sequence of negative characteristics that he believes will affect the individual personality and give rise to socialization difficulties. These psychosocial characteristics are mistrust, shame and doubt, guilt, and inferiority. As you can see, each of these is the opposite of a prosocial behavior discussed earlier in this chapter.

MISTRUST. The child who establishes a tendency for mistrust during the first year of life often shows a continuing pattern of depression and withdrawal from others. This apparent "coldness" toward others is generally based on an individual's subconscious distress at not being able to trust himself and others to establish satisfying mutual relations. Mistrust is characteristic of the child whose early environment is not sufficiently stable for the development of trust.

SHAME AND DOUBT. If the child is ashamed of his level of ability and doubts his capacity to exert control in his life, he may develop many antisocial tendencies including sneakiness, rebelliousness, stubborness, and devious preciseness.

Shame and doubt, which may occur in the two-year-old, often cause the child to desire to be invisible. Have you ever heard a child say "Don't

SOCIAL DEVELOPMENT 283

"HOLD IT, JOEY! Boys don't hit girls!"

"We'll get another GIRL to do it."

(Source: DENNIS THE MENACE® used by permission of Hank Ketcham and © by North America Syndicate)

look," when he's not sure he's going to succeed at something? Repeated instances of shame concerning his ability to control circumstances and do for himself may lead to *sneakiness*—"I don't have to feel ashamed if you don't see me goof up." Conversely, constant adult interference in tasks he is trying to master may lead to outright *rebellion*—"I will do it myself even if I make a terrible mess!"

Shame and doubt may also lead to *stubborness* in the child's relations with others. If the child has serious doubts about his ability to assert some autonomy (control), he may fail to develop a balanced attitude toward authority. He won't know when to stand up for his rights and when to accept the ideas of others without losing his sense of self-direction.

Another outgrowth of shame and doubt is *jealousy*. This intense yearning for something someone else has is frequently accompanied by the child's conviction that the possessor is not nearly as deserving of this "desired something" as he is and that he should "even the score" by taking it or by making the other person so miserable he can't enjoy it. Jealousy is exhibited by a plethora of symptoms.

Finally, the child who doubts his own autonomy may feel that he constantly needs to assert himself. One way to do this is to be deviously precise, to do exactly what is required but not what is obviously wanted. "You said to wipe my feet before coming in; you didn't say anything about a muddy dog." This type of comment may indicate a desire for "safe defiance"—the child asserts autonomy while avoiding punishment by being technically correct.

If the child is provided with many constructive opportunities to develop and exercise autonomy, shame and doubt are not likely to predominate in his personality.

GUILT. Guilt is a feeling of disappointment with oneself for not living up to the ideals or standards one has set. It is likely to begin when the child is three to five years of age. Sometimes this pain is turned inward, and the individual makes himself sick. Often, however, relief from frustration with oneself is sought by attacking others. One such behavior is *rivalry*—a fierce competition with other children. One danger of this behavior is that the child may lose sight of the joy of doing, because he can be happy only when he is best. (He may eventually be afraid to try some activities in which he is interested because he is afraid he can't "outdo"

BOX 9.3

Forms of Aggression

- *Direct physical aggression:* Hitting, throwing, withholding objects, pulling, taking things away from a child (i.e., the use of force toward another person).
- *Direct verbal aggression:* Name calling, jeering, threatening, uttering angry talk, derogating status, commanding vigorously.
- *Injury to objects:* Displaced or non-person-directed aggression, such as smashing constructions or spilling paints.
- *Mischief:* Mischievous disobedience, such as throwing cups in the wrong place or spilling sand.
- *Verbal disapproval of behavior:* "That's bad!"
- *Tattling:* Calling attention to another child's behavior.

SOURCE. Summarized from Sears et al., 1965, p. 117.

...ated to feelings of inadequacy is also expressed ...ward others. The material in Box 9.3 describes the ...ression may take.

A diffe... antisocial response to feelings of guilt is *self-righteous-*... The chil... o feels guilty about "wrong" things he secretly wants ...do will constantly monitor the behavior of others and piously point ...t their every flaw. Tattling is a frequent symptom of this basic problem. ...e child who is encouraged to initiate positive, age-appropriate tasks ...d social exchanges is less likely to develop the frustrations on which ...onic feelings of guilt can be based.

FERIORITY. The child who feels inferior may choose *isolation* from ...ers as a protection against ridicule. This may become a lifelong pattern ... behavior, and the individual may have trouble "coming out of his ...ll" at a later date. Some children, instead of withdrawing, choose *slavish* *formity*. They feel so inferior about their own ideas or products that ...y constantly copy others. Overconformity is a dangerous practice for ...o reasons. First, the child may ultimately be compelled to copy antisocial, ...rmful, or illegal activities if those are the behaviors exhibited by valued ...dels. Second, and even more tragic, the child may lose all the wonderful ...lividualism of which he is capable.

The caregiver should recognize these antisocial behaviors as a cry for ...p rather than behavior deserving punishment. Each child should be ...ured that he is equally loved and has unique abilities that make him ...special value. He should be encouraged to "talk out" these unhappy ...lings and experience warmth and reassurance rather than rejection.

Socialization is one of the most crucial aspects of a child's development. ...children move from self-centeredness to affiliation with other individu-..., they need warmth, direction, consistent standards, and many opportu-...ies for social interaction.

y

...ttachments, which serve as the foundation of all future socialization, ...re based on the warmth and promptness with which the young child's ...eeds are met.

...he child is born in a state of dependency and gradually moves toward ...ndependence as his caregivers provide opportunities for him to meet ...uccess at a variety of carefully scaled activities, as he is given necessary ...ut not overwhelming assistance, and as he is praised and rewarded ...or his efforts.

- Modeling involves copying the behaviors of someone who possesses a desired trait, object, or position. Identification is a relatively permanent form of modeling whereby the child emulates the mannerisms of an individual who represents a number of valued characteristics.
- Significant agents of the child's socialization include parents, siblings, peers, and television personalities.
- Parents are key figures in helping the child achieve trust instead of mistrust, autonomy instead of shame and doubt, initiative instead of guilt, and industry instead of inferiority. They accomplish this through the attitudes they model, the opportunities they facilitate, and the interpersonal relations they encourage.
- The findings of many recent studies have demonstrated that fathers are fully capable of nurturing and rearing children. In addition to playing an increasing role in child care in intact families, single fathering is an increasing phenomenon.
- Siblings are apt to be the first "other children" the young child meets, and they provide experience in cooperation, negotiation, competition, and awareness of the feelings of others. Birth order and number of siblings appear to impact the socialization of all of the children involved.
- Peer friendships are of great value to children as sources of both self-esteem and instruction. Children most desired as friends tend to be helpful, cooperative, and attentive. They are likely to share common interests, have desired possessions, and live close by. Youngsters who are rejected are apt to be aggressive, to violate rules, to ridicule, to ignore or withdraw from peers, or simply "to act weird." Since repeated social failure will hamper development, caregivers should provide children with training in specific socialization skills. Cross-age friendships are important for several reasons: (1) Older children can teach younger ones, (2) less mature older children can repeat needed skills while playing with younger peers without risking loss of status, and (3) younger children who are advanced for their age can tackle new skills while working with older peers.
- Since children are spending an increasing amount of time watching television, this media has become a major socializer. Children absorb televised information through a three-stage process: exposure (viewing the act), acquisition (making a mental note of the act if it appears to be novel or of value to the viewer), and acceptance (repeating the act if it does not violate previous training and/or if circumstances in the present situation seem to warrant it). Some of the negative effects of television include encouragement of violence, exposure to new fears, promotion of stereotypes, discontentment at not being able to purchase an endless variety of new toys, lags in large- and small-muscle

development if televiewing is substituted for exercise, lack of firsthand experience with materials, and reduced interest in reading. On the positive side, television introduces children to people, places, and things they would otherwise never see. The language bombardment can result in increased vocabularies for some children. Finally, many shows contain elements that promote empathy and understanding in relations with others.
- The development of prosocial behavior is based on recognizing the feelings of others, seeing another person's point of view, distinguishing between intentional and accidental behavior, and understanding equity.
- Troubled socialization in young children is often expressed through jealousy and aggression.

Selected Readings

DUNN, J. *Brothers & Sisters.* Cambridge, MA: Harvard University Press, 1985.
   This is a very readable account of sibling relationships including conflict, play, growth of social understandings, and family variables such as birth order, age gap, and sex.

HARTUP, W. W. and RUBIN, Z. (Eds.). *Relationships and Development.* Hillsdale, NJ: Erlbaum, 1986.
   The selections in this book summarize recent research findings concerning social relationships, both in and out of the family, that occur throughout childhood and into the adult years.

Journal of Marriage and Family.
   This periodical offers a continuing source of current information concerning the family.

LAMB, M. E. *The Father's Role: Applied Perspectives.* New York: Wiley, 1986.
   This comprehensive book details the many issues related to fathering. Included are the changing roles of fathers, custody relationships, family therapy, employment-related situations, education, and social services.

LAMB, M. E.; THOMPSON, R. A.; GARDNER, W. and CONNELL, J. P. *Infant-Mother Attachment.* Hillsdale, NJ: Erlbaum, 1985.
   This book includes a comprehensive investigation of the historical development of the attachment theory, individual differences in attachment, and cross-cultural research related to the issue.

PERLMUTTER, M. (Ed.) *Parent-Child Interaction and Parent-Child Relations in Child Development* (Vol. 17).
   This book contains discussion of such socialization issues as imitation and attachment in infancy, day care, maternal employment, multigeneralizational bonds, and family interaction.

Television and Children. Since there are a number of current books related to this important topic, the following list is provided:

BARLOW, G., and HILL, A. (eds.) *Video Violence and Children.* London: Hodder and Stoughton, 1985.
This volume documents and discusses televised violence and aggression.

BERRY G. L., and MITCHELL-KERNAN, C. *Television and the Socialization of the Minority Child.* New York: Academic Press, 1982.
This very readable book analyzes issues related to television and identity, cognition, and socialization of minority children (separate chapters on Asian-, Native-, Hispanic-, and black American children).

DURKIN, K. *Television, Sex Roles, and Children.* Philadelphia: Open University Press, 1985.
Durkin explores the relationships among these factors.

LIEBERT, R. M.; SPRAFKIN, J. N.; and DAVIDSON, E. S. *The Early Window* (2nd ed.). New York: Pergamon Press, 1982.
This book contains a very thorough account of investigations/legislation concerning television and its possible effects on children.

CHAPTER 10

Moral Development and Behavior Management

CHAPTER OUTLINE

    Moral Behavior: Major Components
    Factors That Affect Moral Behavior
    How Moral Behavior Develops
            Through Psychoanalytic Processes
            Through Social Learning
            Through Cognitive Understanding
    Strategies For Developing Moral Behavior
        Sanctions By Reciprocity
        Modeling
        Direct Adult Management
        Behavior Modification through Reinforcement
        Empathy Development
        Self-direction through Verbalization
Summary
Selected Readings

Johnathan was the holy terror of the first grade group. He beat up other children soundly and regularly. My student teacher was quite interested in Transactional Analysis (TA), a system based on helping people improve their interactions with others. Using the book *TA for Tots* (Freed, 1980), Brenda explained that the good things we do for others can be called "warm fuzzies" (they make people feel warm and happy, like stroking a fuzzy kitten). Bad actions are designated as "cold pricklies," since no one enjoys touching things that are either cold or prickly. The children were delighted and spent the next two days in a euphoria of warm fuzzies. (Almost anything new will work for two days.) On the third day, pandemonium broke loose as Johnathan lashed out against one of his peers. After breaking up the fight, Brenda inquired, "Don't you remember what we said about warm fuzzies?" "Uh huh," Johnathan nodded. "And were those warm fuzzies you were giving Josh?" she continued. "Nope," Johnathan answered. Then he explained matter-of-factly, "I saw Josh give cold pricklies to three other children this morning, so I gave them back to him all at once." From that day until Brenda finished her student teaching, Johnathan carefully watched the behavior of the other children and judiciously administered cold pricklies with solemn satisfaction. No amount of "Johnathan, that's naughty!" would deter him. He firmly believed that he was performing a valuable and needed service.

From this example you can see that a child's concept of "being good" may be quite different from that of an adult. What moral behaviors can we reasonably expect from young children? What factors positively correlate with the development of prosocial conduct? How does moral behavior develop, and what strategies may be used by caregivers to guide this process? The answer to these questions will be discussed in this chapter.

Moral Behavior: Major Components

Morality is not a simple matter. If it were, there would be more moral behavior, both by children and by adults. Several prosocial components, however, are involved in our moral decisions: (1) empathy—the ability to feel and understand another person's point of view, (2) altruism—a willingness to help others even if personal sacrifice is involved, (3) self-control—resistance to temptation and the determination to do what is believed to be right, and (4) moral judgment—what is believed to be right or wrong based on one's maturity and experience. These four components interact to produce moral conduct, what the individual actually does in a given situation. The child needs to develop a state of moral autonomy in which she is fair to both herself and others. Autonomy refers to being self-governed. A morally autonomous individual is one who behaves responsibly independent of outside authority, punishment/reward systems, or the probability of being caught. Throughout the chapter, we consider how each of these factors develops and interacts with the others to implement moral behavior.

Factors That Affect Moral Behavior

Since moral behavior is so important in human relations, many studies have been conducted to determine what factors are correlated with such conduct. The following list has been compiled from the findings of several research studies (Burton, 1976; Lickona, 1976; Mischel and Mischel, 1976; Higbee, 1979; Hoffman, 1984):

Group affiliation
- We are apt to behave like the people with whom we associate. We either choose the group because we admire that behavior, copy their actions because we have become accustomed to seeing things done in that manner, or eventually leave the group.

Values
- From our group affiliations, we develop a system of values through which we screen our immediate desires to determine what behavior we will accept from ourselves.

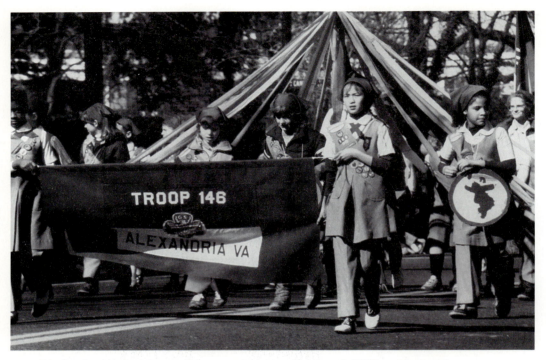

Moral behavior is often learned by association. (*Source: © William Moriarty/Envision*)

Lack of discrepancy	• If all the groups to which we belong behave morally, we are more likely to develop moral conduct. If a discrepancy of standards exists, we are apt to follow the rules that best suit our immediate purposes.
Family responsibility	• Concern for others is strongly affected by active involvement in family welfare if tasks are assigned and work is monitored.
Consequences	• Actions for which we have been punished or for which we have observed others punished are less tempting.
Risk	• The likelihood of being caught or the knowledge that we are being watched

MORAL DEVELOPMENT AND BEHAVIOR MANAGEMENT

                                                         increases conformity to moral standards.

Incentive
- If the gain for dishonest behavior is great and the risk of detection is slight, we are more tempted to cheat.

Delay of gratification
- People who have difficulty resisting temptation tend to be more "now" oriented and can't wait for future rewards. They also have difficuty talking firmly to themselves when tempted. (More details about self-instruction through verbalization are included later in this chapter.)

Distraction
- Wrongdoing often occurs after we get distracted from the activity in which we are supposed to be involved.

Strength of competing motives
- Often the desire both to do good and to do wrong are present at the same time. Behavior depends on which motive is stronger.

IQ
- Although correlations between IQ and morality do exist, the findings are misleading. The brighter individual might be better able to estimate the chances of getting caught, and increased competence may lessen the need to be dishonest.

Age
- With age, the child can better understand both the reasons for rules and the feelings of other persons. Although this increased understanding enables a child to be more moral, it does not guarantee prosocial behavior. (Age-related changes in moral concepts and behavior are discussed in greater detail later in the chapter.)

Self-concept
- People who are secure and self-confident can "dare to be different," if necessary, in order to follow their own conscience. They also can muster the courage to admit error.

BOX 10.1

Derek's Moral Dilemma

Mental Reasoning	Influencing Factor
"Girls are pests! My three sisters pick on me, too."	Social learning through past experience.
"Other boys in this class hit girls."	Imitation.
"I'll be scolded or spanked if I hit her."	Response shaped by reinforcement.
"I shouldn't hit people, because hitting hurts. And besides, it's not nice to hit girls."	Cognitive understanding.
"I'm so mad, I'm going to slug her anyway!" WHAM!	Feeling at the moment.

How do these factors interact to determine the "morality of the moment"? Suppose Derek is in a dispute with Sarah in the block center. Derek's conversation with himself might look something like the behavior analysis in Box 10.1.

How Moral Behavior Develops

Several explanations have been offered as to how moral behaviors develop. The psychoanalytic view stresses the importance of the superego and its subcomponents of conscience and ego-ideal. Social learning theory emphasizes the processes of modeling and operant conditioning. The cognitive-developmental approach identifies the role of advanced ability in understanding in determining moral decisions. Each of these points of view has generated a great deal of research.

Moral Development through Psychoanalytic Processes

Psychoanalytic theorists state that beliefs about what is right and wrong are based on the values and ideas of the particular culture in which a person is reared. These tenets are transmitted to the child through identification with the parents' position of power and through the caregivers' use of rewards and punishments. Freud named this internal moral control the superego and described it as having two parts. The conscience is the subsystem that contains the knowledge of the acts that deserve to be punished. The ego-ideal comprises notions about deeds that should be rewarded. When the youngster accepts these ideas and internalizes them into her personality, her conscience will make her feel bad when she does things she believes are wrong, and her ego-ideal will make her feel happy when she does what she perceives as right.

One of my graduate students was interested in discovering what children understood about this concept we call conscience. She reported that the following definitions were given in response to a news reporter's question, "What do you think a conscience is?":

BOX 10.2

"What Is Conscience?"

"It tells you right from wrong whether you like it or not."

"When you're good, you don't even know you have it, but when you're bad, it hurts."

"It sounds like some kind of Chinese food to me."

"It's this spot in your heart that burns if you're not good."

"I've heard that word before. Seems like it's that man from China who knows all the answers."

"That's what makes you feel sorry for people. Some people don't have one. They must just stuff it in their back pocket."

"I don't know. That's something too big for me, but I think it has something to do with feeling bad about kicking girls or little dogs."

"Your conscience tells you when you're doing something wrong. It's kind of like having a teacher in your brain."

"It's like on "Emergency"—when people are unconscience, they're sick."

"Sometimes, when you want to do something, your conscience will tell you 'No!' Like when I want to beat up my brother. My conscience has saved him a lot of times."

SOURCE. Escabar, 1976.

From the explanations in Box 10.2, you can see that children incorporate social values into their thinking at an early age, often do right when they would rather do wrong, feel guilty for transgressions, and recognize that not all people have uniform consciences. Conscience is not always a reliable guide to moral behavior, however. Pascal observed, "Evil is never done so thoroughly or so well as when it is done with a good conscience" (Lickona, 1976).

Moral Development through Social Learning

Social learning, as you will recall from Chapter 6, is based on the idea that behavior is learned by observing the activities of others in our environment. Two important aspects of observational learning are modeling and use of reinforcement.

MODELING. The child does not model all the things she sees others do. How important she perceives the model to be, her interest in the behavior or activity being demonstrated, the values she has been taught, the opinions of her peers, and physical factors such as energy level and skill development all help to determine whether the child will imitate.

Research has also indicated that a child is more likely to imitate if previous imitations have been rewarded. Suppose Julie joins in every disruption that occurs in her classroom. Her teacher tries to reason with her but sees no improvement in her behavior. When she tries to discuss the situation with Julie's mother, the lady laughingly replies in front of the child, "Oh, Julie's a real pill; we just can't do anything with her." Julie glows with satisfaction. The mother's remark (probably often repeated

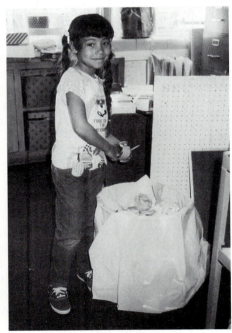

This girl models social responsibility by emptying the pencil sharpener.

MORAL DEVELOPMENT AND BEHAVIOR MANAGEMENT

in Julie's presence) is rewarding to her. It convinces her that she is smarter and stronger than any of the adults with whom she is dealing. No matter which techniques the teacher uses, the child is apt to continue to misbehave because she is constantly being rewarded by her mother's remarks and attitudes. After the habit of imitating certain behaviors has become established, similar or related behaviors will be copied (generalized imitation) even if no reinforcement occurs in a given situation.

USE OF REINFORCEMENT. Our responses are constantly modified by the consequences (rewards or punishments) that occur as a result of our actions. Four conditions are often used to encourage desired behavior:

1. *Positive reinforcement:* rewarding the child immediately with something she especially likes as soon as she exhibits the desired behavior. Concrete reinforcers (tokens, candy, money) and social reinforcers (smiles, pats, praise) have been found to be effective in conditioning.
2. *Negative reinforcement:* terminating a situation that is unpleasant to the child (e.g., getting to rejoin the group after being removed for misbehavior, getting to watch television again after being "grounded").
3. *Nonreinforcement:* ignoring the child; denying attention and other rewards while undesirable behavior is being exhibited.
4. *Punishments:* doing something unpleasant to the child in response to misbehavior (e.g., spanking, scolding, removing from the group).

How effective is the use of positive and negative reinforcement in controlling undesirable behavior? Essa (1978) reported two studies designed to combine reinforcement techniques in an effort to decrease aggressive/disruptive behaviors in three- and four-year-olds. When a child was removed from the group, he was placed in a "time-out" chair. (He remained in the room and could see the other children but was not permitted to participate in class activities.) When desirable behavior was exhibited, he was rewarded with social reinforcers. Since the results, analyzed in Box 10.3, show a drastic drop in undesirable behavior, such combinations of reinforcement techniques may be particularly effective in working with some children.

Since punishment is so frequently used with children, how does it work, and why is it sometimes not effective? Punishment is doing something the child does not like in response to some undesired behavior she has evidenced. Frequently used punishments are spanking, sharp words, and confinement (being sent to her room, being deprived of favored activities). Caregivers should remember that each interaction with a child is a learning

BOX 10.3

Decreasing Aggressive/Disruptive Behaviors

Child's Age	Initial Problem	Treatment	Result
3 years	Screaming, throwing things, whining	During structured class activities, removal from the group was used (not during unstructured periods); teacher attention was given only during good behavior.	Disruptive behavior decreased from 54% to 2%; later behavior checks indicated permanent change.
4½ years	Extreme aggression and temper tantrums	Removal from group was given for physical aggression only (verbal aggression ignored); teacher attention was given for cooperative behavior.	Physical aggression dropped from 15 episodes per day to 3, which usually stopped with warning.

SOURCE. Essa, 1978.

experience. Constant hitting may teach hostility and aggression. Ridicule may demolish self-esteem. By contrast, being deprived of something good is often a natural consequence of misbehavior. The child will discover repeatedly that breaking rules, failing to do scheduled assignments, or being rude to other people carries unwanted penalties.

Kamii (1985) suggests three negative outcomes of punishment. First, the child may develop the habit of evaluating the risks involved in misbehavior. She may become adept at deciding how likely she is to be caught. She also may carefully consider whether the punishment will be as awful as the deed is pleasant. The second problem that may be created is the tendency toward blind conformity. The child may follow negative as well as positive behaviors in order to "do as told" or "be one of the crowd." A third possible problem is revolt. The child may conform for a time, build intense resentment toward authority in general, and later become irresponsible or even delinquent.

As an alternative to punishment, Kamii suggests sharing ideas and helping in problem situations. When a child's misdeed has created trouble, a comment such as "I'll help you, and together we'll fix it" can teach responsible behavior.

Some people view the effects of punishment differently. Eysenck (1976) contends that conscience is actually a conditioned reflex based on the use of punishment.

MORAL DEVELOPMENT AND BEHAVIOR MANAGEMENT

(Source: DENNIS THE MENACE® used by permission of Hank Ketcham and © by North America Syndicate)

- The child says or does something that she has been told is wrong.
- This act is immediately followed by a sharp remark or a swat.
- This punishment is painful, either physically or psychologically, and this act plus the punishment becomes paired in the child's mind.
- Eventually the act or even the thought of it makes the child so uneasy that she refrains from doing the forbidden thing.

Research has indicated that the results of punishment are often unpredictable. Constant use of punishment, rather than techniques for positive self-direction, often results in feelings of hostility and loss of self-esteem. With reference to undesirable behavior, some of the reasons punishment may not achieve desired aims are

- The child may be using "bad" behavior to get attention. (Even getting hit may not be as painful as being ignored.)
- The child may have such a low opinion of herself that she expects to be punished daily.
- There may be a temperament difference between the child and the caregiver. The caregiver may be calm, quiet, and well-organized and the child, by nature, just the opposite.
- The caregiver may have said "Don't!" without indicating the desired behavior. The child's judgment in selecting behavior alternatives may be very immature.
- The overpunished child often feels hostile and unloved.
- The child's behavior may be normal for her age group even though it doesn't measure up to the caregiver's standards. Remember the bumpersticker, "DON'T GIVE UP! GOD ISN'T THROUGH WITH ME YET!"

Although punishment is sometimes effective for some children, a perceptive caregiver will note which methods are effective under which circumstances and learn to use a wide variety of behavioral guides.

A number of techniques for using modeling and reinforcement for the improvement of behavior have been devised. Several of these are discussed later in this chapter in the section titled "Strategies for Developing Moral Behavior."

Moral Development through Cognitive Understanding

Many psychologists have explored the effects of age and experience on moral decision making. How do these two factors affect the child's understanding of rules, her ability to be concerned about another person's point of view (empathy), and her inclination to share and/or help others (altruism)? Will this increased comprehension guarantee moral behavior? To find the answers, let's examine the theories of Piaget and Kohlberg and the research studies these have generated.

PIAGET. The Swiss psychologist Jean Piaget wanted to know how a child came to understand a social order based on rules and justice (Piaget, 1948; Rich and DeVitis, 1985). He was particularly concerned with the child's answers to three basic questions: "Where do rules come from, and can they change?" "Is there a difference between cause and intention?" and "Which punishments are appropriate and under what circumstances?" He used games and story pairs to see how children's answers to these questions changed with age.

MORAL DEVELOPMENT AND BEHAVIOR MANAGEMENT

While involving groups of children in playing marbles, he inquired as to where the rules for the game came from, whether they could be changed, and what would happen to the child who disobeyed a rule. Piaget found the following contrast between the concepts of younger and older children (Piaget, 1948):

Children's Perceptions of Rules

Younger Children	Older Children
• Rules are absolute and must remain unchanged.	• Rules are made by people (not by some ultimate authority), and they can be changed by mutual consent.
• Right is following the rules exactly, regardless of its effects on others.	• Right is justice (fair and equal treatment for all). Some rules need to be modified or scaled to be fair (letting the younger child stand closer to the goal in a game of ring toss).

To investigate the child's understanding of *intent* as a basis for judging good and bad behavior, Piaget used story pairs. In one of these, a child broke one cup while climbing in the cupboard to reach a forbidden crock of jam, and another child broke fifteen cups when he swung a door open and accidentally hit a tray behind it. Younger children center only on the damage done, and they judge the child who broke fifteen cups as naughtier. Older children focus on intent and consider the child engaged in the forbidden act as more guilty.

Piaget checked children's attitudes toward punishment by describing a wrongdoing and asking the child what punishment would be appropriate (Piaget, 1948):

Children's Views of Punishment

Younger Children	Older Children
• Punishment will be immediate from God or some other key person.	• Punishment usually occurs as a natural consequence of wrongdoing. (Getting one's feet wet causes colds.)
• If a person is hurt while committing a wrong, he is being punished from the act itself.	• The fact that punishment does not occur immediately does not mean that what was done was acceptable.
• Punishment should be severe. (Penalties that young children advocate are often more harsh than a caregiver would consider using.)	• Punishment should be related to the wrongdoing (sitting in the "time-out" chair if the child didn't choose to keep her hands off other children).

Piaget discussed the use of "sanctions by reciprocity" as an alternative to punishment (Piaget, 1948; Kamii, 1985). In a punishment, there is no connection between the misdeed and the result. In a sanction by reciprocity, there is a direct relationship. For instance, depriving a child of lunch dessert because she disrupted morning story time is punishment. By contrast, removing a child from the group until she decides she can listen without interrupting is a sanction by reciprocity.

KOHLBERG. After studying Piaget's stages of cognitive development, Kohlberg hypothesized that people also go through a stage sequence in the development of moral behavior. Progression through these stages results from experience, social interaction, feedback from others, and increased ability in reasoning. To check his theory, he conducted a twenty-year longitudinal study in which the subjects were interviewed at three-year intervals. An analysis of the stages he identified is found in Box 10.4.

There are no fixed ages at which people pass from one level to another, since judgment depends on quantity of experience and social interaction. Generally, preschoolers function in Stage 1, and seven- and eight-year-olds begin to enter Stage 2 (Reimer and Hersh, 1983). Some adolescents and many adolescent and adult criminal offenders never advance past

---

BOX 10.4

Kohlberg's Six Moral Stages

PRECONVENTIONAL LEVEL

- *Stage 1*: Emphasis on obedience and avoidance of punishment (outside control).
- *Stage 2*: "What's good for me" considered first; occasional consideration for rights as determined by the welfare of others.

CONVENTIONAL LEVEL

- *Stage 3*: Stress on behavior that pleases or helps others and meets their approval.
- *Stage 4*: Respect for law for its own sake independent of personal desires.

POSTCONVENTIONAL LEVEL

- *Stage 5*: Rights and standards supported by social consensus with the option to change the rules for public good.
- *Stage 6*: Being governed by self-chosen principles relating to justice and the dignity of man.

SOURCE. Kohlberg, 1984. Rich and Devitis, 1985.

this preconventional level of morality (Kohlberg, 1984). Reimer and Hersh (1983) believe that individuals must reach the concrete operational stage of thinking (see Chapter 6) before they can effectively put themselves in another's place, weigh the needs of others against desires of their own, and function consistently at the conventional level. It is at this Level 2 that most adolescents and adults operate; Kohlberg believes that relatively few people ever reach Level 3.

Kohlberg and his associates have now designed a standardized interview form to be used in research (Kohlberg, 1984). The interviews Kohlberg uses to identify the individual's level of moral understanding are based on responses to three story problems. Each story is used to check two of six major moral concepts. In each of these, the main character must make a difficult decision in which there is a conflict of interest or values between herself and others. The person being tested is asked what the main character should do and why. Moral development is indicated not only by the solutions proposed, but also by the reasons given for these decisions. Responses are analyzed in terms of six concepts (Kohlberg, 1984):

1. *Life:* how life is valued.
2. *Property rights and values:* how property is viewed and valued.
3. *Conscience:* what the individual believes is right and wrong.
4. *Punishment and justice:* what happens if the rules are not followed.
5. *Contract, trust, and justice in exchange:* ability to understand different point of view; the extent to which a person should do for others.
6. *Authority:* who is equal or unequal in authority; who is responsible for making and enforcing rules; whether rules can be changed and, if so, how.

Box 10.5 contains a brief summary of the first story used in the 1984 standardized test and scoring form and indicates the two issues checked.

BOX 10.5

Sample Kohlberg Story

FIRST STORY

Heinz's wife is dying of cancer. A local druggist has discovered a drug that might save her. He was charging ten times what the drug cost to make. After raising all the money he could, Heinz offers the druggist $2,000 with the promise to pay out the balance. The druggist refuses, and Heinz steals the drug. (Questions check value of life versus value of property.)

SOURCE. Adapted from Kohlberg, 1984, pp. 640–645.

Let's see how an older child's responses to this story might differ from a preschooler's views. An upper elementary child would probably recognize that life is more important than property, whereas the younger child would think a rule takes precedence over anything else. (Her egocentrism might even cause her to make a different judgment about the importance of a life depending on whether or not she liked a person.) The older child might question in his conscience whether stealing in this case would actually be wrong; the younger child would never consider whether circumstances make this action acceptable. In terms of fair exchange, the older child would feel that the druggist must share the blame, because he was being unreasonable. The preschooler is not able to analyze motive in making judgments. The upper elementary child might even question whether the druggist should have had the authority to withhold a life-sustaining measure. When punishment is to be considered, the older child would take many aspects of the situation into consideration. The younger one would likely "quote the rule" again and be satisfied that uniform punishment for a given crime is appropriate.

Preschool logic can be as amusing as it is complex. A four-year-old became a vegetarian since he decided it was wrong to kill animals. After hearing a story about Eskimos going on a seal hunt, he announced, "There is one kind of meat I would eat—Eskimo meat. It's bad to kill and eat animals so it's all right to eat Eskimos" (Papalia and Olds, 1982).

Kohlberg readily acknowledges that the ability to reason at a certain stage does not ensure that the individual will behave at that moral level. After reviewing many studies, he concludes that factors in an immediate situation are more likely to control a person's behavior than are the moral principles in which the individual says she believes (Reimer and Hersh, 1983).

Kohlberg's theory has generated much research. Some people question the notion that higher levels of morality should be assigned to what may be different cultural or religious values. Others question sex bias. Gilligan (1982) contends that since Kohlberg's original research sample comprises males only, it may not be valid for females. She believes that the morality taught to girls focuses on care and responsibility, whereas the concepts of right and wrong taught to boys are more oriented toward justice and fairness. Many research studies are now being conducted to investigate these ideas and challenges.

The methodology associated with Kohlberg's dilemmas is very adaptable for use in group discussions at the upper elementary level. Berndt (1984) has conducted a number of studies related to this group process. After students have used furnished dilemmas for a period of time, they are likely to begin to devise their own based on the concerns of their group.

MORAL DEVELOPMENT AND BEHAVIOR MANAGEMENT

INVOLVER 10

In your own words, tell a preschool child the following version of Little Red Riding Hood. Little Red Riding Hood's grandmother was sick, so she decided to take her a basket of good things to eat. As she walked through the woods to Grandmother's house, she met a wolf. After she told him she was going to Grandmother's, he ran ahead, chased Grandmother into a closet, dressed up like Grandmother, and waited in her bed. Tell the "big eyes, big ears, big teeth" part, and end with the hunter hearing Red Riding Hood's screams and chasing the wolf away. Now ask the following questions:

1. Why did Little Red Riding Hood want to visit grandmother? (Does the child understand empathy—that grandmother is sick and that attention makes her feel better—or does the child focus only on taking food to satisfy hunger?)
2. Why did the hunter come when he heard Red Riding Hood scream? (Does the child mention helping Red Riding Hood or focus on the excitement of chasing the wolf?)
3. Was the wolf a good person or a bad person? Why? (Note reasons given for judging his behavior.)
4. What should be done to the wolf when he is caught? (Remember Piaget's observations on punishment, and see if the younger child recommends a more drastic penalty than does the older child.)

THINKING IT OVER

- What evidences of empathy and helpfulness were included in the child's answers?
- What did the child tell you about her criteria for classifying people as good or bad?
- How did the child's answer concerning punishment compare with Piaget's observations?
- Retell the story to a child who is about three years older than your first subject. What differences in moral understanding did you note?

Such discussions are found to be positively related to improvement in moral behavior.

Strategies for Developing Moral Behavior

Techniques and activities designed to facilitate the development of moral behavior serve a variety of purposes. First, the child may be introduced to behavior possibilities that she has had no previous opportunity to learn.

Second, growth in the ability to analyze may help the child better understand and appreciate other people. Third, the moral structure provided by parents and caregivers may serve as a framework for the development of the child's own moral standards as she matures. Finally, the mastery of methods involving self-direction may enable the child to change undesirable, self-defeating behaviors. Although the types of strategies that might be effectively used for guiding moral development are endless, the following have been chosen for discussion in this chapter: sanctions by reciprocity, modeling, direct discipline, behavior modification through reinforcement, empathy development (role playing, magic circle, bibliotherapy), self-direction through verbalization, and group management techniques.

Sanctions by Reciprocity

As mentioned earlier in the discussion of Piaget's theories, sanctions by reciprocity stress directly relating adult responses to the nature of the child's misbehavior. The following four examples will illustrate this practice for you (Kamii, 1985, pp. 43, 44):

- *Exclusion from the group.* When a child's behavior disrupts a group activity, she should be removed from the group and told that she may return when she has decided to behave according to group standards.
- *Appeal to direct and material consequences of the act.* Remind the child that if she pushes and shoves, other children may not choose to play with her.
- *Depriving a child of the thing she has misused.* If the child chooses to knock over other children's constructions, she will not be allowed to play with these materials.
- *Restitution.* The child should be taught that if she breaks something, someone will help her to repair it. If she makes a mess, she must clean it up.

Modeling

Modeling is one of the most powerful techniques for affecting behavior, since the child may observe the actions of others during every waking moment. The child does not, however, copy or model all the things she sees others do. If you would like to become a more effective model, consider the following guidelines:

- Discover what characteristics and skills are important to the children with whom you work and become expert in some of these.

MORAL DEVELOPMENT AND BEHAVIOR MANAGEMENT

(*Source: Reprinted with special permission of Cowles Syndicate, Inc. © Bill Keane*)

- Take time to develop warm interactions with the children, since young people tend to model those to whom they are attached.
- Be consistent. Sameness gives children many opportunities to see what behavior is desired and also convinces them that the caregiver sincerely believes that this way is important.
- Don't expect immediate change. If the behavior is new, time may be needed to understand and develop necessary skills. Present undesirable habits may also be hard to change. (For use of modeling in development of physical skills, see Chapter 4.)

   Don't forget that as children get older, peers become an everincreasing source of models. Helping older children become actively involved in a variety of groups in which prosocial behavior is encouraged will help furnish a good supply of high-quality peer models. Such environmental supports have a measurable effect on the behavior of children (Fischer, 1983; Saltzstein, 1983).

Direct Adult Management

On many occasions the caregiver feels that direct adult management is necessary. To make behavior management a positive learning experience, several factors need to be considered. Some of these are the disposition of the caregiver, the disposition of the child, behavior surveillance, possible types of discipline, and special problems involving multiple caregivers.

DISPOSITION OF THE CAREGIVER. Most of us use the discipline methods that were used on us as children. Differences in our own personal temperaments also make it easier for some people to explain and reason whereas others command and swat. (Personality differences should not, however, be used as an excuse for abusive behavior.) Personal warmth is often effective in inducing cooperation and goodwill. This should be balanced, however, with firmness and conviction. It is hardly fair to expect a child to assume responsibility for running a household. Decision making that is appropriate for a teenager is beyond the capacity of a younger child. Rules should be present, fair, consistent, and thoroughly understood. Even the disorganized adult should make a special effort to maintain some reliable routines that can serve as guidelines for the young child in ordering her world and her relationships with others. In conflict situations, the knowledge that a caregiver will punish misbehavior is a deterrent to undesirable behavior (Higbee, 1979). The purpose of punishment, then, is not to inflict pain or embarrassment, but rather to emphasize that the caregiver sincerely believes such behavior will cause harm to the child or to others.

DISPOSITION OF THE CHILD. Anyone who has worked with more than one child knows that there are no two children alike. Ray may be very concerned with a stern look or a low, firm correction. Much stronger methods may be needed to get Shannon's attention. Discipline is a language that needs to be adjusted to the understanding of the individual child.

BEHAVIOR SURVEILLANCE. Many children have great difficulty in establishing acceptable behavior patterns because caregivers fail to observe and give consistent feedback. If Jeremy has a tantrum today and nobody notices, "pitches a fit" tomorrow and Mother thinks it's cute, and creates a ruckus the next day and the sitter paddles him, he's apt to be a little confused as to how people expect him to behave. He simply never knows which day he can get by with what! Research indicates that the probability of disobedience increases as time passes (Higbee, 1979). If the child sees she is being monitored, she will more likely continue to exhibit desirable behaviors than she will if she feels nobody notices whether or not she is complying. Being aware of what the child is doing and giving corrective feedback should be considered essential preventive discipline.

TYPES OF BEHAVIOR MANAGEMENT. When a child is being disciplined, the parent is modeling some type of behavior depending on the kind of discipline he or she selects to use. After extensive research, Hoffman (1970), identified three major types of discipline and their most likely effects on a child's behavior. These are summarized in Box 10.6.

The use of external control in power assertion discipline has three distinct disadvantages (Hoffman, 1976). First, the parent or caregiver will not always be present to guarantee compliance to the rules. Second, the person who is accustomed to being controlled by someone else may fall under the influence of an antisocial individual. Third, if rules are obeyed only to avoid punishment and not because of personal commitment, the individual will constantly try to find a way to avoid or justify noncompliance.

The age of the child is also an important consideration in the use of power assertion. Adult directives should be used more frequently with young children and should gradually be replaced by reasoning as the

---

BOX 10.6

Types of Discipline

Type	Example	Effect
Power assertion (power of bigger authority)	• Physical punishment • Loss of privileges • Interruption of undesired behavior	• Immediate regret from child • Compliance in presence of authority • Tendency to act out when not watched
Love withdrawal (disapproval by loss of warmth)	• Ignoring the child • Making negative remarks to or about the child	• Long-term fear of loss of love • Anxiety and insecurity
Induction (explanations and reasons)	• Explaining the "whys" for requirements • Developing an understanding and concern for the feelings of others	• Security of becoming a responsible decision maker • Desire to cooperate based on understanding

SOURCE: Hoffman, M. L. In *Carmichael's Manual of Child Psychology*, Vol. 2, 3rd ed., P. H. Mussen (Ed.), copyright © 1970, John Wiley & Sons, reprinted by permission of John Wiley & Sons, Inc.

child assumes responsibility for prosocial behavior. Many authorities, in fact, do not recognize punishment as discipline. They define discipline as techniques for helping the child learn to manage her own behavior. Parent power in the form of punishment loses its effectiveness if administered too frequently. The caregiver who is constantly scolding and/or spanking a child needs to analyze the situation: "Have I organized routines for reasonably smooth functioning, or am I blaming the child for uproars that occur from poor planning?" "Are the rules realistic for the age of the child?" The child is more impressed by punishment when it is reserved for important misconduct and preventive measures are used to avoid undesirable behavior. Allowing the child "to express herself" to the point that her behavior causes her to be rejected by others, however, is an injustice to that child. Time and effort should be devoted to finding effective methods for developing self-control and prosocial responses in the child.

Love withdrawal is probably the least desirable method for behavior control. The constant threat of losing the love of a significant person may create lifelong anxiety patterns. The child may also come to feel that she is undesirable and unworthy—that those who mistreat her are justified in their actions. Many abuse victims are trapped in such situations by their own feelings of low self-esteem.

Use of induction or reason is positively correlated with high scores on morality measures (Hoffman, 1976; Saltzstein, 1983; Wertsch, 1985). Discussions related to such questions as "How do you think she feels?" and "Wouldn't you want someone to be kind to you?" help the child increase cognitive understanding and empathy. Practice in putting themselves in the place of others helps young children move from their natural egocentrism to a greater concern for the needs and feelings of others.

Upper elementary children are generally able to use induction and reason to exercise what Keller (1984) calls "a moral orientation." They are able to (1) observe and define the moral rules that should be applied in a given situation, (2) be aware of the consequences should they choose to violate obligations and responsibilities, and (3) negotiate among conflicting claims. This last insight is one that a younger child cannot mentally coordinate. Sometimes there is no clear-cut right or wrong in a situation. Several possible actions and consequences must be considered and either the best or the least harmful solution be used. This level of moral judgment will probably not be developed until a measure of skill in abstract thinking is attained.

Special problems may arise if differences exist between the disciplinary methods used at home and those used at other places where the child regularly stays. Parents and other child-care workers need to plan cooperatively to minimize such differences lest the child be confused.

Behavior Modification through Reinforcement

One of the most positive forms of discipline is the consistent use of behavior modification techniques. Among these strategies are praise, extinction by ignoring, time-out, contingent observation, and relearning group sessions.

PRAISE.   Praise is a verbal form of positive reinforcement. Labeled praise ("I'm so glad Susan is sharing.") is more effective than unlabeled praise ("Susan is such a nice person.") because the labeling specifies exactly what you want Susan to do. (This praise will be effective, of course, only if Susan has the concept of sharing.) When Mother takes Jennifer to the doctor's office, she says, "Sit quietly, and look at a book." Then a friend arrives. Anxious to show off her charming child, Mother says, "Talk to the lady, Jennifer. Don't be so shy!" The signals are mixed. "When does Mother want me to be quiet, and when does she expect me to speak up?" The child often has difficulty generalizing instructions to new situations that may be slightly different from previous ones. How many times has Mother said, "Don't get your dress dirty," only to discover fifteen minutes later that the child's shoes are caked with mud. (Mother said dress, not shoes.) Labeled praise given before the child needs to perform the desired behavior often helps her know what is expected.

EXTINCTION BY IGNORING.   Many children misbehave to get attention. When dealing with such children, ignoring undesirable antics deprives these young people of being noticed and sometimes causes them to give up their disruptive behaviors (Essa, 1978). Please be aware of the following precautions when using this technique: (1) Ignoring may be interpreted by the child as a lack of firmness on the part of the caregiver. ("Since she didn't stop me, I guess it's all right.") (2) If the other children are not ignoring the misbehavior, the child may be reinforced by their comments and attention. They may also feel that since Daren "got by with it," they might as well join in the commotion. (3) Some behaviors cannot be ignored without running the risk of injury either to the disruptive child or to other members of the group.

TIME-OUT.   As previously discussed, time-out involves the temporary removal of the child from the group. This strategy is used (1) to impress upon the child that the behavior being exhibited will not be tolerated, (2) to give the child the opportunity to think about why the present course of action is wrong and what other behaviors are more appropriate (although there is no way to ensure that this type of thinking will always occur), and (3) to help the child make a self-commitment to change her behavior. The restricted time need not be long. Five minutes can seem like an eternity to a young child. Avoid putting the child out of the room, as she may enjoy the freedom and opportunity for getting into mischief and she will miss the chance to see what the others are doing. Interesting ongoing activities can provide a powerful incentive to rejoin the group. The use of time-out is not limited to small children. It is used very effectively with older young people, since they have even greater abilities in mental analysis.

CONTINGENT OBSERVATION. Contingent observation is a combination of direct instruction, time-out, peer observation, and praise. Essa (1978, p. 546) offers the following outline of this procedure:

- a. tell the child what he did wrong and suggest an appropriate alternative,
- b. separate him from the group to the edge of the play area and instruct him to observe the appropriate behavior of the other children,
- c. return him to the group when he has indicated verbally or otherwise that he is under social control, and
- d. praise him for subsequent appropriate behavior.

RELEARNING GROUP SESSIONS. The power of peer influence is utilized in relearning group sessions (Essa, 1978). The disruptive child is placed in a relearning group comprising two or three peers who are her friends and who regularly exhibit desirable behaviors. The caregiver describes some typical real-life situation and asks the group members how they would behave. Prosocial solutions are praised. When aggressive solutions are proposed, the children are asked if they can think of another way to handle the problem. Role playing of desirable behavior solutions may be included.

When using behavior modification through reinforcement, the caregiver should remember the following generalizations (Burton, 1976; Essa, 1978; Nisan, 1984):

- Misbehavior often has some immediate reward in the environment and therefore takes time to extinguish.
- The caregiver may have difficulty finding a reward the child will like as well as the pleasure she is already getting from the mischief itself.
- A combination of techniques is most likely to be effective.
- Don't assume that one particular technique will be equally effective with all children.
- Don't become so attached to one method of behavior management that you continue to use it even when it is not working.

MORAL DEVELOPMENT AND BEHAVIOR MANAGEMENT 313

Empathy Development

Since young children tend to be egocentric and self-centered, they need many opportunities to become involved with the feelings and needs of others. Three techniques that may help them identify with another person's point of view are bibliotherapy, role playing, and magic circle (Webb, 1981). These techniques are also valuable tools for working with older children.

BIBLIOTHERAPY. Bibliotherapy is the use of books and stories to influence behavior. Through identification with story characters, children can learn to exhibit such attributes as friendliness, sharing, helpfulness, and comfort. Stories may also be selected to illustrate solutions to behavior problems that exist in a particular group. Children's librarians serve as invaluable resource persons for helping caregivers find appropriate materials.

The Book Finder is a sourcebook that may be used in locating appropriate

Bibliotherapy is the use of stories to improve behavior. (*Source: © MacDonald/ Envision*)

stories (Dreyer, 1985). It references over a thousand children's books and contains a topical index, age recommendations, and comprehensive abstract summaries. A sample summary is included in Case Study 10.

ROLE PLAYING.   In order to maximize the child's involvement in stories, several types of role playing may be used. The child herself may assume the character role. One of my shyest kindergartners regularly volunteered

---

Case Study 10

Bibliotherapy

The Book Finder indexes over a thousand books dealing with needs and problems of young people from the ages of two to fifteen. The following is a summary from this source:

Klimowicz, Barbara, *The Strawberry Thumb.*

> Anna-May is about three years old. She sucks her thumb—"her strawberry thumb, her munchable, lunchable, sucking-good thumb." She sucks it all day, indoors and out, and she sucks it as she goes to sleep at night. Anna-May's mother, father, and big brother try without success to make her stop. She does not want to play with other children; she would rather suck her thumb. Her family is at wit's end trying to solve the problem. Then grandmother arrives with sympathy and her sewing bag. She says she feels sorry for Anna-May's wrinkled thumb, and she dresses it up as a puppet with a change of clothes. Anna-May is so happy she takes her puppet out to play, puts a nightcap on him at bedtime, and sleeps with him close by her side.
> The little girl in this illustrated poem depends on her thumb for security. It is not until her grandmother arrives with a novel solution that Anna-May gives up sucking her thumb. The book includes patterns and instructions for making a cloth or paper thumb puppet having two hats, a vest, and a nightshirt.

Ages 3–6

SOURCE. Dreyer, S. S., *The Book Finder*, copyright © American Guidance Service, Circle Pines, MN, 1985, reprinted with permission.

to be the bad troll, since role playing allowed her to "try on" behaviors without the fear of rejection. Seeing other children in role playing situations may also demonstrate new prosocial behaviors that you are trying to introduce to the group. Use of puppets is another avenue for role playing. Some children will explore new behaviors more freely with puppets, since if the puppet makes a mistake, the children are laughing at the puppet, not at them! Flannel-graph is another open-ended role-playing technique. The children draw and cut out figures representing the main characters, back them with flannel, and attach them to a flannel board. They may retell the story, or they can explore the question "What would happen if . . . ?" by trying new endings. Many studies have indicated that when children in both early and middle grades are given problem situations and are encouraged to role play or suggest solutions, these young people show an increase in helpfulness in a variety of classroom situations (Shantz, 1981).

MAGIC CIRCLE. "Magic circle" is a term coined to describe the excellent benefits children may derive from talking together about their problems and concerns. The teacher needs no special materials, but an orientation session during which the purpose and procedure are explained to the children is crucial. The following ideas should be stressed:

- All of us want our group to be happy, and each of us has some good ideas to share.
- We can talk about any problem that concerns us, but we cannot call names. (Speak of actions that are liked or disliked, not of people.)
- We must talk one at a time so we can listen to the problems of others and help think of solutions.
- After one problem has been presented, we must suggest some solutions before we go on to another problem in order to be helpful. (Magic circle can be used for sharing feelings and ideas as well as for problem solving.)

After this introduction, the teacher should seat the children in a circle for a few minutes several times a week. Let the children do the talking; teacher talk should be limited to facilitating remarks such as "Can someone help Robert?" or "Jeanie hasn't finished talking yet." The teacher should never offer solutions during magic circle time, since the purpose of this form of activity is to encourage the children to think and be helpful. (The teacher can save her ideas and present them later with no mention of magic circle.) Consistent use of magic circle often results in an increase in concern for others by the children involved.

Self-direction through Verbalization

Initially children are deterred from undesirable behavior by the echo of the parent's voice in the mind saying "Don't!" As children get older, however, they can assume some responsibility for instructing themselves. As you will recall from Chapter 6, the child's understanding of control over her own mental processes is called metacognition. Research has indicated that the particular words that are used in self-instruction are very important.

Based on the findings of research, the following generalizations can be made about the use of self-instruction for behavior control (see Figure 10.1) (Mischel, 1976; Berndt and Heller, 1985; Meichenbaum et al., 1985; Wertsch, 1985):

- Getting temptation out of sight is much more effective than teaching the child to say, "I won't do that."
- Thinking happy thoughts and remembering success experiences help the child resist temptation, continue to work when bored, and share treasured possessions.
- Emphasizing physical consequences ("I must be careful with this telescope; it might break.") is more effective than stressing empathy ("I don't want to make Judy sad.") or property ("It belongs to Judy, so I must be careful.")
- Concentrating on rewards and having them in sight excites the child and makes the waiting harder. ("I'll get to play video games on the

FIGURE 10.1   School rules are often posted as reminders for appropriate behavior.

MORAL DEVELOPMENT AND BEHAVIOR MANAGEMENT

computer as soon as I finish my homework!" will result in more daydreaming about the games than in work on the homework.)
- Imagining a wall between themselves and distraction is possible for an older child. One ingenious teacher developed a technique she called The Turtle. She explained that when a turtle is bothered, he goes inside his shell and thinks until he decides what he needs to do next. She suggested that when a child feels a situation is getting out of control, the child should imagine she is inside a shell, talk to herself about the problem, and then return to the group. Now when trouble starts to brew, some child will point to the disrupter and say, "Do turtle!"
- Giving a child a cue often helps her know when she needs to instruct herself. One mother put a rubber duck under the entry mat ("When you hear the duck squeak, remind yourself to wipe your feet.").

As the child grows older, self-instruction becomes an important base for self-control. Because it is an internal form of regulation, these verbalizations can give stability to behavior as the power of external controls lessens (Yussen, 1985).

Glasser (Charles, 1984) offered concrete guidelines for discussing decision making with children and helping them do their own planning for behavior management. In brief, these are

1. Concentrate on current behavior. (Don't discourage the child with a tirade such as "You always do that!" "That's the third time I've had to tell you!")
2. Don't ask for or accept excuses. (Often the child doesn't know why she did something. What is necessary is to plan appropriate behavior.)
3. Let natural consequences follow whatever behavior the child chooses. (Consequences should be stated in advance and need not be harsh. Reasonable behavior is based on a predictable world in which the child knows what will happen next when she chooses a certain behavior.)
4. Let the child construct a plan for dealing with the problem situation. (Self-planning usually engenders a measure of commitment and follow-through.)

Glasser's plan has been implemented in a number of school systems, and reports indicate positive self-discipline gains for many children.

Summary

- Moral behavior comprises many elements. Chief among these are empathy (understanding another's point of view), altruism (willingness

to help others), self-control (determination to resist temptation and do what is perceived to be good), and moral judgment (a learned system of right and wrong).
- Research has indicated that the following factors affect moral behavior: group affiliation, values, lack of discrepancy, family responsibility, consequences, risk, incentive, delay of gratification, distraction, strength of competing motives, IQ, age, and self-concept.
- According to psychoanalytic theory, moral behavior is controlled by the superego which we develop through early identification with parents and other caregivers. This system contains the conscience (our belief about which acts should be punished) and the ego-ideal (our notion about what the ideal person should do).
- By contrast, social learning theory attributes our behavior patterns to our tendency to model the actions of persons we consider to be powerful and significant. We do not imitate all of the behaviors we see; our choice is controlled by reinforcement. We model those behaviors that we see rewarded and avoid those acts that we see punished.
- Cognitive theorists stress the role of understanding in determining moral behavior. Piaget found that as we get older, we understand the origin of rules and can modify them appropriately in new situations. We also come to evaluate right and wrong in terms of intent rather than with respect to damage done. Kohlberg hypothesized that as we mature, we go through a series of stages. At the preconventional level, we obey out of fear of punishment and have limited regard for the welfare of others. At the conventional level, we are concerned with the approval of others and respect the law even when it conflicts with personal desires. At the postconventional level, we consider rules as standards based on social consensus which may need to be changed for the welfare of those involved, and our major concern is that we follow our own internal convictions relating to justice.
- Many strategies may be used to guide moral development. Among them are modeling, direct discipline, behavior modification through reinforcement, bibliotherapy, role playing, magic circle, and self-direction through verbalization.
- To be chosen by children as a model, the caregiver must possess characteristics and skills valued by these young people. Warm interactions, time and attention, and consistency of behavior increase the probability that children will imitate that individual. Behavior change by modeling requires great patience; even with a consistent model, children cannot alter their actions overnight.
- In planning direct discipline, the personality of the caregiver, the disposition of the child, and the type of discipline must be considered.

- Excessive use of power-assertion discipline may produce an individual who will follow the rules only when someone is looking and may be unduly influenced by any domineering individual with whom she becomes associated. Love-withdrawal techniques often engender anxiety and feelings of unworthiness. Use of induction, or discipline based on explanations and reasons, appears to produce the highest level of morality in children.
- Many techniques for behavior modification through reinforcement have been devised. Labeled praise that specifies the desired behavior is more effective than is unlabeled ("good girl") praise. Ignoring undesirable behaviors will often extinguish them, since this practice deprives the child of the attention she may be seeking. Time-out, the removal of the child from the group for misbehavior, often inspires the young person to improve in order to rejoin her friends. Contingent observation allows the child to observe appropriate behaviors of peers, and in relearning group sessions the child discusses with her peers what behaviors would be appropriate in situations described by the teacher.
- Empathy, or feeling for others, may be developed through bibliotherapy, role playing, and magic circle. Bibliotherapy is the age-old practice of reading stories about how other people feel and react in various situations. Role playing is assuming the character of another person and acting out the behaviors that might be exhibited under specified circumstances. Magic circle is a group experience for children during which they share their feelings and ideas.
- The child can learn to control her own behavior by talking to herself. These self-instructions are most effective when both temptations and rewards are removed from sight, when the child thinks happy thoughts and has success experiences, when physical consequences of misbehavior are verbalized, and when the child is given a cue to be used as a reminder to instruct herself.

Selected Readings

CHARLES, C. M. *Building Classroom Discipline: From Models to Practice* (2nd. ed.). New York: Longman, 1984.
This very readable paperback explores the sources of behavior, misbehavior, motives, and controls and contains concise summaries of seven models of discipline. It is a valuable "why and how-to" book for anyone who works with children.

ESSA, E. L. "The Preschool: Setting for Applied Behavior Analysis Research." *Review of Educational Research* 48(4) 1978, 537–575.
In this article, Essa summarizes extensive research related to the use of

behavior modification with young children. In the description of these studies, the reader will find many interesting techniques for behavior management.

KOHLBERG, L. *The Psychology of Moral Development.* New York: Harper & Row, 1984.
In this book, Kohlberg discusses in great detail the many aspects of his theory and their relationship to the ideas of other authorities.

KURTINES, W. M., AND GEWIRTZ, J. L. (eds.). *Morality, Moral Behavior, and Moral Development.* New York: Wiley, 1984.
This work contains articles relating to the following theoretical approaches: the cognitive-developmental, the stage-constructivist, the learning-behavioral, and the social-personality. This breadth of perspective is very useful in analyzing the issues.

PIAGET, J. *The Moral Judgment of the Child.* Glencoe, IL: Free Press, 1948.
This is the classic account of Piaget's research into the moral development of children.

SIGEL, I. E. *Parental Belief Systems: The Psychological Consequences for Children.* Hillsdale, NJ: Erlbaum, 1985.
The selections in this work document the interaction of parenting beliefs with such diverse aspects of child development as cognitive level, communication, behavior change, academic performance, socialization, socioeconomic status, intervention programs, and sex-typed characteristics.

CHAPTER 11

Integration of Development through Play

"AND NOW, AN IMPORTANT MESSAGE FROM YOUR SPONSOR: GO OUT AND PLAY!"

(Source: DENNIS THE MENACE® used by permission of Hank Ketcham and © by North America Syndicate)

CHAPTER OUTLINE

  What Is Play?
  Developmental Sequence of Play Behavior
    Functional Play
    Symbolic Play
    Games-with-Rules
  Functions of Play
    Emotional Development
    Creativity
    Socialization
    Assimilation of Culture
    Physical Development
    Language Development
    Cognition and Problem Solving
    Academic Achievement
    Pleasure
  Facilitating Children's Play
    Selection of Toys
    Construction of Play Areas
  Summary
  Selected Readings

Play is difficult to define, because it is many things. Consider the following examples:

> A little girl who while on vacation had asked various questions about the mechanics of the bells observed on an old village church steeple, now stood stiff as a ramrod beside her father's desk, making a deafening noise. "You're bothering me, you know," said the father, "can't you see I'm working?" "Don't talk to me," replied the little girl. "I'm a church." (Piaget and Inhelder, 1969, p. 59)

In this incident, the child was playing alone, using action thinking to help her to internalize the characteristics of an unfamiliar object she had seen. Contrast this scene with a group play exchange.

  Two young children were arguing heatedly over what they were going to play. Finally Holland said with solemn emphasis, "I'M COMPANY, so we'll have to play what I want to!" Immediately, Darren snapped back, "Then we'll go to YOUR house and play what I want to!" Here the children give evidence of the cultural and social values of play. Without intervention from adults, children learn to negotiate their differences. Evidently they have already learned customs about how to treat company, but the egocentric "I want my way" is still strong. Through play, they will be confronted with the conflicting desires of others and see the necessity to find solutions that are mutually agreeable.

In this chapter we consider several questions: What is play? Through what sequence do play behaviors develop? What major benefits does the child accrue through play? How can caregivers facilitate children's play? Through all our discussions, I hope we never lose sight of the carefree joyousness of this thing we call play.

What Is Play?

Chance (1979, p. 1) observed, "Play is like love: everybody knows what it is but nobody can define it." Several definitions may be better than one in helping us to understand the scope of this favorite pastime. Based on the writings of many authorities, we may conclude that play is (Piaget, 1962; Sapora and Mitchell, 1971; Vygotsky, 1978; Bruner, 1983):

- doing something for the joy of it
- being free to experiment without having to produce something
- taking a vacation from daily routine
- making free, aimless, and diverting use of time
- having voluntary control of an activity
- doing something that will not be rated for quality of performance

Why is it so important that we define play, since it is a phenomenon that defies a simple definition? In order to reap maximum benefits from play, the child must have active control in planning and implementing his own experiences. The child who is rigidly scheduled from piano to dance to dramatics to little league may not be playing in any of these incidences, though any one of these might be chosen by the child as an avenue of play. Adults may provide stimulating and appropriate conditions for play, but the play experience itself will be most valuable when the child's initiative is paramount. The importance of defining play, therefore, is to help caregivers recognize the importance of play in a child's development and to encourage adults to let play be an area of the child's life in which he is free to explore and to express.

Play may be crowding into a cube or riding the turtle monster.

Developmental Sequence of Play Behavior

The child's developmental capacities are evident in his play activities. This fact implies a reciprocal relationship; the child plays according to the level of his developmental expertise, and his play results in further advancement. Although psychologists have proposed different stage categories, a common sequence of play development has been observed. We incorporate the ideas of several theorists in describing play in three stages: functional play (first two years of life), symbolic play (preschool years), and games-with-rules (elementary level). Please note that each stage builds on the preceding ones. Therefore, the older child or adult continues to use each of these types of play at various times throughout life.

Functional Play

Functional play is typical of the sensorimotor period and is the predominant play form for the child from birth to about the age of two years (Piaget, 1962). As the child acquires sensory abilities (sucking, feeling, listening, looking, vocalizing) and motor skills (grasping, walking, talking, handling objects), he uses these as a basis for play patterns. He repeats simple actions over and over again, sometimes with variations, and seems to delight in a feeling of mastery. In fact, Piaget (1973) feels that the desire to master his own abilities is the child's basic impetus for play. As he plays, the child imitates sounds he has heard and has learned to make, and these early vocalizations serve as a foundation for the language component of play (Smilansky, 1968).

As previously mentioned, solitary sensorimotor play may also occur with an older child. Sometimes such activities can be very useful for internalizing new concepts. An excess of such play, however, can be socially detrimental. Rubin (1982) found that not only do preschool children who spend a large portion of their time playing alone have fewer social contacts and conversations with peers than do age-mates whose play forms are more socialized, but the encounters they do have are more likely to involve conflicts.

Symbolic Play

During the sensorimotor period, the child begins to form mental images or pictures of the experiences he has had. By about the age of one-and-a-half or two years, the child develops the ability to attach symbols to images. He can use a word, a gesture, or an activity to represent an

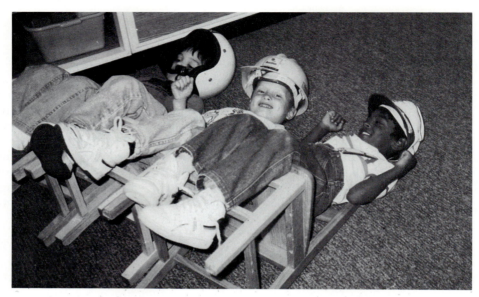
"Pretend play" astronauts may be male or female.

object, a person, or an event with which he has had experience (Piaget, 1973; Isenberg and Jacob, 1983). The child expresses this ability through symbolic play (Bretherton, 1984).

Piaget and Inhelder (1969) cite four behavioral signs of the child's ability to use symbols in play:

1. deferred imitation through repeating the actions of another person after that individual has gone
2. pretend activities such as taking roles and acting out familiar occurrences
3. drawing (showing familiar concepts in picture form)
4. oral statements about past occurrences (remembering details from the past)

Children between the ages of two and four years are particularly fascinated by construction play. After the child has played with materials until he understands some of their characteristics, he is ready to create (Smilansky, 1968). His construction may be meant to represent something he has seen, or it may be something wonderful from his imagination. One word of caution to caregivers. Never assume you know what a construction is. It is much safer to say, "Tell me about what you have made." The child is apt to be a bit disgruntled if you call it a barn when he knows it is a hospital.

Another important distinction that needs to be made is whether the child wants to undo and redo his construction or whether he wants to preserve it. To Eric, for instance, it was the process, not the product, that was important.

> Eric is building a mound of sand. The sand is moist enough to hold the shape the child creates. Shortly after building the mound, Eric smashes it flat with his hand, smooths it out, and begins to build the mound again. (Forman and Kushner, 1983, p. 137)

In a contrasting incident, I made Thanksgiving turkeys with nursery school children. We used an apple for a body, a toothpick topped by a pimento-stuffed olive to the front for a head and gobble, and many toothpicks laced with raisins to the back for tail feathers. The children were delighted with their constructions and looked forward to taking them home. World War III almost broke out when David caught Landon eating his turkey's tail feathers!

During this stage of construction play, the child is apt to be an avid collector. This "beautiful junk" with which he fills his lifespace is very important to him, because it becomes the material for his fabulous creations. Probably compromise is in order. The caregiver should provide or encourage him to accumulate blocks and wood scraps, leaves and rocks, scissors and old magazines, string and construction paper, paste and things to be pasted—all those wondrous things from which treasures are made. In return, the child should learn to organize and store these items in a somewhat orderly manner.

Pretend play is of primary importance from about the age of four to the onset of middle childhood (Butler et al., 1978; McCune-Nicolick and Fenson, 1984). Through this play form, children assume imaginary roles and enact scenes of their own choosing. In many instances, they reenact episodes from their daily lives. Although these events may not correspond to actual facts, they do represent life as the child sees it, and they do incorporate the rules and customs of that child's society as he understands them (Butler et al., 1978; Vygotsky, 1978). The child is also likely to pretend to be a character he fears or admires. While playing such a role, the child may gain the feeling of power he associates with that character. A young child, just beginning pretend play, may simply select several things he especially likes and combine them into a single event. I can still remember the hilarious sight of a little girl, fully decked in a bridal gown and veil, roaring across the nursery room floor on a firetruck!

BOX 11.1
Six Criteria for Sociodramatic Play

1. *Imitative role play.* The child undertakes a make-believe role and expresses it in imitative action and/or verbalization.
2. *Make-believe in regard to objects.* Movements or verbal declarations are substituted for real objects.
3. *Make-believe in regard to actions and situations.* Verbal descriptions are substituted for actions and situations.
4. *Persistence.* The child persists in a play episode for at least ten minutes.
5. *Interaction.* There are at least two players interacting in the framework of the play episode.
6. *Verbal communication.* There is some verbal interaction related to the play episode.

SOURCE. Smilansky, 1968, p. 9.

When pretend play involves only one child, it is called dramatic play. When two or more children pretend together, the play form is called sociodramatic play. Smilansky has identified six criteria for make-believe play. The first four are applicable to all pretend play, but the last two are distinctively related to sociodramatic play. These criteria are listed in Box 11.1

The movement of the child from dramatic play by himself to sociodramatic play with others is very important to his development. Through involvement with others, he is able to explore their experiences and fantasies as well as his own. His language development is accelerated as he exchanges vocabulary words and models sentence patterns of others. He can also refine his language and behaviors as a result of the corrective feedback he receives from peers ("That's not the way you say that word!" "You mustn't do that. It's not nice.").

Although dramatic and sociodramatic play continue during the early elementary years, games-with-rules become an important play form for children from the age of seven to eleven (Butler et al., 1978). These may be very simple games with rules that are so flexible that they are changed to fit each group of players. By contrast, they may be very detailed and involve extensive practice and regular team participation. Bogdanoff and Dolch have catalogued a number of the all-time favorites. A summary of their work is found in Box 11.2. Take a minute to reminisce about the childhood hours you devoted to some of these games.

BOX 11.2
Developmental Guidelines for Choosing Games

Child's Thought Development	Game Requirements	Suggested Games
Early Preoperational		
Limited memory for sequence items	Pattern or sequence game Two-step sequence	Ring around the Rosie Roll the Ball (small group) Hokey Pokey (modified) Humpty Dumpty and other nursery rhymes This is the way the _____ walks (tune of Mulberry Bush)
Very limited verbal understanding	No verbal instruction necessary to teach game	
Strong egocentrism	Continuous participation by all No waiting necessary Two to four children	
Little group awareness involved primarily with adults	Game depends on adult action No role alteration required	
Late Preoperational		
More objective understanding of role in action of game	Players required to make some choices of action	A Tisket-a-Tasket Squirrel in the Trees Charlie over the Water Find My Child London Bridge Knock, Knock
Good verbal understanding	May use verbal cues as well as action	
Egocentrism diminishing	Taking turns can be part of game	
Enjoys coordination with group Will subject own interests to group effort	Understand and enjoy role alternation and some role reversal Eight to twelve children	
Concrete Operational		
Reversible thought and lessened egocentrism Understand rules as objective framework for action	Decisions of strategy determine outcome of game	Word games (G-H-O-S-T) Tag (modified) Hide and Seek Kick the Can Competitive races and relays Follow the Leader Darts Horseshoes Pease Porridge Hot Simon Says
New interest in competition within coordinated effort	Competition may be used Team action may substitute for personal involvement	
Uses language easily for thought	Verbal element can be definitive part of game	

SOURCE. Abstracted from Bogdanoff, R. F. and Dolch, E. T., *Young Children*, 34(2), pp. 42–43, copyright © National Association for the Education of Young Children, Washington, D.C., 1979. Used with permission.

Games-with-Rules

Playing games-with-rules has some important developmental consequences. Consider the following examples (Piaget, 1962; Butler et al., 1978; Chance, 1979):

- Following rules set by others teaches the child to subjugate his own desires in the interest of cooperation and to control his behavior to conform to regulations.
- Making rules helps the child realize and accept personal responsibility for orderly behavior in social situations.
- Making rules may also challenge the child to adjust requirements in order to be fair to younger or less-capable players.
- Learning the rules of a game requires memory and application of ideas to behaviors.
- Playing games-with-rules involves repetition of actions which gives the child a chance to perfect related skills.
- Taking turns is an important social concept embedded in games-with-rules.

BOX 11.3
Parten's Categories of Play

Category	Description
1. Unoccupied	• Not playing; not watching others more than momentarily; may play with own fingers or toes
2. Onlooker	• Watches particular other children and their play sequences; may make comments or ask questions; doesn't directly participate in play
3. Solitary play	• Plays by himself with selected toys; doesn't involve other children
4. Parallel group activity	• Plays by himself, but close to other children; may verbalize about his play, but speaks to no one and expects no answers
5. Associative group play	• Plays actively with others; talks and shares materials; does not have any goal or division of labor
6. Cooperative group play	• Plays with others to achieve goals; divides task and assigns roles; may play games-with-rules

SOURCE. Summarized from Parten, 1932.

- Participating in games gives the child practice in resolving conflicting desires (weighing the desire to win against the desire to be popular).
- Working with several other children in a game situation helps the child relate to different personalities in a goal-oriented situation.

Throughout this developmental sequence of play, the child moves from curious observer to active group participant. Parten chronicled this progression and designed a classic scheme for use in observing children's play. Please carefully consider the data in Box 11.3 for her descriptions of the following six categories: unoccupied, onlooker, solitary play, parallel group activity, associative group play, and cooperative group play. Parten suggested that the observer make particular note of the number of social contacts made by the child, the kinds of groups the child selects, and the role the child plays in these groups.

Functions of Play

Play for the sheer joy of it is a worthwhile use of the child's time. However, in recent years, much research has been devoted to the many ancillary benefits the child reaps from such activities. In this section, we analyze play as a vehicle for many accomplishments.

Emotional Development

One of the great values of play, according to Vygotsky (1978), is the child's ability to use this medium to do all the "big and important" things he is powerless to do as a child. The little boy who has just been rejected by an older brother and his friends as too little to play ball can use his blocks to build a mighty tower that in his imagination reaches to the heavens. If he is still feeling angry, he can even knock it down flat and not be scolded for breaking something. A little girl can don playhouse finery and order dolls, and perhaps even other children, to do her bidding as she imitates her mother's coveted position of authority.

Erikson (1963) stresses the importance of play to emotional well-being in helping the child develop his own "microsphere," a small, private world of toys and objects that he can manage. Successful mastery of small play tasks is very important to the development of the self-concept. Learning to deal with the frustration associated with more difficult play endeavors builds emotional strength which will be of continued value. Erikson believes the microsphere will remain as a safe haven to which the child can return whenever life in the larger world seems too risky or when he needs to regain his feeling of personal worth.

Children sometimes choose small, private "microspheres" for playing or for just thinking.

Play is also a valuable tool for helping the child deal constructively with negative emotions (Piaget and Inhelder, 1969; Milos and Reiss, 1982). Play situations give the child an opportunity to experiment without fear of failure or without having to face higher standards of achievement than he is able to attain. Play can also be used to desensitize frightening situations. Many children play "doctor" to overcome their fear of sickness. Of course, such play may not always be reassuring, as I discovered when

I heard a cry from the far side of the room and found a child orthodontist trying to attach a paper clip to another child's tooth for "braces."

Creativity

Creativity is characterized by flexibility and by the capacity to generate novel responses (Ellis, 1984). Both of these are important elements in play. I once found children seated but bouncing up and down on a new air-filled cushion I had added to the play area. They explained that they were riding down a bumpy road in a new convertible. My kindergartners also made fantastic trips to outer space in helmets made from round ice cream cartons!

From studies relating creativity to play, two findings are of particular importance. First, children who engage in pretend play appear to develop a mental set for creating novel ideas (Dansky, 1975, 1980). Second, imaginative play seems to stimulate the child to find original uses for objects and to combine things in unique ways (Christie and Johnsen, 1983). These mental habits may enable the child to see many more possibilities in the environment. As a result, the child may not only lead a more interesting life but may also be more proficient in problem solving. Watch for more research in this area.

Socialization

Since play so frequently involves other children, what are some of the socialization benefits? Let's consider how corrective feedback, modeling, resolution of conflict, and empathy for those who are different can be accomplished through play activity.

The poet Robert Burns (1897, p. 44) gave us the immortal lines

> O wad some Power the giftie gie us
> To see oursels as others see us!

when, in the middle of church, he observed a bug crawling out of a very prissy lady's hair. The close personal contact of children in play situations affords many opportunities for children to show their peers "how others see them." The child who exhibits poor sportsmanship in a game is likely to be chided by peers, and the domineering child who insists on his own way is apt to be threatened with expulsion from the group. This corrective feedback helps the child understand other points of view (Rubin, 1982). Through modeling the behaviors of others, he may learn such skills as how to behave if he wants to be chosen, how to get his way without clobbering someone, and how to be a "best friend."

Case Study 11

If there is a scene at lunch, for example, one can be sure that an hour or two afterward it will be recreated with dolls and will be brought to a happier solution. Either the child disciplines her doll more intelligently than her parents did her, or in play she accepts what she had not accepted at lunch (such as finishing a bowl of soup she does not like, especially if it is the doll who finishes it symbolically). Similarly, if the child has been frightened by a big dog, in a symbolic game things will be arranged so that dogs will no longer be mean or else children will become brave. Generally speaking, symbolic play helps in the resolution of conflicts and also in the compensation of unsatisfied needs, the inversion of roles (such as obedience and authority) [or] the liberation and extension of the self.

SOURCE. Piaget and Inhelder, 1969, p. 60.

Another value of play in social development is its use in resolving conflicts. See Case Study 11 for a perceptive example from Piaget and Inhelder.

Play is also important in helping the child understand the feelings and needs of the individual who is different (Quinn and Rubin, 1984). In school settings where handicapped and nonhandicapped children have been mainstreamed into the same classrooms, play has been an important vehicle for fostering interactions between the two groups (Levine and McCollum, 1983). Such associations have been mutually beneficial; the unimpaired lose some of their awe and reticence about being near someone who is different, and the children with problems gain a wider choice of models and added self-esteem.

Assimilation of Culture

Through play the child internalizes many of the values and expectations of his culture (Bruner, 1983). Team sports teach competition, fair play, and acceptable behavior in both victory and defeat. Solitary play helps the child develop independence (and perhaps the added bonus of cleaning up after oneself). In pretend play, the child actually models behavior he has seen and, from corrective peer feedback, learns to conduct himself in a more culturally approved manner. This emphasis on equity and manners is well-illustrated by Bruner's (1983, p. 65) account of the child

A child from Colombia demonstrates a native dance.

who said, "If you give me your marbles I'll give you my revolver if you're nice."

The play activities associated with such holidays as Thanksgiving, Halloween, Easter, Cinco de Mayo, and Fourth of July help the child assimilate cultural learnings and values. Celebrations and recreational events (e.g., weddings, Bar Mitzvahs, family reunions) further extend this feeling of affiliation.

The sex-role expectations of the culture are also transmitted through play (Liss, 1983; Pitcher and Schultz, 1983). Boys learn to expect rough-and-tumble encounters from the games in which they are encouraged to participate, and girls are conditioned to be more nurturant through an emphasis on family living play. Years of such differential play exposure may be an important factor in the sex roles assumed later in life. By offering a wider variety of play experiences to both boys and girls, these sex roles may become less stereotyped.

Physical Development

Play is one of the prime developers of physical skills and personal health. As a result of active play, children acquire better muscle tone and nerve functioning, stimulate circulation, improve perceptual-motor coordination, and help maintain proper weight (Chance, 1979).

Often physical action in play is combined with other features. Garvey (1977) offers several examples: Rope play may be accompanied by rhymes, pursuit and escape may occur in a story context such as "cops and robbers," and intricate motor skills may be involved in games that range in complexity from hopscotch to kickball. The benefits of play are multifaceted.

Language Development

Children's play is frequently a noisy affair with chattering and cheering, arguing and explaining, questioning and answering. From all this verbalization, much language development takes place (Smilansky, 1968; Yawkey and Hancia, 1982; Christie and Johnsen, 1983; Williamson and Silvern, 1984). Let us now consider some of the major language opportunities and effects:

- Children attribute roles and characteristics to objects, persons, and happenings and use language to explain these roles to other children ("We are in the hospital, and I'm the doctor taking your tonsils out!").
- They talk and act for their play characters. (Such speech and action opportunities may increase verbal output, encourage use of complete sentences, improve vocal expression, and refine comprehension.)
- Through group play, children expand the number of models they have for language development. (This exposure leads to larger vocabularies, more correct and/or complex sentence structure, and new ideas to which the child has not previously been exposed.)
- When children play games, they integrate a wide variety of language skills. (They listen to directions and mentally repeat them as they try to perfect their skills. They may also explain rules and strategies to new or younger players.)

Cognition and Problem Solving

Very frequently, early childhood educators are confronted by parents who say, "I don't want my child just to play all day in kindergarten, I want him to learn something." What are some of the special cognitive and problem-solving "learnings" we can identify for these people?

Play is a happy medium for the development of coordination and strength.

One of the major cognitive values of play is that it enables the child to learn concepts before he has the words to express them (Piaget, 1962; Pepler and Rubin, 1982). The great German educator Friedrich Froebel recognized this potential for what he referred to as "play tools" when he opened a school he called a kindergarten in 1837 (Ransbury, 1982). He developed a set of objects he referred to as "gifts" which were based on common shapes (square, circle, cylinder, sphere, cube, triangle). He prescribed "occupations"—actions to be performed with each gift designed to enable the child to discover the gift's attributes. The young child's everyday environment is filled with potential toys that can be used for concept learning. Play is also one of the prime mediums for internalizing the meaning of words related to location and direction.

Bruner and Sutton-Smith describe the value of play for "variation seek-

Many computer games combine play with learning. (*Source: Courtesy, National Science Teachers Association, photograph by William E. Mills, Montgomery County Public Schools*)

ing"—learning to use objects in a variety of different ways (Rubin and Pepler, 1982; Copple et al., 1984). The flexibility of thinking developed in this way can help the child in many problem-solving situations. Sylva (1981) found that play experiences greatly improve the ability of three- to-five-year-olds to use tools in accomplishing goals.

Play is also of value in helping the child develop organizational skills (Fowler, 1980; Pellegrini, 1984). Many times the organization is embedded in the material itself. For instance, a puzzle fits together only one way and a model must be assembled in a specific order. At other times, as with games involving rules, an organizational sequence is a part of the activity itself. In any event, organization strengthens cognition and facilitates problem solving by helping the child see relationships.

Academic Achievement

Extensive surveys of the literature have linked ability in symbolic play to school achievement (Pellegrini, 1980; Isenberg and Jacob, 1983). Children who have well-developed skills in symbolic play or who have received training in this area, when compared with children with more limited play skills, have been found to (1) score higher in reading achievement and writing fluency, (2) have increased language skills, (3) be more accurate in constructing story sequences and in making inferences about story content, and (4) score higher in vocabulary and syntax measures. Play has also been used successfully in enhancing school achievement with learning-disabled children (Irwin and Frank, 1977).

Gentile and Hoot (1983) analyzed specific play activities and related them to skills used in reading. The following are examples of their findings:

Painting: details, position (or sequence) of parts, figure-ground relationships
Letter blocks: letter identification, part/whole patterns or configurations, vocabulary expansion
Movement activities: left-to-right sequence
Sociodramatic play: comprehension, vocabulary, feelings, point of view
Field trips: experiential background, reading comprehension
Being read to: vocabulary, comprehension, interest in learning to read

Investigations have also been made concerning the relationship of play activities and development in arithmetic. Zammarelli and Bolton (1977) found high correlations between play and mathematical concept formation.

Pleasure

Aside from any cognitive, physical, social, or emotional rewards, play is of value for the sheer pleasure of it. An individual of any age should be encouraged to spend some time each week in some activity which, for him, is play. A worthwhile goal for the childhood years is that during this time each person should develop the realization that play for pleasure is a respectable use of time and perhaps discover some form of activity that may continue to be a source of play pleasure to him.

Facilitating Children's Play

Two important mediums through which adults facilitate children's play are the selection of toys and the construction of play areas. There are several factors related to each of these which are discussed in this section.

Selection of Toys

What are toys? In the broadest sense, anything a child uses in play is a toy. Some of these implements of play are drawn from the everyday environment and some are purchased by caregivers for the specific purpose of play.

Almost every environment contains many opportunities for play. The average kitchen is a gold mine for activities such as stacking plates, sorting flatware, categorizing canned goods, reading from labels, pouring from pitchers, and seeing science transformations through cooking. The house has clocks for setting and for telling time, bathrooms for endless water play activities, and yard equipment for digging, cutting, and planting. Some children have even discovered that the bed makes a great trampoline (though most parents definitely frown on this pastime)! If all the play possibilities of the home environment are put to maximum use, children will not actually need as vast a supply of special toys as many of them receive.

What qualities should caregivers consider when selecting toys for children? Several good suggestions can be drawn from the writings of Butler and her colleagues (1978) and from Fowler (1980).

Preference should be given to open-ended toys, which are adaptable to many uses. Such toys are more interesting to the child, since their use does not involve constant repetition. Playing with open-ended toys also tends to stimulate the imagination and challenge the child's creativity. Clay can be used for figures or pottery, blocks for houses or counting, paints for

INTEGRATION OF DEVELOPMENT THROUGH PLAY

Paints provide an open-ended experience for creative expression.

pictures or lettering, tinker toys for all sorts of construction, and wheel toys for everything from ambulances to family cars.

Some specific-purpose toys are needed. Toys such as puzzles, form boards, construction kits, balls, and racquets provide a pleasant way to develop particular skills. They can be used to discover relationships (visually discriminate how each puzzle piece fits where), follow a sequence (use the correct order in putting a construction kit together), or develop fine-motor coordination (in a variety of sports).

Three-dimensional toys are of particular value. Any building-type toys that do not snap together help the child understand balance, weight distribution, and gravity. Container-type toys such as cups, pails, or hollow forms give the child an opportunity to experiment with volume. Any three-dimensional object is of value in the development of perceptual skills, particularly those involving depth perception and proportion.

Some toys should be chosen for their potential in the development of large and small muscles. Wheel toys are good for leg muscles and endurance. Various sizes and types of balls can be used to improve eye-hand coordination and manual dexterity. Any toys that involve the placement of small pieces can help in small-muscle development.

The social value of toys should also be considered. Some toys, by their very nature, tend to involve social play. A playhouse or scaled-play furniture may lead to sociodramatic play with friends. Many board games require more than one player. Sports equipment almost always can be used to prepare the child to be a partner or team member. Although solitary play has certain values, a balance of social play is needed.

All play equipment should be sturdy and safe. Active play will test the durability of toys, and they should not break or fall apart with reasonable use. They should also not have small parts that can easily be swallowed, sharp edges that can cut, or paint that is toxic.

As you can see from the foregoing list, a few toys from each category could provide the child with endless hours of happy and wholesome play. The total number of toys is not as important as the variety of type.

Construction of Play Areas

Three types of playgrounds are frequently discussed and compared in research literature (Frost and Klein, 1979; Strickland, 1980; Edwards, 1985). These playgrounds are often labeled traditional, creative, and adventure. Each has distinctive characteristics, and each affects the kinds of play in which the user engages. In this section, we consider each type.

TRADITIONAL PLAYGROUNDS. The traditional playground is the type so frequently seen in parks and at elementary schools. The play equipment generally consists of swings, see-saws, merry-go-rounds, slides, and jungle gyms (assorted bars for climbing). Nearby courts and/or diamonds provide areas for team sports. Although traditional playgrounds provide many opportunities for exercise, most of the equipment is of single-purpose use. Even the team-sports areas are designed specifically for games-with-rules. Such playgrounds, although certainly of value, do restrict creative expression. (There are, of course, exceptions. Some innovative children walk up the see-saw, balance carefully as it tilts, and then continue their walk down the other side.) Although traditional playgrounds facilitate functional play and games-with-rules, dramatic play and constructions are not encouraged.

CREATIVE PLAYGROUNDS. Creative playgrounds are frequently designed by psychologists, educators, and/or architects. There are, in fact, a number of companies that specialize in research and construction of such play areas (Edwards, 1985). These include a wide variety of "landscape adventures." There are such things as staggered railroad ties, suspended rope and log bridges, and tire configurations for fancy footwork and climbing. There are towers that can be anything from the mast of a ship to a lookout for a fort. There may be swings, caves, and tunnels made from all types of materials. Each part of the play landscape is designed for multipurpose use. The types of play inspired by such a setting is as limitless as the imagination of the individual child.

INTEGRATION OF DEVELOPMENT THROUGH PLAY 343

This tower may be the mast of a ship, the lookout of a fort, or whatever else these children can imagine.

ADVENTURE PLAYGROUNDS. Children have always spontaneously used vacant lots and abandoned structures for adventure play. In recent years, child development specialists have begun to arrange such free-expression play areas. For play equipment, a vast array of scrap materials—from boards to old boats or cars—is collected to be used creatively by the children to make their own structures and configurations. In 1976, a group of interested professionals organized the American Adventure Playground Association to encourage the development of more playgrounds of this type (Frost and Klein, 1979).

Summary

- Play is the free use of time in voluntary activities. In play, the child has control over the planning and implementation of his experiences.
- The child's play is characteristic of his developmental level. During the first two years of life, the child strengthens his sensorimotor abilities through functional play. He handles objects and internalizes their characteristics. He perfects many skills with extensive repetition. After about two years of age, the child has developed a store of symbols to

which he has attached images. Then the child moves into symbolic play—he can use objects, words, and gestures to represent persons, events, and things in his play sequences. From age two to four, the child takes particular delight in constructions. Such creations give him a sense of mastery and an opportunity to express creativity. From about the age of four, pretend play predominates. Through pretend play the child may practice the social skills of his cultural group, or he may embody those characteristics he admires or fears in others. When pretend play involves only one child, it is called dramatic play; when more than one child is involved, the term "sociodramatic play" is used. Games-with-rules develop self-pride and self-reliance, facilitate social participation, and strengthen such cognitive skills as memory, judgment, and problem solving.

- Play serves many functions. The autonomy and control the child exercises in play enhances emotional development. Opportunities for making things and for developing pretend episodes extend the child's creative abilities. Much socialization is gained through interactions in group play. The child reinforces the values of his culture as he relives personal experiences in pretend play. He extends this value system through his observations and his interactions with others. Many play activities provide the exercise necessary for large- and small-muscle development. Language enrichment, cognitive development, and problem-solving practice are natural outgrowths of play sequences. Academic achievement is enhanced through a variety of play experiences that involve subskills related to school learning. Finally, play for the sheer pleasure of it is, in itself, a worthwhile function of play.

- Caregivers can facilitate children's play through judicious selection of toys and construction of play areas. A child's collection of toys should be balanced as to type and purpose. Many toys should be open-ended and adaptable to many uses. Some should be designed to develop some specific skill such as perception or coordination. Some three-dimensional toys are needed for an understanding of scientific principles such as weight, balance, and volume. Some toys should be chosen for large- and small-muscle development and some for encouragement of social participation. Quality of safety and sturdiness should be considered for all toys.

- Three types of playgrounds are often seen. The traditional playground includes such single-purpose equipment as swings, see-saws, and merry-go-rounds. They are most effective in facilititating functional play and games-with-rules. Creative playgrounds contain a much greater variety of objects (towers, bridges, caves, rope constructions). Here symbolic play and constructions as well as functional play and rule games are encouraged. A final type of play environment, the adventure playground, comprises scrap materials from which the children can construct their own play structures.

Selected Readings

Bretherton, I. (ed.). *Symbolic Play: The Development of Social Understanding.* New York: Academic Press, 1984.
    These readings include information concerning theories, cooperative symbolic play, and words and toys used with symbolic play.

Frost, J. L., and Klein, B. L. *Children's Play and Playgrounds.* Boston: Allyn & Bacon, 1979.
    One of the outstanding characteristics of this book is that it contains photo essays and diagrams of all the concepts it presents. Various types of playgrounds are illustrated, and helpful suggestions for the construction of play areas are included.

Frost, J. L., and Sunderlin, S. (eds.). *When Children Play.* New York: ACEI, 1986.
    The functions of play and the relationship of play to areas of child development are described in this book.

Liss, M. B. (ed.). *Social and Cognitive Skills: Sex Roles and Children's Play.* New York: Academic Press, 1983.
    The book explores the relationships between play, sex roles, and many areas of development.

Piaget, J. *Play, Dreams, and Imitation in Childhood.* New York: Norton, 1962.
    This book contains Piaget's ideas concerning the developmental sequence of play and its importance to the child's development.

Smilansky, S. *The Effects of Sociodramatic Play on Disadvantaged Preschool Children.* New York: Wiley, 1968.
    This classic work details the author's observations concerning the various types of and uses for sociodramatic play. Also included are the relationships of age, IQ, and socioeconomic status to these play episodes.

Yawkey, T. D., and Pellegrini, A. D. *Child's Play: Developmental and Applied.* Hillsdale, NJ: Erlbaum, 1984.
    These readings present play as a vital vehicle in the developmental process.

CHAPTER 12

The Child and the Socioculture: Contributions of Society to Development

CHAPTER OUTLINE

Sociocultural Shaping
    Group Traditions
    Family Structure
    Socioeconomic Status
    Communication Patterns
    Educational Opportunities
Current Concerns for which Society Needs Support Systems
    Child Care Facilities
    Divorce
    Child Abuse
Summary
Selected Readings

> Little Indian, Sioux, or Crow,
> Little Frosty Eskimo,
> Little Turk or Japanese—
> Oh! don't you wish that you were me?
>
> You have seen the scarlet trees,
> And the lions overseas;
> You have eaten ostrich eggs,
> And turned the turtles off their legs.
>
> Such a life is very fine,
> But it's not as nice as mine;
> You must often, as you trod
> Have wearied not to be abroad.
>
> You have curious things to eat,
> I am fed on proper meat;
> You must dwell beyond the foam,
> But I am safe and live at home.
>
> Little Indian, Sioux, or Crow,
> Little Frosty Eskimo,
> Little Turk or Japanese—
> Oh! don't you wish that you were me?

("Foreign Children" by Robert Louis Stevenson, in Untermeyer, 1985.)

In this light and humorous verse, Stevenson underscores our tendency to see the people of other cultures as strange and less desirable while viewing our own ways as safe, comfortable, and "proper." The effects of the child's culture on development cannot be overestimated, since beliefs, values, and behavior are formed as children absorb the ways and attitudes of those around them. In this chapter, we consider the answers to two important questions: (1) How does socioculture shape the child's development? (2) What current social concerns exist for which society needs support systems? Much related research is considered in exploring these concerns.

Sociocultural Shaping

Culture may be defined as a pattern of behavior or a way of life learned by an individual while growing up with a particular group. This environment is composed of many sociocultural elements. The five important facets of culture to be explored in this section are group traditions, family structure, socioeconomic status, communication patterns, and educational opportunities.

Group Traditions

Certain basic needs are common to all cultures. As people live in groups, they develop traditions related to the meeting of these needs. What traditions might be considered by people from different groups when faced with the following questions?

- *Shall we live in a single-family unit or an extended-family arrangement?* Many minority groups prefer a family cluster that includes other relatives and friends, since such a unit enables them to be with others who share their traditions, to maintain their second language, and to share finances and family responsibilities (Miller, 1978; Valentine, 1980).
- *What are the traditional food favorites of my group?* These have often developed historically from foods available to the group. In some groups, certain foods are forbidden.
- *What shall I wear?* Fashion in the United States is an amalgam of many cultures, with everything from west Texas cowboy boots to Mexican sombreros.
- *Do I want to be part of the "melting pot," or do I want to retain the ways of my birth culture?* Groups differ in the degree to which they want to change their ways. For example, about 50 percent of the Native Americans who move to the city return to the reservation (White, 1979).

These are only a few sample questions. As you think about group traditions, you can add many more.

Group traditions are passed from one generation to another in many

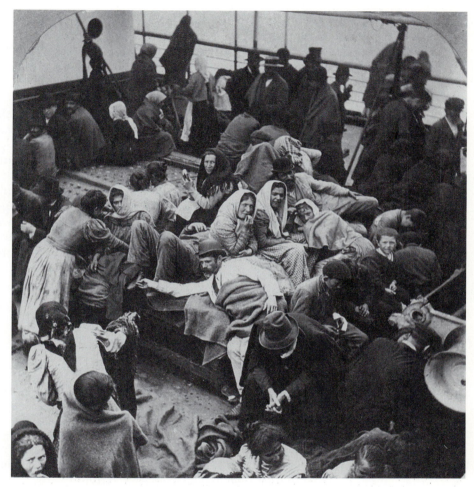

People from many culture groups came to America bringing with them a variety of traditions   (*Source: Library of Congress [LC-USZ62-7307]*)

ways. Raths and his colleagues (1978, pp. 39, 40) describe seven of these in their book on values:

1. *Setting an example* (demonstrating by modeling a behavior that is valued),
2. *Persuading and convincing* (showing the advantages of one set of values and the disadvantages of another),
3. *Limiting choices* ("You can do this or this but not that!"),
4. *Inspiring* (making an emotional appeal for some value),

5. *Rules and regulations* (molding behavior through rewards and punishments),
6. *Cultural or religious dogma* ("Our people have always done it this way!"),
7. *Appeals to conscience* (teaching the child to feel good when he does "right" and bad when he does "wrong").

All of these methods of inculcating group traditions into the behavior of children have both advantages and disadvantages. Some of these are listed in Box 12.1.

The traditions and values for a particular cultural group must never be considered fixed or permanent. The entire group may change gradually or rapidly as a result of such factors as new economic opportunities, increased educational advantages, or social legislation. Stereotyped ideas about other cultures also do not take into account in-group variations. Many circumstances may cause some individuals to be very different from the more traditional or the more liberal members of their culture.

BOX 12.1

Methods of Transmitting Traditions: Pros and Cons

Method	Pros	Cons
Setting an example	May show how to do something (is likely to copy behavior of someone admired)	May learn only one way (may refuse to copy behavior of a model not liked)
Persuading and convincing	May give good reasons	May be perceived as nagging
Limiting choices	May teach self-discipline; may keep child from harm	May stifle initiative and/or creativity
Inspiring	May get the child enthused about an idea or behavior	May annoy or disgust the child with the thing being promoted
Rules and regulations	May teach a "sense" of right and wrong; may help establish good habits	May create resentment and the intent to defy when not watched
Cultural and religious dogma	May show how to become an accepted member of a particular group; may teach goodness toward others	May teach prejudice; may encourage intolerance toward other groups
Appeals to conscience	May make child considerate and empathetic toward others	May cause child to feel constantly guilty and miserable

SOURCE. Summarized from Raths et al., 1978.

Margaret Mead discussed the effects of speed of cultural change on child development (Mead, 1978). In some societies, change is so slow that a child's cultural needs can be predicted at birth. Personal adjustments in these groups are more simple, since the generation gap is small and all members know and agree on expected behaviors. In societies with a moderate rate of change, the present can serve as a guide to future expectations. Here caregivers can estimate with reasonable accuracy the future needs of the next generation and can prepare its members accordingly. In societies where rapid changes are occurring, however, the parents must learn from their children about experiences they have not personally had. In such instances, insecurity, confusion of values, and tension between generational groups often ensues as members of all ages struggle to create new and appropriate cultural structures.

In the United States, all ethnic and socioeconomic groups are undergoing rapid cultural transition. Each generation presents its own distinct lifestyles and values. Many young people can no longer expect to equal or exceed the economic level enjoyed by their parents. All groups must face escalation of such problems as drug abuse and teenage pregnancy. New solutions will have to be found, as current institutions are not meeting many vital social needs.

Family Structure

Family structure is very important in shaping a child's development. Each set of parents has beliefs concerning what its children will need to know and be able to do in order to be successful members of their society (Ogbu, 1981). In order to better understand the impact of the family on children, we consider family composition and changes in family living patterns.

The traditional family as pictured for many years in the first-grade reader was Mother and Father, Dick and Jane, little sister Sally, a dog named Spot, and a cat named Puff. Much has changed. Although many children still live with both father and mother, a host of others live in "single-parent families" headed by either mother or father, in "blended" families which may include a raft of "steps" (parent, brothers, sisters), or in "extended families" which include other relatives or nonfamily members. A child should never be made to feel that his or her family arrangement is "bad." With careful management, each of these constellations can produce children who are healthy and happy.

TWO-PAYCHECK FAMILIES. The number of women working outside the home is steadily increasing. Reasons frequently cited include financial need, new professional opportunities for women, the declining birthrate, and single-parent families (Easterlin, 1982). What effect will this phenomenon have on the development of children? Extensive reviews of research related to physical, cognitive, social, and emotional development have indicated that "the fact that the mother works has no universally predictable effect on the child" (Crouter, 1982, p. 25).

When mothers work outside the home, other family members must learn new roles (Voydanoff, 1984). Both parents generally share the responsibility for child care and household tasks. In very traditional homes of all culture groups, men may hesitate to perform such duties. Cazenave (1983) states, however, that this division of labor is not likely to create contention in black middle-class homes, since middle-class black males generally have supported women's professional endeavors and traditionally have shared both work and home responsibilities. In black families, regardless of socioeconomic level, both partners frequently have worked outside the home for necessary financial security. Strategies they have learned about shared parenting responsibilities could be very valuable to all groups in this time of transition to the two-paycheck family (Hale, 1982). Research studies need to tap the expertise of these black families.

Academic achievement, socialization, and adherence to family values need not be affected if three criteria are met: (1) that the parents both feel good about the mother's employment outside the home, (2) that high-quality child-care arrangements are made, and (3) that the parents plan for regular times with the children in pleasant, constructive interaction through which personal attachment and transmission of ideas can occur. The section on "Child-Care Facilities" which appears later in this chapter contains additional information on current trends.

SINGLE-PARENT FAMILIES. Moving from a two-parent to a one-parent family requires considerable adjustment, as such families are often plagued by financial problems, emotional upheavals, and new role responsibilities. These difficulties are compounded if the single parent is a female head of household. By combining the findings from several research studies, we can profile some of these problems (Valentine, 1980; Ferber, 1982; Tienda and Angel, 1982; Hanson, 1983; Voydanoff, 1984).

- Families headed by women are more apt to be poor than are families containing two parents. This is particularly true if the woman is a minority person.
- Women generally have less education and/or job training than do men.
- Women usually work a fewer number of years and have disconnected work experiences because of pregnancies and child-care responsibilities. (This has a negative effect on both salaries and promotions.)

CONTRIBUTIONS OF SOCIETY TO DEVELOPMENT   353

- Women are often victims of stereotyping concerning the kinds of work they can do. (Many labor jobs and managerial positions frequently are not offered to women.)
- Women may be subject to job discrimination because of the number or ages of their children. (Since minority groups often have larger families, this fact poses special problems for them.)
- Women are less likely to be able to move to take advantage of job opportunities. (They often lack necessary funds for relocation, and they often hesitate to give up child-care assistance available from their families.)

An increasing number of single-parent households are being headed by men. Data concerning these situations are discussed in Chapter 9.

EXTENDED FAMILIES.   When confronted with the problems of single parenting, many people choose extended family arrangements. Such a family generally includes one parent, at least one other related or nonrelated adult, and an assortment of children. One of the advantages of the extended

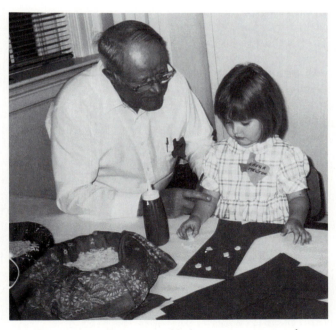

Happiness is having a grandfather come to open house at school.

family is that each child becomes the shared responsibility of the group rather than of one individual (Bilge and Kaufman, 1983). Other pluses frequently cited are the division of household chores among many hands and the combining of incomes for a higher standard of living (Tienda and Angel, 1982). According to the United States Census Bureau, the

---

INVOLVER 12

What Is a Family?

This involver is designed to help you understand a child's concept of family. First, study the questionnaire that follows, so you can speak casually with the children being interviewed. (You will use only the questions, not the italic heading, with your participants.) Next, select six children from four to six years of age. After talking with them for a few minutes to get them to relax, ask the questions and record their answers. Finally, give each child a piece of paper on which to draw his or her family. Answering the "Thinking It Over" questions with their responses should be both amusing and informative!

WHAT IS A FAMILY?

Family membership: Who is in your family? Who else? Tell me about where you live.
Family function: Tell me about how moms and dads help children grow up. What do you learn? What do you do together?
Family effect: In your family, what good feelings (happy, funny, loving) can you tell me about? What sad or angry ones? How do you help each other with these feelings?
Changes in families: How are other families the same or different? Do they change? Will you be a mother or father?

THINKING IT OVER

- From the children's variations in remarks and drawings, what different family constellations did you find? (Any pets?)
- List and tally the items mentioned about how parents help children learn and which activities the family does together.
- How did the children's comments on good and bad feelings help you picture the home climate? Describe any child who had mostly positive or mostly negative responses.
- What concepts of change did the children have? Did they seem happy or apprehensive about these changes?

SOURCE. From *Journal of Research and Development in Education,* 16 (4), Cataldo, C. and Geismar, L. "What Is a Family" Questionnaire, copyright © 1983, University of Georgia. Used with permission.

total number of extended families in this country is decreasing. Another interesting statistic is that, contrary to popular opinion, most Mexican-Americans do not live in extended families (Miranda, 1977; Miller, 1978). This arrangement is, however, still considered an important way to meet financial and family needs and is frequently used by members of all culture groups as a short-term solution in times of difficulty.

What is the child's concept of family and family interaction? This is the subject of the Involver for Chapter 12 and is based on an interview technique developed by Cataldo and Geismar (1983). After interviewing children and analyzing their answers, you should have a refreshing and first-hand impression of the modern American family from the child's point of view.

Socioeconomic Status

What differences presently exist between middle-class and lower-class families? How does ethnic affiliation affect socioeconomic status, and what related problems do minority groups face? These are the questions we shall seek to answer as we examine the relationship between socioeconomic status and four factors: financial position of minorities, parental aspirations, personal attributes, and family relations.

FINANCIAL POSITION OF MINORITIES. A disproportionately large number of minority families fall into the working class. Many negative characteristics attributed to Afro-Americans, Mexican-Americans, and Native Americans result from their socioeconomic status rather than from their ethnic origin (McFadden and Cook, 1983). In an effort to alleviate this situation, two important pieces of legislation were passed (Freeman, 1976). The Civil Rights Act of 1964 prohibits discrimination in wages and working conditions because of race, color, religion, sex, or national origin. The Federal Affirmative Action Order Number 4 states that employers must survey their hiring practices and if a deficient percentage of minorities is being selected, they must develop and follow a plan to eliminate this discrimination. As a result, more minority families are reaching the middle class. Unfortunately, many of the provisions of the Civil Rights Act have been rescinded. Persons who would have benefited from such parts of this legislation are still in difficult straits.

The difference between blacks and Anglos in levels of income and education has diminished sharply (Collins, 1983). The black middle class is in a tenuous position, however, since so many of their professional positions are tied either to government programs or to business ventures in the black community and may be vulnerable to recessions. Another problem faced by blacks is that their unemployment rate is significantly higher than that of Anglos (Pinkney, 1975). The distribution of this unemployment is even more troubling to the black family. Males are more likely to be out of work than are females, and young workers, perhaps just starting families, have more difficulty finding jobs than older blacks do. Racial discrimination is still a vital force in employment patterns. Black males are taught a strong work ethic within the family. Each family member is encouraged to develop talents and use the benefits derived from these efforts for the good of their family units. The inability to find work and to provide financial assistance to their families is a source of great frustration to black men (Hale, 1982).

The socioeconomic plight of the migrant worker is of special concern (Wells, 1976). Although a large number are Mexican-American, all ethnic groups are found among these people. As they trek from the South through the Midwest and back, they draw low salaries and live in poor housing. Their children are likely not to attend school for a full year, since these young people often help their parents work in the harvest. When these families eventually leave the migrant life and move to the city, they are often troubled by lack of trade skills, limited English, and job discrimination (Wells, 1976).

How and where are the Native Americans (Indians) living today? Native Americans are probably the most economically impoverished group in the United States. Estimates indicate that approximately two-thirds of these families are living below the poverty level (Keloe, 1981). Contrary to popular concept, the majority of them do not live on reservations but rather are living in cities (Nichols, 1981). In fact, Native Americans are migrating to the cities at a more rapid pace than any other ethnic group (Steele, 1979). Better jobs and housing are the reasons most often cited for these moves (Steele, 1979).

Native Americans remaining on reservations face special problems (White, 1979). In many cases the land is poor, hunting tribes dislike the limitations of space, and the population is young and expanding. Attempts to bring industry to the reservations have met with little success, since the location of reservations often makes transportation and distribution of goods very difficult (Hagan, 1979).

Poverty is not an ethnic-linked state of existence. Many people fail to recognize that the largest group of poor people in the United States are the poor and lower-working-class white Americans. At the present time, many earlier financial gains made by all groups have become recessed.

Regardless of socioeconomic status or ethnic affiliation, chronic parental unemployment may create special material and emotional stresses. Madge (1983) estimates that one father out of six will be unemployed for an extended period during the time the children are in the home. Although sickness or fluctuating markets account for some cases, many of these

Many families in all ethnic groups live in poverty. (*Source:* © 1988 Ulrike Welsch)

persons are chronically unemployed or underemployed because of lack of basic job skills. Box 12.2 summarizes a review of research concerning the multiple effects of unemployment on the family.

PARENTAL ASPIRATIONS. To what extent does socioeconomic status affect what parents want for their children and what they believe they will accomplish? Marotz-Baden and Tallman (1978) made an extensive survey of existing literature and concluded that there is no clear indication that social class alone greatly affects parental aspirations and expectations. Fotheringham and Creal (1980) concurred and stated that "achievement press of the parents, home language models, academic home guidance, and social participation of the parents are more important predictors of school achievement than are parents' education, occupation, and income" (Fotheringham and Creal, 1980, p. 317).

PERSONAL ATTRIBUTES. Which personal attributes of children currently seem to be related to socioeconomic level? There is some evidence to support the idea that middle-class children may be more future oriented than are their lower-class counterparts. Research activities involving mid-

BOX 12.2
Effects of Unemployment on the Family

Material Deprivation
- Men who are frequently unemployed are apt to be in the lowest-paying jobs when they are working.
- They are more likely than the general population to have wives who do not work outside the home.
- They often have larger-than-average families and subsist with poor food, shelter, and clothing.

Psychological Impact
- Family members feel a sense of social stigma and embarrassment.
- Mothers are often bored, apathetic, and/or depressed.
- Fathers are more subject to psychosomatic reactions such as alcoholism and suicide.

Family Roles
- Even if family members have little to do, they may not spend much time interacting with other family members.
- Fathers often lose their positions of authority in the family and are viewed as failures.

Children's Health and Behavior
- The child of an unemployed breadwinner has twice the risk of an illness that requires hospitalization.
- Research findings concerning effects on behavior and on school progress vary. Lower grades, aimlessness, and delinquency are often mentioned.

Child Abuse
- The abused child is three to six times more apt to have a father who is unemployed.

SOURCE. Summarized from *Journal of Child Psychology and Psychiatry*, 24(2), Madge, N. Unemployment and Its Effects on Children, copyright © 1983, Pergamon Press plc. Used with permission.

dle- and lower-class Anglo, black, and Puerto Rican children indicated that those from higher socioeconomic backgrounds were more able to postpone immediate pleasure in order to win future gains (Freire et al., 1980). In another study, children from middle and lower classes were asked to choose wish items from among twenty categories. Children from white-collar backgrounds tended to choose things related to future plans, whereas children from blue-collar settings showed more interest in tangible things they could use immediately (Guarnaccia and Vane, 1979). A possible explanation for these findings is that lower-class families have less control over their lives and, therefore, feel the need to take advantage of any opportunity immediately lest it not be available tomorrow.

Many research studies have also indicated that children from lower socioeconomic backgrounds are more impulsive than are youngsters from more affluent circumstances (Meade, 1981). This impulsiveness may cause them to respond with the first answer that occurs to them and thus make more errors, lower grades, and lower scores on test batteries. Lack of impulse control, rather than lack of ability or background, may account for the lower achievement levels of some of these children.

FAMILY RELATIONS. Space does not permit a comprehensive investigation of family relations for each ethnic group within the national population. The black family was chosen for analysis because its strengths are representative of the nurturance family relations can provide. Hill has cited five basic strengths in the black family: intense kinship bonds, strong achievement orientation, adaptability of family roles, commitment to a religious orientation, and a strong work ethic (Hale, 1982). Strong kinship bonds are expressed by the "mutual aid" orientation that motivates the black person always to be available to assist her group. These bonds are also found in the "oneness" of those who have become close friends. Black parents have always stressed achievement as a matter of family and ethnic pride. Families sacrifice to give their young better opportunities than were enjoyed by the previous generation. The black family stresses flexibility of family roles by encouraging each family member to contribute to the good of the whole. The assignment of tasks depends on circumstances, not necessarily on sex or age. The strong religious orientation of the black family is due both to religious interest and to the fact that the black church serves as a focal point for social and special talent development. The blacks' strong commitment to the work ethic is evidenced by their quality of work and their efforts to seek employment.

Communication Patterns

Cultural differences in speech patterns can sometimes create total misunderstanding. When my sister was teaching in a predominantly German community, an aspiring first-grade scholar inquired, "Miz Harrison, how do you spell 'day'?" She replied, "D-A-Y," to which the youngster protested, "No, no, Miz Harrison! Not dat kind of day. Dey, like 'Dey went to dah pahk.'" In multicultural settings, you should always remember that the speaker and the listener may or may not be understanding the same content in any given conversation. An equally important consideration is that not all communication is verbal. Facial expressions, gestures, and manners are also used to convey messages. We shall explore how both verbal and nonverbal communication varies according to a person's cultural background.

VERBAL COMMUNICATION. Communication patterns in language emerge as the members of a given culture agree on such things as the meaning of words, the order of sentences, and the gestures that will accompany words to emphasize or clarify their meanings (Longstreet, 1978). Although some words and motions have common meanings to all who speak a particular language, many phrases are unique to individual culture groups. The ability of a person to use these idioms fluently indicates the degree to which this person has been successfully socialized in the group and affects both communication and acceptance to this group (Wright, 1983).

Although we realize that there is no single "standard English," of what use is the more formal, analytical style of the language? One advantage of fluency in this mode is that of versatility. It enables the speaker to communicate with persons who may not fully understand the vernacular of a special group. The second advantage is in writing. When nonverbal cues are absent, the words must have sufficient detail to convey the meaning. A third consideration is that more formal language is frequently used in schools and in business. Success in these areas is often enhanced by ability to use this style. Many varieties of English are used in various parts of the United States. Language fluency requires the ability to choose a communication style that is appropriate for the situation.

NONVERBAL COMMUNICATION. Does Graciela feel lonely and rejected if you never touch her? Is John embarrassed when you try to get him to raise his hand to respond to a question his friends cannot answer? Both students are giving evidence of nonverbal communication patterns that they learned in their respective cultures. Many minority groups are more inclined to touching than Anglos are, and the absence of touching is, to them, an indication of unfriendliness or rejection (Ford and Graves, 1977). In John's Native-American peer group, no one wants to shame his friends by "showing them up." He may be glad, however, to write the correct answer if no one but you sees it, and you don't tell. Meeting children's needs in a multicultural setting involves learning a complex system of nonverbal cues on which much behavior and feelings are based. This can best be accomplished in an individual classroom by (1) very carefully watching the interactions among children of a particular group, (2) talking with them about how they feel in certain situations, and (3) talking with them about how they use words and actions to let other people know what they are thinking and feeling.

Poor communication causes many conflicts between groups. Papagiannis discusses the effects of such misunderstandings on the child's educational experience: "Teachers may respond by regarding students as indifferent, unintelligent, willfully unresponsive, and even belligerent. Students may view teachers' judgments as markedly inconsistent with their own out-of-school experience" (Papagiannis et al., 1983). If a caregiver is conscious of both verbal and nonverbal communication, many problems can be avoided.

Educational Opportunities

Many cultural forces interact to affect educational opportunities. In this section we consider the impact of parental achievement and aspirations, cultural patterning of mental abilities, home-school discrepancies, and guided intervention on the educational achievement of children.

PARENTAL ACHIEVEMENT AND ASPIRATIONS. Parental achievement (what the parent has actually accomplished) and aspirations (what the parent would like to do or see the child do) are both of vital importance to the child. If the parents' achievement levels have been high, they may have the knowledge and resources to provide the child with an enriched and stimulating environment. They may also serve as powerful models, causing the child to want to be like Mom or Dad and showing her how to accomplish this goal. Some high-achieving parents, however, are so busy with their own careers that they have little time for parenting. By the same token, many parents who have had limited educational opportunities strive very conscientiously to give their children educational opportunities they never enjoyed. Dillard and Campbell (1982) investigated the career aspirations of parents from three ethnic groups (black, Anglo, Puerto Rican) and found no pattern of preference or significant difference among their choices. Many factors such as career information services on television, increased job opportunities for minorities and women, and the challenge of upward mobility have caused parents from all socioeconomic and ethnic backgrounds to become very aware of the importance of education in the lives of their children. The extent to which parents encourage and support educational activities for their children greatly affects the level of their educational development.

CULTURAL PATTERNING OF MENTAL ABILITIES. Each culture group values certain skills and enjoys certain activities. These preferences affect the amount of time its members spend doing these things. For this reason, a child growing up in a particular culture gets more practice related to some mental skills and less to others. These differences in emphasis may create definite strengths for some children. Some studies indicate that a child who becomes bilingual or multilingual will be more flexible intellectually than will be the monolingual young person (Duncan and DeAvila, 1979). The dual socialization of the black child enables her to function successfully in two social contexts (Hale, 1982).

Uhlig and Vasquez (1982, p. 46) reviewed research over a ten-year period and concluded that "patterns of mental abilities are the best cross-cultural evidence for the effects of environment and culture on memory development." They found that the child varies in ability in the following areas depending on the culture group to which she belongs:

- recall memory (ability to repeat things seen or heard)
- cognitive tempo (speed of thinking)
- verbal elaboration (ability given to relevant details about a topic under discussion)
- test formats (ability to find correct answers in multiple-choice, cloze, and maze tests)
- causation (correct conclusion about what caused something)
- concept learning (ability to see relationships among ideas in order to understand what something is)
- auditory speech (listening skills)

By examining the foregoing list, you can see that these cultural skills are directly related as to whether the school tasks would be easy or hard for a child.

HOME-SCHOOL DISCREPANCIES. What other discrepancies exist for some children between what is customary at home and what is expected at school? What effects do these differences have on learning and on children's feelings about school? These questions have served as the basis for Ogbu's research. He has identified several cultural areas in which such discrepancies exist. These are summarized in Box 12.3. Ogbu has concluded that the number and degree of educational problems experienced by the child are directly related to the amount of discontinuity between home and school practices.

GUIDED INTERVENTION. A number of instruments and programs have been designed to help parents prepare their children for educational experiences. A notable example is the Home Observation for Measurement of the Environment (HOME) developed at the Children's Center at Syracuse University. This instrument is used to analyze the level of intellectual stimulation and emotional support in the home and to determine how environmental features within the home relate to future educational achievement (Doorninck et al., 1981). This inventory contains six subscales: (1) emotional and verbal responsiveness of the mother, (2) avoidance of restriction and punishment, (3) organization of the physical and temporal environment, (4) provision of appropriate play materials, (5) maternal in-

BOX 12.3

Home-School Differences

Factor	Home	School
Educational (learning) setting	Intimacy, individual standards, degree of dependency	Impersonality (many children), uniform standards, independence
Language	A particular code known and understood by members of the family/culture group	A standard code requiring much more detail (often unfamiliar) for precise communication
Subject areas	Related to everyday life, to some degree familiar	Learning symbols for which child may have no parallel in everyday life
Learning process	Learning how to do things for which student has immediate need (motivation), individual, 1 to 1	Learning group (often large) "how-tos" (how to read, how to write) on which most future advancement will be based but for which many students see no need

SOURCE. Summarized from Ogbu, 1982, pp. 290–307.

volvement with the child, and (6) opportunities for variety in daily stimulation. Dr. Bettye M. Caldwell has been active in the development and use of this instrument over a period of several years. She has concluded that the child's cognitive development is more affected by the quality of the home environment than by social status or family composition (Erickson, 1981). She has further discovered that if the parents are given constructive feedback about the home environment when the HOME inventory is used, they can make changes that will enhance the cognitive development of their children.

Well-meaning caregivers should be careful not to violate the child's cultural identity. Parents should not be made to feel that their ways are wrong and that what they have to offer is inferior. Although home enrichment is very important to cognitive development, such programs should always be based on the interests and values of the group being served.

As we have seen from this portion of the chapter, the socioculture plays an important role in shaping the development of the child. Group traditions, family structure, socioeconomic status, communication patterns, and educational opportunities all are important facets in this shaping process.

The child's cultural identity must always be respected.   (Source: © MacDonald/Envision)

Current Concerns for Which Society Needs Support Systems

Several changes in society are of such magnitude that parents may need community understanding and assistance in order to meet special family needs. Three important concerns receiving current attention are child-care facilities, divorce, and child abuse. What facts are available about each of these areas, and what forms of societal assistance should be initiated? These are the questions to be answered in the following section.

Child-Care Facilities

Over the past few years, the number of child-care placements outside the home has risen dramatically. Why are more child-care spaces needed? Who is sponsoring and/or funding them? What variations are available? What developmental effects may result from these placements? These are only a few of the many pertinent questions that need to be answered.

NEED FOR CHILD-CARE SPACE. Most of the mothers who have entered the work force have reported that they have done so out of economic necessity. For this reason, they cannot afford many of the currently available child-care facilities. There is a critical shortage of good quality, economically priced child-care arrangements (Bridgman, 1985; Mirga, 1985; Sirkin, 1985).

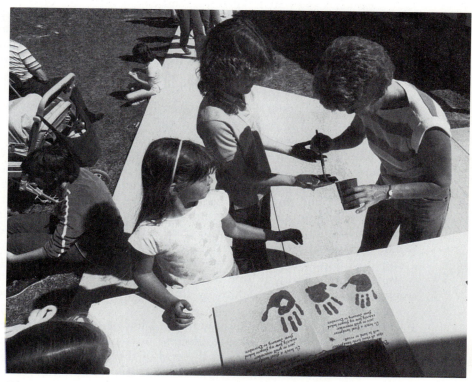

There is an ever increasing need for child care, particularly for low-cost arrangements. (*Source: © MacDonald Photography/Envision*)

Out-of-home child care has also been designed to meet other needs. Some parents take their children to a nursery school or playgroup setting for a few hours a week to provide the child with specific cognitive, physical, or social enrichment. Other children with measurable developmental problems are placed in compensatory programs designed to offset their deficits. Community child-care programs have been sponsored to provide care for the children of parents who are attempting to break the poverty cycle and their dependency on welfare. Finally, a number of facilities offer available space on an hourly basis for "mother's day out"—released time for a mother to transact family business or enjoy a time of recreation.

CHILD-CARE SPONSORS. Child-care centers are sponsored under the auspices of many groups—private individuals, churches, local or national franchises, community agencies, public schools, and places of employment (Fernandez, 1986). Some in each of these categories do a very good job; others do not. Private proprietors may have specialized training in some areas of child development and may offer unique programs. Such programs are often expensive. Churches frequently have the financial advantage of having a portion of the operating expenses underwritten by the congregation. In such cases they can offer outstanding programs at lower tuition rates. Franchises provide funding and training for persons who could not otherwise enter the child-care business. Community agencies combine local, state, and federal grants to provide high-quality low-cost care for families in need of help. There are never enough of these spaces to fill the community needs, and waiting lists are common. Because of declining enrollments, many public schools have available space and staff, and many of these systems offer innovative programs, often on a tuition basis. Finally, many companies, particularly those that employ large numbers of women, have established child-care facilities on their premises. Industrial child care is becoming increasingly popular with both parents and employers, since on-site child-care programs tend to reduce worker absenteeism, provide an opportunity for the parent to see the child at some time during the day, facilitate flexible scheduling in case of overtime, and offer the convenience of a "one-stop" job and child-care arrangement. Unfortunately, there are relatively few of these programs at the present time.

A recurring child-care problem faced by many parents is the fact that there is approximately a ten-to-fifteen-hours-per-week difference between the end of the school day and the end of the adult work day (Rubin and Medrich, 1979). For this reason, almost half of the parents surveyed used multiple-care strategies. (The child is placed in several settings per day or week to meet scheduling needs.) For these parents, the task of evaluating facilities and maintaining firm arrangements is at least doubled. From

CONTRIBUTIONS OF SOCIETY TO DEVELOPMENT

the child's point of view, many adjustments must be made, particularly if there are variations of standards in the different placements.

VARIATIONS OF CHILD-CARE ARRANGEMENTS. When the child is being placed for the major part of a day because of the employment needs of the parent, what child-care arrangements are commonly used? Studies have consistently shown that the majority of children are cared for in a home setting rather than in a child-care center. This home care comes in a variety of forms. Often the child is kept in his or her own home by a babysitter or housekeeper. In extended families, relatives living in the home may provide this service. Brothers and sisters are frequently used for after-school care, and, in extreme cases, these older siblings may be kept home from school to look after preschool youngsters. In most cases, as a matter of economic necessity, the parents have very few options. They have to accept whatever arrangements they can afford.

One variation of home care that has been used by many families is that of "split-shift care." In this arrangement both parents work different shifts, and both care for the children. There are two major advantages

Parents often share child-care responsibilities. (*Source:* © *1988 Brent Jones*)

to this system: (1) Children spend most of their time with their own parents, and (2) the arrangement is dependable except during times of illness or overtime at work. The major problem faced by couples who elect this plan is that they greatly limit the time they have available to spend with each other and with the child together.

Another type of at-home arrangement commonly used is that of the "child-care home." Many women who need additional income but for some reason prefer not to seek outside employment care for children in their homes. Sometimes not more than four children including those of the caregiver are involved. Such a plan provides the small-group setting that many parents want for their children. At other times, the number of children served in a home may be large. Many children whose families have limited incomes are involved in such settings.

Some parents prefer to place their children in child-care centers for several reasons. First, these centers offer a variety of special programs. Some stress skill development with emphasis on cognitive, language, physical, emotional, and/or social enrichment. Others are designed to facilitate creativity through providing a vast variety of stimulating free-play equipment. This abundance of material and equipment is often cited by parents as the deciding factor in choosing a center over a home placement. A second factor often considered is that some centers use only trained child-care workers. Such persons may be more sensitive to special developmental needs of children. In perhaps a majority of the centers, however, the low pay scale results in the hiring of persons with little or no background in the principles of child development. A third plus experienced by center children may be a scheduled variety of community activities such as field trips to the zoo, children's theater, or swimming lessons. Although these same experiences are available to children in home care, many parents find comfort in the regularity with which some centers schedule these events. Finally, many parents who are concerned about socialization prefer that their children meet a larger number of children than they do in a home-care setting. This is particularly true as the children get older. In fact, parents often choose home care for younger children and transfer them to child-care facilities as they get older and nearer the age at which they will enroll in school.

Many children are enrolled in overcrowded, understaffed centers, because the fees are within the family budget. These parents desperately need community support systems. The Perry Preschool Project documented that society recovered $7 for every $1 spent on preschool programs (Bridgman, 1985).

EFFECTS OF CHILD-CARE PLACEMENTS. Since so many children are being enrolled in child-care centers, much research has been devoted to studying

BOX 12.4
Developmental Effects of Group Childcare

Advantages	Disadvantages	No Significant Difference
* (Blusiewicz, in Watson et al., 1984; Doyle, 1975 Golden et al., 1978; Howes, in Watson et al., 1984; Robinson and Robinson, 1978; Rubenstein et al., 1981)	* (Blusiewicz, in Watson et al., 1984; Powell, 1978; Rubenstein, 1981; White and Glode, in Watson et al., 1984)	* (Etduscon, 1977; Kagan, in Watson, 1984; Moore, 1975; Rubenstein et al., 1981)
• Enhanced cognitive development • Expanded verbal proficiency • Earlier development of social skills and the ability to form friendships • More cooperation • Less fear of unfamiliar peers though more apprehension of unfamiliar adults	• High child-to-staff ratios • Competition for caregiver's time • Incompatible models between home and school • Inconsistent reinforcement of behavior • Less compliant and more assertive behavior • High personnel turnover which may necessitate many child/caregiver adjustments • Exposure to infectious diseases	• Attachment to the mother • Cognitive development/mental skills • Language acquisition • Emotional adjustment • Social development • Motor ability • Behavior problems • Aggression level

* Please note: The chart is a summary; not all researchers found each item listed in the column which bears his or her name.

the developmental effects of such placements. Box 12.4 summarizes recent findings. As you can see from examining this box, authorities do not always agree as to effects on the child's development, and both advantages and disadvantages must be considered in selecting a facility.

Divorce

The number of children under eighteen affected by divorce has tripled over the past twenty years. Since 75 percent of all divorces in the United States occur in families with children under eighteen, it is predicted that by 1990, approximately 44 percent of the children in America will live part of their lives before age eighteen with one parent (Albrecht et al., 1983). What life-style changes are likely to occur as a result of divorce, what effects may these changes have on development, and how can society best help these children?

The most basic change in the child's life involves custody. Traditionally the child is placed with the mother, and the father is given visiting rights. Sometimes, however, neither parent is able to assume this responsibility, and custody is given to a third party (relative, friend, foster home). Two other child-care patterns are becoming more common: split custody (in which each parent gets some of the children) and joint custody (in which the child lives alternately with each parent in a somewhat even division of time). Split custody is most frequently used to place children with the same-sex parent. Joint custody was devised to give the child more even exposure to both parents and appears to be successful only if the parents live close together, have similar life-styles, and get along with each other (Luepnitz, 1982).

The problems that exist in the aftermath of divorce have been analyzed by a number of research authorities (Hetherington et al., 1978; Albrecht et al., 1983). The following is a summary of these findings:

CONDITIONS IN THE HOME

- Homes were often more chaotic.
- Meals often occurred at irregular times.
- Mothers were less likely to have dinner with the children.
- Bedtimes varied and the bedtime story was more likely to be omitted.
- Children were more likely to be late for school.

CONDITION OF THE PARENTS

- Both parents, at time of divorce, expressed more feelings of anxiety, depression, anger, rejection, incompetence, loss of attractiveness, and hopelessness.
- Parents suffered most during the first year after divorce.
- After two years, the father's involvement with children greatly diminished (providing less chance for the father to serve as a model or teacher).

SOCIALIZATION PRACTICES

- The custodial parent was often less warm and affectionate with the children because of increased responsibilities and time limitations.
- Children exhibited more negative behavior (especially boys).
- After two years, this negative behavior leveled off for girls but not for boys (although aggression in boys diminished during this time).
- Children exhibited negative behavior most frequently in response to pressure from the mother (haggling, whining, dependency).

Although divorce is a time of great stress for all involved, not all homes fit the disorganized picture just described. If confusion and bitterness are rampant in the home prior to the termination of the marriage, conditions may be calmer after the couple parts (Troyer, 1979). The effects of divorce on a child's life depend on (1) the severity of the problem between the parents, (2) the individual personality of the child, (3) the child's previous experiences with each parent, (4) the preparation the child is given for the divorce, (5) the way the parents behaved during the crisis, (6) the support systems available (other family members, neighborhood, friends), and (7) the age of the child at the time of the separation. Hanson and Reynolds (1980) reported the findings of a four-year research project conducted by Wallerstein and Kelley. The developmental impact of divorce by age is found in Box 12.5.

What can a parent or a caregiver do to help a child deal with divorce (Troyer, 1979; Palker, 1980; Allers, 1981)? First, listen to her fears and feelings. Let the child initiate the conversations, since she may feel very shy about her "different" situation. Try to avoid making judgmental statements about parental disagreements and concentrate on helping the child see that she is accepted, loved, and capable. Second, keep well-written books on the subject of divorce available to the child, as such materials may give helpful suggestions and make her feel that others have successfully faced similar problems. Third, be aware of the child's moods and preoccupations with change and give an extra measure of patience. Fourth, try to divert her attention from her problems to other activities. Redirecting behavior into constructive channels is better than excusing all misbehaviors as reactions to stress. A caregiver must accept the fact that the divorce

---

BOX 12.5

Developmental Impact of Divorce

Age	Behaviors	Age	Behaviors
2½–3¼ years	• Acute regression in toilet training • Increased irritability • Whining, crying • General fearfulness, acute separation anxiety • Variety of sleep problems • Escalation of aggressive behavior and tantrums	3½–4½ years 5–6 years 7–8 years	• Less regression than earlier, more adaptive • Heightened anxiety • Restlessness, whininess, moodiness, sadness • General sadness • Variety of responses (e.g., denial, seeking support from others)

SOURCE: Adapted from research reported by Hanson and Reynolds, 1980.

has occurred, assure the child that the event was not his or her fault, and help the child start a new life.

Perhaps the best insight into children's feelings about divorce comes from their own words. Case Study 12 contains excerpts from "Listen, Divorced Kids Speak!"

Caregivers have no control over the incidence of divorce. What they can do, however, is make a helpful impact on the adjustment of the children in their care who are experiencing this traumatic event.

Case Study 12

Listen! Divorced Kids Speak!

DIVORCE NOTICE

- "I came home from camp and found out Daddy had been gone for three weeks" (Almost every one of 300 to 400 children interviewed complained the divorce occurred without any warning.), p. 26.

CUSTODY

- "I felt like a piece of baggage and they just decided where was the best place to store me," p. 27.

FATHERS WHO DON'T VISIT

- *Wendy is nine:* "I make my Dad a card at school for Father's Day every year. And I bring it home. I've got three cards, now, in my room. I'm keeping them. So if I ever see my Dad again I can give them to him," p. 51.

SHAME

- "And when I filled out the first form, at my new school . . . I just wrote in 'Deceased.' And everyone was very nice about it, and I didn't have to feel guilty anymore," p. 52.

REDUCED FINANCES

- "We don't have much money now and I don't get an allowance, like I used to. So, after school I always have to come home and do chores 'cause I haven't got any money to buy a drink or things like that with the other guys," p. 72.

EQUITY

- "I think my mother got the better of the whole deal. After all, she has us . . . ," p. 96.

NEED FOR DIVORCE

- "Look. Here's the question you have to ask yourself: Is it better to be from a broken home, or to be in a broken home? So pretty often, separation is best for kids, even when it's tough for them," p. 147.

SOURCE. Quotations from Troyer, 1979.

Child Abuse

Another societal problem that is receiving extensive attention today is that of child abuse. It is estimated that more than 1 million children in the United States are victims of physical harm and that at least 2,000 children die from maltreatment annually (Copans et al., 1979). The problem of child abuse is many-faceted, and several key questions concerning abuse and abusers need to be answered (Pagelow, 1984).

What constitutes child abuse? In 1974, the Federal Child Abuse Prevention and Treatment Act defined child abuse as "the physical or mental injury, sexual abuse, negligent treatment, or maltreatment of a child under the age of eighteen by a person who is responsible for the child's welfare under circumstances which indicate that the child's health or welfare is harmed or threatened thereby" (U. S. Office of Human Development, 1976). Each of these categories has been the subject of considerable research.

PHYSICAL ABUSE. Physical abuse may involve both external and internal injury. Hitting is the most commonly reported form of abuse, as it leaves telltale marks. Since a large portion of our population believes in spanking for discipline, it is sometimes difficult to distinguish between overzealous correction and chronic abuse. Other forms of physical abuse are more clear-cut—large bruises, bites, burns, fractures, contusions, lacerations, swellings, lost teeth (Halperin, 1979; Mayhall and Norgard, 1983). Internal injuries are often undetected unless the child is examined by medical personnel. Such examinations frequently reveal evidence of previous and repeated injuries. Children suffering physical abuse may try to hide the marks by wearing long-sleeved clothes or by being absent until the marks heal. When questioned, these children are apt to misrepresent the cause

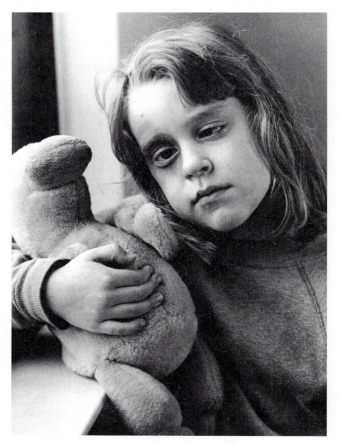

The prevention of child abuse is a major challenge to society. (*Source: Bob Kalman/The Image Works*)

of injury in order to protect themselves from further abuse from the parents for reporting the incident.

SEXUAL ABUSE. Sexual abuse is probably the most hidden form of maltreatment toward children, but research findings have provided some insight into the problem (Halperin, 1979; Mayhall and Norgard, 1983). Seventy-five percent of all sexual abuse involves family members and most frequently is perpetrated by adult males with female children. Such abuse is hard to detect, since no external marks are evident. Indications of the onset of sexual abuse may include sudden changes in behavior—withdrawal, frequent crying, sudden hostility or apparent fear of adults, and extreme anxiety when asked to undress for play activities or physical examinations. Why do children submit to such treatment? Fear of physical punishment, threats of love withdrawal, and desirable presents are often cited as reasons for submission. The mother is frequently aware of the sexual encounters but either ignores the situation or actually encourages the child to submit in order to hold the attention of the man involved.

EMOTIONAL ABUSE. Emotional abuse may be defined as behavior or speech that hinders the personal growth of children (U. S. Office of Human Development, 1976). Many parents do not recognize their emotionally abusive behaviors. They want their children to "do their best." In an effort to propel the youngsters along the road to success, these caregivers set unrealistically high goals, make love and acceptance dependent on conforming to these parental demands, and use criticism or ridicule as means of pressure. Emotionally abused children often become convinced that they are personally worthless and either withdraw and daydream excessively or imitate the critical, aggressive attitudes of the parents. Unfortunately, most emotionally abused children do not realize that the behavior of their caregivers is abnormal; therefore, they are quite apt to model these actions.

CHILD NEGLECT. Child neglect refers to living conditions that endanger the physical, emotional, or mental development of the child (Mayhall and Norgard, 1983). Signs of physical neglect include such things as dirty clothes, cluttered living conditions, and lack of health care. Emotional neglect involves limited or inappropriate interactions between caregiver and child. Some parents are always too busy to share the triumph or crises, listen to children's interests, or participate in nurturing activities with their youngsters. Other parents emotionally neglect their children by failing to provide organization and structure in daily living (teaching the children how to be dependable and how to perform necessary daily tasks). Still others neglect to provide the consistent discipline necessary for social acceptability. Mental neglect includes such actions as failure to provide a stimulating home environment, negligence in ensuring regular school attendance, and disregard for setting a good example by showing personal interest and involvement in educational endeavors.

What personal characteristics and conditions are frequently found to be related to child abusers? After extensive research, Helfer (1974) identified the following:

- Neglect or abuse during childhood
- Low self-esteem and feelings of worthlessness
- Extreme isolation with few friends and emotional support systems (family, church, organization)

- Unhappy marriage relations
- Failure to develop strong attachment to the child during infancy
- Reversal of parent-child roles (use of the child for emotional support and satisfaction)
- Responsibility for a child who is unwanted, ill, different (handicapped, hyperactive, or withdrawn), of the wrong sex (parent wanted child of other sex), or likely to interfere with parent's affiliations or activities (companion doesn't want child around)

No one of these factors causes child abuse, as many persons who live with such conditions do not become abusers. However, if a number of these items are present in a person's life, the chances for child abuse are increased.

What can be done to prevent child abuse? Techniques for dealing with child abuse involve either removal from the abuse setting or in-home treatment for the family (Baxter, 1985). If the physical or emotional welfare of the child is in danger, the child may be removed from the home. Two major problems related to this procedure are (1) foster homes are in short supply and (2) the child may be quite attached to the abusing parent since that is the only model the child has ever known. More often, case workers attempt to counsel the parents while leaving the child in the home setting. Although such professional help often lessens the incidence of abuse, these programs are often so understaffed that workers are not able to adequately monitor family relations to ensure that further abuse does not occur. Public awareness programs and legislation may help gain the support for finding more effective ways to deal with this problem (Nelson, 1984).

In this section, we have explored three major problems a child may face. In each incidence, knowledgeable and conscientious effort by other members of society can make a difference in the child's development.

The importance of the various elements of the socioculture discussed in this chapter to the child's nurturance is well stated by Hilliard (1979, p. 3): "We know, or ought to know, that the child's culture is never a deficit. Rather it is learning's chief asset."

Summary

- Culture is a way of life learned as one grows up as a member of a particular group.
- The socioculture shapes the individual through a number of media. Some of the most important of these are group traditions, family

CONTRIBUTIONS OF SOCIETY TO DEVELOPMENT *377*

    structure, socioeconomic status, communication patterns, and educational opportunities.
- Group traditions relate to every facet of life—for example, what to eat and wear, where to live, whether or not to be open to change. Group traditions are passed from one generation to another by such methods as setting an example, persuading and convincing, limiting choices, inspiring, rules and regulations, cultural or religious dogma, and appeals to conscience.
- Family structure is important since it provides the original setting for development. Family composition may be a family containing only parent and children, a single-parent family headed by either father or mother, or an extended family including other relatives and/or friends. If both parents work outside the home, new challenges must be faced.
- Because of differences in socioeconomic opportunities, many minority persons have less opportunity for middle-class status. Class status does not, however, appear to affect the aspirations parents have for their children's futures. Some personal attributes do appear to be related to socioeconomic level; middle-class children of all ethnic groups appear to be more future oriented and less impulsive.
- There are significant cultural differences in communication patterns. These differences often result in misunderstanding and negative feelings.
- Two major areas of communication are verbal and nonverbal. Individuals who speak an elaborate code rather than a restricted one can express themselves more precisely and are able to communicate about more-complex ideas. Nonverbal communication, such as facial expressions and motor gestures, are also important in conveying messages.
Some ethnic groups rely more on nonverbal communication than on words.
- Educational opportunities for children are related to such cultural forces as parental achievement and aspiration, cultural patterning of mental abilities, similarity or difference between home and school expectations, and the quality and amount of guided intervention afforded.
- There are many concerns for which society needs support systems. The three major ones discussed in this chapter are child-care facilities, divorce, and child abuse.
- Quality child care is a major need as more mothers seek employment outside the home. This care may be provided in the child's own home by a hired caregiver or by parents working in shifts. It may also be given in the home of a relative or friend or in a child-care center. Child-care centers are sponsored by many groups—private individuals,

churches, franchises, community agencies, public schools, and places of employment. Each has special advantages and disadvantages.
- The incidence of divorce continues to increase. When divorce occurs, custody of the child may be given to one parent (usually the mother), both parents (in split or joint custody), or a third party (relative, friend, or foster parent). Many problems are apt to occur. The home may become disorganized; the parents may be hurt or bitter. The home situation may result in conflicts among family members, and the children may exhibit more negative behaviors. Fortunately, not all families involved in divorce will evidence these reactions; many may be more peaceful than when the parents were still together. Caregivers can help children through these hard times by listening, by providing related reading materials, by being aware of moods and feelings, by providing diversions, and by assuring the child that the divorce was not her fault.
- Child abuse occurs far more frequently than had previously been recognized. Child abuse may be physical, sexual, or emotional, or it may involve gross neglect that endangers the well-being of the child. Some recognized causes include neglect or abuse during the parent's childhood, low parental self-esteem, isolation and limited friendships, unhappy marriages, failure to develop attachment to the child during infancy, reversal of parent-child roles, and responsibility for a child who is, for some reason, unwanted. Removal of the child from the home and parental counseling are the ways most frequently used to counteract child abuse.

Selected Readings

ALBRECHT, S. L.; BAHR, H. M.; AND GOODMAN, K. L. *Divorce and Remarriage.* Westport, CT: Greenwood Press, 1983.
    This book gives a comprehensive overview of problems, adaptations, and adjustments related to divorce and/or remarriage.

FERNANDEZ, J. P. *Child Care and Corporate Productivity.* Lexington, MA: Heath, 1986.
    In Part I, the author discusses many issues related to child care and family-work problems. In Part II, suggested solutions are posed.

PAGELOW, M. D. *Family Violence.* New York: Praeger, 1984.
    This work is a comprehensive treatment of the various forms of violence and abuse that occur within the family setting.

POWELL, G. J. (ED.). *The Psychosocial Development of Minority Group Children.* New York: Brunner/Mazel, 1983.
    This collection of readings about minority group children is divided into six categories: health status, psychosocial development, family life patterns,

mental health issues, educational issues, and research and social policy issues. Information about many different minorities is included.

VOYDANOFF, P. (ED.). *Work and Family: Changing Roles of Men and Women.* Palo Alto, CA: Mayfield, 1984.
This book focuses on the changing roles of men and women and the many adjustments that are being made in the family.

PART IV

The Special Child

CHAPTER 13

Cognitive and Physical Differences

Muscle training and use of braces often help the cerebral palsied child. (*Source: © Ben Asen/Envision*)

CHAPTER OUTLINE

    Cognitive Variations
        Giftedness
        Retardation
        Learning Disabilities
    Physical Variations
        Visual Handicaps
        Hearing Impairments
        Speech and Language Disabilities
        Neurological Impairments
        Orthopedic Handicaps
    Summary
    Selected Readings

Until recently, if Peter couldn't hear and was slow in developing language, if Marcus was partially sighted and needed special instructional materials, and if Dennis needed therapy to overcome stuttering, the family was solely responsible for finding and financing the necessary help. Now the education of special children has become a national responsibility and priority.

With the passage of Public Law 94-142, Education for All Handicapped Children Act, the handicapped child has five major assurances (Ingram, 1980, p. 346):

1. The handicapped child must be placed in the least restrictive environment.
2. A free and appropriate education must be provided for each child.
3. A plan and documentation for the evaluation and placement of children into an appropriate education setting must be given.
4. There must be an Individual Education Program (IEP) written that illustrates the direction and outlines the goals and objectives to be met by the program in assisting the child.
5. There must be evidence of due process or procedural safeguards in which the child can contest being placed in or being kept from attending a specially designed educational program.

In the wake of these mandates, parents and child-care workers are cooperatively seeking the answers to the following questions: What are the major characteristics of various mental and physical impairments? What related causes have been identified? What educational strategies can be designed to ameliorate related disabilities? In this chapter, we review research findings related to these questions.

Cognitive Variations

There are three types of cognitive variations that warrant special educational attention. These are giftedness, retardation, and learning disabilities. What are the distinguishing characteristics of children in each of these categories? How may such children correctly be identified? What educational opportunities will enable each child to reach his maximum potential? These are the questions to be answered in this section.

Giftedness

For centuries there has been great interest in those individuals who show special potential in particular areas (Kirk and Gallagher, 1983). Over 2,000 years ago in ancient Greece, Plato stressed the need to identify outstanding children and to educate them in science, philosophy, and metaphysics so they could become leaders in Greek democracy. The sixteenth-century Turkish ruler Suleiman the Magnificent sent scouts throughout his empire to locate talented Christian subjects to be converted to the Moslem faith and trained in art, philosophy, science, and war, so the Ottoman Empire would exceed the accomplishment of its neighbors. Most recently in our own country, a revival of interest in programs of the gifted is occurring. In order to recognize giftedness in many areas, the United States Commissioner of Education recommended that consideration of giftedness not be limited to those who possess high intelligence quotients or accelerated academic achievement records (Roedell et al., 1980). He felt that outstanding ability in the performing arts, sports, creative thinking, and leadership should also be included in the gifted classification.

CHARACTERISTICS OF THE GIFTED.   Since these children are so diverse in their talents, what characteristics do gifted children frequently have in common? By combining the findings of many studies, we can construct a descriptive profile. Please remember, however, that all gifted children are not alike; no single child will excel in each of the dimensions mentioned. Also recognize that these characteristics are found to some degree in most children. Those who are considered gifted possess a greater degree of the attribute and generally evidence it at an earlier age than do most children.

Gifted children are generally above average in health and physical condition (Kirk and Gallagher, 1983). They often exceed their peers in height,

A child may be gifted in any one of many areas. (*Source: Courtesy UNICEF*)

weight, coordination, physical endurance, muscle strength, and lung capacity. They also tend to mature at an accelerated pace; they often talk about three months earlier and walk about one month sooner. Gifted children are also less likely to have physical defects (e.g., sight or hearing problems) or nervous disorders (e.g., stuttering or tics), and they have fewer childhood illnesses.

Although gifted children have sometimes been described as loners and misfits, research has indicated that these children are actually more likely to be emotionally secure and socially well liked than are their nongifted peers (Janos and Robinson, 1985). They are less aggressive and withdrawn and are less inclined to immature behaviors. They participate in more extracurricular activities and possess higher levels of social competence. Because of their ability to organize social situations, gifted children often excel in leadership (Tuttle and Becker, 1983). Arnold has described the personal qualities that make this leadership likely (Kirk and Gallagher, 1983).

1. A strong drive for responsibility and task completion
2. Vigor and persistence in the pursuit of goals
3. Venturesomeness and originality in problem solving
4. Self-confidence and sense of personal identity
5. The willingness to absorb interpersonal stress
6. The willingness to tolerate frustration and delays
7. The ability to influence other persons' behavior
8. The capacity to structure social interaction systems to the purpose at hand

Although these children are flexible and adaptable and can relate well to their peers, they particularly enjoy the companionship of other gifted children or of older friends.

What are the intellectual characteristics of gifted children? First, these children acquire new knowledge with great speed (Roedell et al., 1980). They can process large amounts of information quickly and accurately, form rapid generalizations, and learn the use of abstract symbols to which they are exposed at an accelerated rate. Second, they have superior memories (Roedell et al., 1980). Many of these children have almost automatic retention for material that has been presented in a learning situation or has been observed in a daily life setting. Third, gifted children have a high level of curiosity (Tuttle and Becker, 1983). They are likely to immerse themselves in a topic of interest and explore it in great detail. They constantly seek to understand the how and why of the things they observe, and their seeking nature causes them to absorb more from the environment. These children are also particularly adept at seeing relationships (Kirk and Gallagher, 1979; Roedell et al., 1980; Tuttle and Becker, 1983). They excel in generating both analytic and unique problem solutions. Their perception of relationships also enhances their ability to transfer information learned in one situation to related incidences. Finally, these children have usually developed at an accelerated rate; they perform tasks at an earlier age than expected. When their progress is monitored into later years, they have been found to maintain this high level of intellectual functioning. One word of caution should be included, however. The child with a high IQ may experience a gap between his mental ability to plan and his physical ability to execute it. As with any child, the caregiver should strive to help the gifted young person plan realistically and be proud of his accomplishments.

IDENTIFICATION OF THE GIFTED. Many resources are used in identifying the gifted, and Hagan (1980, pp. 11–12) listed the following examples:

1. School records
2. Teachers and other school personnel who have worked with the child
3. Parents or guardians
4. Other adults in the community who have worked with the child
5. The individual student
6. Products of the child
7. Peers

School records may include the results of several types of measurement. The Stanford-Binet (Form L-M) is frequently administered to young children who are believed to be intellectually gifted (Roedell et al., 1980). It can be used for older children also; the examiner can test until the child's intellectual ceiling has been reached. Stafford (1978) found that the following scores were widely used for designating degree of giftedness: 110–119, high average; 120–139, superior; 140 up, very superior. Tests for creativity may also be included (Roedell et al., 1980). *The Torrance Tests for Creative Thinking* (Torrance, 1974) contain tasks that require either verbal response or figural arrangement. These are evaluated in terms of fluency, flexibility, originality of response, and elaboration. Another instrument, the *Educational Testing Services CIRCUS Battery* (1979), involves asking the child to make a tree from a pile of colored stickers. One week later, the subject is asked to "make a tree as different as possible from the other tree." The test is then scored on its resemblance to a tree, its unique features, and its difference from the first tree. A third type of instrument used to evaluate giftedness is a behavioral rating scale. Such scales are often used to help caregivers be more objective and systematic in their observations of children. Box 13.1 includes a sample from the Renzulli and Hartman "Scale for Rating Behavioral Characteristics of Superior Students." As you can see from examination of this instrument, the use of such a scale might broaden the base of student characteristics considered in identifying giftedness in students.

Although tests and scales are very useful in documenting certain types of giftedness, most educators place great importance on the personal descriptions of those who have interacted with a child who is being consid-

BOX 13.1
Sample Rating Scale Items: Superior Students

Part I:	Learning characteristics	• Has unusually advanced vocabulary for age or grade level; uses terms in a meaningful way; has verbal behavior characterized by "richness" of expression, elaboration, and fluency
Part II:	Motivational characteristics	• Strives toward perfection; is self-critical; is not easily satisfied with own speed or products
Part III:	Creativity characteristics	• Displays a great deal of curiosity about many things; is constantly asking questions about anything and everything
Part IV:	Leadership characteristics	• Is self-confident with children his own age as well as adults; seems comfortable when asked to show work to the class; generally directs the activity in which he is involved

SOURCE. Scale for Rating Behavioral Characteristics of Superior Students by Renzulli, J. and Hartman, R., *Exceptional Children*, 38, 1971, pp. 245–246, Copyright © 1979 by The Council for Exceptional Children. Reprinted with permission.

ered for a program for the gifted. These commentaries may include qualities not included on a test or scale, or they may explain interactions among strengths or compensations for weaknesses that greatly affect the child's functional capacity.

For certain types of giftedness, an interview with the child or an examination of his creative products is a necessary part of the identification process. The personal magnetism of a child gifted in leadership or the dramatic arts can best be witnessed by direct observation of the child, and the quality of the child's creations needs to be determined by seeing samples of these products.

EDUCATION OF GIFTED CHILDREN. Several types of educational arrangements have been used with gifted children. These include acceleration, special classes or programs, and enrichment within the regular classroom (Tuttle and Becker, 1983; Horowitz and O'Brien, 1985).

An early adaptation for giftedness was the practice of skipping grades. Two problems frequently resulted: (1) The child was not gifted in all areas and missed many needed skills, and (2) the child was not developmentally able to compete with older children. (These age differences are particularly important in the areas of physical coordination and social development.)

Special classes and programs and enrichment within the classroom have both provided opportunities for gifted children to have special learning opportunities tailored to their interests and abilities. In many school systems, these programs are scheduled on a part-time basis for a few hours each week, so the young children will not be isolated from their peers.

Retardation

The American Association on Mental Deficiency defines retardation as "substantially subaverage general intellectual functioning existing concurrently with deficits in adaptive behavior, and manifested during the developmental period" (Brewer and Kakalik, 1979, p. 88). Thus, a retarded individual is one who is unable to achieve the level of independence and social responsibility that is typical of his age group. Mental deficiency is sometimes obvious during infancy when the child is quite late in reaching several developmental landmarks such as sitting up, walking, or talking. Milder retardation is often not noticed until the child has difficulty in school.

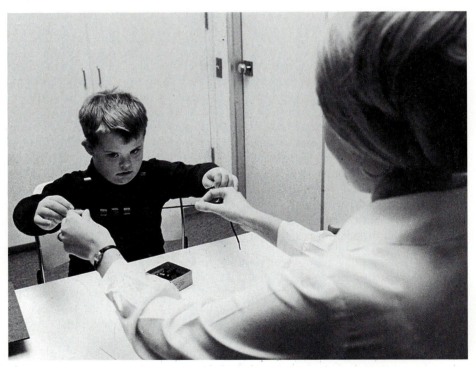

Many new methods are available for working with children who have learning limitations. (*Source: United States Department of Health and Human Services*)

CLASSIFICATION OF MENTAL RETARDATION. Mentally retarded individuals are often classified into the following four categories (Weiss and Weisz, 1986):

MILD MENTAL RETARDATION (IQ 55–69)
- About 80 percent of all retarded persons are in this category.
- Social and communication skills are near normal.
- These children can eventually master academic subjects to about the sixth-grade level and can become self-supporting.

MODERATE MENTAL RETARDATION (IQ 40–55)
- These children are likely to have noticeable physical disabilities.
- They may learn some basic academic concepts.
- They generally cannot live independently as adults.

SEVERE MENTAL RETARDATION (IQ 25–39)
- These children have definite speech and motor impairments.
- They may eventually learn basic self-help skills.

PROFOUND MENTAL RETARDATION (IQ < 25)
- These children frequently cannot walk or communicate in speech.
- They generally require lifetime custodial care.

Children with mild mental retardation are often referred to as the educable mentally retarded (EMR), and children in the moderate category are called the trainable mentally retarded (TMR). Since children in the lower ranges of intelligence are difficult to measure, the difference between classification as an EMR or a TMR is often that of expected potential (Macmillan, 1982). The EMR will likely master basic subjects such as reading and arithmetic and ultimately will become an independently functioning citizen. A TMR, however, will generally learn only basic words and numbers and will require continuous supervision and financial support.

CAUSES OF MENTAL RETARDATION. Berlin (1978) has charted the problem of mental deficiency in terms of when the damage occurs. His findings are summarized in this section.

Before conception, the mother's health and physical condition are of paramount importance. Any medical treatment over a prolonged period which necessitated the use of strong drugs may cause structural damage to chromosomes or ova and may result in retardation in future children. Long-term maternal diseases such as diabetes, childhood acute leukemia, kidney disease, or high blood pressure also have been identified as contributing factors in mental impairment. Finally, diet of the mother and its relation to her overall general health over a period of years is most important in the production of a healthy child.

At the time of conception, two circumstances increase the risk of retardation. First, if the mother is over thirty-five years of age, the risk of producing a Down's syndrome child is significantly increased. Second, if recessive genes for disorders associated with retardation are carried by both parents, an impaired child may be conceived. Both of these factors are discussed in detail in Chapter 3.

Conditions during pregnancy should be carefully monitored. Maternal diseases and disorders, toxins, radiation, and infections can cause irreversible brain damage. Inadequate nutrition during this period may also retard brain development.

Labor/delivery is another crucial period. A major cause of retardation in children is the loss of blood supply and oxygen to the brain at this time. Cerebral palsy is one of the disorders that often result from such oxygen deprivation. Mental impairment may also occur if infections such as herpes, tuberculosis, or streptococcus are transmitted to the child as he passes through the birth canal.

Extensive neonatal care is needed for some children in order to prevent impairment. Prematurity is one such condition, since it is a leading cause of mental retardation. Children who weigh above 1,500 grams have a good chance for adequate physical and mental development. Children who weigh less than this amount, however, run a great risk of retardation. Premature children need to be carefully monitored to be sure that adequate oxygen, temperature, nutrition, and freedom from infection are provided.

Environmental hazards may result in mental retardation at any time. Approximately 1,500,000 children are involved in accidents each year. Many of these incur brain damage. An additional million suffer mental impairment from swallowing toxins. Many others catch infections such as meningitis, diptheria, and measles which can result in loss of mental ability. Safety training, careful observation, and regular immunization could reduce these numbers.

Some children develop functional retardation as a result of environmental conditions. Neisworth and Smith (1978) refer to these as "at-risk" children. When they surveyed the effects of enriched environments on the development of these children, they concluded that:

1. At-risk children placed in more stimulating environments are likely to show intelligence score gains (sometimes as much as ten to thirty points).
2. Such children not provided with enriched environment are apt to evidence IQ losses.

COGNITIVE AND PHYSICAL DIFFERENCES

3. Enrichment, when provided, should be offered during the early preschool years, as later intervention does not result in large gains.
4. Increases in intellectual functioning appear to be maintained over a period of years.

WORKING WITH MENTALLY RETARDED CHILDREN. Nurturance is particularly important to children of limited learning capacity. A successful program for working with mentally retarded children should contain several essential elements:

1. Teachers should understand the learning processes and problems typical of these children. Such knowledge can enable them to plan and execute appropriate learning experiences.
2. A large number of curricular materials that are of high interest level must be available for each task to be taught. Use of these aids will provide an opportunity for much needed repetition without boredom.
3. Individual instruction and/or small class size is necessary for extensive teacher-pupil interaction.
4. Concepts and skills should be presented at a pace that is slower than would be used for non-learning-impaired children. Positive reinforcement including praise and immediate rewards or feedback should be used to sustain attention and cooperation.
5. A strong parenting component should be implemented to ensure continuous opportunities for progress.

Learning Disabilities

For years, child-care workers have noted that some children of normal intelligence have learning difficulties in specific areas. A term to designate these children and a definition to describe them has created much controversy for two reasons: (1) There are so many different learning problems involved, and (2) determination of the exact cause of these variations is often impossible. A working definition that is widely used was suggested by the National Advisory Committee on Handicapped Children (1968):

> Children with special learning disabilities exhibit a disorder in one or more of the basic psychological processes involved in understanding or using spoken or written language. These may be manifested in disorders of listening, talking, reading, writing, spelling or arithmetic.

CAUSES OF LEARNING DISABILITIES. Learning disabilities may be caused by a variety of conditions or circumstances (Ysseldyke and Stevens, 1986).

One of the major causes is believed to be brain malfunction. Damage to some area of the brain may cause perceptual problems or difficulty in making mental associations. A great problem in diagnosing minimal brain dysfunction is that brain injury is very difficult to measure and to prove. Most children with learning disabilities are believed to be of average or above average intelligence, because their functional level in some areas is much higher than in others. For example, if a child has advanced speech and reasoning but cannot trace letters provided to him, there is good reason to suspect a learning disability. Box 13.2 provides details about a new procedure for mapping electrical activity in the brain.

A genetic component is sometimes present in a learning disability. Twin studies and analyses of family learning patterns have demonstrated that language learning disabilities such as dyslexia often run in families and most frequently affect males.

Environmental factors account for some learning disabilities. Malnutrition during the first two years of life may reduce the number of brain cells, thus creating permanent brain damage. Insufficient stimulation may also retard mental development.

A new frontier in the search for factors relating to learning disabilities is the investigation of biochemical elements and their effects on learning behavior. Learning disabilities may occur because of an imbalance in body chemistry. Megavitamins, drugs, and diets free of food additives, food colors, and excess sugar are sometimes used to correct this perceived biochemical problem.

DESCRIPTIONS OF LEARNING DISABILITIES. Wide variation exists in the classification of learning disabilities. Kirk and Chalfant (1984), highly recognized authorities in this area, have organized these deficits into five

---

BOX 13.2

Brain Research

Two Harvard research specialists are using the new Brain Electrical Activity Mapping (BEAM) technique to analyze different patterns of brain activity in the diagnosis of learning disabilities. BEAM can summarize information on brain activity from twenty different locations and make statistical comparisons between the learning-disabled sample and a control group. Such data may lead to a better understanding of brain involvement in various types of learning disabilities.

SOURCE. Summarized from Torello and Duffy, 1985.

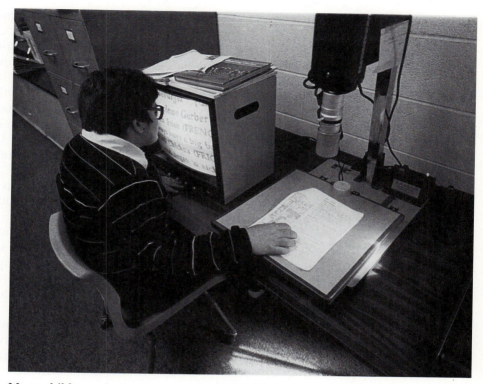

Many children who have perceptual difficulties may experience difficulty in learning to read.   (*Source: © MacDonald Photography/Envision*)

categories: attention, memory, perceptual, thinking, and oral language. The data included in the following paragraphs are based on their work.

An *attention disability* is a problem in focusing on a selected activity. The child may be highly distractable (constantly shifting attention to various things occurring in the environment) or overly attentive to some irrelevant detail (concentrating so much on one insignificant part that he misses the main idea). He may have a very short attention span and be unable to concentrate for the duration of a lesson. He may also have trouble shifting attention at appropriate times. The child may become so deeply engrossed in whatever activity he is doing that he cannot go on to the next topic or lesson.

Memory disabilities occur because the child cannot hold a thought in short-term memory long enough to transfer the idea to long-term memory. The ability to recognize items to which they have been previously exposed, to recall information, and to engage in rote memory are all diminished in children with memory deficits. These memory impairments may be for things that have been seen, heard, or experienced by touch.

Several types of *perceptual deficits* are common among learning-disabled children. Some have discrimination problems. They may have visual difficulty seeing differences in letters (b,d) or words (was, saw) or auditory problems in distinguishing between similar sounds (t,d; p,b). Other children find closure difficult; they cannot readily recognize a whole when parts are missing. These children may try to spell out letters in order to read and have trouble noticing the order of letters in spelling. Children with visual-motor problems may have poor eye-hand coordination or left-right awareness.

Thinking disabilities may affect concept formation or problem solving. Children with conceptual deficits may have difficulty in noticing likenesses and differences, in selecting common characteristics that determine that something does or does not belong to a group, and in retaining criteria in mind long enough to examine the things to be classified. Problem-solving deficits may cause children to have difficulty designing and/or remembering logical problem-solving steps. If their thinking is impulsive, they may also respond to their first impression rather than thinking the problem through.

Oral language disabilities may be receptive, expressive, or integrative. Children with receptive language disorders have trouble receiving language information from others. They may have difficulty associating words with their meanings and following instructions. Children with expressive language problems understand what is said to them, but they have difficulty putting their own thoughts into words for communication with others. Children with integrative language deficits have trouble understanding word associations. They often cannot reflect on the independent meaning of a word and at the same time consider its relationship to other words in the sentence. For example, when working with analogies, the teacher said "Father is a man; Mother is   ?" "Fat!" chirped the child whose mother was on a diet.

WORKING WITH LEARNING-DISABLED CHILDREN. Since there are so many different variations involved in learning disabilities, comprehensive suggestions for each type go beyond the scope of this book. There are, however, several general guidelines that will help caregivers who work with these children:

- Structure carefully so that learning tasks are sequenced to build on past experiences.
- Present materials at a slower pace when necessary with many parallel activities for reinforcement. (Avoid setting time limits.)

COGNITIVE AND PHYSICAL DIFFERENCES

- Teach the child to clear his work space each time he begins a new activity in order to minimize distractions.
- Use teaching materials that tap different modalities (sight, sound, touch) to compensate for any modal deficits the child may have.
- Use warmth and praise to encourage best efforts.

Physical Variations

Many children have physical variations that must be considered by their caregivers when planning developmental experiences for them. In this section, we consider the special needs of children who are visually handicapped, hearing impaired, speech and language disabled, neurologically impaired, and orthopedically handicapped.

Visual Handicaps

Since many visual handicaps go undetected, caregivers need more information concerning types of visual impairment and the special needs of children who have these problems. Consider the following important questions that need to be answered.

How is visual ability classified? Sabatino (1979) described visual performance in three basic levels, each with subcategories:

NORMAL: NORMAL, NEAR-NORMAL

A designation of normal or near-normal vision indicates that the individual can perform tasks related to seeing without any special aids.

LOW VISION: MODERATE, SEVERE

The low-vision category comprises those who need visual correction in order to perform daily vision-related activities. At the moderate level, sight is near normal with correction; at the severe level, vision is impaired even with the use of an aid.

BLINDNESS: MODERATE, SEVERE, TOTAL

The term "blindness" does not indicate a total lack of sight, but rather a visual ability of less than 20/200 in the better eye after correction. The ability to perceive some light and/or some shapes and forms is very important in the education of such children.

What are some of the major visual disorders and their causes? There are two major types of visual disorders—refractive errors and muscle defects

Many visual problems can be corrected by wearing glasses. (*Source: United States Department of Health and Human Services*)

(Sabatino and Miller, 1979; Kirk and Gallagher, 1983). Refractive errors refer to distortions in the way the light enters the eye. In hyperopia (farsightedness), the light hits beyond the retina, and the individual has difficulty seeing things close up. Many young children are farsighted until about the age of six or seven years. This is the reason that close eye work, such as reading, is often postponed until sight is more mature. In myopia (nearsightedness), the light hits the eye before it reaches the retina, and the person has difficulty seeing at a distance (e.g., items on a chalkboard across the room). Astigmatism, caused by irregular curve of the eye lens, results in distortion and indistinct visual images. Eye muscle defects may cause (1) a lack of coordination between eye muscles that results in crossed eyes, (2) an eye that wanders from the usual position and creates a blurred image instead of a clear one, and (3) jerky eye movements that also impair clarity of vision.

Kirk and Gallagher surveyed the literature relating to initial causes of visual impairments. According to their findings, major causes of visual disabilities include infectious diseases, accidents and injuries, poisonings, tumors, prenatal environment, and heredity (Kirk and Gallagher, 1983).

What are the signs of visual impairment? Fallen and Umansky (1984) have listed nine behaviors that can alert a caregiver to possible visual problems:

1. Chronic eye irritations as evidenced by watery eyes or sensitive eyelids
2. Complaints about visual blurring or the inability to see
3. Rubbing of eyes, frowning, squinting, excessive blinking
4. Tilting head when reading or holding reading matter in an unusual position
5. Nausea, double vision, or blurring when reading
6. Avoiding reading-related activities
7. Inattention to visual tasks
8. Lack of gross- or fine-motor coordination
9. Crossed eyes

When any of these symptoms are noted, the child should be examined by an eye specialist to determine the cause of the problem and necessary remediation.

What are the special needs of visually impaired children? There are several measures that need to be taken when working with children who have visual limitations. First, be sure the best correction for the visual problem is made. This may involve glasses, eye exercises, or even surgery. Second, place the child in an appropriate learning environment. If the child is in a classroom setting, seat him near the front of the room, make sure lights do not glare on either the chalkboard or the face of the teacher when instruction is being given, and use enlarged print for learning materials whenever possible. Use many "hands-on" manipulatives from which he can learn concepts through his sense of touch.

Visually impaired children have particular difficulty in developing cognitive concepts and social skills. Lowenfeld observed that blind or partially sighted children experience problems because (1) their inability to see limits the number and variety of their experiences, and (2) their difficulty in locomotion adversely affects their interactions with objects in the environment (Kirk and Gallagher, 1983). Social skills are hard for blind children to acquire, since so many of these attributes are learned modeling behavior that has been seen (Hersen, 1983).

Hearing Impairments

"It is generally estimated that between 14 and 20 percent of school age children have some difficulty hearing" (Sabatino and Miller, 1979, p. 32). These hearing impairments often go undetected, since there is no way to directly observe hearing losses (Reed, 1984). When hearing-impaired children go to school, they may be misclassified as mentally retarded because of the limited quality and quantity of their responses (Reed, 1984). What does the caregiver need to know in order to meet the needs of these children?

CAUSES OF DEAFNESS. Some children are born deaf and others become deaf as a result of illness, injury, or accident. The site of impairment may be the outer, middle, or inner ear.

There are two major types of hearing impairment: conductive deafness and sensorineural deafness (Reed, 1984; Bordley et al., 1986). Conductive deafness is caused by deformities of the outer and/or middle ear. These malformations occur when drugs such as thalidomide are taken during pregnancy. They may also result from infections, enlarged adenoids, fluids in the middle ear, and objects poked in the ear by the individual. Total deafness will not occur from damage to the outer and middle ear; the bones of the skull conduct some sound, although at much less intensity (Reed, 1984; Bordley et al., 1986). In such cases, hearing aids to amplify the sound or lipreading to give an additional clue to what is being said can be used, and the child is likely to be assigned to a regular classroom. Sensorineural deafness may occur in the inner ear, to the nerves between the ear and the brain, or to nerves within the brain itself. This type of hearing loss may be caused by genetic defects, German measles during the first trimester of pregnancy, viral infections, drugs, prematurity, anoxia (loss of oxygen), or environmental noise. Such losses cannot be corrected, and the child will need to be placed in a special class for the deaf.

SIGNS OF HEARING LOSS (Fallen and Umansky, 1978). How can the caregiver detect a hearing loss in a child? First, chronic inattention may indicate that the child is not hearing enough of what is being said to motivate sustained listening. Second, failure to respond when addressed may indicate a problem. This is particularly true if the child is not looking at the speaker at the time the utterance is made. Many children lip-read rather than hear and caregivers fail to notice that they have a loss. Third, unusually delayed speech and/or significantly poor articulation may also

COGNITIVE AND PHYSICAL DIFFERENCES

Amplification can improve hearing if the impairment is not in the inner ear. (*Source:* © *Marilyn M. Pfaltz*)

provide a clue to impairment, since the child had not been able to hear distinctly enough to model the sounds to which he has been exposed.

TESTING FOR DEAFNESS. A hearing test must always check for two things: (1) how loud or soft a sound can be heard by the individual and (2) how loud the sound registers at different sound frequencies (Reed, 1984). If the child cannot hear a soft sound, a hearing aid can be used to amplify the sound. If, however, he has an imbalance in hearing sounds produced at different frequencies, he will hear a distortion rather than comprehensible speech. Vowels are louder and are of lower sound frequency; consonants are softer and of higher sound frequency. Since the English language comprises vowels and consonants, disabilities in volume and/or sound frequency could make the following sentence incomprehensible (sentence patterned after Reed, 1984):

"Good morning; I'm glad to see you."
"oo o i I a o ee you"   (hearing vowels only).
"G d m rn ng; m gl d t s"   (hearing consonants only).

The initial screening for hearing impairment should be done by a school hearing specialist (audiologist). Children who are identified as having a loss should then be referred to a doctor who specializes in hearing problems (otologist) for diagnosis and possible treatment.

WORKING WITH HEARING-IMPAIRED CHILDREN. Two important factors must be considered in helping children with hearing loss. First is the age at which the impairment occurs. If the hearing problem happens after the child has begun to develop speech, it is far less serious. He has heard speech and had the concept that words are related to things and ideas. A loss that occurs before the onset of language requires much more intensive training. The second critical factor is the extent of the impairment. Hearing loss may occur to any degree—slight, moderate, or severe. It may affect one side only or both sides. It may also be for only certain frequencies (very high or low pitches). If the loss is slight or moderate and if amplification can be used to make an adequate correction, the child can stay in the regular classroom. If the problem is more severe, special facilities and teachers are needed. Box 13.3 contains suggestions from Safford concerning work with hearing-impaired children in the regular classroom.

When the child is placed in a special classroom, three systems of communication may be used. Some children are taught manual sign language (American Sign Language—ASL). Others are encouraged to rely more heavily on lipreading. The current trend, however, is that of total communication—manual sign language, lipreading, amplification (if the loss is conductive), and training of any traces of natural hearing. In this way, the hearing-impaired child uses every available modality for language comprehension. Special training designed to help parents work with their children

---

BOX 13.3

Working with Hearing-Impaired Children

1. Make visual cues available to the child.
   - *Stand so the child can see you.*
   - *Use a wide variety of audiovisuals.*

2. Be sure the child's position is optimal.
   - *The light should be on the speaker's face.*
   - *Stand in such a position that the sound will go toward the child's good ear.*

3. Speak in clear, well-modulated tones.
   - *Enunciate carefully.*
   - *Don't talk too fast.*

SOURCE. Safford, 1978.

usually begins early as soon as the disability is diagnosed. All three of the methods just described may be included (Krantz, 1985; Rodel, 1985).

Speech and Language Disabilities

When the child's speech is noticeably different and he has difficulty making himself understood, the child is said to have a speech or language disability (Fallen and Umansky, 1984). The variations considered in this section are articulation differences, stuttering, voice problems, and delayed or absent speech. One word of caution is needed: Always consider the age of the child before deciding he has a speech or language disorder. Language development continues throughout a lifetime, and rigid timetables for the acquisition of particular skills are not valid.

ARTICULATION DIFFERENCES. Faulty articulation is the most common communication disorder and accounts for about 60 percent of all speech-related clinical referrals (Safford, 1978). The most common errors are substitution, omission, addition, and distortion (Kirk and Gallagher, 1983). Young children often substitute an easy sound for one they find hard to make. (My nephew lovingly referred to me as Aunt Bat instead of Pat. "Boff" for "both" is also frequently used by children who have not yet developed the "th" sound.) Omission is likely to involve the letters at the end of words (gimme/give me, cah/car). Such omissions may make language difficult to understand. Some children add sounds to words, such as "sumber" for "summer" or "on-a the table." Finally, distortions of sounds occur when the child either fails to hear the correct sound or has difficulty making it.

What are the major causes of faulty articulation? One of the most common problems is that of incorrect models. The child may be replicating the sounds he has heard and still be mispronouncing words. Another source of difficulty is impaired hearing. The child may not be able to discriminate small differences between sounds if hearing is faulty. In other cases, structural malformation or neurological problems make some sounds very difficult to make. Children with cleft palate have defects involving the palate, mouth, and lips that cause them to have poor articulation and a distinct nasal quality to their speech. Cerebral palsied children may omit or slur sounds because of spastic movements.

STUTTERING. Stuttering has been described as "a disfluency of speech which involves blocks, hesitations, prolongations, and repetitions" (Fallen and Umansky, 1984). The child may show signs of this problem as early as during the second year. The speech impairment is not necessarily con-

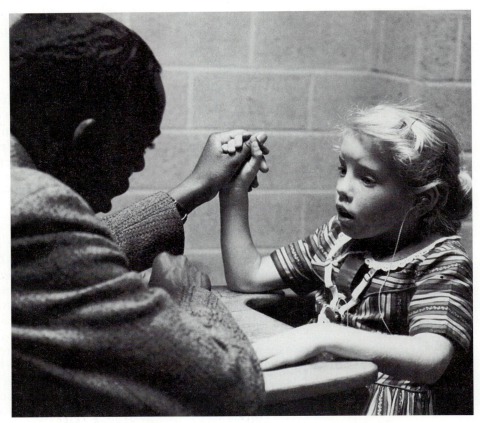

Faulty articulation, the most common speech disability, may result from incorrect models, hearing impairment, structural differences, or neurological problems. (*Source: From Armstrong*)

stant. Many children alternate between fluent speech and stuttering. This speech impairment can result from any one of several causes. Many times an organic problem is suspected, since stuttering occurs more frequently in left-handed persons, twins, individuals whose beginning speech was delayed, or those who suffered illnesses that could have resulted in damage to the central nervous system. Certain psychological factors may also cause stuttering. Early anxiety problems between parent and child, self-concept conflicts, and modeling of a stuttering friend or relative are common examples.

Treatment of stuttering varies. Primary emphasis is given to relaxation techniques, since stuttering is often more frequently manifested when the individual feels stress. Behavior modification is also used. The individual is taught specific behaviors to use in connection with speech.

VOICE PROBLEMS. There are several types of voice problems that often come to the attention of speech therapists. Among these are voice quality, voice pitch, and voice loudness (Kirk and Gallagher, 1983). Structural differences in the nasal passages, the mouth, or the tongue may cause some of these speech variations. After any necessary or possible medical corrections are made, the speech specialist may use intensive one-to-one modeling with corrective feedback to help the individual achieve more normal speech. Inappropriate voice pitch often self-corrects with age.

DELAYED OR ABSENT SPEECH. Most children begin to talk between the ages of two and three years. Several conditions, however, may cause a delay in speech production. Among these are hearing impairment, environmental deprivation, behavioral disorders, mental retardation, and cerebral malfunctions (Fallen and Umansky, 1984). Amplification and verbal training often can facilitate speech for a child with a hearing problem. Language-enriched preschool programs can be used to compensate for limited early language exposure. Speech delays caused by such behavioral disorders as autism and childhood schizophrenia require intensive language therapy, and even then normal speech may not fully develop. In cases of retardation or cerebral malfunction, speech is likely to develop, but at a much slower rate. The length of the delay and the extent to which the child ever develops verbal fluency depend on the degree of the retardation or cerebral malfunction.

Neurological Impairments

Impairment of the central nervous system can create a variety of physical, mental, and psychosocial problems. Two of the most common handicapping conditions related to neurological variance are cerebral palsy and epilepsy. Both of these disorders are being widely researched, and the debilitating effects of each can be lessened through knowledge and understanding on the part of parents and other caregivers.

CEREBRAL PALSY. Cerebral palsy is a term used to designate a variety of conditions that (1) result from damage to the motor center in the brain and (2) most frequently occur early in life and impair normal brain function and (3) involve lack of coordination, weakness, and/or paralysis (Gamstorp, 1985). It is one of the most prevalent of all handicapping conditions. Cerebral palsy may be caused by problems that occur before, at, or after birth (Martin, 1983). During pregnancy, toxins or Rh incompatibility may cause damage. During the birth process, the child may suffer loss of oxygen (anoxia) or receive a head injury at the time of delivery (particularly from forceps). During childhood, a disease such as encephalitis or spinal meningitis or a blow to the head as a result of an accident or abuse can cause cerebral damage. Cerebral palsy is not a progressive disease; whatever disability results from the damaging incident does not get continually worse (Gamstorp, 1985).

There are several types of cerebral palsy, but two are most common: spastic and dyskinetic. The *spastic* condition occurs when a constant increase of muscle tone causes such a stiffness that the person cannot straighten his hand, foot, or whatever part is affected (Gamstorp, 1985; Molnar, 1985). If a leg is affected, a halting walk results. This tension is so intense that it even continues during sleep. The *dyskinetic* condition is characterized by excess movement. This may be manifest in slow, writhing movements or twisting disorders; in rapid, irregular jerky movements of the face and/or other parts of the body; or in wide, flailing movements of arms and legs. Thus, all types of cerebral palsy involve some distortion of appropriate muscle tone or movement.

Several modes of treatment are used with the cerebral palsied. Muscle training through childhood and adolescence can sometimes check excess movement and give greater muscle control. Surgery can often be used to improve position and function of body parts. The use of braces may give the necessary support to improve coordination. If seizures are present, drug therapy can be successfully used. Finally, speech therapy is often needed because of impairments of muscles in language-production areas.

EPILEPSY.   Epilepsy is a disorder characterized by seizures that are caused by irregularities in the electrical impulses in the brain. The brain injuries that result in epilepsy may be caused by genetics, head injuries, faulty metabolism that affects the functioning of certain brain cells, nutritional deficiencies, diseases or infections involving the brain, or high fever (Fallen and Umansky, 1984).

There are two major types of epileptic seizures (grand mal and petit mal) and two other forms which occur less frequently (myoclonic and akinetic). In a *grand mal seizure,* the individual loses consciousness and often twitches violently. People who have this form of epilepsy report that they frequently have advanced warning of an oncoming attack. Such signs include strange sensations, nausea, and cramping (Safford, 1978). By contrast, *petit mal seizures* do not involve a loss of consciousness. The episodes last from about three to ten seconds during which time the individual usually just stares. Since no disruptions occur, these seizures

Case Study 13

When the first-grade teacher asked for guidance in working with a child who had epilepsy, the school nurse gave her the following set of guidelines from The Epilepsy Foundation of America (Gearheart and Weishann, 1976, p. 81; Safford, 1978, p. 190). These ideas will be of value to all who work with children.

1. Remain calm. Students will assume the same emotional reaction as their teacher. The seizure itself is painless to the child.
2. Do not try to restrain the child. Nothing can be done to stop a seizure once it has begun. It must run its course.
3. Clear the area around the student so he does not injure himself on hard objects. Try not to interfere with his movements in any way.
4. Do not force anything between his teeth. If his mouth is already open, a soft object such as a handkerchief may be placed between his side teeth.
5. When the seizure is over, let the child rest if he needs to.
6. The child's parents and physician should be informed of the seizure.
7. Turn the incident into a learning experience for the entire class. Explain what a seizure is, that it is not contagious, and that it is nothing to be afraid of. Teach the class understanding toward the child, not pity, so that his classmates will continue to accept him as "one of the gang."

---

are very hard to detect. *Myoclonic seizures* are characterized by a sudden jerk that lasts for only about a second, and *akinetic seizures* involve a sudden loss of muscle strength which may cause the person to stumble, fall, or drop something.

When a seizure occurs, many caregivers are at a loss to know how to respond. Case Study 13 offers concrete suggestions.

Orthopedic Handicaps

An orthopedic handicap is described as a crippling condition that impairs the functions of bones, joints, or muscles to such a degree that the individual needs some form of special education (Fallen and Umansky, 1984). Some of these orthopedic problems are apparent at birth; others occur postnatally as a result of diseases, disorders, or injuries.

ORTHOPEDIC BIRTH DEFECTS. One of the most common birth defects involving orthopedic impairment is spina bifida (Safford, 1978; Badell-Ribera, 1985). This condition is caused by a failure of the vertebrae to close around the spinal cord or by the reopening of this closure during the first three months of pregnancy. A cystlike formation containing part of the spinal cord or its covering tissues may protrude from the spinal column, or a vertebral malformation may exist without such a sac. Since paralysis occurs below the location of the malformation, the higher on the spinal column the vertebral fault occurs, the greater the damage. Even if the sac is removed, the damage cannot be reversed. Paralysis of legs and lack of bladder and bowel control are frequent associated problems. Hydrocephalus (fluid on the brain) often occurs with spina bifida. A medical process called "shunting" is used to drain the excess fluid from the brain in an attempt to prevent extensive brain damage and/or retardation. Many spinal bifida children are not learning impaired, and they can be placed in the regular classroom if problems related to their dysfunctions can be managed by school personnel.

Some orthopedic impairments visible at birth can be corrected by surgery. Some examples are clubbed foot (misshaped appendage), polydactyly (extra fingers or toes), and cleft lip and/or cleft palate (structural deformity of the mouth area). With therapy and physical training, children with these defects can function well in the regular educational settings.

POSTNATAL ORTHOPEDIC PROBLEMS. Many children develop orthopedic handicaps at some time during the childhood years. The following chart summarizes data concerning some of these debilities:

Defect	Cause/Description	Prognosis
Polio	Viral infection of the motor cells in the spinal cord causing paralysis and crippling	Therapy and/or braces may restore some movement; damage usually permanent
Muscular dystrophy	Disease of the muscles causing weakness and/or atrophy	Progressive impairment; exercise, medication, and braces may help
Multiple sclerosis	Disease that attacks the central nervous system, impairs nerve transmission, and results in loss of muscle coordination and sometimes blindness	Often involves periods of wellness alternating with times of acute illness; rest and physical therapy may help

COGNITIVE AND PHYSICAL DIFFERENCES

Defect	Cause/Description	Prognosis
Rheumatoid arthritis	Disease causing swelling, stiffness, and deformities in many joints	Progressive, results in severe crippling
Leg-calve-perthes	Degeneration of material in the femur that can cause flattening and lack of fit in the hip joint	Cast or brace used to keep body weight off joint until disease is over
Injury or amputation	Accidents; diseases causing impairment of circulation	Cast, brace, or (in case of amputation) prothesis; therapy as needed

As a result of PL 94-142, many special children will find their way into regular classrooms. With knowledge, patience, and planning, the needs of these children can be met. In order to better understand about working with exceptional children, follow the instructions in Involver 13.

INVOLVER 13

Working with exceptional children involves careful identification, assessment, and planning. To gain firsthand knowledge from professionals in the field, follow these three steps:

1. Pick a category of exceptionality.
2. Design an interview questionnaire including such information as:
   - how children are identified (parents, teachers, community agency referral)
   - how children are assessed (medical tests or records used, descriptions of psychological tests and informal assessments such as inventories, checklists, and observation guides administered)
   - how intervention is conducted (copies of IEPs and ARD meeting records).
3. Make an interview appointment with a public school consultant specializing in your area of interest or with personnel at a school noted for work with children having that exceptionality.

THINKING IT OVER

- Review your notes on identification, assessment, and intervention.
- Write a short paper summarizing your findings.

Summary

- Three significant types of cognitive variation are giftedness, mental retardation, and learning disability.
- Gifted children frequently are accelerated in physical, mental, emotional, and social growth. They may be identified through referrals from caregivers or peers or through examination of their school records and/or creative products.
- Mental retardation may be classified as mild (educable to about a sixth-grade level), moderate (trainable in simple concepts and activities), severe (significantly impaired in mental or motor functions), and profound (without capacity for such functions as speech or walking). Mental retardation may be caused by poor maternal physical condition prior to pregnancy, prenatal complications, injury at birth, or accidents later in life.
- Learning-disabled children exhibit problems in one or more of the basic communication processes (e.g., reading, writing, speaking). Education of these children often focuses on structured work related to attention, memory, perception, thinking, or oral communication.
- Physical variations among children include visual handicaps, hearing impairments, speech and language disabilities, neurological problems, and orthopedic handicaps.
- A child's vision level may be classified as normal/near-normal (can perform tasks without special aids), low (needs correction for daily activities), or blind (may see light and shapes or nothing). Evidence of visual impairment may include self-reports of seeing difficulties, squinting/blinking, nausea, or avoidance of or inattention to visually related tasks.
- Two major types of hearing impairments are conductive deafness (malformations of the outer or middle ear) and sensorineural deafness (problems in the inner ear or in nerves to the brain). Conductive deafness can be partially corrected through the use of a hearing aid that amplifies sound; sensorineural losses cannot be corrected.
- A person is said to have a speech or language disability if he has difficulty making himself understood in spoken words. Such impairments include faulty articulation, stuttering, voice problems, and delayed or absent speech.
- Neurological impairments involve damage to the central nervous system. Persons with cerebral palsy have movement difficulties characterized by poor coordination and/or by paralysis of certain muscles. Those who

are epileptic are subject to seizures caused by irregular electrical impulses in the brain.
- An orthopedic handicap is one that involves crippling in bones, muscles, or joints. One of the most common disorders in this category is spina bifida (prenatal failure of vertebrae to close around the spinal cord). Other examples include polio, muscular dystrophy, multiple sclerosis, rheumatoid arthritis, and injury or amputation.

Selected Readings

BROWN, R. T., AND REYNOLDS, C. R. (EDS.). *Psychological Perspectives on Childhood Exceptionality: A Casebook.* New York: Wiley, 1986.
This comprehensive work includes information on many areas of exceptionality including both gifted and disabled.

FALLEN, N. H., AND UMANSKY, W. (EDS.). *Young Children with Special Needs.* Columbus, OH: Merrill, 1984.
This book contains separate chapters about each of a number of developmental variations.

HOROWITZ, F. D., AND O'BRIEN, M. (EDS.). *The Gifted and Talented: Developmental Perspectives.* Washington, D. C.: American Psychological Association, 1985.
Current research related to many facets of giftedness are contributed by various authors.

KIRK, S. A., AND GALLAGHER, J. J. *Educating Exceptional Children* (4th ed.). Boston: Houghton-Mifflin, 1983.
In this work, the authors describe various types of exceptionalities and appropriate educational strategies.

CHAPTER 14

Relational Dysfunctions

"MY MOM SAYS I COME FROM HEAVEN. MY DAD SAYS HE CAN'T REMEMBER AN' MR. WILSON IS POSITIVE I CAME FROM MARS!"

All children exhibit a variety of behaviors. Only those behaviors that are consistently extreme may be classified as relational dysfunctions. (*Source: DENNIS THE MENACE® used by permission of Hank Ketcham and © by North America Syndicate*)

CHAPTER OUTLINE

    Excessive Reaction: Attention Deficit Disorder: Hyperactivity
    Lack of Relatedness (Autism)
    Hesitant Relatedness
        Phobias
        Depression
        Withdrawal
        Extreme Shyness
    Hostile Relatedness (Aggressive Disorders)
    Summary
    Selected Readings

Many children who are neither mentally nor physically handicapped have behavioral problems that hinder their relations with others. Consider the contrasting portraits of two children. The first is a description by the distraught teacher of a hyperactive child:

> While I attempted to take attendance, Philip hopped from desk to desk in a frenzy of motion. He squealed and grunted, clapped his hands, grabbed other children's crayons and bumped against their arms as they tried to color pictures. . . . If his large leg muscles were not being used in running around, his smaller hand muscles were in motion. Even the muscles of his mouth were in constant movement as he blew scraps from his desk. . . . I asked [Philip's mother] how long he had been this way. "He was born with his mainspring wound too tight," she answered. (Schasre, 1978, pp. 156–158)

The second is an account by the concerned parent of a very reticent child:

> I have a daughter who is extremely shy, and who has an extremely low opinion of herself. Her excessive shyness has caused her a great deal of discomfort in peer as well as adult relationships. She has been placed in pre-first instead of first grade because of her inability to deal confidently with others her own age. . . . She can be a lovely, sensitive child, but I'm afraid she'll find the world a hostile place unless someone can help her. (Zimbardo, 1981, p. 2)

In this chapter we examine data concerning relational dysfunctions that affect the well-being of children and their associations with others. We also evaluate strategies for working with these young people.

Excessive Reaction: Attention Deficit Disorder (Hyperactivity)

The American Psychiatric Association now uses the term "attention deficit disorder" to connote the child who is inattentive, impulsive, and hyperactive. Many professional writers, however, still use the term "hyperactive" to describe such children.

Children who are in perpetual motion will have a variety of relational problems partly because their constant movements and impulsive behaviors bother other people and partly because their inattentiveness keeps them from being able to develop the skills expected of children their age. They may also develop low self-concepts because of their academic and social failures (Loffredo et al., 1984). In order to better understand this disorder, answers to questions concerning description, diagnosis, causes, effects, and management strategies will now be discussed.

What is considered hyperactive behavior? One professional jokingly stated

Not all very active children should be labeled hyperactive.   (*Source: Envision*)

that hyperactivity exists when the activity level of the child exceeds that of the caregiver! Although many exhausted adults might agree with this definition, some children exhibit activity patterns that are excessive even for normally active children. The American Psychiatric Association estimates that about 3 percent of our children have attention deficit disorders accompanied by hyperactivity (DSM-III-R, 1987). The behavior patterns are usually observable by the age of three, although they may not present social or learning problems until these children start school.

Hyperactive children characteristically are overly or inappropriately active, impulsive, unduly responsive to nonrelated aspects of a situation, and of low frustration tolerance. Even during a structured learning situation, hyperactive children tend to engage in more excessive, nonrelated motions such as eye movements and head turns than do their nonhyperactive peers (Ceci and Tishman, 1984). Hyperactive children talk and move more during quiet, low-stimulation times or when several alternatives are available and no clear preference is shown. They have difficulty inhibiting movement during periods of low stimulation (Zentall et al., 1983). My mother says that she can distinctly remember, as a child, pushing her books off the edge of her desk when the room got too quiet, because the stillness made her extremely edgy.

In order to help you more precisely picture the hyperactive child, the diagnostic description of attention deficit disorder published by the American Psychiatric Association is included in Box 14.1. Symptoms must have been manifested by the child for more than a year for a classification of deficient attention to be rendered.

As you can see from examining the box, the characteristics of hyperactivity are so typical of many active children that many disagreements can occur when diagnosing these children. When teachers rated children using three different diagnostic scales, the percentage of children identified as hyperactive varied from 5.6 to 12 percent (Holborow et al., 1984). Since labels often become self-fulfilling prophecies, great care should be taken to avoid mistaken identification.

What causes some children to be hyperactive? Hyperactivity may result from brain damage or dysfunction, neurological problems, or biochemical disorders (Kauffman, 1977; DSM-III-R, 1987). It may be associated with mental retardation, epilepsy, some forms of cerebral palsy, or perhaps even food additives and sugar levels. Some studies have shown a relationship between hyperactivity and heredity. Since children tend to imitate the significant persons in their lifespace, however, the relative effects of heredity and environment are hard to separate.

Gender also appears to be a factor in hyperactivity. Approximately ten times as many boys are identified as hyperactive as are girls (DSM-

BOX 14.1

Attention Deficit Disorder

Note: Consider a criterion met only if the behavior is considerably more frequent than that of most people of the same mental age.

A. A disturbance of at least six months during which at least eight of the following are present:
   (1) often fidgets with hands or feet or squirms in seat (in adolescents, may be limited to subjective feelings of restlessness)
   (2) has difficulty remaining seated when required to do so
   (3) is easily distracted by extraneous stimuli
   (4) has difficulty awaiting turn in games or group situations
   (5) often blurts out answers to questions before they have been completed
   (6) has difficulty following through on instructions from others (not due to oppositional behavior or failure of comprehension), e.g., fails to finish chores
   (7) has difficulty sustaining attention in tasks or play activities
   (8) often shifts from one uncompleted activity to another
   (9) has difficulty playing quietly
   (10) often talks excessively
   (11) often interrupts or intrudes on others, e.g., butts into other children's games
   (12) often does not seem to listen to what is being said to him or her
   (13) often loses things necessary for tasks or activities at school or at home (e.g., toys, pencils, books, assignments)
   (14) often engages in physically dangerous activities without considering possible consequences (not for the purpose of thrill-seeking), e.g., runs into street without looking

Note: The above items are listed in descending order of discriminating power based on data from a national field trial of the DSM-III-R criteria for Disruptive Behavior Disorders.

B. Onset before the age of seven.
C. Does not meet the criteria for a Pervasive Developmental Disorder.

Reprinted with permission from the *Diagnostic and Statistical Manual of Mental Disorders, Third Edition, Revised,* Copyright 1987 American Psychiatric Association.

III-R, 1987). Both physical differences and cultural expectations have been cited as reasons for this finding. Research concerning hyperactive girls is very limited. A review of the studies that have been published indicate that such girls are more impulsive and less well-adjusted than their male counterparts (perhaps because active behavior is considered more normal and acceptable in males than in females). Although they are overactive in kindergarten, girls may tend to become assertive learners as they get older. Whereas some hyperactive boys are quite aggressive, hyperactive girls are likely to express a tendency for depression (Ackerman et al., 1983).

Maturation sometimes has an effect on hyperactive manifestations (DSM-III, 1987). For about one-third of all hyperactive people, all symptoms continue for a lifetime; for another third, symptoms disappear at about the time of puberty; and for the final third, hyperactivity disappears at puberty but inattention and impulsivity remain.

How does hyperactivity affect academic progress and social relations? Hyperactive children frequently experience difficulty in schoolwork and in peer interactions. The three major characteristics of their disorder—constant movement, impulsivity, and inattention—each contribute to their problems. Kirk and Chalfant (1984) identified three attention factors related to learning tasks that are problematic for hyperactive children:

1. Attention selection (the ability to screen out all distractions and concentrate on the task at hand)
2. Duration of attending behavior (the ability to maintain attention focus for the amount of time necessary to accomplish the task)
3. Attention shifts (the ability to move attention from one aspect of learning to another as necessary to follow a lesson or accomplish an assignment)

A child with a significant attention deficit would be unable to control behavior to the extent necessary to accomplish these three tasks of learning. After repeated failures, the lowered self-concept may cause her to feel that school success is not worth the effort.

The findings of extensive research indicate that hyperactive children frequently experience difficulty in relations with their peers (Pelham and Milich, 1984). Their rowdiness and clumsiness make them undesirable companions when control and skill are needed, as in performance or game situations. Their impulsiveness often makes them less reliable and/or more apt to make needless mistakes. The hyperactive child's greatest social debit, however, may be aggression. Although not all hyperactive children are aggressive, it is a characteristic common to many of these young people (Trites and La Prade, 1983; Hinshaw et al., 1984). Medication such as Ritalin may reduce disruptive classroom behavior; however, it does not reduce negative social behavior or increase prosocial tendencies.

What can be done to foster control and boost achievement in hyperactive children? A number of different strategies have been used to help hyperactive children (Kauffman, 1977; Ceci and Tishman, 1984; Loffredo et al., 1984). I have summarized their findings in the following chart:

Method	Description
Medication	• Stimulant drugs such as Ritalin and amphetamines are used to slow hyper children. Little is known about long-term effect, relationship to conceptual learning, or later predisposition for drug abuse.
Relaxation techniques	• Relaxation techniques have been taught to hyperactive boys and their mothers. Techniques are to be used at least once a day and always before the boys must sit still. Personal, social, and intellectual self-concepts have improved for the boys involved.
Behavior modification	• Rewards are given for desired behavior; nonreward or punishment is paired with undesirable behavior. Much success has been reported in the literature.
Structured environment	• A minimum-distraction environment is created in which clear, consistent expectations and a nonvarying classroom routine are maintained. The teacher is highly directive. Research reports indicate a high rate of success.
Self-instruction	• Children are taught to verbalize each behavior before acting on it. Both talking aloud and to oneself are used. This approach shows good promise.
Modeling	• Much hyperactive behavior is learned. As hyperactive children interact with nonhyperactive peers, new and less-distracting behavior is often acquired.
Biofeedback	• Children can be trained to control muscle tension. Although this method is now limited to the laboratory, related methods may be adapted to natural settings.
Mega-vitamin therapy	• Massive doses of vitamins and withdrawal from certain foods (especially those containing certain dyes or additives) have been used to control hyperactivity. Results have not conclusively established success.

Lack of Relatedness: Autism

Autism is a relatively rare disorder affecting about two to four children in 10,000. "The essential features are lack of responsiveness to other people, gross impairment in communication skills, and bizarre responses to various aspects of the environment, all developing within the first 30 months of age" (DSM-III-R, 1987, p. 87). Autism was once considered a form of childhood schizophrenia. Now authorities believe that there are several types of autism that have similar symptoms and that autism may vary greatly in its severity. They further classify it as a developmental disorder probably present from birth. The following discussion of autism

RELATIONAL DYSFUNCTIONS

is based on data gleaned from the research findings of the American Psychiatric Association (DSM-III, 1987).

DESCRIPTIONS OF AUTISTIC BEHAVIOR. The autistic child's lack of response to people is often first noticed in infancy by a lack of attachment behaviors such as cuddling, eye contact, and facial expression. Later, the disorder is evidenced by an inability to engage in cooperative play and to form friendships. Sometimes social involvement may develop as the child grows older in less-severe cases of autism.

Many types of treatment are used to help autistic children. (Source: President's Committee on Mental Retardation. Courtesy United States Department of Health and Human Services)

Often communication disorders are reflected in IQ scores. Since language skills are extremely limited for many autistic children, 40 percent score below 50 on IQ measures, and only 30 percent score above 70.

When speech is present, the listener notes rudimentary grammar structure, echolalia (repetition of words or short phrases), confused switching of the words "you" and "I," and strange voice pitches. These children are apt to be strongest in manipulative or visual-spatial skills and in immediate memory. They are most likely to have difficulty in verbal tasks, particularly those involving abstract thought or sequential logic.

Much has been written about the bizarre behavior of these children. They are often either highly responsive to stimulation or completely unaffected by it. (Those who have limited perception of pain often must wear a football helmet to prevent them from beating their heads against things.) Autistic children appear to be very uncomfortable with change. They often react violently to any alterations in their lifespace. They are also noted for their unchanging behavior. (Rocking back and forth for extended periods and establishing elaborate and unvarying procedures to mealtime or bedtime are common.) These children generally show an intense interest in moving objects. Tops and other things that whirl particularly seem to fascinate them. Perhaps this love of movement accounts for their enjoyment of music. Because of their responsiveness, music therapy is important in working with some of these children.

CAUSES OF AUTISM. Since authorities believe there are different types of autism, a number of possible causes must be explored. These include biogenic, biochemical, genetic, and psychogenic factors (Paluszny, 1979; DSM-III, 1987). Biogenic brain damage or dysfunction is indicated by the fact that many autistic children show abnormal brain wave patterns. Epilepsy is more common in autistic children than in the general population. Brain damage with autistic symptoms has also been linked to the effects of phenylketonuria, meningitis, encephalitis, tuberous sclerosis, and maternal rubella. Faulty biochemistry in some autistic children includes malfunctions of the neurotransmitters that cause interference between nerve impulses and muscle contractions and chemical imbalances that make the body unable to use some of its chemical substances. Evidence of genetic factors in some cases of autism is based on the fact that three times as many boys are autistic as are girls and that a couple has a fifty times greater chance of having another autistic child if they already have one. At one time, autism was believed to be caused by parents who had "refrigerator personalities." Authorities now believe that a very small percentage of cases of this disorder are related to defective parental personalities.

TREATMENT FOR AUTISM. A number of types of treatment have been initiated with autistic children (Paluszny, 1979). At present, none of these restore large numbers of these children to normal functioning. Frequently, a number of approaches are used with a given child in the hope that there will be a favorable response to one of them. Changes in biochemistry may be induced by mega-vitamin therapy (often using massive doses of the B vitamins) or by hormone supplements (e.g., thyroid derivatives). In a large number of cases, progress in language development and specific behavior changes are accomplished through behavior modification. Some children suspected of having oral language deficits have been successfully reached through the use of American Sign Language, which is used with deaf children. In severe cases, a total environmental change is recommended, and the child is placed in a residential facility where she can receive consistent monitoring and conditioning on a continuous basis.

According to figures collected by the American Psychiatric Association, the prognosis for autistic children is disheartening at this time (DSM-III, 1987). Only one in six will make sufficient adjustment to be able to work and to relate socially. Another one in six can be expected to make only fair progress. The remaining two-thirds will remain severely handicapped and will require custodial care for life.

Hesitant Relatedness

Some children seem reluctant to relate to their environments. They are not so withdrawn that they have lost contact with reality, but their social and cognitive functions are impaired by emotional problems. Four categories of disturbance that are frequently seen by parents and child-care workers are phobias, depression, withdrawal, and extreme shyness. What causes these difficulties and what can be done to alleviate them is the focus of this section.

Phobias

A phobia is an intense and ever-present fear of a particular person, place, or thing that is grossly out of proportion to any harm that is apt to come from that source (DSM-III-R, 1987; Kellerman, 1981). Young children often have such exaggerated anxieties because of their limited understanding of cause and effect. Until they have had more experience, they cannot determine how likely something is to hurt them or how severe the damage may be. Animals and the dark are two common examples of things that evoke phobic fears in children. When phobias occur, the child should never be teased or shamed. Several avenues of treatment may be tried. Sometimes a cognitive approach involving talking about

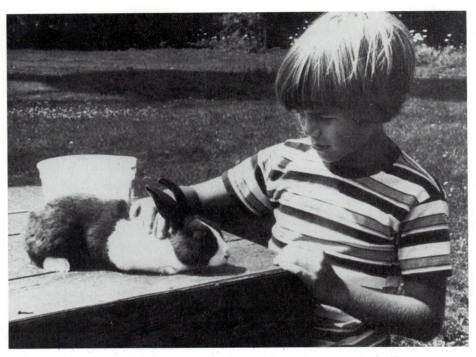
A child with a phobia for furry animals would not enjoy petting this rabbit. (*Source: Courtesy, National Science Teachers Association, photograph © 1988 Joanne Meldrum*)

the fear may be successful. Bibliotherapy (use of books or stories) may be combined with these discussions. (*Where the Wild Things Are* by Maurice Sendak has often been used to reduce fear of the dark in small children.) Sometimes desensitization is helpful. In this approach, the child is exposed for greater durations of time to the thing feared while receiving reinforcement and encouragement from a supportive caregiver. If phobias persist, professional help should be arranged.

As children get older and are placed in organized group settings such as nurseries or schools, about 1.7 percent will experience school phobia (Morris and Kratochwill, 1985). This malady often manifests itself after weekends, holidays, or illnesses (Kellerman, 1981). It may be characterized by open resistance to leaving home or by signs of physical distress such as vomiting, dizziness, or abdominal pain. Even though the symptoms are of psychological origin, the pain and discomfort to the child may be very real.

What causes school phobia? The answer may lie in maternal relationships, peer experiences, school conditions, or the personality of the individual child (Harris, 1980; Kellerman, 1981). Many children feel intense anxiety about leaving their mother. This may be caused by such factors as a fear that the mother will not be home when the child returns or that a younger child will get all of the mother's love and attention while the schoolchild is gone. Separation anxiety may also be a function of the mother's behavior. Many child-care workers avow that children would be happy if their mother didn't make such an emotional scene as she leaves. If the child has had limited exposure to other children before starting to school, the children themselves may look ominous. Particularly for the child from a small family, the classroom may look frightfully crowded. A further reason the school may be disliked is that it is very likely to involve more structure and discipline than the home situation does. Finally, many school-phobic children have what the American Psychiatric Association describes as an avoidant personality disorder. Such children are very sensitive to rejection, are apt to feel they are being ridiculed, are hesitant to become involved in social interactions unless full acceptance can be guaranteed, and have a tendency to withdraw from social situations because of low estimates of their own worth and that of their achievements (DSM-III-R, 1987).

Several guidelines may be helpful in preventing school phobia from occurring:

- Provide early experiences with peers.
- Don't dwell on how much Mother will miss the child during school hours.
- Don't recite all the fascinating things that are done at home during the child's absence.
- Involve the child in part-time group child-care arrangements before full-time placement is necessary.
- Select a preschool similar to home for less-stressful transition.
- Use a positive approach. The child must go to school, and he or she must not come to feel that malingering can change that fact. Each day that the child is out of the classroom, anxiety rises and adjustment to routine is more difficult (Kellerman, 1981).
- If intense resistance to school persists, confer with a specialist to determine whether the child has other psychological problems.

Depression

How can a parent or a caregiver distinguish between the child who is quiet and orderly as a result of disposition or early training and one who is depressed? (Since all the children in my family had been extremely active, I misdiagnosed all the quiet ones as depressives my first year of teaching and worked untiringly to activate them!) In this section, we see the characteristics of depression, factors related to this unhappy state, and suggestions for helping the child to overcome this problem.

CHARACTERISTICS OF DEPRESSION IN CHILDREN. The child may evidence depression by internalizing anxiety and hurting herself or by externalizing

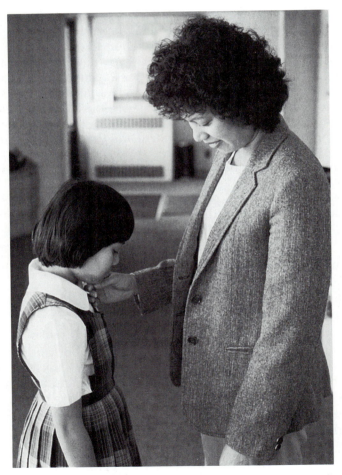

Talking with a nurturant adult often can help a depressed child to feel better. (*Source: © MacDonald Photography/ Envision*)

her feelings and jeopardizing her achievement and relations with others. Internalized depression may surface as changes in appetite or weight, insomnia at night or extreme sleepiness during the day, chronic fatigue or lack of energy, negative self-feelings such as worthlessness or unjustified guilt, or even illnesses of emotional rather than physical origin (Clarizio, 1984; Reynolds, 1984). Some of the indicators of externalized depression are changes in activity level (hyperactivity or apathy), loss of interest in previously favored activities, impaired concentration, and conduct disorders ranging from temper tantrums to moping (Clarizio, 1984; Reynolds, 1984).

FACTORS RELATED TO DEPRESSION. What causes a child to slide into a state of depression? First, many children react with depression when they suffer a loss (McGuire and Ely, 1984). Death, divorce, or even a quarrel with a best friend may set a grieving process in motion. Kindness, understanding, and a chance to talk about it will help this type of depression to lift in time. A second common instigator of depression is developmental change (Clarizio, 1984). When a child is struggling with a new developmental task, stress may lead to depression. The four-year-old who is "not quite" potty trained or the shy kindergartner who gets pushed around by her more-aggressive peers is apt to become depressed. Third, the child who can realistically observe that her skills are different or not equal to those of her peers is a likely candidate for depression (Stevenson, 1984). When a bilingual child cannot make herself understood or a second-grader who had trouble with reading last year faces the reading circle again, depression is a natural outcome. A fourth reason that some children become depressed is that their self-image is so low that they have little faith in their ability to do better (Layne and Berry, 1983). A final factor implicated in some instances of depression is that of minimal brain dysfunction (Stevenson, 1984). When such a condition is indicated, medication sometimes can help to restore more normal behavior.

HELP FOR DEPRESSED CHILDREN. Several techniques for helping depressed children have been suggested in the literature. Each of the following has a particular strength:

- *Information* (Renshaw, 1974): Give the child additional data about the things that are troubling her. Such information may include reassurance that you understand, that others have had the same problem, that the situation is only temporary (if it is), and that you will be happy to help as long as the problem persists.
- *Exploration of feelings* (Jewett, 1982): A "five feelings technique" helps some children express their depressions. When the child identifies the

source of her depression, ask a series of short questions based on the five most common feelings (sad, mad, glad/happy, scared, and lonely). For example, "When the new baby came, tell me about the sad [mad, and so forth] feelings you had." Sympathetic listening to the child's troubles is a good beginning to the mediation of the child's problems.

- *Role playing* (Reynolds, 1984):   Through seeing peers in different roles and having the personal opportunities to try new behaviors, many children gain the confidence to overcome depression.
- *Rehearsal* (Renshaw, 1974):   Knowing what you are going to do in advance helps relieve anxiety. When children rehearse how they will behave in frightening or depressing situations, they can trade some of their fear for a sense of control.
- *Family therapy* (Reynolds, 1984):   Some of the depression problems children have require professional counseling. In such cases, therapists generally work with the family as well as the child, since home conditions and interactions generally are involved.

Withdrawal

One teacher aptly described withdrawn children as "hermits in residence" (Kauffman, 1977). These young people remain aloof both physically and emotionally. Common behaviors include playing by themselves, saying little to peers and caregivers, and failing to respond when other people make social overtures. In more severe cases, these children may suffer from what the American Psychiatric Association designates as a schizoid disorder of childhood (DSM-III-R, 1987). Such children are characterized as (1) having no close friend who is near the same age, except perhaps a family member or an equally troubled peer, (2) showing no evidence of enjoying the company of age-mates, trying to make friends, or pursuing social contacts outside the family, and (3) maintaining such behaviors for more than three months. What causes children to withdraw, and what can caregivers do to reintegrate them socially? A look at the findings of research may help us find some answers.

CAUSES OF WITHDRAWAL.   A frequent cause of withdrawal is immaturity (Kauffman, 1977). The "late bloomer" is a little behind her age-mates in the development of many skills. These inadequacies often cause her to be released and rejected. In reaction, she withdraws and hopes her deficits will not be so noticeable. A second impetus to withdrawal is stress (DSM-III-R, 1987). When a child goes through a stressful event (new school, family move, death, divorce), the child may not feel like interacting with other people and may prefer to spend some time alone. Sudden withdrawal on the part of a usually happy child generally occurs within three months of the onset of a particularly stressful event or condition and often abates when the stress is removed or when time for adjustment has transpired.

Sometimes, when stress is prolonged, the child may develop such negative thoughts about herself or others that she remains detached until the caregivers initiate some type of intervention or treatment (Evans et al., 1984). Parental behavior is a third possible cause of withdrawal in some children. The parents may have set such high standards or so many prohibitions that the child is afraid to act lest she do something wrong. (One child tearfully begged me to give him a *2* instead of a *1* on his report card, because if he made a *1* that time and not at the next reporting period, he would be spanked "for goofing off.") A fourth major cause of withdrawal in children is that they have not been taught sufficient social skills to enable them to interact successfully with others. For example, they may not know how to become a part of a new group, how to recognize friendly overtures from peers, or how to behave acceptably once they have a social opportunity.

Many suggestions have been made for helping withdrawn children to become more socialized. The following are drawn from my own experience and from the writings of Kratochwill and French (1984), Litz (1983), and Essa (1978):

- Model warmth and acceptance to all children. They are likely to eventually follow your lead.
- Give the withdrawn child many opportunities to express her feelings to a warm and accepting adult.
- Teach the child the necessary social skills to enable her to function appropriately in social situations.
- Enlist the aid of other children. Use discussions, books, and role playing to develop concern for the feelings of others. When small-group activities are planned, pair the withdrawn child with active, accepted peers.
- Enlist the aid of the withdrawn child herself. Help her identify the problems that are causing the withdrawal and to make and execute plans to overcome these drawbacks.
- Use behavior modification techniques. For specific suggestions, consider the procedures described in Case Study 14.

Extreme Shyness

Some people consider the shy child as ideal; she never causes anybody any trouble. Others recognize that this child may want closer social relations and need help in achieving this goal. Stanford University now operates

Case Study 14

Behavior Modification: Increasing Peer Interaction

Child's Age	Initial Problem	Treatment	Result
4 years	Rejected by peers	Received adult attention only when interacting with peers	Went from 10% peer/40% adult interaction to 60% peer/20% adult contacts
3½ years	Rejected by peers	*First phase*—peers were verbally or physically rewarded for each interaction with isolate; *second phase*—isolate reinforced for socializing	Increased social interactions over 400%
4½ years	Poor play skills, little peer interaction	*First phase*—systematically taught child to use each play material, then reinforced for interacting with material; *second phase*—reinforced for peer interaction using materials	Peer interactions increased; later checks showed gain permanent even when placed in new group
6 preschool children	Limited peer interaction; average of only 2 peer interactions per session	Showed modeling film—a series of 11 scenes involving peer interaction; first the child in the film observed the group, then joined in activities and received obvious rewards	Averaged over four times as many peer interactions (control group showed no change)

SOURCE: Based on findings reviewed by Essa, 1978.

RELATIONAL DYSFUNCTIONS

the Stanford Shyness Clinic, which is dedicated to research the causes of shyness and to develop strategies for helping shy individuals overcome any debilitating effects of their shyness. The data included in this section are drawn from the findings of the clinic's research (Zimbardo and Radl, 1981).

What is shyness? Shyness is an attitude that causes a person to be overly concerned with what others think about her. Shy people often fear ridicule and rejection, and they will go to great lengths to avoid the limelight (or even casual notice). A very quiet second-grader once asked me why another boy in the class was being so aggressive. I explained to him that the other child wanted attention; he wanted us to notice him. "Why would anybody want that?" the shy child replied in amazement, shaking his head.

Based on their research, Zimbardo and Radl (1981) state that the shy child

- Is conforming, timid, and easily embarrassed
- Talks little and speaks in a soft voice
- Rarely shares problems or ideas
- Is timid when meeting strangers
- Rarely initiates social interactions

This avoidance of social contacts, which is characteristic of shy children, tends to compound their social problems, since such behavior denies them the opportunity to practice the social skills necessary for successful interpersonal interactions.

Shy children have two problems that are both caused by their shyness and compounded by their limited social encounters: (1) They often fail to develop needed assertiveness, and (2) they may have a poor sense of social timing (knowing when to say what and how much). These debits may cause shy children to be unduly influenced, controlled, or even exploited by their more-aggressive peers.

Contrary to popular opinion, not all shy children are introverts. Those who are introverts cannot hide the signs of their shyness. By contrast, the extroverted child is outgoing in her behavior but feels her shyness very keenly inside. Many famous and public figures report that they have intense feelings of shyness and reticence that never show.

What causes shyness? Much research now indicates that people are born with certain personality predispositions (Willerman, 1979; Zimbardo and Radl, 1981; Plomin and Daniels, 1986). Although shyness is not directly inherited, some people probably are more likely to develop this tendency under certain social conditions than are others.

The fact that a child sometimes enjoys being alone is not an indication of shyness.

Early childhood experiences are very important in the development of shyness. How these events are seen and interpreted by the child is of equal importance to what actually happens. According to Zimbardo and Radl (1981), some of the precursors of shyness in children are

- Painful memories of specific failures
- Negative comparisons with siblings or peers
- Loss of support systems (e.g., death, moving)
- Shy parent models
- Lack of experience in social settings
- Shame used as a tool for control and discipline

Research studies involving middle and late childhood indicate that the shy child is neither favored nor disliked; she is merely unnoticed in the group. The preadolescent is particularly shy when the situation involves entering a new group of peers.

How can shyness be overcome? Many of the suggestions in the previous section that were designated for working with the withdrawn can also be used successfully with the shy child. To these we can add the following findings from the Stanford Shyness Clinic's research (Zimbardo and Radl, 1981) and other research studies (Jones et al., 1986). Love unconditionally. (Such support gives security which helps the child overcome shyness.) Discipline fairly. (Behaviors, not children, may be disliked, and intent as well as act should be considered.) Give attention in stressful situations. (Immediate attention often averts failures that are particularly painful to shy children.) Set realistic expectations. (Standards that are neither too high nor too low give the shy child a sense of pride without undue fear of failure.)

Hostile Relatedness: Aggressive Disorders

In our society, we place great value on assertiveness and frown on undue aggression. Determining the difference between the two is apt to be quite confusing to many young children. (One of my college students made the following wise distinction: "If I do it to someone else, I'm being assertive; if they do it to me, they're definitely being aggressive!" What are the major types of aggression? Why do people behave this way? How can we help children divert their behavior into more prosocial channels? The answers to these questions are of interest to all caregivers.

TYPES OF AGGRESSION. Several types of aggressive behavior common to young children have been identified (DSM-III, 1987; Miller, 1982). Among them are

Physical violence: shoving, fighting, stomping
Verbal violence: screaming, use of forbidden words, arguing, unkind remarks
Defiance: refusing to do the required or insisting on doing the forbidden
Destructiveness: breaking or tearing up things, or being cruel to animals
Passive aggression: deliberately delaying, being inefficient, "forgetting," or engaging in stubborn behavior

As you can see from the foregoing list, some of these behaviors are done openly; others are done secretly. In some cases, even the child may not recognize that aggression is the reason for her actions.

CAUSES OF AGGRESSION. What causes the child to behave aggressively? Research has indicated that many factors are involved. We shall consider some of the major instigators of these behaviors.

One of the most commonly used explanations for aggressive behavior is that of social learning. Chronic and daily exposure to aggressive behavior teaches this type of response (Renshaw, 1974). If children grow up in a cultural environment in which acts of violence are condoned or encouraged, they will even feel that these actions are right and justified. They will identify with aggressive models and emulate their methods of dealing with life situations (Lefkowitz et al., 1977). Finally, parents are a powerful force in determining the frequency of aggression. Their own behavior toward the child and the manner in which they either reward or punish

Aggression may be verbal as well as physical. (Source: DENNIS THE MENACE® used by permission of Hank Ketcham and © by North America Syndicate)

aggression greatly influences the aggressive levels of their children (Kauffman, 1977).

Another explanation for aggression is that it results from frustration. Dollard, Miller, and Sears contend that aggression usually occurs when some important goal has been blocked and the individual is having difficulty dealing with the inner tension (Lefkowitz et al., 1977). Intense frustration may also occur when a person is subjected to unpredictable or unjustified attacks (Renshaw, 1974). In either case, engaging in aggressive behavior reduces this tension.

Low self-esteem often leads to aggression. Some children are pushy and aggressive to assert their importance and control in a situation (Miller, 1982). Others use aggression as a form of grieving when feelings of rejection threaten their sense of self-worth (Lefkowitz et al., 1977).

In some cases of continued aggression, biological irregularities may be at fault. Disorders in certain areas of the brain, hormone variations, low blood sugar level, and genetic difference (having an extra male chromosome in the XYY syndrome) all may cause an increased level of aggressive behavior.

REDUCING AGGRESSIVE BEHAVIOR. Although many forms of treatment have been used to reduce the incidence of aggression, three types have emerged as being particularly effective. These are arranged environment, cognitive reasoning, and behavior modification.

Parents and other caregivers have the opportunity and the responsibility to arrange an environment that contains necessary structure and minimal stress. This environment should be based on age-appropriate expectations, so the child can have a reasonable chance for success. Rules should be both clear and fair, and monitoring of these regulations should be consistent. In such a situation, the child knows what to do and is sure that order will be maintained. Such firmness helps eliminate the temptation to try aggressive behavior to see what will happen. Discipline based on natural consequences rather than on aggressive behavior toward the child will further help reduce aggression. In this way, the caregiver models behaviors that accomplish goals without resorting to aggression.

Cognitive reasoning is an important tool for reducing aggression. Discussions about the feelings and needs of others coupled with a genuine concern for the welfare of the child being counseled should eventually lead to the development of empathy. Many caregivers, however, become discouraged when results of reasoning are not immediately forthcoming. Always try to remember: children do not become extremely aggressive overnight. (Hopefully, it won't take you as long to get them to change their aggressive behavior patterns as it did for the children to develop them.)

Discussions with peers play a vital role in shaping behavior. Many of these are spontaneous as children talk about their problems with each other. Other sessions may be initiated through the use of some stimulus device such as a story, a role-playing incident, or a sentence-completion list. Involver 14 illustrates this possibility.

Behavior modification is one of the most widely used methods for changing undesirable behaviors in children. Since we have discussed this approach previously, a brief summary of major principles should be sufficient. Behaviorists believe that no matter what caused a behavior, the probability of its being repeated depends on what occurs immediately following the action. If what happens next is viewed by the doer as good or rewarding, the individual will repeat the act. If punishment or the absence of any desirable reinforcement occurs, the person will eventually abandon that action. Behavior cannot go from poor to perfect instantly, but gets better by degrees. A caregiver "shapes" behavior by setting up a series of "successive approximations" (intermediate levels of behavior that become closer

INVOLVER 14

Small-Group Discussion: Aggression

Children are very interested in the opinions of their peers. Therefore, they usually enjoy talking over their feelings and ideas with friends. Involver 14 gives you a chance to be a part of such a discussion.

Construct a list of five incomplete sentences dealing with anger. (You may add three original ones to the following two samples.)

1. I always get angry when . . .
2.
3.
4.
5. The best thing to do when I'm angry is . . .

Select three to six children (include both boys and girls) for a group discussion about what makes them angry and what they do when they feel this way. After you have explained the activity to the children, present each question and let them discuss it. (Try not to lead the conversation; their ideas are what you want to hear.)

THINKING IT OVER

- What did you learn about children's anger?
- What (if any) differences did you note between boys and girls?

and closer to the desired state). Over a period of time, the individual learns to perform in an acceptable manner.

The most important way to deal with relational dysfunctions of all kinds is to deal, whenever possible, with the causes. Many changes in the lifespace of children can be made with beneficial results.

Summary

- The behavior of hyperactive children is characterized by excessive movement, impulsiveness, and lack of attention. Some of the causes of this condition include damage or dysfunction of the brain as a result of prenatal or postnatal conditions, neurological impairments, faulty body chemistry, or gender (physical differences and cultural expectations). Hyperactive children are also likely to experience difficulties with their peers as a result of their rowdiness, clumsiness, and impulsivity. Strategies used to help hyperactive children include medication, relaxation techniques, behavior modification, structured environment, self-instruction, modeling, biofeedback, and mega-vitamin therapy.
- Autism is a developmental disorder apparent from shortly after birth. An autistic child is unresponsive to people and to the environment, has very limited language skills, and is apt to evidence strange repetitive motions. Brain damage, viral illnesses, imbalances in body chemistry, and genetics are some of the causes that thus far have been identified. Drugs, hormones, vitamins, behavior modification, and even American Sign Language have been used in efforts to reach these children. Only about one in six will recover sufficiently to work and to relate socially even on a limited basis.
- Phobias are prolonged and unrealistic fears. Some are developmental and disappear with age; others result from some traumatic event. School phobia affects almost 2 percent of all children. This phobia is usually based on a fear of rejection or a lack of self-confidence. Strategies that build self-esteem are often useful in eliminating this phobia.
- Depression in children is characterized by changes in activity level and loss of interest in the environment. Some of the factors related are severe loss of something loved, stress related to a developmental change, lack of needed skills, and low self-image. Information, exploration of feelings, role playing, rehearsal, and family therapy have been successfully used in working with such children.
- Some children react to troubled feelings by withdrawing either physically or emotionally from those around them. Limited academic or social skills, stress, and parental overstrictness or neglect have been identified

as causes of withdrawal in children. Caregiver warmth, an opportunity to learn needed skills, peer encouragement, individual counseling, and behavior modification are often used to help withdrawn children to reintegrate.
- Some children are painfully shy. They are timid, soft-spoken children who are reluctant to express their ideas, meet new situations, or initiate social relations. They may have experienced failure, felt inferior to others, lost support systems, had shy parents, lack social experience, or been victims of ridicule or shame. Love, attention, and realistic expectations can often help these children.
- Aggressive children often resort to physical or verbal violence, defiance, destructiveness, or passive aggression to get their way. They may have learned aggressive behaviors from watching the people in their environments, experiencing frustration, failing to develop positive self-esteem, or suffering from some biological disorder. Through the use of carefully structured environments, cognitive reasoning, and behavior modification, excessive aggression in children often can be changed.

Selected Readings

HINSHAW, S. P.; HENKER, B.; AND WHALEN, C. K. "Cognitive Behavioral and Pharmacologic Interventions for Hyperactive Boys: Comparative and Combined Effects." *Journal of Consulting and Clinical Psychology* 52(5) 1984, 739–749.

JEWETT, C. L. *Helping Children Cope with Separation and Loss*. Cambridge, MA: Harvard University Press, 1982.
   This excellent book contains many specific suggestions for telling the child about a loss and for helping her express her sadness, anger, and aggression and to repair damaged self-esteem and behavior control.

JONES, W. H.; CHEEK, J. M.; AND BRIGGS, S. R. (eds.). *Shyness: Perspectives on Research and Treatment*. New York: Plenum Press, 1986.
   This comprehensive work includes development, personal and social aspects, and therapeutic interventions related to shyness.

MORRIS, R. J., AND KRATOCHWILL, T. R. Behavioral Treatment of Children's Fears and Phobias: A Review. *School Psychology Review,* 14(1) 1985, 84–93.
   The authors analyze various treatment conditions and describe them in detail.

PLOMIN, R., AND DUNN, J. (eds.). *The Study of Temperament: Changes, Continuities, and Challenges*. Hillsdale, NJ: Erlbaum, 1986.
   This work contains a collation of studies related to temperament. Issues explored include cultural and biological bases for temperament, stability or change in temperament over time, and various interactions between temperament and other factors.

VARMA, V. P. (ed.). *Anxiety in Children.* New York: Methuen, 1984.
 The authors describe various characteristics of anxiety and suggestions for interventions.

ZIMBARDO, P. G., AND RADL, S. L. *The Shy Child.* New York: McGraw-Hill, 1981.
 This book is based on the findings of research at the Stanford University Shyness Clinic. It includes chapters on causes of shyness, suggested parenting styles, strategies for minimizing shyness, and special chapters on each of four age levels (2–6, 6–12, 12–17, 17 on).

Bibliography

ACKERMAN, P. T.; DYKMAN, R. A.; AND OGLESBY, D. M. "Sex and Group Differences in Reading in Attention Disordered Children with and without Hyperkinesis." *Journal of Learning Disabilities* **16**(7), 1983, 407–415.

AINSWORTH, M.D.S.; BLEHAR, M. C.; WATERS, E.; AND WALL, S. *Patterns of Attachment.* Hillsdale, NJ: Erlbaum, 1978.

ALBRECHT, S. L.; BAHR, H. M.; AND GOODMAN, K. L. *Divorce and Remarriage.* Westport, CT: Greenwood Press, 1983.

ALLEN, V. L. "The Role of Nonverbal Behavior in Children's Communications." In Dickson, W. P. (ed.), *Children's Oral Communication Skills.* New York: Academic Press, 1981.

ALLERS, R. D. "Helping Children Understand Divorce." *Education Digest* **46**, 1981, 20–23.

ALLPORT, G. W. *Becoming.* New Haven, CT: Yale University Press, 1955.

ALMY, M., AND GENISHI, C. *Ways of Studying Children: An Observational Manual for Early Childhood Teachers* (2nd ed.). New York: Teachers College Press, Columbia University, 1979.

AMERICAN PSYCHIATRIC ASSOCIATION. *Diagnostic and Statistical Manual of Mental Disorders, Third Edition, Revised.* Washington, DC.: American Psychiatric Association, 1987.

AMES, L. B.; GILLESPIE, C.; HAINES, J.; AND ILG, F. L. *The Gesell Institute's Child from One to Six.* New York: Harper & Row, 1979.

ANDERSON, D. R.; LORCH, E. P.; FIELD, D. E.; AND SANDERS, J. "The Effects of TV Program Comprehensibility on Preschool Children's Visual Attention to Television." *Child Development,* **52**, 1981, 151–157.

ANDERSON, S. B. *CIRCUS Manual and Technical Report.* Princeton, NJ: Educational Testing Service, 1979.

APGAR, V., AND BECK, J. *Is My Baby All Right?* New York: Pocket Books, 1978.

ARNHEIM, D. D., AND PESTOLESI, R. A. *Developing Motor Behavior in Children.* St. Louis: Mosby, 1977

ASENDORPF, J. "Shyness in Middle and Late Childhood." In Jones, W. H.; Cheek, J. M.; and Briggs, S. R. (eds.), *Shyness: Perspectives on Research and Treatment.* New York: Plenum Press, 1986.

AUTRY, L. B., AND LANGENBACK, M. "Locus of Control and Self-Responsibility for Behavior." *Journal of Educational Research* **79**(2), 1985, 76–84.

BADELL-RIBERA, A. "Myelodyplasia." In Molnar, G. E. (ed.), *Pediatric Rehabilitation.* Baltimore: Williams & Wilkins, 1985.

BANDURA, A.; ROSS, D.; AND ROSS, S. A. "Transmission of Aggression through Imitation of Aggressive Models." *Journal of Abnormal and Social Psychology* **63**, 1961, 575–582.

BARBIERI, M. S., AND DEVESCOVI, A. "Different Ways of Explanation in Two Social Classes: Story Telling to Children from 18 to 36 months." In Johnson, C. E., and Thew, C. L. (eds.), *Proceedings of the Second International Congress for the Study of the Child Language,* Vol. 1. Washington, DC, University Press of America, 1982.

BARLOW, G., AND HILL, A. (eds.). *Video Violence and Children.* London: Hodder and Stoughton, 1985.

BASKITT, L. M. "Ordinal Position Differences in Children's Family Interactions." *Developmental Psychology* **20**(6), 1984, 1026–1031.

———. "Sibling Status Effects: Adult Expectations." *Developmental Psychology* **21**(3), 1985, 441–445.

BAUMRIND, D. "Socialization and Instrumental Competence in Young Children." In Kaplan-Sanoff, M., and Yablans-Magid, R., *Exploring Early Childhood: Readings in Theory and Practice.* New York: Macmillan, 1981.

BAVELAS, J. B. *Personality: Current Theory and Research.* Monterey, CA: Brooks/Cole, 1978.

BAXTER, A. *Techniques for Dealing with Child Abuse.* Springfield, IL: Thomas, 1985.

BEARD, R. M. *An Outline of Piaget's Developmental Psychology for Students and Teachers.* New York: Routledge & Kegan, 1983.

BEATTY, J. J. *Observing Development of the Young Child.* Columbus, OH: Merrill, 1984.

BECK, J. *Best Beginnings: Giving Your Child a Head Start in Life.* New York: Putnam, 1983.

BELL, C. "Ameliorating the Impact of Teen-Age Pregnancy on Parent and Child." *Child Welfare* **62**(2), 1983, 167–173.

BERGMAN, B. "Children's Sleep Patterns." Personal interview, 1987a.

———. "Immunization Schedule." Personal interview, 1987b.

BERLIN, C. M. "Biology and Retardation." In Neisworth, J. T., and Smith, R. M. (eds.), *Retardation: Issues, Assessment, and Intervention.* New York: McGraw-Hill, 1978.

BERLYNE, D. E. *Conflict, Arousal and Curiosity.* New York: McGraw-Hill, 1960.

BERNDT, T. J. "The Influence of Group Discussions on Children's Moral Decisions." In Masters, J. C., and Yarkin-Levin, K. (eds.), *Boundary Areas in Social and Developmental Psychology.* New York: Academic Press, 1984.

———. "Lack of Acceptance of Reciprocity Norms in Preschool Children." *Developmental Psychology* 15(6), 1979, 662–663.

BERNDT, T. J., AND BERNDT, E. G. "Person Perception and Moral Judgment." *Child Development* 46(4), 1975, 904–912.

BERNDT, T. J., AND HELLER, K. A. "Measuring Children's Personality Attributions." In Yussen, S. R. (ed.), *The Growth of Reflection in Children.* New York: Academic Press, 1985.

BERNSTEIN, B. *Class, Codes, and Controls.* Vol. 3, *Towards a Theory of Educational Transmissions.* London: Routledge & Kegan Paul, 1977.

BERRY, G. L., AND MITCHELL-KERNAN, C. *Television and the Socialization of the Minority Child.* New York: Academic Press, 1982.

BEST, J. W., AND KAHN, J. V. *Research in Education* (5th ed.). Englewood Cliffs, NJ: Prentice-Hall, 1986.

BIEHLER, R. F., AND SNOWMAN, J. *Psychology Applied to Teaching* (4th ed.). Boston: Houghton-Mifflin, 1982.

BILGE, B., AND KAUFMAN, G. "Children of Divorce and One-Parent Families: Cross-Culture Perspectives." *Family Relations* 32(1), 1983, 59–71.

BOGDANOFF, R. F., AND DOLCH, E. T. "Old Games for Young Children: A Link to Our Heritage." *Young Children* 34(2), 1979, 42–43.

BONNEY, M. E. *Mental Health in Education.* Boston: Allyn & Bacon, 1969.

BORDLEY, J. E.; BROOKHAUSER, P. E.; AND TUCKER, G. F. *Ear, Nose, and Throat Disorders in Children.* New York: Raven Press, 1986.

BORG, W. S., AND GALL, M. D. *Educational Research: An Introduction* (3rd ed.). New York: Longman, 1983.

BORKOWSKI, J. G. "Impulsivity and Strategy Transfer: Metamemory as Mediator." *Child Development* 54(2), 1983, 459–473.

BRADLEY, R. H., AND CALDWELL, B. M. "The Home Inventory and Family Demographics." *Developmental Psychology* 20(2), 1984, 315–320.

BRAY, G. "The Nutrition Message Must Be Spread." *The Journal of the American Medical Association* 241(13), 1979, 1320–1321.

BRAZELTON, T. B. *Doctor and Child.* New York: Delta, 1976.

———. *Infants and Mothers: Differences in Development.* New York: Dell, 1983.

———. *Neonatal Behavioral Assessment Scale* (2nd ed.). Philadelphia: Lippincott, 1984.

BREGER, L. *Freud's Unfinished Journey: Conventional and Critical Perspectives in Psychoanalytic Theory.* London: Routledge & Kegan Paul, 1981.

BRENDER, J. D. "Fiber Intake and Childhood Appendicitis." *American Journal of Public Health* 75(4), 1985, 399–400.

BRETHERTON, I. (ED.). *Symbolic Play: The Development of Social Understanding.* New York: Academic Press, 1984.

BREWER, G. D., AND KAKALIK, J. S. *Handicapped Children: Strategies for Improving Services.* New York: McGraw-Hill, 1979.

BRIDGMAN, A. "Early-Childhood Education: States Already on the Move." *Education Week* 5(7), October 16, 1985, 1, 14–15.

BRIGGS, G. M., AND CALLOWAY, D. H. *Bogart's Nutrition and Physical Fitness* (11th ed.). New York: Holt, Rinehart & Winston, 1984.

BROWN, R. *A First Language.* Cambridge, MA: Harvard University Press, 1973.

———. *Psycholinguistics.* New York: Free Press, 1970.

BROWN, R. T., AND REYNOLDS, C. R. (EDS.). *Psychological Perspectives on Childhood Exceptionality: A Casebook.* New York: Wiley, 1986.

BRUNER, J. "The Course of Cognitive Growth." *American Psychologist* 19, 1964, 1–15.

———. "Play, Thought, and Language." *Peabody Journal of Education* 60(3), 1983, 60–69.

BURNS, R. *The Complete Poetical Works of Robert Burns.* Boston: Houghton-Mifflin, 1897.

BURTON, R. V. "Honesty and Dishonesty." In T. Lickona (ed.), *Moral Development and Behavior.* New York: Holt, Rinehart & Winston, 1976.

BUSS, A. H., AND PLOMIN, R. *Temperament.* Hillsdale, NJ: Erlbaum, 1984.

BUTLER, A. L.; GOTTS, E. E.; AND QUISENBERRY, N. L. *Play as Development.* Columbus, OH: Merrill, 1978.

BYRNE, D., AND KELLEY, K. *An Introduction to Personality* (3rd ed.). Englewood Cliffs, NJ: Prentice-Hall, 1981.

CALHOUN, G., AND MORSE, W. C. "Self-Concept and Self-Esteem: Another Perspective." *Psychology in the School* 14(3), 1977, 318–322.

CALVERT, S.; HUSTON, A. C.; WATKINS, B. A.; AND WRIGHT, J. C. "The Relation between Selected Attention to Television Forms and Children's Comprehension of Content." *Child Development* 53(2), 1982, 601–610.

CARNATION COMPANY. *Pregnancy in Anatomical Illustrations.* Los Angeles, CA, 1962.

CASSETTY, J. (ED.). *The Parental Child-Support Obligation.* Lexington, MA: Heath, 1983.

CATALDO, C., AND GEISMAR, L. "Preschoolers' Views of Parenting and the Family." *Journal of Research and Development in Education* 16(4), 1983, 8–14.

CAZENAVE, N. A. "A Woman's Place: The Attitudes of Middle-Class Black Men." *Phylon* 44(1), 1983, 12–32.

CECI, S. J., AND TISHMAN, J. "Hyperactivity and Incidental Memory: Evidence for Attentional Diffusion." *Child Development* 55(6), 1984, 2192–2203.

CHANCE, P. *Learning through Play.* New York: Gardner Press, 1979.

CHARLES, C. M. *Building Classroom Discipline: From Models to Practice* (2nd ed.). New York: Longman, 1984.

CHESS, S., AND THOMAS, A. *Origins and Evolution of Behavior Disorders: From Infancy to Young Adult Life.* New York: Brunner/Mazel, 1984.

CHOMSKY, N. *Aspects of the Theory of Syntax.* Cambridge: MIT Press, 1965.

———. *Language and the Mind.* New York: Harcourt, Brace & World, 1972.

———. *Syntactic Structures.* The Hague: Mouton, 1957.

CHRISTIE, J. F., AND JOHNSEN, E. P. "The Role of Play in Social-Intellectual Development." *Review of Educational Research* 53(1), 1983, 93–115.

CLARIZIO, H. F. "Childhood Depression: Diagnostic Considerations." *Psychology in the Schools* 21(2), 1984, 181–197.

CLARK, E. V. "Convention and Contract in Acquiring the Lexicon." In Seiler, T. B., and Wannenmacher, W. (eds.), *Concept Development and the Development of Word Meaning.* New York: Springer-Verlag, 1983, 67–89.

CLARK, M.; BEGLEY, S.; AND HAGER, M. "The Miracles of Spliced Genes." *Newsweek* 95(11), March 17, 1980, 62–71.

COHEN, L. *Educational Research in Classrooms and Schools: A Manual of Materials and Methods.* New York: Harper & Row, 1976.

COLLINS, S. M. "The Making of the Black Middle Class." *Social Problems* 30(4), 1983, 369–382.

COMMISSION ON NUTRITION, AMERICAN ACADEMY OF PEDIATRICS. *Pediatric Nutrition Handbook* (2nd ed.). Elk Grove Village, IL: Academic Press, 1985.

CONNOR, W. E. "Too Little or Too Much: The Case for Preventive Nutrition." *The American Journal of Clinical Nutrition* 32(10), 1979, 1976–1977.

COOPER, C. R., AND COOPER, R. G., JR. "Skill in Peer Learning Discourse: What Develops?" In Kuczaj, S. A. (ed.), *Discourse Development: Progress in Cognitive Development Research.* New York: Springer-Verlag, 1984.

COOPERSMITH, S. *The Antecedents of Self-Esteem* (2nd ed.). San Francisco: Freeman, 1981.

COPANS, S.; KRELL, H.; GUNDY, J. H.; REGAN, J.; AND FIELD, F. "The Stresses of Treating Child Abuse." *Children Today* 8, 1979, 22.

COPPLE, E. E.; COCKING, R. R.; AND MATTHEWS, W. S. "Objects, Symbols, and Substitutes: The Nature of Cognitive Activity during Symbolic Play." In Yawkey, T. D., and Pellegrini, A. D. (eds.), *Child's Play: Developmental and Applied.* Hillsdale, NJ: Erlbaum, 1984.

CORLESS, C. E. *Patten's Human Embryology.* New York: McGraw-Hill, 1976.

COX, M. V. *The Child's Point of View.* New York: St. Martin's Press, 1986.

CRATTY, B. J. *Perceptual and Motor Development in Infants and Children* (3rd ed.). Englewood Cliffs, NJ: Prentice-Hall, 1986.

CRAVIOTO, J., AND DELICARDIE, E. R. "Nutrition and Behavior and Learning." In Rechcigl, M. (ed.), *Food, Nutrition, and Health.* Basel, Switzerland: S. Karger, 1973.

CROMER, R. F. "The Acquisition of Word Knowledge: Gradual Learning or Sudden Recognition?" In Seiler, T. B., and Wannenmacher, W. (eds.), *Concept*

Development and the Development of Word Meaning. New York: Springer-Verlag, 1983, 34–53.

CROUTER, A. C. "The Children of Working Parents." *Children Today* 11(4), 1982, 25–28.

CRUTTENDEN, A. *Language in Infancy and Childhood.* New York: St. Martin's Press, 1979.

CULLINGFORD, C. *Children and Television.* New York: St. Martin's Press, 1984.

CURTISS, S. *Genie: A Psycholinguistic Study of a Modern-Day "Wild Child."* New York: Academic Press, 1977.

DALE, P. S. *Language Development: Structure and Function.* New York: Holt, Rinehart & Winston, 1976.

DANSKY, J. L. "Make-Believe: A Mediator of Relationship between Play and Associative Fluency." *Child Development* 51, 1980, 576–579.

DANSKY, J. L., AND SILVERMAN, I. W. "Play: A General Facilitator of Associative Fluency." *Developmental Psychology* 11, 1975, 104.

DECI, E. L. "Intrinsic Motivation and Personality." In Staub, E. (ed.), *Personality: Basic Aspects and Current Research.* Englewood Cliffs, NJ: Prentice-Hall, 1980, 35–80.

DE VILLIERS, P. A., AND DE VILLIERS, J. G. *Early Language.* Cambridge, MA: Harvard University Press, 1979.

DICKSTEIN, E. "Self and Self-Esteem: Theoretical Foundations and Their Implications for Research." *Human Development* 20(7), 1977, 129–140.

DILL, S. R. *Child Psychology in Contemporary Society.* Boston: Holbrook Press, 1978.

DILLARD, J. M., AND CAMPBELL, N. J. "Career Values and Aspirations of Adult Female and Male Puerto Ricans, Blacks, and Anglos." *Journal of Employment Counseling* 19(4), 1982, 163–170.

DONAHUE, M. "Phonological Constraints on the Emergence of Two-Word Utterance." *Journal of Child Language* 13(2), 1986, 209–218.

DOORNINCK, W. J.; CALDWELL, B. M.; WRIGHT, C.; AND FRANKENBURG, W. K. "The Relationship between Twelve-Month Home Stimulation and School Achievement. *Child Development* 52, 1981, 1080–1082.

DOYLE, A. "Infant Development in Day Care." *Developmental Psychology* 11, 1975, 655–656.

DRAHMAN, R. S.; DORDUA, G. D.; HAMMER, D.; JARVIE, G. J.; AND HORTON, W. "Developmental Trends in Eating Rates of Normal and Overweight Preschool Children." *Child Development* 50(1), 1979, 221–226.

DREYER, S. S. *The Book Finder.* Circle Pines, MN: American Guidance Service, 1985.

DUNCAN, S., AND DEAVILA, E. "Bilingualism and Cognition: Some Recent Findings." *Journal of the Association for Bilingual Education* 4, 1979, 43.

DUNN, J. *Brothers and Sisters.* Cambridge, MA: Harvard University Press, 1985.

DURKIN, K. *Television, Sex Roles, and Children.* Philadelphia: Open University Press, 1985.

EASTERLIN, R. A. "The Changing Circumstances of Child-Rearing." *Journal of Communication* **32**(3), 1982, 86–98.

EDWARDS, S., "Sensitive Play Spaces." *International Designs*, 1985, 40–45, 80.

EISENBERG, N. "The Development of Prosocial Behavior and Cognitions in German Children." *Journal of Cross-Cultural Psychology* **16**(1), 1985 69–82.

EISENBERG, N. "Sex Differences in the Relationship of Height to Children's Actual and Attributed Social and Cognitive Competencies." *Sex Roles* **11**(7–8), 1984, 719–734.

EISENBERG-BERG, N., AND HAND, M. "The Relationship of Preschoolers' Reasoning about Prosocial Moral Conflicts to Prosocial Behavior." *Child Development* **50**(2), 1979, 356–363.

ELARDO, R.; BRADLEY, R.; AND CALDWELL, B. M. "A Longitudinal Study of the Relation of Infants' Home Environments to Language Development at Age Three." *Child Development* **38**, 1977, 595–603.

ELKIND, D., AND WEINER, I. *Development of the Child.* New York: Wiley, 1978.

ELLIS, P. "Play, Novelty, and Stimulus Seeking." In Yawkey, T. D., and Pellegrini, A. D. (eds.), *Child's Play: Developmental and Applied.* Hillsdale, NJ: Erlbaum, 1984.

EME, R., AND SCHMIDT, D. "The Stability of Children's Fears." *Child Development* **49**(4), 1978, 1277–1279.

EPSTEIN, L. H.; VALOSKI, M. S.; KOESKE, R.; AND WING. R. R. "Family-Based Behavioral Weight Control in Obese Young Children." *The Journal of the American Dietetic Association* **86**(4), 1986, 481–484.

EPSTEIN, S. "The Self-Concept: A Review and the Proposal of an Integrated Theory of Personality." In Staub, E. (ed.), *Personality: Basic Aspects and Current Research.* Englewood Cliffs, NJ: Prentice-Hall, 1980.

ERICKSON, M. P. "Assessment of the Child's Environment." In Tudor, M. (ed.), *Child Development.* New York: McGraw-Hill, 1981.

ERIKSON, E. H. *Childhood and Society* (2nd ed.). New York: Norton, 1963.

———. *The Life Cycle Completed: A Review.* New York: Norton, 1985.

ERNST, C., AND ANGST, J. *Birth Order: Its Influence on Personality.* New York: Springer-Verlag, 1983.

ESCABAR, L. "The Development of Conscience." Unpublished paper, Southern Methodist University, 1976.

ESSA, E. L. "The Preschool: Setting for Applied Behavior Analysis Research." *Review of Educational Research* **48**(4), 1978, 537–575.

ETDUSON, B. T. "Single versus Multiple Parenting: Implications for Infancy." Paper presented at the 85th annual meeting of the American Psychological Association, San Francisco, CA, 1977.

EVANS, S. S.; EVANS, W. H.; AND MERCER, C. D. "Counseling Approaches Used with Emotionally Disturbed Children." *Journal of School Health* **54**(7), 1984, 250–252.

EYSENCK, H. J. "The Biology of Morality." In T. Lickona (ed.), *Moral Development and Behavior.* New York: Holt, Rinehart & Winston, 1976.

Eysenck, H. J., and Kamin, L. *The Intelligence Controversy*. New York: Wiley, 1981.

Falbo, T. "Only Children in America." In Lamb, M. E., and Sutton-Smith, B., *Sibling Relationships: Their Nature and Significance over a Lifetime*. Hillsdale, NJ: Erlbaum, 1982.

Fallen, N. H., and McGovern, J. E. *Young Children with Special Needs*. Columbus, OH: Merrill, 1978.

Fallen, N. H., and Umansky, W. (eds.). *Young Children with Special Needs*. Columbus, OH: Merrill, 1984.

Farber, S. L. *Identical Twins Reared Apart: A Reanalysis*. New York: Basic Books, 1981.

Faw, T. *Theories and Problems of Child Psychology*. New York: McGraw-Hill, 1980.

Feingold, B. F. "Food Additives and Child Development." *Hospital Practice* 14, 1973, 11–12.

———. *Why Your Child Is Hyperactive*. New York: Random, 1985.

Ferber, M. A. "Women and Work: Issues of the 1980s." *Signs: Journal of Women in Culture and Society* 8(2), 1982, 273–295.

Fernandez, J. P. *Child Care and Corporate Productivity*. Lexington, MA: Heath, 1986.

Fischer, J. W. "Illuminating the Process of Moral Development." *Monographs of the Society for Research in Child Development* 48, 1983, 97–107.

Fitzgerald, M.J.T. *Human Embryology*. New York: Harper & Row, 1978.

Flanagan, G. L. *The First Nine Months of Life* (2nd ed.). New York: Simon and Schuster, 1987.

Flavell, J. H. *Cognitive Development*. Englewood Cliffs, NJ: Prentice-Hall, 1977.

Fogel, A., and Melson, G. F. *Origins of Nurturance: Developmental, Biological, and Cultural Perspectives in Caregiving*. Hillsdale, NJ: Erlbaum, 1986.

Fomon, S. J. "Breast-Feeding and Evolution." *The Journal of the American Dietetic Association* 86(3), 1986, 317–318.

———. *Infant Nutrition* (2nd ed.). Philadelphia: Saunders, 1974.

Fomon, S. J.; Anderson, T. A.; and Ziegler, E. K. "Recommendations for Feeding Normal Infants." *Pediatrics* 63, 1979, 52.

Ford, J. G., and Graves, J. R. "Differences between Mexican and White Children in Interpersonal Distance and Social Touching." *Perceptual and Motor Skills* 45(3), 1977, 779–785.

Forman, G. E., and Kushner, D. S. *The Child's Construction of Knowledge: Piaget for Teaching Children*. New York: National Association for the Education of Young Children, 1983.

Fotheringham, J. B., and Creal, D. "Family Socioeconomic and Educational-Emotional Characteristics as Predictors of School Achievement." *Journal of Educational Research* 73, 1980, 311–317.

Fowler, W. *Infant and Child Care*. Boston: Allyn & Bacon, 1980.

Freed, A. M. *TA for Tots*. Rolling Hills Estate, CA: Galmar Press, 1980.

Freeman, R. B. *Black Elite.* New York: McGraw-Hill, 1976.

Freire, E.; Gorman, B.; and Wessman, A. E. "Temporal Span, Delay of Gratification, and Children's Socioeconomic Status." *The Journal of Genetic Psychology* **137**, 1980, 247–255.

Freud, A. *The Ego and the Mechanisms of Defense.* New York: International Universities Press, 1967.

———. *The Writings of Anna Freud.* Vol. 6, *Normality and Pathology in Childhood: Assessments of Development.* New York: International Universities Press, 1973.

Freud, S. *An Outline of Psychoanalysis.* New York: Norton, 1970.

———. *The Problem of Anxiety.* New York: Norton, 1936.

Frost, J. L., and Klein, B. L. *Children's Play and Playgrounds.* Boston: Allyn & Bacon, 1979.

Frost, J. L., and Sunderlin, S. (eds.). *When Children Play.* New York: ACE1, 1986.

Gallahue, D. L. *Understanding Motor Development in Children.* New York: Wiley, 1982.

Galton, L. "Special Treatment for Obese Children." *Parade Magazine, Dallas Times Herald,* February 26, 1978.

Gamstorp, I. *Paédiatric Neurology* (2nd ed.). Boston: Butterworths, 1985.

Garcia, E. E. (ed.). *The Mexican-American Child.* Tempe, AZ: Center for Bilingual Education, 1983.

Garger, S., and Guild, P. "Learning Styles: The Crucial Differences." *Curriculum Review* **23**, 1984, 9–12.

Garn, S. M.; Ridella, S. A.; and Kramer, A. "Effect of Smoking during Pregnancy on Mother and the Conceptus." In Committee on Nutrition of the Mother and Preschool Child, *Alternative Dietary Practices and Nutritional Abuses in Pregnancy.* Washington, DC: National Academic Press, 1982.

Garvey, C. *Play.* Cambridge, MA: Harvard University Press, 1977.

Gearheart, B. R., and Weishann, M. W. *The Handicapped Child in the Regular Classroom.* St. Louis: Mosby, 1976.

Gentile, L. M., and Hoot, J. L. "Kindergarten Play: The Foundation of Reading." *Reading Teacher* **36**(4), 1983, 436–439.

Gerber Consultant Committee. "Guidelines: Child Safety." Fremont, MI: Gerber Products Company, Medical Marketing Services, 1980.

Gerhard, M. M. "Brain Research and Education." *Connecticut Journal of Science Education* **22**(2), 1985, 19–23.

Gesell, A. *The Embryology of Behavior.* New York: Harper, 1945.

Gesell, A., and Ilg, F. L. *The Child from Five to Ten.* New York: Harper and Row, 1986.

Ghiselin, B. *The Creative Process.* New York: Mentor Books, 1955.

Gibson, J. J. *The Senses Considered as Perceptual Systems.* Westport, CT: Greenwood, 1983.

GILLIGAN, C. *In a Different Voice.* Cambridge, MA: Harvard University Press, 1982.

GLOGER-TIPPELT, G. "A Process Model of the Pregnancy Course." *Human Development* **26**(3), 1983, 134–149.

GOLDEN, M.; ROSENBLUTH, L.; GROSSI, M.; POLICARE, H.; FREEMAN, H.; AND BROWNLESS, E. *The New York City Infant Day Care Study.* New York: Medical and Health Research Association of New York City, Inc., 1978.

GOLDIN-MEADOW, S. "The Resilience of Recursion: A Study of the Communication System Developed without a Conventional Language Model." In Wanner, E., and Gleitman, L. R. (eds.), *Language Acquisition.* Cambridge: Cambridge University Press, 1982, 51–77.

GOLDMAN, J.; STEIN, C. L.; AND GUERRY, S. *Psychological Methods of Child Assessment.* New York: Brunner/Mazel, 1983.

GRANT, J. P. *The State of the World's Children in 1985.* Oxford: Oxford University Press, 1985.

GREER, D.; POTS, R.; WRIGHT, J. C.; AND HUSTON, A. C. "The Effects of Television Commercial Form and Commercial Placement on Children's Special Behavior and Attention." *Child Development* **53**(3), 1982, 611–619.

GUARNACCIA, V. J., AND VANE, J. R. "Children's Wishes." *Journal of School Psychology* **17**(2), 1979, 126–133.

GUILFORD, J. P., AND HOEPFNER, R. *The Analysis of Intelligence.* New York: McGraw-Hill, 1971.

GUTHRIE, H. *Introductory Nutrition* (5th ed.). St. Louis: Mosby, 1983.

GUTTMACHER, A. F. *Pregnancy, Birth, and Family Planning.* New York: Viking Press, 1984.

HAGAN, E. *Identification of the Gifted.* New York: Teachers College, Columbia University, 1980.

HAGAN, W. T. *American Indians.* Chicago: University of Chicago Press, 1979.

HALE, J. E. *Black Children: Their Roots, Culture, and Learning Styles.* Provo, UT: Brigham Young University, 1982.

HALPERIN, M. *Helping Maltreated Children.* St. Louis: Mosby, 1979.

HAMILTON, W. J., AND MOSSMAN, H. W. *Human Embryology.* Baltimore: Williams & Wilkins, 1972.

HANSON, R. A., AND REYNOLDS, R. *Child Development: Concepts, Issues, and Readings.* St. Paul, MN: West Publishing Co., 1980.

HANSON, S. L. "A Family Life-Cycle Approach to the Socioeconomic Attainment of Working Women." *Journal of Marriage and the Family* **45**(2), 1983, 323–338.

HARRIS, S. R. "School Phobic Children and Adolescents: A Challenge to Counselors." *The School Counselor* **27**, 1980, 263–269.

HARRISON, R. F. *In Vitro Fertilization, Embryo Transfer and Pregnancy.* London: Kluwer Academic, 1984.

HARTUP, W. W., AND RUBIN, Z. (EDS.). *Relationships and Development*. Hillsdale, NJ: Erlbaum, 1986.

HARTY, H., AND BEALL, D. "Reactive Curiosity of Gifted and Nongifted Elementary School Youngsters." *Roeper Review* **7**(4), 1985, 214–217.

HAVIGHURST, R. J. *Developmental Tasks and Education* (3rd ed.). New York: Longman, 1979.

HAYES, D. S. "Cognitive Bases for Liking and Disliking among Preschool Children." *Child Development* **49**(3), 1978, 906–909.

HAYS, J. R. "Legal Aspects of Psychological Testing." In Weaver, S. J. (ed.), *Testing Children*. Kansas City: Test Corporation of America, 1984.

HELFER, R. "The Relationship between Lack of Bonding and Child Abuse and Neglect. Maternal Attachment and Mothering Disorders: A Round Table." Sausalito, CA: Johnson & Johnson, 1974.

HENNESSEE, M. J., AND DIXON, S. D. "The Development of Gait: A Study in African Children Ages One to Five." *Child Development* **55**, 1984, 844–853.

HERSEN, M.; VAN HASSELT, V. B.; AND MATSON, J. L. *Behavior Therapy for the Developmentally and Physically Disabled*. New York: Academic Press, 1983.

HETHERINGTON, E. M.; COX, M. J.; AND COX, R. D. "The Aftermath of Divorce." In J. H. Stevens and M. V. Matthews (eds.), *Mother-Child, Father-Child Relations*. Washington, DC: NAEYC, 1978.

HIGBEE, K. L. "Factors Affecting Obedience in Preschool Children." *The Journal of Genetic Psychology* **134**(2), 1979, 241–253.

HILLIARD, A. G. "Respect the Child's Culture." *Young Children* **34**(5), 1979, 2–3.

HIMES, J. H. "Infant Feeding Practices and Obesity." *The Journal of the American Dietetic Association* **75**(2), 1979, 122–125.

HINSHAW, S. P.; HENKER, B.; AND WHALEN, C. K. "Cognitive Behavioral and Pharmacologic Interventions for Hyperactive Boys: Comparative and Combined Effects." *Journal of Consulting and Clinical Psychology* **52**(5), 1984, 739–749.

HOEK, D. "Some Possible Causes of Children's Early Word Overextensions." *Journal of Child Language* **13**(3), 1986, 477–494.

HOFFMAN, M. L. "Empathy, Its Limitations, and Its Role in a Comprehensive Moral Theory." In Kurtines, W. M., and Gerwitz, J. L. (eds.), *Morality, Moral Behavior, and Moral Development*. New York: Wiley, 1984.

———. "Empathy, Role-Taking, Guilt, and Development of Altruistic Motives." In Lickona, T. (ed.), *Moral Development and Behavior*. New York: Holt, Rinehart & Winston, 1976.

———. "Moral Development." In P. H. Mussen (ed.), *Carmichael's Manual of Child Psychology* (Vol. 2, 3rd ed.). New York: Wiley, 1970.

HOLBOROW, P. L.; BERRY, P.; AND ELKINS, J. "Prevalence of Hyperkinesis: A Comparison of Three Rating Scales." *Journal of Learning Disabilities* **17**(7), 1984, 411–417.

Holland, J. G., and Skinner, B. F. *The Analysis of Behavior.* New York: McGraw-Hill, 1961.

Holte, C. S. "Influence of the Child's Positive Perceptions on Donating Behaviors in a Naturalistic Setting." *Journal of School Psychology* **22**(4), 1984, 145–153.

Horowitz, F. D., and O'Brien, M. (eds.). *The Gifted and Talented: Developmental Perspectives.* Washington, DC: American Psychological Association, 1985.

Hull, F. M., and Hull, M. E. "Children with Oral Communication Disabilities." In Dur., L. M. (ed.), *Exceptional Children in the Schools: Special Education in Transition* (2nd ed.). New York: Holt, Rinehart & Winston, 1976.

Humphrey, J. H. (ed.). *Stress in Childhood.* New York: AMSA Press, 1984.

Hurlock, E. B. *Developmental Psychology: A Life-Span Approach.* New York: McGraw-Hill, 1980.

Hutchins, B. *Child Nutrition and Health.* New York: McGraw-Hill, 1979.

Ilg, F. L., and Ames, L. B. *Child Behavior.* New York: Harper & Row, 1981.

———. *Child Behavior from Birth to Ten.* New York: Barnes & Noble, 1980.

Ingram, C. F. *Fundamentals of Educational Assessment.* New York: A. Van Nostrand, 1980.

Inhelder, B., and Piaget, J. *The Growth of Logical Thinking.* New York: Basic Books, 1958.

Iosub, S. "Incidence of Major Congenital Malformations in Offspring of Alcoholics and Polydrug Abusers." *Alcohol* **2**(3), 1985, 521–523.

Irwin, E. C., and Frank, M. I. "Facilitating the Play Process with LD Children." *Academic Therapy* **12**(4), 1977, 435–443.

Isenberg, J., and Jacob, E. "Literacy and Symbolic Play: A Review of the Literature." *Childhood Education* **59**(4), 1983, 272–276.

Janos, P. M., and Robinson, N. M. "Psychosocial Development in Intellectually Gifted Children." In Horowitz, F. D., and O'Brien, M. (eds.), *The Gifted and Talented: Developmental Perspectives.* Washington, DC: American Psychological Society, 1985.

Jewett, C. L. *Helping Children Cope with Separation and Loss.* Cambridge, MA: Harvard Press, 1982.

Johnson, P. "The Miracle of Dolly." *The Dallas Morning News,* May 31, 1979.

Jones, W. H.; Cheek, J. M.; and Briggs, S. R. (eds.). *Shyness: Perspectives on Research and Treatment.* New York: Plenum Press, 1986.

Joos, S. K. "The Bacon Chow Study: Maternal Nutritional Supplementation and Infant Behavioral Development." *Child Development* **54**(3), 1983, 669–676.

Jordan, B. E.; Radin, N.; and Epstein, A. "Paternal Behavior and Intellectual Functioning in Preschool Boys and Girls." *Developmental Psychology* **99**(3), 1975, 407–408.

Journal of Marriage and Family. Various issues.

Journal of the American Dietetic Association. Various issues.

Kail, R. *The Development of Memory in Children* (2nd ed.). New York: Freeman, 1984.

Kamii, C. *What Do Children Learn When They Manipulate Objects?* Edwardsville, IL: University Press, 1980.

———. *Young Children Reinvent Arithmetic.* New York: Columbia University Press, 1985.

Kauffman, J. M. *Characteristics of Children's Behavior Disorders.* Columbus, OH: Merrill, 1977.

Keerdoja, E., and Manning, R. "Son of Washoe Learns to Talk." *Newsweek*, May 28, 1979, p. 17.

Keller, J., and Shanahan, D. "Robots in Kindergarten." *Computing Teacher* 10(9), 1983, 66–67.

Keller, M. "Resolving Conflicts in Friendship: The Development of Moral Understanding in Everyday Life." In Kurtines, W. M., and Gerwitz, J. L. (eds.), *Morality, Moral Behavior, and Moral Development.* New York: Wiley, 1984.

Kellerman, J. *Helping the Fearful Child.* New York: Norton, 1981.

Keloe, A. B. *North American Indians.* Englewood Cliffs, NJ: Prentice-Hall, 1981.

Kemper, S. "The Development of Narrative Skills: Explanations and Entertainments." In Kuczaj, S. A. (ed.), *Discourse Development: Progress in Cognitive Development Research.* New York: Springer-Verlag, 1984.

Kerchner, E. P., and Vondrack, S. I. "Perceived Sources of Esteem in Early Childhood." *Journal of Genetic Psychology* 126(2), 1975, 169–176.

Kerr, M. A.; Bogues, J. L.; and Herr, D. S. "Psychosocial Functioning of Mothers of Malnourished Children." *Pediatrics* 62(5), 1978, 778–784.

Kirk, S. A., and Chalfant, J. C. *Academic and Developmental Learning Disabilities.* Denver: Love Publishing, 1984.

Kirk, S. A., and Gallagher, J. J. *Educating Exceptional Children* (4th ed.). Boston: Houghton-Mifflin, 1983.

Klatzky, R. L. *Human Memory: Structures and Processes.* San Francisco: W. H. Freeman, 1980.

Kogan, N. *Cognitive Styles in Infancy and Early Childhood.* New York: Wiley, 1976.

Kohlberg, L. *The Psychology of Moral Development.* New York: Harper & Row, 1984.

Kotelchuck, M. "WIC Participation and Pregnancy Outcomes: Massachusetts Statewide Evaluation Project." *American Journal of Public Health* 74(10), 1984, 1086–1092.

Kowtaluk, H. *Discovering Nutrition.* Peoria, IL: Charles Bennett, 1980.

Krantz, M. "Parent-Infant Programs for the Hearing Impaired." In Katz, J. (ed.), *Handbook of Clinical Audiology* (3rd ed.). Baltimore: Williams & Wilkins, 1985.

Kratochwill, T. R., and French, D. C. "Social Skills Training for Withdrawn Children." *School Psychology Review* 13(3), 1984, 331–338.

Kurtines, W. M., and Gerwirtz, J. L. (eds.). *Morality, Moral Behavior, and Moral Development.* New York: Wiley, 1984.

Lamb, M. E. *The Father's Role: Applied Perspectives.* New York: Wiley, 1986.

Lamb, M. E.; Thompson, R. A.; Gardner, W.; and Connell, J. P. *Infant-Mother Attachment.* Hillsdale, NJ: Erlbaum, 1985.

Langlois, J. H., and Downs, A. C. "Peer Relation as a Function of Physical Attractiveness." *Child Development* **50**(2), 1979, 409–418.

Langman, J. *Medical Embryology* (3rd ed.). Baltimore: Williams & Wilkins, 1975.

Layne, C., and Berry, E. "Motivational Deficit in Childhood Depression and Hyperactivity." *Journal of Clinical Psychology* **39**(4), 1983, 523–531.

Lee, T. R. "Nutritional Understanding of Preschool Children Taught in the Home or a Child Development Laboratory." *Home Economics Research Journal* **13**(1), 1984, 52–60.

Lefcourt, H. M. "Locus of Control and Coping with Life's Events." In Staub, E. (ed.), *Personality: Basic Aspects and Current Research.* Englewood Cliffs, NJ: Prentice-Hall, 1980.

Lefkowitz, M. M.; Eron, L. D.; Walder, L. O.; and Huesmann, L. R. *Growing Up to Be Violent: A Longitudinal Study of Development of Aggression.* New York: Pergamon Press, 1977.

Lenneberg, E. *Biological Foundations of Language.* New York: Wiley, 1967.

———. "The Natural History of Language." In Smith, F., and Miller, G. A. (eds.), *The Genesis of Language.* Cambridge, MA: MIT Press, 1966, p. 22–29.

Leve, R. *Childhood: The Study of Development.* New York: Random House, 1980.

Leventhal, B. L., and Dawson, G. "Middle Childhood: Normalcy as Integration and Interaction." In Offer, D., and Sabskin, M. *Normalcy and the Life Cycle.* New York: Basic Books, 1984.

Levine, M. H., and McCollum, J. A. "Peer Play and Toys: Key Factors in Mainstreaming Infants." *Young Children* **38**(5), 1983, 22–26.

Lewis, M. (ed.). *Origins of Intelligence* (2nd ed.). New York: Plenum Press, 1983.

Lickona, T. *Moral Development and Behavior.* New York: Holt, Rinehart & Winston, 1976.

Liebert, R. M., and Poulos, R. W. "Television as a Moral Teacher." In Lickona, T. (ed.), *Moral Development and Behavior.* New York: Holt, Rinehart & Winston, 1976.

Liebert, R. M.; Sprafkin, J. N.; and Davidson, E. S. *The Early Window* (2nd ed.). New York: Pergamon Press, 1982.

Lindberg, L., and Swedlow, R. *Early Childhood Education: A Guide for Observation and Participation* (2nd ed.). Boston: Allyn & Bacon, 1980.

Lindholm, B. W. "Predicting Changes in Nutrition Knowledge and Dietary Quality in Ten- to Thirteen-Year-Olds Following a Nutrition Education Program." *Adolescence* **19**(74), 1984, 367–375.

Lipstein, B. "Log for Psychology 138, Brandeis University, Spring 1979." In

Rubin, Z. (ed.), *Children's Friendships*. Cambridge: Harvard University Press, 1980.

Liss, M. (ed.). *Social and Cognitive Skills: Sex Roles and Children's Play*. New York: Academic Press, 1983.

Litz, C. S. "Emotional Disturbance in Preschool Children." *Teaching Exceptional Children* 15(3), 1983, 164–167.

Locke, J. L. *Phonological Acquisition and Change*. New York: Academic Press, 1983.

Loffredo, D. A.; Amizo, M.; and Hammett, V. L. "Group Relaxation Training and Parental Involvement with Hyperactive Boys." *Journal of Learning Disabilities* 17(4), 1984, 210–213.

Longo, L. M. "Health Consequences of Maternal Smoking: Experimental Studies and Public Policy Recommendations." In Committee on Nutrition of the Mother and Preschool Child, *Alternative Dietary Practices and Nutritional Abuses in Pregnancy*. Washington, DC: National Academic Press, 1982.

Longstreet, W. S. *Aspects of Ethnicity: Understanding Differences in Pluralistic Classrooms*. New York: Teachers College Press, 1978.

Lokare, V. G. "Anxiety in Children: A Cross-Cultural Perspective." In Varma, V. P. (ed.), *Anxiety in Children*. New York: Methuen, 1984.

Lowenberg, M. E.; Todhunter, E. N.; Wilson, E. D.; Savage, J. R.; and Lubawski, J. L. *Food and People* (3rd ed.). New York: Wiley, 1979.

Luepnitz, D. A. *Child Custody*. Lexington, MA: Heath, 1982.

Lundberg, I.; Olofsson, A.; and Wall, S. "Reading and Spelling Skills in the First School Years." *Scandinavian Journal of Psychology* 21, 1980, 159–173.

Lynn, D. *The Father: His Role in Development*. Belmont, CA: Brooks/Cole, 1974.

Lyon, R. K. "Moral and Personal Value Judgments of Preschool Children." *Child Development* 49(4), 1978, 1197–1207

McCall, R. B. "Environmental Effects on Intelligence: The Forgotten Realm of Discontinuous Nonshared Within-Family Factors." *Child Development* 54(2), 1983, 408–415.

McClenaghan, B. A., and Gallahue, D. L. *Fundamental Movement: A Developmental and Remedial Approach*. Philadelphia: Saunders, 1978.

Maccoby, E. E. "Social Emotional Development and Response to Stressors." In Garmezy, N., and Rutter, M. (eds.), *Stress, Coping, and Development in Children*. New York: McGraw-Hill, 1983.

Maccoby, E. E., and Jacklin, E. N. *The Psychology of Sex Differences*. Palo Alto, CA: Stanford University Press, 1974.

McCune-Nicolick, L., and Fenson, L. "Methodological Issues in Studying Early Pretend Play." In Yawkey, T. D., and Pellegrini, A. D. (eds.), *Child's Play: Developmental and Applied*. Hillsdale, NJ: Erlbaum, 1984.

McFadden, J., and Cook, J. A. "The Hydra-Headed Nature of Prejudice: Research Perspectives concerning Cross-Cultural Counseling with Elementary Age Children." *Elementary School Guidance & Counseling* 17(4), 1983, 294–304.

McGhee, P. E. *Humor: Its Origin and Development.* San Francisco: Freeman, 1979.

McGhee, P. E., and Chapman, A. J. (eds.). *Children's Humor.* New York: Wiley, 1980.

McGuire, D. J., and Ely, M. "Childhood Suicide." *Child Welfare* 63(1), 1984, 17–26.

McKusick, V. A. *Mendelian Inheritance in Man: Catalog of Autosomal Dominant, Autosomal Recessive, and X-Linked Phenotypes* (6th ed.). Baltimore: Johns Hopkins Press, 1983.

Macmillan, D. L. *Mental Retardation in School and Society* (3rd ed.). Boston: Little, Brown, 1982.

McNeill, D. "The Development of Language." In Mussen, P. H. (ed.), *Carmichael's Manual of Child Psychology* (Vol. 1, 3rd ed.). New York: Wiley, 1970, 1086–1089.

Madge, N. "Unemployment and Its Effects on Children." *Journal of Child Psychology and Psychiatry* 24(2), 1983, 311–319.

March of Dimes. *Genetic Counseling.* White Plains, NY: March of Dimes Birth Defects Foundation, 1987.

Marotz-Baden, R., and Tallman, I. "Parental Aspirations and Expectations for Daughters and Sons: A Comparative Analysis." *Adolescence* 13(59), 1978, 251–268.

Martin, J. A. "Physical Handicaps." In Hersen, M.; Van Hasselt, V. B.; and Matson, J. L., *Behavior Therapy for the Developmentally and Physically Disabled.* New York: Academic Press, 1983.

Mathews, W. W. *Atlas of Descriptive Embryology* (4th ed.). New York: Macmillan, 1986.

Mayhall, P. D., and Norgard, K. E. *Child Abuse and Neglect: Sharing Responsibility.* New York: Wiley, 1983.

Mead, M. *Culture and Commitment.* New York: Columbia University Press, 1978.

Meade, E. R. "Impulse Control and Cognitive Functioning in Lower- and Middle-Socioeconomic Children: A Developmental Study." *Merrill-Palmer Quarterly* 27(3), 1981, 271–285.

Meadows, S. (ed.). *Developing Thinking.* New York: Methuen, 1983.

Medeiros, D. C.; Porter, B. J.; and Welch, I. D. *Children under Stress.* Englewood Cliffs, NJ: Prentice-Hall, 1983.

Medinnus, G. R. *Child Study and Observation Guide.* New York: Wiley, 1976.

Meichenbaum, D.; Burland, S.; Gruson, L.; and Cameron, R. "Metacognitive Assessment." In Yussen, S. R. (ed.), *The Growth of Reflection in Children.* New York: Academic Press, 1985.

Mercer, J. R. "What Is a Racially and Culturally Nondiscriminatory Test? A Sociological and Pluralistic Perspective." In Reynolds, C. R., and Brown, R. T. (eds.), *Perspectives on Bias in Mental Testing.* New York: Plenum Press, 1984.

Meredith, H. V. "Body Size of Contemporary Groups of One Year Old

Infants Studied in Different Parts of the World." *Child Development* **41**, 1970, 551–600.

———. "Body Size of Contemporary Groups of Preschool Children Studied in Different Parts of the World." *Child Development* **39**, 1968, 335–377.

MILLER, M. S. *Child-Stress.* Garden City, NY: Doubleday, 1982.

MILLER, M. U. "Variations in Mexican-American Family Life: A Review Synthesis of Empirical Research." *Aztlan-International Journal of Chicago Studies Research* **9**, 1978, 209–231.

MILLER, N. E., AND DOLLARD, J. *Social Learning and Imitation.* New Haven, CT: Yale University Press, 1941.

MILNER, D. *Children and Race.* Beverly Hills, CA: Sage, 1983.

MILOS, M. E., AND REISS, S. "Effects of Three Play Conditions on Separation Anxiety in Young Children." *Journal of Consulting and Clinical Psychology* **50**(3), 1982, 389–395.

MIRANDA, A. "The Chicano Family: A Reanalysis of Conflicting Views." *Journal of Marriage and Family* **39**(4), 1977, 747–755.

MIRGA, T. "Reform Has Ignored 'At-Risk' Students, Inquiry by Advocacy Group Concludes." *Education Week* **5**(1), October 16, 1985, 1, 10

MISCHEL, W., AND WISCHEL, H. N. "A Cognitive Social-Learning Approach to Morality and Self-Regulation." In T. Lickona (ed.), *Moral Development and Behavior.* New York: Holt, Rinehart & Winston, 1976.

MODGIL, S.; MODGIL, C.; AND BROWN, G. *Jean Piaget: An Interdisciplinary Critique.* London: Routledge & Kegan Paul, 1983.

MOLNAR, G. E. "Cerebral Palsy." In Molnar, (ed.), *Pediatric Rehabilitation.* Baltimore: Williams & Wilkins, 1985.

MONTAGU, A. *Touching the Human Significance of the Skin.* New York: Columbia University Press, 1971.

MOODY, K. *Growing Up on Television.* New York: Time Books, 1980.

MOOK, D. G. *Psychological Research: Strategy and Tactics.* New York: Harper & Row, 1982.

MOORE, K. L. *Before We Are Born: Basic Embryology and Birth Defects* (2nd ed.). Philadelphia: Saunders, 1983.

MOORE, T. "Exclusive Early Mothering and Its Alternatives: The Outcome to Adolescence." *Scandinavian Journal of Psychology* **16**, 1975, 255–272.

MORRIS, D. H., AND LUBIN, A. H. "A Review of the Symposium: Diet and Behavior—A Multidisciplinary Evaluation." *Contemporary Nutrition* **10**(5), 1985, 1–2.

MORRIS, R. J., AND KRATOCHWILL, T. R. *Treating Children's Fears and Phobias.* New York: Pergamon Press, 1983.

———. "Behavioral Treatment of Children's Fears and Phobias: A Review." *School Psychololgy Review* **14**(1), 1985, 84–93.

MOSENTHAL, P. "Language and Thought." *Theory into Practice* **145**(5), 1975, 306–311.

MOULY, G. J. *Psychology for Teaching.* Boston: Allyn & Bacon, 1982.

MUSINGER, H. "The Adopted Child's IQ: A Critical Review." *Psychological Bulletin* 82, 1975, 623–659.

NADELMAN, L., AND BEGIN, A. "The Effect of the Newborn on the Older Sibling: Mothers' Questionnaires." In Lamb, M. E., and Sutton-Smith, B. (eds.), *Sibling Relationships: Their Nature and Significance across a Lifespan.* Hillsdale, NJ: Erlbaum, 1982.

NAOUR, P. "Brain/Behavior Relationships, Gender Differences, and the Learning Disabled." *Theory into Practice* 24(2), 1985, 100–105.

NATIONAL ADVISORY COMMITTEE ON HANDICAPPED CHILDREN. "First Annual Report." Washington, DC: U. S. Office of Education, 1968.

NEISWORTH, J. T., AND SMITH, R. M. *Retardation: Issues, Assessment, and Intervention.* New York: McGraw-Hill, 1978.

NELSON, B. J. *Making an Issue of Child Abuse.* Chicago: University of Chicago Press, 1984.

NICHOLS, R. L. *The American Indian: Past and Present* (2nd ed.). New York: Wiley, 1981.

NILSSON, L. A. *A Child Is Born.* New York: Dell (Delacorte Press), 1977.

NISAN, M. "Content and Structure in Moral Judgment: An Integrative View." In Kurtines, W., and Gerwirtz, J. L. (eds.), *Morality, Moral Behavior, and Moral Development.* New York: Wiley, 1984.

NOLES, S. W. "Body Image, Physical Attractiveness, and Depression." *Journal of Consulting and Clinical Psychology* 53(1), 1985, 88–94.

ODEN, S.; HERZBERGER, S. D.; MANGIONE, P. L.; AND WHEELER, V. A. "Children's Peer Relationships: An Examination of Social Processes." In Masters, J. C., and Yarkin-Levin, K. (eds.), *Boundary Areas in Social and Developmental Psychology.* New York: Academic Press, 1984.

OETTINGEN, G. "The Influence of the Kindergarten Teacher on Sex Differences in Behavior." *International Journal of Behavioral Development* 8(1), 1985, 3–13.

OGBU, J. U. "Cultural Discontinuities and Schooling." *Anthropology and Education Quarterly* 13(4), 1982, 290–307.

———. "Origins of Human Competence: A Cultural Ecological Perspective." *Child Development* 52, 1981, 413–439.

OKSAAR, E. *Language Acquisition in the Early Years.* (Trans. Turfler, K.) New York: St. Martin's Press, 1983.

OLSON, R. K.; DAVIDSON, B. J.; KLIEGL, R.; AND DAVIS, S. E. "Development of Phonetic Memory in Disabled and Normal Readers." *Journal of Experimental Child Psychology* 37, 1984, 187–206.

OPPENHEIMER, S. B., AND LEFEVRE. *Introduction of Embryonic Development* (2nd ed.). Boston: Allyn & Bacon, 1984.

ORNSTEIN, R., AND THOMPSON, R. F. *The Amazing Brain.* Boston: Houghton-Mifflin, 1984.

PAGELOW, M. D. *Family Violence.* New York: Praeger, 1984.

PALKER, P. "How to Deal with the Single-Parent Child in the Classroom." *Teacher* 98, 1980, 51–54.

PALUSZNY, M. J. *Autism: A Practical Guide for Parents and Professionals.* Syracuse, NY: Syracuse University Press, 1979.

PAPAGIANNIS, G.; BICKEL, R. N.; AND FULLER, R. H. "The Social Creation of School Dropouts." *Youth and Society* 14(3), 1983, 363–392.

PAPALIA, D., AND OLDS, S. W. *A Child's World* (3rd ed.). New York: McGraw-Hill, 1982.

PARKE, R. *Father-Infant Interaction, Maternal Attachment and Mothering Disorders.* Sausalito, CA: Johnson and Johnson, 1975.

PARTEN, M. "Social Participation among Preschool Children." *Journal of Abnormal and Social Psychology* 27, 1932, 243–369.

PARTRIDGE, R. P. "Learning Styles: A Review of Selected Models." *Journal of Nursing Education* 22, 1983, 243–248.

PASSMORE, R.; NICOL, B. M.; AND RAO, M. N. *Handbook on Human Nutritional Requirements.* Geneva: World Health Organization, 1974.

PATTERSON, C. J., AND KISTNER, M. C. "The Development of Listener Skills for Referential Communication." In Dickson, W. P. (ed.), *Children's Oral Communication Skills.* New York: Academic Press, 1981.

PELHAM, W. W., AND MILICH, R. "Peer Relations in Children with Hyperactivity/Attention Deficit Disorder." *Journal of Learning Disabilities* 17(9), 1984, 560–567.

PELLEGRINI, A. D. "The Effects of Exploration and Play on Young Children's Associative Fluency: A Review and Extension of Training Studies." In Yawkey, T. D., and Pellegrini, A. D. (eds.), *Child's Play: Developmental and Applied.* Hillsdale, NJ: Erlbaum, 1984.

———. "The Relationship between Kindergartners' Play and Achievement in Prereading, Language, and Writing." *Psychology in the Schools* 17(4), 1980, 530–535.

PEPLER, D. J., AND RUBIN, K. H. "Current Issues in the Study of Children's Play." *Human Development* 25(6), 1982, 443–447.

PERKINS, S. A. "Malnutrition and Prenatal Development." *Exceptional Children* 43(4), 1978, 214–219.

PERLMUTTER, M. (ed.) *Parent-Child Interaction and Parent-Child Relations in Child Development* (Vol. 17).

PERRY, S. *Casebook of Differential Therapeutics: A Guide to Treatment Selection (DSM-III).* New York: Brunner/Mazel, 1985.

PETERS, A. M. *The Units of Language Acquisition.* Cambridge: Cambridge University Press, 1983.

PETERSON, P. "How Pro-nutrition Television Programming Affects Children's Dietary Habits." *Developmental Psychology* 20(1), 1984, 55–63.

PEUGH, D. "Nutrition Education in Kindergarten." Unpublished research paper for National Dairy Council, 1976.

PHINILLOS, J. L. "The Modification of Intelligence." *Prospects* 12(1), 1982, 5–17.

PIAGET, J. *The Child's Conception of Physical Causality.* New York: Harcourt-Brace, 1930.

———. *The Construction of Reality in the Child.* New York: Basic Books, 1954.

———. *The Equilibration of Cognitive Structures: The Central Problem of Intellectual Development.* Chicago: University of Chicago Press, 1985.

———. *Judgment and Reasoning of the Child.* New York: Harcourt-Brace, 1928.

———. *Language and Thought of the Child.* London: Routledge and Kegan Paul, 1952.

———. *Memory and Intelligence.* New York: Basic Books, 1973.

———. *The Moral Judgment of the Child.* Glencoe, IL: Free Press, 1948.

———. *The Origins of Intelligence in Children.* New York: Norton, 1963.

———. *Play, Dreams, and Imitation in Childhood.* New York: Norton, 1962.

———. *The Psychology of the Child.* New York: Basic Books, 1969.

———. *The Psychology of Intelligence.* New York: Harcourt-Brace, 1950.

PIAGET, J., AND INHELDER, B. *The Psychology of the Child.* New York: Basic Books, 1969.

PILKIN, R. M. "Megadose Nutrients during Pregnancy." In Committee on Nutrition of the Mother and Preschool Child, *Alternative Dietary Practices and Nutritional Abuses in Pregnancy.* Washington DC: National Academic Press, 1982.

PINKNEY, A. *Black-Americans* (2nd ed.). Englewood Cliffs, NJ: Prentice-Hall, 1975.

PISSANOS, B. W. "Sex, Age, and Body Composition as Predictors of Children's Performance on Basic Motor Abilities and Health Related Fitness Items." *Perceptual and Motor Skills* 56(1), 1983, 71–77.

PITCHER, E. G., AND SCHULTZ, L. H. *Boys and Girls at Play: The Development of Sex Roles.* New York: Praeger, 1983.

PLANT, M. *Women, Drinking, and Pregnancy.* London: Tavistock Publications, 1985.

PLOMIN, R., AND DANIELS, D. "Genetics and Shyness." In Jones, W. H.; Cheek, J. M.; and Briggs, S. R. (eds.), *Shyness: Perspectives on Research and Treatment.* New York: Plenum Press, 1986.

PLOMIN, R., AND DEFRIES, J. C. *Origins of Individual Differences in Infancy.* New York: Academic Press, 1985.

PLOMIN, R., AND DUNN, J. (eds.). *The Study of Temperament: Change, Continuities, and Challenges.* Hillsdale, NJ: Erlbaum, 1986.

POLLITT, E. "Nutrition and Educational Performance." *Prospects: Quarterly Review of Education* 14(4), 1984, 443–460.

POWELL, D. R. "The Interpersonal Relationship Between Parents and Caregivers in Day Care Settings." *American Journal of Orthopsychiatry* **48**(4), 1978, 680–689.

Powell, G. J. (ed.). *The Psychosocial Development of Minority Group Children.* New York: Brunner/Mazel, 1983.

Powell, R. C., and Batters, J. D. "Pupils' Perception of Foreign Language Learning at 12: Some Gender Differences." *Educational Studies* **11**(1), 1985, 11–23.

Powers, H., and Presley, J. *Food Power: Nutrition and Your Child's Behavior.* New York: St. Martin's Press, 1978.

Public Health Nutritionist's Dietetic Practices Group. "Statement on Nutrition and Your Health: Dietary Guidelines for Americans." *The Journal of the American Dietetic Association* **86**(1), 1986, 107–108.

Quinn, J. M., and Rubin, K. H. "The Play of Handicapped Children." In Yawkey, T. D., and Pellegrini, A. D. (eds.), *Child's Play: Developmental and Applied.* Hillside, NJ: Erlbaum, 1984.

Rallison, M. L. *Growth Disorders in Infants, Children, and Adolescents.* New York: Wiley, 1986.

Ransbury, M. K. "Friedrich Froebel 1782–1982: A Reexamination of Froebel's Principles of Childhood Learning." *Childhood Education* **59**(2), 104–106.

Rapoport, R. N. (ed.). *Children, Youth and Families: The Action Research Relationship.* New York: Cambridge University Press, 1985.

Rapoport, R., and Rapoport, R. *Fathers, Mothers, and Society.* New York: Random House, 1980.

Raths, L. E.; Merrill, H.; and Simon, S. B. *Values and Teaching* (2nd ed.). Columbus, OH: Charles Merrill, 1978.

Read, M. S. *Relationships of Hunger and Malnutrition to Learning Ability and Behavior.* Lakeland: State of Florida, 1979.

Rechcigl, M., Jr. *Man, Food, and Nutrition.* Melbourne, FL: Krieger, 1982.

Reed, M. *Educating Hearing Impaired Children.* Milton Keyes, Eng.: Open University Press, 1984.

Reimer, J., and Hersh, R. *Promoting Moral Growth: From Piaget to Kohlberg.* New York: Longman, 1983.

Reinisch, E. H., and Minear, R. E. *Health of the Preschool Child.* New York: Wiley, 1978.

Reisinger, K.; Rogers, K. D.; and Johnson, O. "Nutrition Survey of Lower Greasewood, Arizona Navajos." In Moore, W. M.; Silverbery, M. M.; and Read, O.M.S., (eds.), *Nutrition, Growth and Development of North American Indian Children.* DHEW Publication No. (NIH) 12-26, 1972.

Renshaw, D. C. *The Hyperactive Child.* Chicago: Nelson-Hall, 1974.

Renzulli, J., and Hartman, R. "Scale for Rating Behavioral Characteristics of Superior Students." *Exceptional Children* **38**, 1971, 243–248.

Reynolds, C. R., and Brown, R. T. (eds.). *Perspectives on Bias in Mental Testing.* New York: Plenum Press, 1984.

Reynolds, W. M. "Depression in Children and Adolescents: Phenomenology, Evaluation and Treatment." *School Psychology Review* 13(2), 1984, 171–182.

Rice, M. L. "Contemporary Accounts of the Cognition/Language Relationship." *Journal of Speech and Hearing Disorders* 48, 1983, 347–359.

Rich, M., and DeVitis, J. L. *Theories of Moral Development.* Springfield, IL: Thomas, 1985.

Richey, S., and Taper, L. J. *Maternal and Child Nutrition.* New York: Harper & Row, 1983.

Riley, D., and Cochran, M. M. "Naturally Occurring Child-Rearing Advice for Fathers: Utilization of Personal Social Network." *Journal of Marriage and Family* 47(2), 1985, 275–286.

Rinne, C. H. "Low-Profile Classroom Controls." *Phi Delta Kappan* 64(1), 1982, 52–54.

Robinson, E. "Metacognitive Development." In Meadows, S. (ed.), *Developing Thinking.* New York: Methuen, 1983.

Robinson, H. B., and Robinson, N. M. "Longitudinal Development of Very Young Children in a Comprehensive Day-Care Program: The First Two Years." In H. Bee, *Social Issues in Developmental Psychology* (2nd ed.). New York: Harper & Row, 1978.

Rodel, M. J. "Children with Hearing Impairment." In J. Katz (ed.), *Handbook of Clinical Audiology* (3rd ed.). Baltimore: Williams and Willkins, 1985.

Roedell, W. C.; Jackson, M. E.; and Robinson, H. B. *Gifted Young Children.* New York: Teachers College, Columbia University, 1980.

Rogers, C. R. *Client-Centered Therapy: Its Current Practice, Implications, and Theory.* Boston: Houghton-Mifflin, 1951.

———. *On Becoming a Person.* Boston: Houghton-Mifflin, 1961.

Rosenthal, R.; and Rosnow, R. L. *Essentials of Behavioral Research: Methods and Data Analysis.* New York: McGraw-Hill, 1984.

Rosett, H. L. *Alcohol and the Fetus.* New York: Oxford Press, 1984.

Rubenstein, J. L.; Hower, C.; and Boyle, P. "A Two-Year Follow-Up of Infants in Community-Based Day Care." *Journal of Child Psychology & Psychiatry* 22, 1981, 209–218.

Rubin, K. H. "Nonsocial Play in Preschoolers: Necessary Evil?" *Child Development* 53(3), 1982, 651–657.

Rubin, K. H., and Pepler, D. J. "Children's Play: Piaget's Views Revisited." *Contemporary Education Psychology* 7(3), 1982, 289–299.

Rubin, U., and Medrich, E. A. "Child Care, Recreation and the Fiscal Crisis." *The Urban and Social Change Review* 12(1), 1979, 22–28.

Rubin, Z. *Children's Friendships.* Cambridge, MA: Harvard University Press, 1980.

Rutter, M. *Maternal Deprivation Reassessed.* Baltimore: Penguin, 1972.

Sabatino, D. A., and Miller, T. L. *Describing Learner Characteristics of Handicapped Children and Youth.* New York: Grune & Gratton, 1979.

Safford, P. L. *Teaching Young Children with Special Needs.* St. Louis: Mosby, 1978.

Sagal, P. T. *Skinner's Philosophy.* Washington, DC: University Press of America, 1981.

Saltzstein, H. D. "Critical Issues in Kohlberg's Theory of Moral Reasoning." *Monographs of the Society for Research in Child Development* **48**, 1983, 108–119.

Samuels, S. J. "Factors Influencing Listening: Inside and Outside the Head." *Theory into Practice* **23**(3), 1984, 183–189.

Sapora, A. V., and Mitchell, M. D. *The Theory of Play and Recreation.* New York: Ronald Press, 1971.

Sarafino, E. P., and Armstrong, J. W. *Child and Adolescent Development.* Glenview, IL: Scott, Foresman, 1980.

Satter, E. M. "Childhood Eating Disorders." *The Journal of the American Dietetic Association* **86**(3), 1986a, 357–361.

———. "The Feeding Relationship." *The Journal of the American Dietetic Association* **86**(3), 1986b, 352–356.

Sattler, J. M. *Assessment of Children's Intelligence and Special Abilities* (2nd ed.). Boston: Allyn & Bacon, 1982.

Savic, S. *How Twins Learn to Talk.* London: Academic Press, 1980.

Schasre, J. M. *Helping Children with Problems.* New York: Walker, 1978.

Schave, B., and Ciciello, J. "Identity and Intimacy in Twins." *Journal of the American Academy of Child Psychiatry* **24**, 1985, 245–246.

Scheinfeld, A. *Heredity in Humans.* Philadelphia: Lippincott, 1971.

Schlesinger, I. M. "The Role of Cognitive Development and Linguistic Input in Language Acquisition." *Journal of Child Language* **4**, 1977, 153–169.

Science and Education Foundation *Family Fare: A Guide to Good Nutrition.* Washington, DC: United States Department of Agriculture, 1987.

Sears, R. R.; Ran, L.; and Alpert, R. *Identification and Child Rearing.* Stanford, CA: Stanford Press, 1965.

Seligmann, J.; Gosnell, M.; and Shapiro, D. "New Science of Birth." In Fitzgerald, H. E. (ed.), *Human Development: Annual Editions 80/81.* Guilford, CT: Duskin, 1980.

Selkow, P. *Assessing Sex Bias in Testing.* Wesport, CT: Greenwood, 1984.

Sells, C. J.; and Bennett, F. C. "Prevention of Mental Retardation: The Role of Medicine." *American Journal of Mental Deficiency* **82**(2), 1977, 117–129.

Shanklin, D. R., and Hodin, J. *Maternal Nutrition and Child Health.* Springfield, IL: Thomas, 1979.

Shantz, C. U. "The Role of Role-Taking in Children's Referential Communication." In Dickson, W. P. (ed.), *Children's Oral Communication Skills.* New York: Academic Press, 1981.

SHATZ, M. "Contributions of Mother and Mind to the Development of Communicative Competence: A Status Report." In Perlmutter, M. (ed.), *Parent-Child Interaction and Parent-Child Relations in Child Development* (Vol. 17). Hillsdale, NJ: Erlbaum, 1984.

SHELDON, W. H. *Varieties of Physique.* New York: Harper & Row, 1940.

SHERMAN, J. "An Analysis of Software Preferences of Preschool Children." *Educational Technology* 25(5), 1985, 39–41.

SIGEL, I. E. *Parental Belief Systems: The Psychological Consequences for Children.* Hillsdale, NJ: Erlbaum, 1985.

SILVA, P. A. "Experiences and the Preschool Child." *Journal of Early Childhood* 5(2), 1980, 13–19.

SIMPSON, G. B., AND LORSBACK, I. C. "The Development of Automatic and Conscious Components of Contextual Facilitation." *Child Development* 54(3), 1983, 760–772.

SIRKIN, J. E. "Foundation Heads Urged to Support Children's Issues." *Education Week* 5(4), September 25, 1985, 5.

SKINNER, B. F. *About Behaviorism.* New York: Knopf, 1974.

———. *Verbal Behavior.* New York: Appleton-Century-Crofts, 1957.

SLOBIN, D. I. *Psycholinguistics* (2nd ed.). Glenview, IL: Scott, Foresman, 1979.

SLOBIN, D. I. "They Learn the Same Way All around the World." *Psychology Today* 6(2), 1972, 71–76, 82.

SMILANSKY, S. *The Effects of Sociodramatic Play on Disadvantaged Preschool Children.* New York: Wiley, 1968.

SMITH, M. C. "Cognizing the Behavioral Stream: The Recognition of Intentional Action." *Child Development* 49(3), 1976, 736–743.

SNOWMAN, M. K., AND DIBBLE, M. V. "Nutrition Component in a Comprehensive Child Development Program." *The Journal of the American Dietetic Association* 43(2), 1979, 119–124.

SPENCER, H. "Minerals and Mineral Interactions in Human Beings." *The Journal of the American Dietetic Association* 86(2), 1986, 864–867.

STALLINGS, L. M. *Motor Learning: From Theory to Practice.* St. Louis: Mosby, 1982.

STAUB, E. (ed.). *Personality: Basic Aspects and Current Research.* Englewood Cliffs, NJ: Prentice-Hall, 1980.

STEELE, C. H. *American Indians and Urban Life: A Community Study.* Ann Arbor, MI: University Microfilms, 1979.

STEELMAN, L. C., AND DOBY, J. T. "Family Size and Birth Order as Factors on the IQ Performance of Black and White Children." *Sociology of Education* 56(2), 1983, 101–109.

STEELMAN, L. C., AND POWELL, B. "The Social and Academic Consequences of Birth Order." *Journal of Marriage and the Family* 47(1), 1985, 117–124.

STEVENS, R. *Erik Erikson: An Introduction.* New York: St. Martin's Press, 1983.

STEVENSON, D. T., AND ROMNEY, D. M. "Depression in Learning Disabled Children." *Journal of Learning Disabilities* 17(1), 1984, 579–582.

Stevenson, R. L. "Foreign Children." In Untermeyer, L. (ed.), *Rainbow in the Sky.* New York: Harcourt Brace Jovanovich, 1985, p. 99.

Stini, W. A.; Weber, C. W.; Kemberling, S. R.; and Vaughan, L. A. "Lean Tissue Growth and Disease Susceptibility in Bottle-Fed versus Breast-Fed Infants." In Green, L. S., and Johnston, F. E. (eds.), *Social and Biological Predictors of Nutritional Status, Physical Growth, and Neurological Development.* New York: Academic Press, 1980.

Stockbauer, J. W. "Evaluation of the Missouri WIC Program: Prenatal Components." *The Journal of the American Dietetic Association* 86(1), 1986, 61–67.

Strickland, E. "The Effect of Contrasting Play Environment on the Free Play of Third Grade Children: Four Case Studies." Unpublished paper. University of Texas at Arlington, 1980.

Tan, L. E. "Laterality and Directional Preferences in Preschool Children." *Perceptual and Motor Skills* 55(3), 1982, 863–870.

Taylor, B. J. *A Child Goes Forth.* Minneapolis: Burgess, 1985.

———. *Dear Mom and Dad: Parents and the Preschooler.* Provo, UT: Brigham Young University Press, 1978.

Thomas, A., and Chess, S. *Temperament and Development.* New York: Brunner/Mazel, 1977.

Thomas, A.; Chess, S.; and Birch, H. G. "The Origin of the Personality." *Scientific American* 223(2), 1970, 102–109.

Tienda, M., and Angel, R. "Headship and Household Composition among Blacks, Hispanics, and Other Whites." *Social Forces* 61(2), 1982, 508–531.

Torello, M. W., and Duffy, F. H. "Using Brain Electrical Activity Mapping to Diagnose Learning Disabilities." *Theory into Practice* 24(2), 1985, 95–99.

Torrance, E. P. *Torrance Tests for Creative Thinking: K–Graduate School.* Los Angeles: Western Psychological Services, 1974.

Touliatos, J., and Compton, N. H. *Approaches to Child Study.* Minneapolis: Burgess, 1983.

Trites, R. L., and La Prade, K. "Evidence for an Independent Syndrome of Hyperactivity." *Journal of Child Psychology and Psychiatry and Allied Disciplines* 24(4), 1983, 573–586.

Troyer, W. *Divorced Kids.* New York: Harcourt, Brace, Jovanovich, 1979.

Tsai, L. Y., and Stewart, M. A. "Etiological Implication of Maternal Age and Birth Order in Infantile Autism." *Journal of Autism and Developmental Disorders* 13(1), 1983, 57–65.

Tuttle, F. B., and Becker, L. A. *Characteristics and Identification of Gifted and Talented Students* (2nd ed.). Washington, DC: National Educational Association, 1983.

Uhlig, G. E., and Vasquez, A. G. "Cross-Cultural Research and Multicultural Education: 1970–1980." *Journal of Teacher Education* 33(4), 1982, 45–58.

UNITED STATES OFFICE OF HUMAN DEVELOPMENT. *Child Abuse and Neglect: The Problem and Its Management.* DHEW Pub. # 75-30073. Washington, DC: Department of Health, Education, and Welfare, 1976.

VALENTINE, B. *Hustling and Other Hard Work.* New York: Free Press, 1980.

VALIAN, V. "Syntactic Categories in the Speech of Young Children." *Developmental Psychology* **22**(4), 1986, 562–579.

VAN HEERDEN, J. R. "Early Undernutrition and Mental Performance." *International Journal of Early Childhood* **16**(1), 1984, 10–16.

VARMA, V. P. (ed.). *Anxiety in Children.* New York: Methuen, 1984.

VASTA, R. *Strategies and Techniques in Child Study.* New York: Academic Press, 1982.

VOLPE, E. P. *Patient in the Womb.* Macon, GA: Mercer University Press, 1984.

VOYDANOFF, P. (ed.). *Work and Family: Changing Roles of Men and Women.* Palo Alto, CA: Mayfield, 1984.

VYGOTSKY, L. S. *Mind in Society.* Cambridge, MA: Harvard University Press, 1978.

WADSWORTH, B. J. *Piaget of the Classroom Teacher.* New York: Longman, 1979.

———. *Piaget's Theory of Cognitive and Affective Development* (3rd ed.). New York: Longman, 1984.

WAGNER, R. K., AND STERNBERG, R. J. "Alternative Conceptions of Intelligence and Their Implications for Education. *Review of Educational Research* **54**(2), 1984, 179–223.

WALKER, D. K. *Socioemotional Measures for Preschool and Kindergarten Children.* San Francisco: Jossey-Bass, 1973.

WATSON, J. *The Darker Side of Childhood.* Austin: Texas Department of Community Affairs, 1974.

WATSON, R.; COPPOLA, V.; WANG, P.; MOREAU, R.; COPELAND, J.; CARDWELL, D.; McDonald, D.; Sandza, R.; Robinson, T.; Burgower, B.; and Bailey, E. "What Price Day Care?" *Newsweek,* September 10, 1984, 14–21.

WATSON, R. R., AND LEONARD, T. K. "Selenium and Vitamins A, E, and C: Nutrients with Cancer Prevention Properties." *The Journal of the American Dietetic Association* **86**(4), 1986, 505–510.

WEBB, P. K. "Becoming: Affective Development in Early Childhood." In Lundsteen, S. W., and Tarrow, N. B. (eds.), *Guiding Young Children's Learning.* New York: McGraw-Hill, 1981.

WEBER, E. *Ideas Influencing Early Childhood Education: A Theoretical Analysis.* New York: Teachers College, Columbia University Press, 1984.

WEISS, B., AND WEISZ, J. R. "General Cognitive Deficits: Mental Retardation." In Brown, R. T., and Reynolds, C. R., (eds.), *Psychological Perspectives on Childhood Exceptionality: A Casebook.* New York: Wiley, 1986.

WELLS, M. J. "Emigrants from the Migrant Stream: Environment Land Incentives in Relocation." *Aztlan-International Journal of Chicano Studies* **7**(2), 1976, 267–290.

WERTSCH, J. V. "Adult-Child Interaction as a Source of Self-Regulation in

Children." In Yussen, S. R. (ed.), *The Growth of Reflection in Children.* New York: Academic Press, 1985.

WHITE, B. L. *The First Three Years of Life.* New York: Avon Books, 1984.

WHITE, J. M. *Everyday Life of the North American Indian.* New York: Holmes & Meier, 1979.

WHITE-GRAVES, M. U., AND SCHILLER, M. R. "History of Foods in the Caries Process." *Journal of the American Dietetic Association* 86(2), 1986, 241–245.

WHORTON, J. E. "Comparing Ability and Achievement in Three Academic Areas for Upper Elementary Gifted Students." *Journal for the Education of the Gifted* 8(2), 1985, 149–154.

WIERSMA, W. *Research Methods in Education* (3rd ed.). Boston: Allyn & Bacon, 1985.

WILLERMAN, L. *The Psychology of Individual and Group Differences.* San Francisco: Freeman, 1979.

WILLIAMS, H. G. *Perceptual and Motor Development.* Englewood Cliffs, NJ: Prentice-Hall, 1983.

WILLIAMSON, P. A., AND SILVERN, S. B. "Creative Dramatic Play and Language Comprehension." In Yawkey, T. D., and Pellegrini, A. D. (eds.), *Child's Play: Developmental and Applied.* Hillsdale, NJ: Erlbaum, 1984.

WINCH, R. F., AND GORDON, M. T. *Familial Structure and Function as Influence.* Lexington, MA: Heath, 1974.

WINICK, M. "Early Malnutrition: Brain Structure and Function." *Preventive Medicine* 6, 1977, 358–360.

———. *Malnutrition and Brain Development.* New York: Oxford University Press, 1976.

WINN, M. *The Plug-In Drug.* New York: Viking, 1985.

WITHERSPOON, R. "Birth Defects: A Risk Even before Conception." *The Dallas Morning News,* November 22, 1980, 1–3.

WOLFF, P. H. "The Natural History of Crying and Other Vocalizations in Infancy." In Stone, L. J.; Smith, H. T.; and Murphy, L. B., (eds.), *The Competent Infant.* New York: Basic Books, 1973.

WOLMAN, B. B. *The Unconscious Mind: The Meaning of Freudian Psychology.* Englewood Cliffs, NJ: Prentice-Hall, 1968.

WOOD, B. S. *Children and Communication: Verbal and Nonverbal Language Development.* Englewood Cliffs, NJ: Prentice-Hall, 1981.

WOOLRIDGE, P., AND RICHMANN, C. L. "Teachers' Choice of Punishment as a Function of the Student's Gender, Age, Race, and IQ Level." *Journal of School Psychology* 23(1), 1985, 19–29.

WRIGHT, R. L. "Functional Language, Socialization, and Academic Achievement." *Journal of Negro Education* 52(1), 1983, 3–14.

YAWKEY, T. D., AND HANCIA, E. J. "Pretend Play Tools for Oral Language Growth in the Preschool." *Journal of Creative Behavior* 16(4), 1982, 265–271.

YAWKEY, T. D., AND PELLEGRINI, A. D. *Child's Play: Developmental and Applied.* Hillsdale, NJ: Erlbaum, 1984.

YORE, L. D., AND OLLILA, L. O. "Cognitive Development, Sex, and Abstractness in Grade One Word Recognition." *Journal of Educational Research* 78(4), 1985, 242–247.

YSSELDYKE, J. E., AND STEVENS, L. J. "Specific Learning Deficits: The Learning Disabled." In Brown, R. T., and Reynolds, C. R. (eds.), *Psychological Perspectives and Childhood Exceptionality: A Casebook.* New York: Wiley, 1986.

YUSSEN, S. R. (ed.). *The Growth of Reflection in Children.* New York: Academic Press, 1985.

ZAHN-WAXLER, C.; RADKE-YARROW, M.; AND BRADY-SMITH, J. "Perspective-Taking and Prosocial Behavior." *Developmental Psychology* 13(1), 1977, 87–88.

ZAHN-WAXLER, C.; RADKE-YARROW, M.; AND KING, R. "Child-Rearing and Children's Prosocial Initiations toward Victims of Distress." *Child Development* 50(2), 1979, 319–330.

ZAMMARELLI, J., AND BOLTON, N. "The Effects of Play on Mathematical Concept Formation." *British Journal of Educational Psychology* 47(2), 1977, 155–161.

ZEISER, E. L., AND HOFFMAN, S. "Computers: Tools for Thinking." *Childhood Education* 59(4), 1983, 251–254.

ZENTALL, S. S.; GOHS, D. E.; AND CULATTA, B. "Language and Activity of Hyperactive and Comparison Children during Listening Tasks." *Exceptional Children* 50(3), 1983, 255–266.

ZILL, N. *National Survey of Children.* New York: Foundation for Child Development, 1977.

ZIMBARDO, P. G., AND RADL, S. L. *The Shy Child.* New York: McGraw-Hill, 1981.

ZURCHER, L. A. *The Mutable Self: A Self-Concept Change.* Beverly Hills, CA: Sage Publications, 1977.

Subject Index

Academic achievement, and play, 339
Accidental acts, understanding, 281
Accommodation, Piaget's theory, 21–22
Action thinking, 169
Adoption studies, 67, 69
Adventure playgrounds, 343
Aggression/Aggressive disorders, 431–434
    causes of, 432
    and television viewing, 276–277
    treatment approaches, 298, 433–434
    types of aggression, 284, 431
Alcohol abuse, and prenatal development, 78
Altruism, 291
Amniocentesis, 68
Anal stage, 9
Anecdotal records, 43
Antisocial behavior, 282–285
    aggression, forms of, 284
    Erikson's theory and, 282–285
        guilt, 284–285
        inferiority, 285
        mistrust, 282
        shame/doubt, 282–284
Anxiety, 6
    increases, in children, 248
    origins of, 247
    and personality development, 247–248
    responses to, 6–7, 247
    See also Stress/anxiety.
Articulation differences, 403
Assessment instruments, 46–49
    cognitive development, 46–47
    motor development, 48
    socioemotional measures, 47–48
Assimilation, Piaget's theory, 21, 22
Attachment, formation of, 259–260

Attention, 173–174
    educational implications, 174, 175
    ethnic affiliation, 174–175
Attention deficit disorder, 395, 414–418
    attention problems, types of, 417
    causes of, 415
    characteristics of, 415
    DSM-III-R criteria, 416
    effects of, academic/social, 417
    incidence of, 415
    and nutrition, 150
    sex differences, 416–417
    strategies for, 417–418
Autism, 418–421
    causes of, 420
    characteristics of, 418–420
    incidence of, 418
    prognosis, 421
    treatment approaches, 421
Automobile related accidents, 107
Autonomy
    autonomy versus shame and doubt, 11, 265
    and dependency, 261

Babbling, 206–207
Balance, and motor development, 108
Basic trust versus basic mistrust, 11
Behavioral problems and nutrition, 149–150
    attention deficit disorder, 150
    specific deficiencies, 150
Behaviorist theory, 13–17
    language development, 197–199
        environmental stimuli, 197–198
        inhibition of, 198–199
        positive reinforcement, 197

Behaviorist theory (continued)
    successive approximations, 198
    verbal models, 198
  operant conditioning, 13–15
  social learning theory, 15–17
Behavior management
  discipline, 308–312
  empathy development, 313–315
  influencing factors
    behavior surveillance, 308–309
    disposition of caretaker, 308
    disposition of child, 308
  self-instruction, 316–317
  See also specific topics.
Behavior modification techniques, 311–312
  aggressive behavior, 434–435
  contingent observation, 312
  extinction, 311
  guidelines for use, 312
  praise, 311
  relearning group sessions, 312
  time-out, 311–312
  withdrawn children, increasing peer interaction, 428
Bibliotherapy, empathy development, 313–314
Birth
  Apgar Scale, newborn evaluation, 84
  delivery settings, 82–84
    birthing rooms, 83–84
    home deliveries, 84
    hospital delivery, 83
  prepared childbirth classes, 79–81
  siblings, explaining birth to, 81–82
Birth order
  characteristics of first/second/youngest children, 235
  influencing factors, 235
  and language development, 222–223
  and personality development, 235–236
  and socialization, 285
Blended families, 351
Body type
  ectomorph, 99
  endomorph, 99
  mesomorph, 99
  and personality characteristics, 99–100
  and physical development, 99–100
Bones, growth of, 96
Book Finder, 314
Brain/nervous system
  growth of, 95–96
  and malnutrition, 148–149

Case study approach, 34, 36
Causal comparative studies, 36
Cavities, 146–147
Cerebral palsy, 405–406
  dyskinetic, 406
  spastic, 406
  treatment, 406
Child abuse, 373–376
  child abusers, characteristics of, 375–376
  child neglect, 375
  definition of, 373
  emotional abuse, 375
  physical abuse, 373–374
  prevention of, 376
  sexual abuse, 374–375
Child care
  child care centers, 368
  child care home, 368
  effects of, 368–369
  home-care, 367
  multiple-care strategies, 366–367
  need for, 365–366
  split-shift care, 367–368
  sponsorship of, 366
Childhood and Society (Erikson), 10
Child safety, 105–107
  automobile related accidents, 107
  falls, 105–106
  fire, 106
  home hazards, 105
  poisons, 106
  water, 107
Circular reactions, Piagetian, 163
Classification, concrete operational period, 171
Client-centered therapy, 24, 25
Cognitive development
  assessment instruments, 46–47
  community programs for, 179
  information processing approach, 173–179
  issues related to, 187–188
  and malnutrition, 148–149
  and maternal nurturance, 149
  Piaget's theory, 163–172
  and play, 336, 338
Cognitive learning styles
  category breadth, 182–183
  distraction, susceptibility/resistance to, 183
  field orientation, 180–182
  impulsiveness, 180
  reflectiveness, 180

SUBJECT INDEX

Cognitive theory, 21–24
  language development, 203–206
    collective monologues, 205
    echolalia, 204
    monologues, 204–205
    socialized speech, 205–206
    See also Piaget's theory.
Collective monologues, language development, 205
Communication patterns, 359–361
  nonverbal communication, 360–361
  verbal communication, 360
Conception, 70–71
  process in humans, 59–60
Concrete operational period, 170–172
  classification in, 171
  conservatism in, 170
  numbering in, 171–172
  seriation in, 171
Conformity, 285
Conscience, 295
  and punishment, 298–299
Conservation, concrete operational period, 170
Construction play, 326–327
Content analysis, 36–37
Contingent observation, behavior modification techniques, 312
Control group, 38
Convergence, vision, 118
Conversational skills, elementary years, 216–217
Coordination, and motor development, 108
Coping ability, 240–243
  locus of control, 240–243
Copying, 16
Creative activities, research, 49–50
Creative playgrounds, 342
Creativity, and play, 333
Critical period, language development, 202–203
Cross-sectional research, 34
Cues, 15–16
Culture, assimilation of, and play, 334–335
Cumulative health records, 103–104

Defense mechanisms, 6
Delayed speech production, 405
Dependency, and autonomy, 261
Dependent variable, 38
Depression, 423–426
  characteristics of, 424–425
  factors related to, 425
  treatment approaches, 425–426
Descriptive research
  case study, 34, 36
  casual comparative studies, 36
  content analysis, 36–37
  cross-sectional research, 34
  ethnographic research, 36
  follow-up studies, 37
  longitudinal research, 34
  survey, 34
Development, theories of
  behaviorist theory, 13–17
  cognitive theory, 21–24
  developmental tasks, 18–21
  maturational theory, 17
  psychoanalytic theory, 4–13
  self theory, 24–25
Developmental forces
  environmental stimulation, 86–87
  family/peer relations, 87
  individual characteristics, 85–86
  societal/ethnic affiliations, 87–88
Developmental tasks, 18–21
  educational implications, 20–21
  infancy/early childhood tasks, 19
  mastery of tasks, 17–18
    failure and, 17–18
  task analysis, 20
  teachable moment, 21
  types of tasks, 19–20
Difficult children, 230
Discipline, 308–312
  behavior modification techniques, 311–312
    contingent observation, 312
    extinction, 311
    guidelines for use, 312
    praise, 311
    relearning group sessions, 312
    time-out, 311–312
  induction, 310
  love withdrawal, 310
  power assertion, 309–310
Distraction, susceptibility/resistance to, 183
Divorce, 369–373
  custody patterns, 370
    joint-custody, 370
    split-custody, 370
  dealing with, 371–372
  effects of, 370–371
    developmental impact, 371
Dominant/recessive genes, 63–64

Down's syndrome, 75
   special nutrition program, 144
Dramatic play, 328
Drive, 15
Dual-worker families, 351–352

Early experiences
   and attachment, 259–260
   and locus of control, 242–243
   and personality development, 236–237
Easy children, 230
Echolalia, language development, 204
Ectomorph, 99
Educational opportunities, 361–363
   cultural factors
      cultural patterning of mental abilities, 361–362
      guided intervention, 362–363
      home-school discrepancies, 362, 363
      parental achievement and, 361
Educational Testing Services CIRCUS Battery, 388
Ego, 5
Egocentrism, 166, 278
Elaborated code, language style, 223
Embedded figures test, 181
Embryonic period, 72
Emotional abuse, of children, 375
Emotional development, and play, 331–333
Empathy development, 291, 313–315
   bibliotherapy, 313–314
   magic circle, 315
   role playing, 314–315
Endocrine system, growth of, 96
Endomorph, 99
Environmental stimulation
   as developmental force, 86–87
   language development, 197–198
Epilepsy, types of seizures, 406
Episodic memory, 176
Erikson's theory
   and antisocial behavior, 282–285
   autonomy versus shame and doubt, 11
   basic trust versus basic mistrust, 11
   industry versus inferiority, 12–13
   initiative versus guilt, 11–12
   and social development, 264–266
Ethical factors, research, 50–51
Ethnic affiliation
   and development, 87–88
   and personality development, 233–235

   and physical development, 100–101
   See also Sociocultural shaping.
Ethnographic research, 36
Events sampling, 43–44
Experimental group, 38
Experimental research
   cause, determination of, 39
   control group in, 38
   dependent variable in, 38
   experimental group in, 38
   independent variable in, 37–38
   overgeneralization error, 40
   randomization in, 39–40
   reliability in, 40
   validity in, 40
Extended families, 353–355
External locus of control, 241, 242
Extinction, behavior modification technique, 311

Fairness, development of, 281–282
Family Development Research Project, 151
Family histories, 69
Family/peer relations, as developmental force, 87
Family size, and language development, 223
Family structure, 351–355
   blended families, 351
   dual-worker families, 351–352
   extended families, 353–355
   single-parent families, 351, 352–353
Fathers, nurturant fathers, 267–269
Fears
   and personality development, 248–251
   sources of
      cause/effect misunderstandings, 251
      imitation of others, 251
      lack of experience, 250–251
      unpleasant experiences, 249–250
Fetal period, 73–74
Field orientation, 180–182
   cultural factors, 181
   educational implications, 181
   embedded figures test, 181
   field-dependence, 180–182
   field-independence, 180–182
Figure-ground discrimination, 118, 119
Fixation, vision, 117–118
Flexibility, and motor development, 108
Follow-up studies, 37
Formal operational period, 172
Form constancy, 118, 120

SUBJECT INDEX

Freudian theory
  anal stage, 9
  anxiety, 6
    adjustments to anxiety, 6–7
  critique of, 10
  defense mechanisms, 6
  ego, 5
  id, 4–5
  implications for relating to children, 7–9
  latency period, 9–10
  oral stage, 9
  phallic stage, 9
  superego, 5
Frustration
  and aggression, 433
  and personality development, 248
  responses to, 248
  temper tantrums, 248
Functional play, 325

Gender
  sex chromosome variations, 62
  sex determination, 62
  sex-linked characteristics, 62–63
Genetic counseling
  amniocentesis, 68
  estimation of risk and, 68
Genetic studies
  adoption studies, 67, 69
  family histories, 69
  twin studies, 67, 69
German measles (rubella), and prenatal development, 77
Gifted children, 385–390
  characteristics of, 385–388
    emotional, 387
    intellectual, 387–388
    leadership qualities, 387
    physical, 386
  education of, 389–390
  identification of, 388–389
    observation, 389
    tests/scales, 388
Government-sponsored programs, nutrition, 151
Group traditions, 348–351
  speed of cultural change, 351
  transmitting
    methods of, 349–350
    pros/cons of methods, 350
Guilford model, intelligence, 160
Guilt, in children, 284–285

Hands-on learning, 162
Health care, 101–104
  cumulative health records, 103–104
  daily care, 101–103
  illness, early detection of, 104–105
  immunizations, 103
Hearing, 120–122
  auditory acuity, 120–121
  auditory discrimination, 121
  auditory memory, 121–122
  auditory-visual integration, 122
  functions of, 120
Hearing impaired child, 400–403
  deafness, causes of, 400
  education of, 402–403
  signs of hearing loss, 400–401
  testing of, 401–402
Heredity
  cell development, 62
  dominant/recessive genes, 63–64
  genetic components, 60–62
    DNA, 61–62
    genes, 61
  genetic counseling, 68
  genetic studies
    adoption studies, 67, 69
    family histories, 69
    twin studies, 67, 69
  heritability
    intelligence, 67, 69
    mental illness, 70
    personality traits, 68–70
    physical defects, 66
    physical traits, 64–65
  sex chromosome variations, 62
  sex determination, 62
  sex-linked characteristics, 62–63
Historical research
  improving accuracy, guidelines for, 33
  primary source materials, 32
  secondary source materials, 32–33
Holophrases, 209
Home environment, and language development, 224
Home Observation for Measurement of the Environment (HOME), 362–363
Humor, sense of, 244–245
  development of, 244
  individual differences, 245
Hyperactivity. *See* Attention deficit disorder

Id, 4–5
Identification, modeling, 263–264
Identity development, 237–240
  self-awareness in, 238
  self-concept in, 238–239
  self-confidence in, 240
  self-esteem in, 239
Illness, early detection of, 104–105
Immunizations, 103
Impulsiveness, cognitive learning styles, 180
Independent variable, 37–38
Individual characteristics, as developmental force, 85–86
Industry, development of, 243–244
Industry versus inferiority, 12–13, 265–266
Inferiority, in children, 285
Information processing approach, 173–179
  attention in, 173–174
  memory in, 175–177
  perception in, 173
  problem solving in, 177–179
Initiative, 241
Initiative versus guilt, 11–12, 265
Innate theory
  critical period, 202–203
  language acquisition device (LAD), 200
  language development, 199–203
  primate speech, 202
  transformations, 201
  universal language characteristics, 200–201
Intelligence
  factor analysis of, 160
    Guilford model, 160
  heritability, 67, 69
  IQ, components of, 159–160
Intelligence measures
  issues related to, 187–188
  Stanford-Binet Intelligence Scale, 183–184
  Wechsler Intelligence Scale for Children–Revised (WISC-R), 187
  Wechsler Preschool and Primary Scale of Intelligence (WPPSI), 184–186
Intentionality, understanding of, 281
Internal locus of control, 240–241
Internal motivation, initiative, 241
Interviews, 45–46
  Piaget's interviewing technique, 47
Introjection, 264
Isolation, 285

Jealousy, 283–284
Joint-custody, 370

Kinethesis, 124
Knowledge, construction of, 160–162
  facilitation of, 162
  impetus for, 161–162
  logico-mathematical knowledge, 160–161
  physical knowledge, 160
  social knowledge, 161
Kohlberg's theory of moral development, 302–304
  criticism of, 304
  interview used, 303
  stages of moral development, 302–303, 304
Kwashiorkor, 145

Lamaze method, 80
Language
  components of
    phonology, 194–195
    semantics, 196
    syntax, 195–196
  functions of, pragmatics, 196–197
Language development
  elementary years
    conversational skills, 216–217
    nonverbal communications, 217–218
    storytelling, 218
    vocabulary, 216
  influencing factors
    birth order, 222–223
    family size, 223
    home environment, 224
    multiple births, 223
    sex of child, 222
    socioeconomic class, 223–224
  motherese, 198
  overgeneralization, in speech, 209
  and play, 336
  rapid language expansion, 211
    relational meanings, development of, 213
    "whip," 213–214
    word formations, modifications of, 211–213
  sequence of, 206–218
    first words, 208–210
    language understanding, 207–208
    prelanguage sounds, 206–207
    two-word sentences, 210–211
  theories of
    behaviorist theory, 197–199
    cognitive theory, 203–206
    innate theory, 199–203
Latency period, 9–10

SUBJECT INDEX

Leadership qualities, gifted children, 387
Learning, and television viewing, 277–278
Learning disabilities, 393–397
  causes of, 393–394
  definition of, 393
  diagnosis of, 394
  education of, 396–397
  types of, 394–396
    attention disability, 395
    memory disability, 395–396
    oral language disability, 396
    perceptual disability, 396
    thinking disability, 396
Leboyer method, 80
Locomotion, sequence of
  climbing, 111
  creeping, 109
  cross-pattern crawling, 109
  hopping, 109
  jumping, 109
  leaping, 111
  precrawling, 109
  running, 109
  skipping, 109, 111
  walking, 109
Locus of control, 240–243
  early experiences and, 242–243
  external locus of control, 241, 242
  initiative and, 241
  internal locus of control, 240–241
    development of, 241–242
Logico-mathematical knowledge, 160–161
Longitudinal research, 34
Long-term memory, 176

Magic circle, empathy development, 315
Manipulation
  grasping, 111
  handedness, 111
  kicking, 112
  throwing/catching, 111–112
Marasmus, 145
Matched-dependent behavior, 16
Maturational theory, 17
  criticism of, 18
  cyclical development, 17
Medications/drugs, and prenatal development, 77
Memory, 175–177
  age factors, 177

  long-term memory, 176
    episodic memory, 176
    semantic memory, 176
  rehearsal, 176
  short-term memory, 175, 176
Memory disability, 395–396
Mental development
  cognition, 160
  intelligence, 159–160
  See also specific topics.
Mental illness, heritability, 70
Mental retardation, 390–393
  at-risk children, 392–393
  causes of, 391–393
  classification of, 390
  definition of, 390
  education of, 393
Mesomorph, 99
Metacognition, 316
Minorities, socioeconomic status, 355–357
Mistrust, in children, 282
Modeling, 261–264
  aggression, 432–433
  identification, 263–264
  language development, 198
  models, factors in choice of, 262–263
  moral behavior, 306–307
  moral development, 296–297
  selectivity of child in, 261–262
Monologues, language development, 204–205
Moral behavior
  components of, 291
  facilitation of, 305
    modeling, 306–307
    sanctions by reciprocity, 302, 306
  influencing factors, 291–294
  See also Behavior management.
Moral development
  Kohlberg's theory, 302–304
    criticism of, 304
    interview used, 303
    stages of moral development, 302–303, 304
  Piaget's theory, 300–302
  psychoanalytic theory, 294–295
    conscience, 295
    superego, 295
  social learning theory, 296–300
    modeling, 296–297
    reinforcement, 297–300
Moral judgment, 291
Motherese, 198

Motor development
　assessment instruments, 48
　importance for children, 107–108
　instruction and, 113–115
　　feedback, 115
　　guidance phase, 115
　　task presentation, 114–115
　locomotion, 109–111
　manipulation, 111–112
　movement exploration and, 112–113
　　equipment used for, 114
　readiness for, 108
　　balance, 108
　　coordination, 108
　　flexibility, 108
　　strength, 108
Multiple births, and language development, 223
Muscles, growth of, 96

Nativist theory. *See* Innate theory
Negative reinforcement, 14, 297
Neurologically impaired child, 405–407
　cerebral palsy, 405–446
　epilepsy, 405–406
Nonverbal communication, 360–361
Numbering, concrete operational period, 171–172
Nutrition
　breast/bottle feeding, 142
　deficiency profiles, 130
　deficient diets, results of, 133
　digestion, process in, 135–136
　Down's syndrome, special nutrition program, 144
　early childhood, 143
　eating disorders, 143
　eating habits, influencing factors, 130
　food groups, 136–138
　good nutrition, basic guidelines, 154
　inadequate nutrition
　　behavioral problems, 149–150
　　characteristics related to, 146
　　cognitive problems, 148–149
　　and deficiency disorders, 146
　　obesity, 147–148
　　tooth decay and, 146–147
　　vitamin deficiencies, 146
　infant diet, 142
　labels of cans, checking, 138, 140
　major nutrients, listing of, 131–133
　maternal nutrition, 141–142
　meal planning, 140
　nutritional supplements, dangers of, 134
　and physical development, 101
　and prenatal development, 76–77
　programs promoting, 151–154
　　government-sponsored programs, 151
　　parent programs, 151
　　programs for children, 152–154
　　public awareness projects, 151

Obesity, factors related to, 147–148
Observation techniques, 41–45
　anecdotal records, 43
　events sampling, 43–44
　observation sheets, 41–42
　pitfalls to avoid, 44–45
　time sampling, 44
　types of information gained, 41
Operant conditioning
　basics of, 13
　conditions for success, 15
　punishment, 15
　reinforcement, 14
　　negative reinforcement, 14
　　positive reinforcement, 14
Oral language disability, 396
Oral stage, 9
Organizational skills, and play, 339
Orthopedically impaired child, 407–409
　birth defects, 408
　education of, 409
　postnatal orthopedic problems, 408–409
Overgeneralization, in speech, 209

Parent programs, nutrition, 151
Parent's role, social development, 264–269
Peers
　friendships, 271–274
　　cross-age friendship, 273–274
　　importance of, 272–273
　　reasons for liking/disliking, 271
　and self-esteem, development of, 239
　social failures, results of, 272
Perception, 173
　and age, 173
　definition of, 173
Perceptual development
　hearing, 120–122
　taste/smell, 124
　touch, 123–124
　vision, 117–120
　See also specific areas.

SUBJECT INDEX

Perceptual disability, 396
Personality development
  basic components
    birth order, 235–236
    early experience, 236–237
    ethnic affiliation, 233–235
    inborn temperament, 229–231
    physical appearance, 231–232
    sexual identity, 232–233
  blocks to development, 245–251
    anxiety, 247–248
    fears, 248–251
    frustration, 248
    stress/tension, 245–247
  coping ability, 240–243
  facilitating healthy development, 251–253
  humor, sense of, 244–245
  identity development, 237–240
  industry, 243–244
Personality traits, heritability, 68–70
Phallic stage, 9
Phobias, 421–423
  characteristics of, 421
  school phobia
    causes of, 422–423
    prevention of, 423
    treatment approaches, 422
Phonology, language, 194–195, 208
Physical abuse, of children, 373–374
Physical defects, heritability, 66
Physical development
  affecting factors
    body type, 99–100
    ethnic affiliation, 100–101
    nutrition, 101
    sex, 100
  of body
    bones, 96
    brain/nervous system, 95–96
    endocrine system, 96
    muscles, 96
  child safety, 105–107
  health care, 101–104
  and personality development, 231–232
  and play, 336
  principles of growth/development, 95
  toilet training and, 97–98
  See also Motor development.
Physical knowledge, 160
Physical traits, heritability, 64–65
Piaget's theory
  accommodation, 21–22

assimilation, 21, 22
concrete operational period, 170–172
construction of knowledge, 24
formal operational period, 172
moral development, 300–302
  sanction by reciprocity *versus* punishment, 302, 306
Piaget's interviewing technique, 47
preoperational period, 165–169
schemas, 21
sensorimotor period, 165–169
stages of development, 22, 23
  movement through stages, 22–24
See also specific stages.
Play
  categories of, 330
  definitions of, 323
  functional play, 325
  functions of, 331–340
    academic achievement, 339
    cognition, 336, 338
    creativity, 333
    culture, assimilation of, 334–335
    emotional development, 331–333
    language development, 336
    physical development, 336
    pleasure, 340
    social development, 333–334
  games
    developmental guidelines for choice of, 329
    games with rules, 330–331
  play areas
    adventure playgrounds, 343
    creative playgrounds, 342
    traditional playgrounds, 342
  symbolic play, 325–328
    behaviors related to, 326
    construction play, 326–327
    dramatic play, 328
    pretend play, 327–328, 333, 334
    sociodramatic play, 328
  toys, 340–342
    open-ended toys, 340–341
    social value of, 341–342
    specific-purpose toys, 341
    three-dimensional toys, 341
Pleasure, and play, 340
Positive reinforcement, 14, 297
  language development and, 197
Praise, behavior modification techniques, 311

SUBJECT INDEX

Prenatal development
  affecting factors
    age of father, 76
    age of mother, 75–76
    harmful substances, 78
    maternal diseases, 77
    maternal emotions, 79
    maternal nutrition, 76–77
    number of pregnancies, 76
    radiation, 78–79
    spacing of pregnancies, 76
  conception, 70–71
  embryonic period, 72
  fetal period, 73–74
  monthly milestones (chart), 74
  zygote, 70–71
Preoperational period, 165–169
  action thinking, 169
  characteristics of, 166–169
  egocentrism in, 166
  representational thought, 166
Prepared childbirth classes, 79–81
Pretend play, 327–328, 333, 334
Primate speech, 202
Problem solving, 177–179
  adult involvement in, 177–179
  and construction of knowledge, 177
  learning materials for, 179
Problem-solving, thinking disability, 396
Prosocial behavior. *See* Social development
Psychoanalytic theory, 4–13
  Erikson's theory, 10–13
  Freudian theory, 4–10
  moral development, 294–295
  See also individual theories.
Psychosocial theory. *See* Erikson's theory
Public awareness projects, nutrition, 151
Punishment, 297–299
  children's views of, 301
  and conscience development, 298–299
  versus discipline, 310
  negative outcomes of, 298, 299–300
  operant conditioning, 15
  sanction by reciprocity *versus* punishment, 302, 306
  use in behavior control, 297–298

Racial attitudes
  development of, 234
  fostering better relations, guidelines for, 234–235

Radiation, and prenatal development, 78–79
Randomization, experimental research, 39–40
Readiness
  for entering school, 266
  motor development, 108
  toilet training, 97–98
Rebelliousness, 283
Recessive genes, 63–64
Reflectiveness, cognitive learning styles, 180
Reflexes, 163
Rehearsal, memory, 176
Reinforcement, 14
  moral development, 297–300
  negative reinforcement, 14, 297
  nonreinforcement, 297
  positive reinforcement, 14, 297
  punishment, 297–299
    and conscience development, 298–299
    negative outcomes of, 298, 299–300
    use in behavior control, 297–298
Relational dysfunctions
  aggressive disorders, 431–434
  attention deficit disorder, 414–418
  autism, 418–421
  depression, 423–426
  phobias, 421–423
  shyness, 427–431
  withdrawn children, 426–427
  See also specific disorders.
Relational meanings, language development, 213
Relearning group sessions, 312
Reliability, experimental research, 40
Research
  assessment instruments, 46–49
  creative activities, 49–50
  descriptive research, 34–37
  ethical factors, 50–51
  experimental research, 37–40
  historical research, 31–33
  interviews, 45–46
  observation techniques, 41–45
  See also specific topics.
Response, 16
Restricted code, language style, 223
Reversibility, 167
Reward, 16
Rh blood factor, and prenatal development, 77
Rogerian theory. *See* Self theory
Role playing, empathy development, 314–315

SUBJECT INDEX

Safety. *See* Child safety
Sanctions by reciprocity, 302, 306
Schemas, Piaget's theory, 21, 163
School phobia, 246
  causes of, 422–423
  prevention of, 423
Self-awareness, development of, 238
Self-concept
  development of, 238–239
  and play, 331
Self-confidence, development of, 240
Self-control, 291
Self-esteem, development of, 239
Self-instruction, 316–317
  guidelines for use, 316–317
Self-righteousness, 285
Self theory, 24–25
  basic concepts in, 24–25
  client-centered therapy, 24, 25
Semantic memory, 176
Semantics, language, 196
Sensorimotor period, 163–164
  invention of new means, 164
  primary/secondary/tertiary circular reactions, 163
  reflexes, 163
  secondary schemas, 163
Sensorimotor play, 325
Seriation, concrete operational period, 171
Sex of child
  and language development, 222
  and physical development, 100
Sex roles, and play, 331
Sexual abuse, of children, 374–375
Sexual identity
  and personality development, 232–233
  sex differences, 233
  sex-role identity, 232
Shame/doubt, in children, 282–284
Sharing, development of, 280–281
Short-term memory, 175, 176
Shyness, 427–431
  causes of, 429–431
  characteristics of child, 429
  debits of shy child, 429
  intervention methods, 431
  Stanford Shyness Clinic, 429, 431
Siblings
  explaining birth to, 81–82
  and socialization, 269–271
  See also Birth order.

Single-parent families, 351, 352–353
Slow-to-warm up children, 230–231
Smoking, and prenatal development, 78
Sneakiness, 283
Social development
  antisocial behavior, 282–285
  attachments, 259–261
  dependency and autonomy, 261
  modeling, 261–264
  parent's role, 264–269
    and Erikson's stages, 264–266
    guidelines for parents, 264–269
    nurturant fathers, 267–269
  peers/friendships in, 271–274
  and play, 333–334
  presocial behavior, 278–282
    fairness, 281–282
    intentionality/accidents, distinguishing between, 281
    others point of view, seeing, 279–280
    sharing, 280–281
    sympathetic feelings, 278
  siblings, role in, 269–271
  television and, 274–278
Social failures, results of, 272
Social issues
  child abuse, 373–376
  child care, 365–369
  divorce, 369–373
Socialized speech, language development, 205–206
Social knowledge, 161
Social learning theory, 15–17
  copying, 16
  cues in, 15–16
  drive in, 15
  matched-dependent behavior, 16
  moral development, 296–300
  response in, 16
  reward in, 16
Sociocultural shaping
  communication patterns, 359–361
  educational opportunities, 361–363
  family structure, 351–355
  group traditions, 348–351
  socioeconomic status, 355–359
  See also specific topics.
Sociodramatic play, 328
Socioeconomic status, 355–359
  family relationships and, 359
  and language development, 223–224

Socioeconomic status (continued)
  minorities, 355–357
  parental aspirations and, 357
  personal attributes and, 357–359
  unemployment, effects on family, 358
Socioemotional measures, assessment instruments, 47–48
Spatial relationships, 118–119
Special children
  gifted children, 385–390
  hearing impaired child, 400–403
  learning disabilities, 393–397
  mental retardation, 390–393
  neurologically impaired child, 405–407
  orthopedically impaired child, 405–407
  speech/language disabilities, 403–405
  visually handicapped child, 397–400
  See also specific topics.
Special Supplemental Food Program for Women, Infants, and Children (WIC), 151
Speech/language disabilities, 403–405
  articulation differences, 403
  delayed speech production, 405
  stuttering, 403–405
  voice problems, 405
Split-custody, 370
Stanford-Binet Intelligence Scale, 183–184
Storytelling, elementary years, 218
Strength, and motor development, 108
Stress/anxiety
  dealing with, 246
  home-related, 246
  and older children, 246–247
  and personality development, 245–247
  and prenatal development, 79
  responses to, 246
  withdrawn children and, 426–427
Stubbornness, 283
Stuttering, 215, 403–405
Successive approximations, language development, 198
Superego, 5, 295
Survey, 34
Symbolic play, 325–328
Symbols and signs, 166
Sympathetic feelings, development of, 278
Syntax, 211
  language, 195–196

Tasks, developmental task theory, 17–21
Taste/smell, 124

Television
  and behavior, 276–277
  internalizing content
    acceptance in, 276
    acquisition in, 275–276
    exposure in, 275
  and learning, 277–278
  physical effects of, 277
Temperament, 229–231
  difficult children, 230
  easy children, 230
  persistent dimensions of, 231
  slow-to-warm up children, 230–231
Temper tantrums, 248
Thinking disability, 396
Time-out, behavior modification techniques, 311–312
Time sampling, 44
Toilet training
  and physical development, 97
  readiness cues, 97–98
Tooth decay, 146–147
Torrance Tests for Creative Thinking, 388
Touch, 123–124
  development of, 123–124
  kinethesis, 124
Toxoplasmosis, and prenatal development, 77
Toys, 340–342
Traditional playgrounds, 342
Traditions. See Group traditions
Transformations, language, 201
Trust versus mistrust, 264–265
Twin studies, 67, 69
Two-word sentences, 210–211

Ultrasound, 68
Unemployment, effects on family, 358

Validity, experimental research, 40
Verbal communication, 360
Viruses, and prenatal development, 77
Vision, 117–120
  age/sex differences and visual skills, 119–120
  convergence, 118
  figure-ground discrimination, 118, 119
  fixation, 117–118

SUBJECT INDEX

Vision (continued)
  form constancy, 118, 120
  spatial relationships, 118–119
  and television viewing, 277
  visual acuity, 117, 119
  visual coordination, 117, 119
  visual discrimination, 118
  visual memory, 118
  visual-motor coordination, 119
  visual tracking, 118
Visually handicapped child, 397–400
  classification of handicaps, 397
  eye muscle defects, 398–399
  refractive errors, 398
  signs of impairment, 399
  special needs of, 399–400

Vitamins
  dangers of, 134
  deficiencies, 146, 150
Vocabulary, elementary years, 216
Voice problems, 405

Wechsler Intelligence Scale for Children - Revised (WISC-R), 187
Wechsler Preschool and Primary Scale of Intelligence (WPPSI), 184–186
Withdrawn children, 426–427
  causes of, 426–427
  characteristics of, 426
  intervention methods, 427–428

Zygote, 70–71

Name Index

Ackerman, P.T., 417
Ainsworth, M.D.S., 259
Albrecht, S.L., 369, 370
Allen, V.L., 218
Allers, R.D., 371
Allport, G.W., 229, 237
Almy, M., 41, 44, 49
Ames, L.B., 17, 46, 100, 245, 246, 248
Amizo, M., 414, 417
Anderson, D.R., 175
Anderson, T.A., 142
Angel, R., 352
Angst, J., 235
Apgar, V., 63, 76, 83, 84
Armstrong, J.W., 222
Arnheim, D.D., 109, 111, 117, 120, 122, 123, 124

Badell-Ribera, A., 408
Bahr, H.M., 369, 370
Bandura, A., 276
Barbieri, M.S., 224
Barlow, G., 276
Baskitt, L.M., 235
Baumrind, D., 269
Bavelas, J.B., 247
Baxter, A., 376
Beard, R.M., 166, 169, 170
Beatty, J.J., 41
Beck, J., 63, 76, 83, 84
Becker, L.A., 387, 389
Begin, A., 270
Begley, S., 61
Bell, C., 80
Bergman, B., 102
Berlin, C.M., 391

Berlyne, D.E., 174
Berndt, E.G., 281
Berndt, T.J., 281, 282, 304, 316
Bernstein, B., 223
Berry, E., 425
Berry, G.L., 276, 277
Berry, P., 415
Best, J.W., 34
Bickel, R.N., 361
Biehler, R.F., 173, 175
Bilge, B., 354
Birch, H.G., 231
Blehar, M.C., 259
Bolton, N., 339
Bordley, J.E., 400
Borg, W.S., 34
Borkowski, J.G., 180
Bradley, R., 224
Bradley, R.H., 235
Brady-Smith, J., 279
Bray, G., 147
Brazelton, T.B., 97, 260, 264
Breger, L., 10
Brender, J.D., 146
Bretherton, I., 326
Brewer, G.D., 390
Bridgmen, A., 365, 368
Briggs, G.M., 142, 143
Briggs, S.R., 431
Brookhauser, P.E., 400
Brown, G., 21
Bruner, J., 219, 323, 334, 338
Burland, S., 316
Burns, R., 333
Burton, R.V., 291, 312
Buss, A.H., 67

481

Butler, A.L., 327, 328, 330, 340
Byrne, D., 238

Caldwell, B.M., 224, 235, 362, 363
Calhoun, G., 237
Calloway, D.H., 142, 143
Calvert, S., 174, 176
Cameron, R., 316
Campbell, N.J., 361
Cataldo, C., 354, 355
Cazenave, N.A., 352
Ceci, S.J., 415, 417
Chalfont, J.C., 173, 177, 178, 394, 417
Chance, P., 323, 330, 336
Chapman, A.J., 244
Charles, C.M., 317
Cheek, J.M., 431
Chess, S., 69, 85, 230, 231
Chomsky, N., 199, 200, 201
Christie, J.F., 333, 336
Ciciello, J., 64, 67, 69
Clarizio, H.F., 425
Clark, E.V., 211, 212
Clark, M., 61
Cocking, R.R., 339
Cohen, L., 41
Collins, S.M., 355
Commission on Nutrition, 131
Connell, J.P., 260, 264
Connor, W.E., 148
Cook, J.A., 355
Cooper, C.R., 217
Cooper, R.G., Jr., 217
Coopersmith, S., 239, 248
Copans, S., 373
Copple, E.E., 339
Corless, C.E., 59
Cox, M.J., 370
Cox, M.V., 198
Cox, R.D., 370
Cratty, B.J., 96, 101, 113
Cravioto, J., 149
Creal, D., 357
Cromer, R.F., 213
Crouter, A.C., 352
Cruttenden, A., 200, 203, 206, 209, 213
Culatta, B., 415
Cullingford, C., 277
Curtiss, S., 203

Dale, P.S., 208, 210
Daniels, D., 429

Dansky, J.L., 333
Davidson, B.J., 195
Davidson, E.S., 276, 277
Davis, S.E., 195
Dawson, G., 216, 272
De Villiers, J.G., 208, 211
De Villiers, P.A., 208, 211
DeAvila, E., 361
Deci, E.L., 237
DeLicardie, E.R., 149
Devescovi, A., 224
DeVitis, J.L., 300
Dibble, M.V., 151
Dickstein, E., 247
Dill, S.R., 99
Dillard, J.M., 361
Dixon, S.D., 101
Doby, J.T., 223
Dollard, J., 15
Donahue, M., 211
Doorninck, W.J., 362
Dordua, G.D., 142
Downs, A.C., 232, 234
Drahman, R.S., 142
Dreyer, S.S., 314
Duncan, S., 361
Dunn, J., 230, 269, 270, 273
Durkin, K., 276, 277
Dykman, R.A., 417

Easterlin, R.A., 352
Edwards, S., 342
Eisenberg, N., 100, 278, 282
Eisenberg-Berg, N., 280
Elardo, R., 224
Elkind, D., 271
Elkins, J., 415
Ellis, P., 333
Eme, R., 250
Epstein, A., 187
Epstein, L.H., 147, 148
Epstein, S., 238
Erickson, M.P., 363
Erikson, E.H., 4, 10, 11, 12, 13, 87, 243, 258, 264, 282, 331
Ernst, C., 235
Eron, L.D., 432, 433
Essa, E.L., 297, 311, 312, 427
Evans, S.S., 427
Evans, W.H., 427
Eysenck, H.J., 159, 160, 298

NAME INDEX

Falbo, T., 270
Fallen, N.H., 399, 400, 403, 405, 406, 407
Farber, S.L., 64, 67, 69
Faw, T., 64
Feingold, B.F., 150
Fenson, L., 327
Ferber, M.A., 352
Fernandez, J.P., 366
Field, D.E., 175
Fischer, J.W., 307
Fitzgerald, M.J.T., 78
Fogel, A., 239, 260, 265
Fomon, S.J., 142
Ford, J.G., 360
Forman, G.E., 327
Fotheringham, J.B., 357
Fowler, W., 339, 340
Frank, M.I., 339
Frankenburg, W.K., 362
Freed, A.M., 290
Freeman, R.B., 355
Freire, E., 358
French, D.C., 427
Freud, A., 7
Freud, S., 4, 6, 9, 10, 13, 247
Frost, J.L., 342, 343
Fuller, R.H., 361

Gall, M.D., 34
Gallagher, J.J., 385, 387, 398, 399, 403, 405
Gallahue, D.L., 107, 109, 111
Galton, L., 129
Gamstorp, I., 405, 406
Garcia, E.E., 181
Gardner, W., 260, 264
Garger, S., 180
Garn, S.M., 78
Garvey, C., 336
Gearheart, B.R., 407
Geismar, L., 354, 355
Genishi, C., 41, 44, 49
Gentile, L.M., 339
Gerber Consultant Committee, 105
Gesell, A., 17, 18
Ghiselin, B., 219
Gibson, J.J., 120
Gillespie, C., 17, 46, 100
Gilligan, C., 303
Gloger-Tippelt, G., 80
Gohs, D.E., 415
Goldin-Meadow, S., 202
Goldman, J., 46, 183

Goodman, K.L., 369, 370
Gordon, M.T., 262
Gorman, B., 358
Gosnell, M., 68, 79
Gotts, E.E., 327, 328, 330, 340
Grant, J.P., 76
Graves, J.R., 360
Greer, D., 174
Gruson, L., 316
Guarnaccia, V.J., 358
Guerry, S., 46, 183
Guild, P., 180
Guilford, J.P., 160
Gundy, J.H., 373
Guthrie, H., 142, 143, 146, 147
Guttmacher, A.F., 83

Hagan, W.T., 356, 388
Hager, M., 61
Haines, J., 17, 46, 100
Hale, J.E., 18, 181, 187, 223, 352, 356, 359, 361
Halperin, M., 373, 374
Hammer, D., 142
Hammett, V.L., 414, 417
Hancia, E.J., 336
Hand, M., 280
Hanson, R.A., 371
Hanson, S.L., 352
Harris, S.R., 423
Hartup, W.W., 266
Havighurst, R.J., 18, 19, 20, 21, 97
Hayes, D.S., 271
Hays, J.R., 50
Helfer, R., 375
Heller, K.A., 316
Henker, B., 417
Hennesee, M.J., 101
Hersch, R., 302, 303
Hersen, M., 400
Herzberger, S.D., 272
Hetherington, E.M., 370
Higbee, K.L., 291, 308
Hill, A., 276
Hilliard, A.G., 376
Himes, J.H., 142
Hinshaw, S.P., 417
Hoek, D., 209
Hoepfner, R., 160
Hoffman, M.L., 278, 291, 309, 310
Hoffman, S., 179
Holborow, P.L., 415

Holland, J.G., 13
Holte, C.S., 278, 281
Hoot, J.L., 339
Horowitz, F.D., 389
Horton, W., 142
Huesmann, L.R., 432, 433
Humphrey, J.H., 246
Hurlock, E.B., 222
Huston, A.C., 174, 176
Hutchins, B., 105, 131

Ilg, F.L., 17, 46, 100, 245, 246, 248
Ingram, C.F., 48, 384
Inhelder, B., 21, 160, 166, 170, 171, 322, 326, 332, 334
Iosub, S., 78
Irwin, E.C., 339
Isenberg, J., 326, 339

Jacklin, E.N., 233
Jackson, M.E., 385, 387, 388
Jacob, E., 326, 339
Janos, P.M., 387
Jarvie, G.J., 142
Jewett, C.L., 425
Johnsen, E.P., 333, 336
Johnson, O., 101
Jones, W.H., 431
Joos, S.K., 76
Jordan, B.E., 187
Journal of the American Dietetic Association, 154

Kahn, J.V., 34
Kail, R., 176
Kakalik, J.S., 390
Kamii, C., 167, 172, 178, 298, 302, 306
Kamin, L., 159, 160
Kauffman, J.M., 415, 417, 426, 433
Kaufman, G., 354
Keller, J., 179
Keller, M., 310
Kellerman, J., 421, 422, 423
Kelley, K., 238, 371
Keloe, A.B., 356
Kemberling, S.R., 142
Kemper, S., 218
Kerchner, E.P., 239
Kerr, M.A., 149
King, R., 278
Kirk, S.A., 173, 177, 178, 385, 387, 394, 398, 399, 403, 405, 417
Kister, M.C., 217

Klatzky, R.L., 174, 176
Klein, B.L., 342, 343
Kliegl, R., 195
Koeske, R., 147, 148
Kogan, N., 180
Kohlberg, L., 302, 303
Kotelchuck, M., 151
Kramer, A., 78
Krantz, M., 403
Kratochwill, T.R., 422, 427
Krell, H., 373
Kushner, D.S., 327

La Prade, K., 417
Lamb, M.E., 260, 264, 268
Langlois, J.H., 232, 234
Langman, J., 74
Layne, C., 425
Lee, T.R., 153
Lefcourt, H.M., 241, 242
Lefkowitz, M.M., 432, 433
Lenneberg, E., 221, 222
Leonard, T.K., 131, 133
Leve, R., 96
Leventhal, B.L., 216, 272
Levine, M.H., 334
Lewis, M., 159
Lickona, T., 291, 295
Liebert, R.M., 275, 276, 277
Lindberg, L., 41, 42, 50
Lindholm, B.W., 153
Lipstein, B., 271
Liss, M., 335
Litz, C.S., 427
Locke, J.L., 208
Loffredo, D.A., 414, 417
Lokare, V.G., 248
Longo, L.M., 78
Longstreet, W.S., 360
Lorch, E.P., 175
Lorsback, I.C., 173
Lowenberg, M.E., 149, 150
Lubawski, J.L., 148
Lubin, A.H., 149
Luepnitz, D.A., 370
Lundberg, I., 194
Lynn, D., 268
Lyon, R.K., 281

McCall, R.B., 187
McClenaghan, B.A., 107, 109, 111
Maccoby, E.E., 233, 246

NAME INDEX

McCollum, J.A., 334
McCune-Nicolick, L., 327
McFadden, J., 355
McGhee, P.E., 244, 245
Macmillan, D.L., 391
McNeill, D., 200
Madge, N., 356
Mangione, P.L., 272
Marotz-Baden, R., 357
Martin, J.A., 406
Mathews, W.W., 72
Matson, J.L., 400
Matthews, W.S., 339
Mayhall, P.D., 373, 374, 375
Mead, M., 351
Meade, E.R., 359
Medeiros, D.C., 246, 248
Medinnus, G.R., 41, 42, 44
Medrich, E.A., 366
Meichenbaum, D., 316
Melson, G.F., 239, 260, 265
Mercer, C.D., 427
Meredith, H.V., 101
Merrill, H., 349
Milich, R., 417
Miller, M.S., 431, 433
Miller, M.U., 348, 355
Miller, N.E., 15
Miller, T.L., 398, 400
Milner, D., 234
Milos, M.E., 332
Minear, R.E., 104, 146
Miranda, A., 355
Mirga, T., 365
Mischel, H.N., 291, 316
Mischel, W., 291, 316
Mitchell, M.D., 323
Mitchell-Kernan, C., 276, 277
Modgil, C., 21
Modgil, S., 21
Molnar, G.E., 406
Montagu, A., 236
Moody, K., 274, 275, 277
Mook, D.G., 31, 41, 160
Moore, K.L., 72, 73
Morris, D.H., 149
Morris, R.J., 422
Morse, W.C., 237
Mosenthal, P., 219, 220, 221
Mouly, G.J., 33
Musinger, H., 67

Nadelman, L., 270
National Advisory Committee on Handicapped Children, 393
Neisworth, J.T., 392
Nelson, B.J., 376
Nichols, R.L., 356
Nicol, B.M., 146
Nisan, M., 312
Noles, S.W., 232
Norgard, K.E., 373, 374, 375

O'Brien, M., 389
Oden, S., 272
Oettingen, G., 233
Ogbu, J.U., 351, 362
Oglesby, D.M., 417
Oksaar, E., 206, 208, 209, 222, 223
Olds, S.W., 303
Olofsson, A., 194
Olson, R.K., 195
Oppenheimer, S.B., 72
Ornstein, R., 96

Pagelow, M.D., 373
Palker, P., 371
Paluszny, M.J., 420, 421
Papagiannis, G., 360, 361
Papalia, D., 303
Parke, R., 267
Partridge, R.P., 180, 182
Passmore, R., 146
Patterson, C.J., 217
Pelham, W.W., 417
Pellegrini, A.D., 339
Pepler, D.J., 338, 339
Perkins, S.A., 149
Perry, S., 148
Pestolesi, R.A., 109, 111, 117, 120, 122, 123, 124
Peters, A.M., 208
Peterson, P., 153
Peugh, D., 150
Phinillos, J.L., 187
Piaget, J., 21, 22, 23, 24, 47, 116, 122, 159, 160, 161, 162, 163, 165, 166, 167, 170, 171, 173, 196, 203, 204, 206, 213, 219, 300, 301, 302, 306, 322, 323, 325, 326, 330, 332, 334, 338
Pilkin, R.M., 76
Pinkney, A., 356
Pissanos, B.W., 111
Pitcher, E.G., 335

Plant, M., 78
Plomin, R., 67, 230, 429
Pollitt, E., 149
Porter, B.J., 246, 248
Pots, R., 174
Poulos, R.W., 275, 276
Powell, B., 235
Powers, H., 150
Presley, J., 150

Quinn, J.M., 334
Quisenberry, N.L., 327, 328, 330, 340

Radin, N., 187
Radke-Yarrow, M., 278, 279
Radl, S.L., 429, 430, 431
Rallison, M.L., 95, 96, 146
Ransbury, M.K., 338
Rao, M.N., 146
Rapoport, R., 268
Raths, L.E., 349
Read, M.S., 149
Reed, M., 400, 401
Reichcigl, M., Jr., 142, 147
Reimer, J., 302, 303
Reinisch, E.H., 104, 146
Reisenger, K., 101
Reiss, S., 332
Renshaw, D.C., 425, 426, 432, 433
Reynolds, R., 371
Reynolds, W.M., 426
Rice, M.L., 219, 221
Rich, M., 300
Richey, S., 100, 130, 131, 148, 151
Richmann, C.L., 233
Ridella, S.A., 78
Rinne, C.H., 175
Robinson, E., 217
Robinson, H.B., 385, 387, 388
Robinson, N.M., 387
Rodel, M.J., 403
Roedell, W.C., 385, 387, 388
Rogers, C., 24, 25
Rogers, K.D., 101
Rosenthal, R., 31, 34
Rosett, H.L., 78
Rosnow, R.L., 31, 34
Ross, D., 276
Ross, S.A., 276
Rubin, K.H., 325, 333, 334, 338, 339
Rubin, U., 366

Rubin, Z., 266, 270, 271, 272, 273
Rutter, M., 260

Sabatino, D.A., 397, 398, 400
Safford, P.L., 388, 403, 406, 407, 408
Saltzstein, H.D., 307, 310
Samuels, S.J., 200, 216
Sanders, J., 175
Sapora, A.V., 323
Sarafino, E.P., 222
Satter, E.M., 143, 144
Sattler, J.M., 184, 187
Savage, J.R., 149, 150
Savic, S., 223
Schasre, J.M., 413
Schave, B., 64, 67, 69
Scheinfeld, A., 60
Schiller, M.R., 147
Schlesinger, I.M., 219
Schmidt, D., 250
Schultz, L.H., 335
Science and Education Foundation, 131
Seligmann, J., 68, 79
Shanahan, D., 179
Shantz, C.U., 315
Shapiro, D., 68, 79
Shatz, M., 198
Sheldon, W.H., 99
Silvern, S.B., 336
Simon, S.B., 349
Simpson, G.B., 173
Sirkin, J.E., 365
Skinner, B.F., 13, 197
Slobin, D.I., 200, 219, 221
Smilansky, S., 325, 326, 328, 336
Smith, M.C., 281
Smith, R.M., 392
Snowman, M.K., 151, 173, 175
Spencer, H., 131
Sprafkin, J.N., 276, 277
Stallings, L.M., 108
Staub, E., 237
Steele, C.H., 356
Steelman, L.C., 223, 235
Stein, C.L., 46, 183
Sternberg, R.J., 159
Stevens, L.J., 393
Stevens, R., 11
Stevenson, D.T., 425
Stevenson, R.L., 347
Stewart, M.A., 75
Stini, W.A., 142

NAME INDEX

Stockbauer, J.W., 151
Strickland, E., 342
Swedlow, R., 41, 42, 50

Tallman, I., 357
Tan, L.E., 111
Taper, L.J., 100, 130, 131, 148, 151
Taylor, B.J., 117, 124
Thomas, A., 69, 85, 230, 231
Thompson, R.A., 260, 264
Thompson, R.F., 96
Tienda, M., 352
Tishman, J., 415, 417
Todhunter, E.N., 149, 150
Torrance, E.P., 388
Trites, R.L., 417
Troyer, W., 371
Tsai, L.Y., 75
Tucker, G.F., 400
Tuttle, F.B., 387, 389

Uhlig, G.E., 362
Umansky, W., 399, 400, 403, 405, 406, 407
U.S. Office of Human Development, 373, 375

Valentine, B., 348, 352
Valian, V., 211
Valoski, M.S., 147, 148
Van Hasselt, V.B., 400
Van Heerden, J.R., 145
Vane, J.R., 358
Varma, V.P., 247
Vasquez, A.G., 362
Vaughan, L.A., 142
Volpe, E.P., 78
Vondrack, S.I., 239
Voydanoff, P., 352
Vygotsky, L.S., 221, 323, 327, 331

Wadsworth, B.J., 166, 170
Wagner, R.K., 159
Walder, L.O., 432, 433
Walker, D.K., 41, 46, 48
Wall, S., 194, 259
Waters, E., 259
Watkins, B.A., 174, 176

Watson, J., 130
Watson, J.B., 13, 219
Watson, R.R., 131, 133
Webb, P.K., 313
Weber, C.W., 142
Weber, E., 18
Weiner, I., 271
Weishann, M.W., 407
Weiss, B., 391
Weisz, J.R., 391
Welch, L.D., 246, 248
Wells, M.J., 356
Wertsch, J.V., 310, 316
Wessman, A.E., 358
Whalen, C.K., 417
Wheeler, V.A., 272
White, B.L., 122, 123
White, J.M., 348, 356
White-Graves, M.U., 147
Wiersma, W., 33
Willerman, L., 232, 429
Williams, H.G., 109, 117, 119, 121, 122
Williamson, P.A., 336
Wilson, E.D., 149, 150
Winch, R.F., 262
Wing, R.R., 147, 148
Winick, M., 101, 148, 149
Winn, M., 276, 277
Witherspoon, R., 141
Wolff, P.H., 206
Wood, B.S., 203, 221
Woolridge, P., 233
Wright, C., 362
Wright, J.C., 174, 176
Wright, R.L., 360

Yawkey, T.D., 336
Ysseldyke, J.E., 393
Yussen, S.R., 317

Zahn-Waxler, C., 278, 279
Zammarelli, J., 339
Zeiser, E.L., 179
Zentall, S.S., 415
Ziegler, E.K., 142
Zill, N., 250
Zimbardo, P.G., 413, 429, 430, 431
Zurcher, L.A., 247